PROPAGANDA
AND THE ETHICS OF PERSUASION

PROPAGANDA
AND THE ETHICS OF PERSUASION

Randal Marlin

broadview press

To my mother, Hilda van Stockum, for all her help,
encouragement, and discussions.

NATIONAL LIBRARY OF CANADA CATALOGUING IN PUBLICATION DATA

Marlin, Randal, 1938-
Propaganda and the ethics of persuasion/Randal Marlin.

Includes bibliographical references and index.
ISBN 1-55111-376-7

1. Propaganda.
2. Persuasion (Psychology).
3. Propaganda—Canada.
I. Title.

HM1231.M37 2002   303.3'75   C2002-901699-1

BROADVIEW PRESS, LTD.
is an independent, international publishing house, incorporated in 1985.

North America
Post Office Box 1243,
Peterborough, Ontario, Canada K9J 7H5

3576 California Road,
Orchard Park, New York, USA 14127
TEL (705) 743-8990; FAX (705) 743-8353

www.broadviewpress.com
customerservice@broadviewpress.com

United Kingdom and Europe
Plymbridge North (Thomas Lyster Ltd.) Units 3
& 4a Ormskirk Industrial Park,
Old Boundary Way, Burscough Rd, Ormskirk,
Lancashire L39 2YW
TEL (1695) 575112; FAX (1695) 570120; E-MAIL
books@tlyster.co.uk

Australia
UNIREPS University of New South Wales
Sydney, NSW 2052
TEL 61 2 9664099; FAX 61 2 9664520
infopress@unsw.edu.au

Broadview Press gratefully acknowledges the support of the Ministry of Canadian
Heritage through the Book Publishing Industry Development Program.

Cover design by Black Eye Design.
Typeset by Liz Broes, Black Eye Design.

Printed in Canada

10 9 8 7 6 5 4 3 2

CONTENTS

PREFACE

The draft of this book was completed before the terrorist attacks of 9/11, but much of it has relevance to events surrounding that tragedy. The forms of prior and ensuing propaganda have many historical antecedents; hopefully, this book will provide illuminating parallels and analytical tools with which to assess it. Some of the ideas here draw inspiration from Albert Camus, who grew up in Algeria, a country that lived through as intense and vicious a terrorist war as has occurred anywhere. As the US and its allies decide how to handle Al-Qa'ida or other prisoners from Afghanistan, they might bear in mind Camus' sage remarks: "Torture has perhaps saved some, at the expense of honour, by uncovering thirty bombs, but at the same time it arouses fifty new terrorists who, operating in some other way and in another place, will cause the death of even more innocent people."[1] A primary purpose of this book is to arouse a critical spirit among readers against being corralled by forces and emotions of the moment into supporting actions that in conscience they will or should later come to regret. There are many special interests skilful at manipulating circumstances and communications in such a way as to benefit their own ends and not necessarily the public good. Hopefully this book will serve as an eye-opener to those who are not yet media-savvy.

My indebtedness goes back a long way, and to many different people: acknowledgement is a pleasure. I learned about the impact of layout and typography on consciousness while working on the student newspaper at Princeton University. Larry DuPraz initiated countless generations of Princeton undergraduates to the intricacies of the journalistic art, and I was lucky to be one of those to benefit, in the late 1950s, from his enthusiasm. That was also a time when James Ridgeway, Bill Greider, Bob Sklar, Don Kirk, and others got sufficiently under the university administration's skin that it organized a series of talks by some of the most distinguished journalists of the time, who left behind a lasting impression on matters of journalistic ethics. Even before that, Rev. Timothy Horner, OSB and the late Rev. Columba Cary-Elwes OSB had started me on the path of philosophy while I was at Ampleforth College in England; we kept in touch over the decades. Father Timothy steered me towards Quintus Cicero and away from false etymologies. Of the many different professors along the way who have supported my career through inspiration or practical assistance I owe special thanks to Gregory Vlastos, Raymond Klibansky, Ronald Butler, Robert McRae, and the late G.E.L. Owen, H.L.A. Hart, A.J. Ayer, and John Hunter. More directly connected with this book was my encounter with Jacques Ellul in 1979-80, and I have the Department of National Defence to thank for the year in Bordeaux where this took place. Contact with Robert Escarpit was also inspiring, and I have Jacques and Nicole Palard to thank for vital practical advice and help. In the same year William Shawcross kindly gave me an interview, sharing some of his insights concerning media manipulation by Henry Kissinger. DND agreed with my argument that a country's defence requires it to be knowledgeable about propaganda as well as military matters. Since propaganda is a tool that can also be misused by officials with their own axes to grind, my concern was to pursue the goal of educating the public about the nature of propaganda, rather than to restrict the knowledge to a controlling group. I chose the path of educating the public by giving the course "Truth and Propaganda" at Carleton University, one that has attracted a generous supply of good students for over two decades. This book is largely the outcome of that teaching. I have the students to thank for bringing me up to date on trends I would otherwise have missed.

Carleton has been especially generous in letting me follow my bent, even though this involved straying from the constraints of traditional disciplinary boundaries. Along the way various deans have provided financial support: Aviva Freedman, Janice Yalden, Stuart Adam, and Naomi Griffiths. The Canada Council supported work on Fitzjames Stephen in 1974, and the Social Sciences and Humanities Research Council provided a grant in 2000 for the present work; thanks to both of these councils. Among colleagues at other universities I am grateful for the stimulation provided by members of the International Association for Philosophy of Law and Social Philosophy. Stan Cunningham has communicated helpfully on our shared interest in propaganda. Numerous colleagues at Carleton, from many different disciplines, deserve thanks: these include Henry Mayo, Patrick Fitzgerald, Bert Halsall, Trevor Hodge, George Frajkor, Bob Gould, Basil Mogridge, Jutta Goheen, Doug Wurtele, Josh Beer, Carter Elwood, Duncan McDowell, Jacob Kovalio, Lloyd Strickland, Roland Jeffreys, Tom and Marilyn Henighan, Bruce MacFarlane, Sidney Wise, Jean-Jacques van Vlasselaer, Klaus Pohle, and Patrick MacFadden, as well as current and former members of my own Department of Philosophy.

From outside the university I am grateful for information and ideas from many current or former civil servants, in particular Keith Wilde, Arthur Cordell, and others in a group organized by Ray Jackson. Fellow members of the executive of the Civil Liberties Association, National Capital Region, have spurred my interest in issues such as the media treatment of David Levine, and Errol Sharpe has my thanks for publishing my work on that subject. Peter Calamai went out of his way to show me the inner sanctum of the *Ottawa Citizen* and put me in touch with members of the editorial staff. The sparring with Peter and other contributors (they know who they are) to the Propaganda and Media bulletin board at the National Capital Freenet has been instructive. Clyde Sanger kindly read and commented on a portion of the present manuscript. Librarians have given generously of their time and expertise; Nancy Peden, Frances Montgomery, and Barbara Harris among those most involved in my area of study.

A sabbatical spent in Oxford in 1987-88 put me in communication with helpful philosophers and classicists. C.C.W. Taylor, G.A. Cohen, and John Flemming facilitated library or personal contacts. The Ockham Society provided incisive criticism of some of my initial thoughts on propaganda. The late Sybil Wolfram was most encouraging in an editorial capacity during this time. Trinity College helped with lodgings, and St. Benet's Hall brought contact with some pertinent medieval scholarship. In the same year an invitation from the University of York provided incentive for more work on Fitzjames Stephen.

Another sabbatical at Trinity College, Dublin, in 1994-95, gave me a new set of valuable colleagues in philosophy and library access to materials that have become important for the ethical core of the present work. Thanks here are due to then-Dean Barbara Wright. I have the Irish Philosophy Club to thank for good criticism of some of the present thoughts on propaganda, at its annual meeting at Ballymascanlon. While visiting Queen's University in Belfast, I came in touch with Jonathan Gorman and his thoughts on William Joyce, useful for the present study. The same year brought valuable contact with Robert Fisk and the *Irish Times* cartoonist, Martyn Turner.

I owe thanks to the helpful staff of many other institutions: Tony Richards and others at the Imperial War Museum, the Public Record Office, and the British Library, particularly Colindale; Frans Van Wijnsberghe of the Bibliothèque Royale de Belgique; Ben Primer and the Princeton University Seely G. Mudd Manuscript Library; the Bordeaux University Library; the Cambridge University Library; the National Library of Canada; the Biblioteca Nazionale Braidense in Milan; and various smaller libraries.

I am most grateful to Michael Harrison of Broadview Press and its reviewers for helping this book along. Betsy Struthers did an outstanding job of copy-editing, and I have to thank her especially for pruning a lot of distracting material and thus making arguments clearer. She tightened up a lot of unnecessary verbosity and made valuable suggestions for modifications and additions. Whatever merits this book may have owe a lot to her substantial efforts.

A conference on "Truth and Propaganda" organized by the Centre of Professional Ethics at Strathmore College in Nairobi, Kenya took place only a few days after the events of 9/11 and gave me added reason to draw connections between those events and the concerns in this book. I would like to thank Strathmore and the many thoughtful participants at that conference for giving me much to mull over for the future.

My family have been most helpful with comments over the years: parents, sisters and brothers, wife and children. My daughter Christine made many good editorial suggestions. I have to give special thanks to my wife Elaine for putting up with all the absences and distractions that work on a book requires, as well as providing most valuable criticisms and suggestions. I credit her with first getting me interested in the incubator babies story and much else.

None of these acknowledgements should of course be construed as tainting anyone else with any share in the deficiencies that remain; for those I, of course, take full responsibility.

NOTE

1   Albert Camus, "Preface," *Algerian Reports, Resistance, Rebellion and Death*, trans. Justin O'Brien (New York: Modern Library, 1963), 84.

ONE
WHY STUDY PROPAGANDA?

INTRODUCTION

Out of the last two centuries a globally interconnected, mass-mediated society has emerged. The events of the twentieth century in particular have shown the enormous power, for good or evil, possessed by those who directly control or know how to manipulate the mass media. World War I left millions of soldiers killed on the battlefield. Why? Both sides seemed to think God was on their side. Britain pioneered techniques of propaganda during that war, techniques imitated by other countries and adapted in some cases to commercial interests.[1] In the 1920s and 1930s, the Nazi Party rose to power, riding a tide of nationalism and anti-Semitism, which it promoted as well as exploited. Hitler quite explicitly outlined the central role propaganda was to play in his party's successes. Lenin came to power through his understanding of the importance of communications with the masses and of harnessing their interests to his own ends. Leaders of democracies opposing these dictators, such as US President Franklin D. Roosevelt and British Prime Minister Winston Churchill, were also highly skilled at influencing public opinion. Not only in politics, but in the commercial realm as well, sophisticated techniques of manipulation have been used to market goods, promote corporate images, and generally protect the interests of the privileged. Advertising and public relations have become pervasive in the industrialized world. It is fair to say, as some have, that this has been an "age of propaganda." Techniques of persuasion are everywhere used, for the reason that, to a large extent, they work.

Once we recognize the power of propaganda, we need to ask whether its exercise is consistent with those democratic ideals to which lip-service is commonly accorded. Should we not want to study the techniques used so that truth gets a fair hearing? One excellent reason for studying propaganda is to try to avoid being led into war unnecessarily. As long as some powerful groups within society stand to benefit from war, we need to be vigilant against the possibility that they may encourage a military solution to world problems when, perhaps, diplomatic or other less costly means have not been entirely exhausted. It seems almost axiomatic that, if two sides go to war believing in the rightness and justice of their cause, then there has been a failure to communicate fully the position of the other side.

The price of freedom, it has been well said, is eternal vigilance. Others go further and claim that freedom must be purchased through blood, through sacrifices of a military kind to guard against armed aggressors. However, resort to military power can be misplaced and self-defeating if the enemy has been misrepresented and if the grounds for intervention are based on misinformation, disinformation, or just plain misunderstanding. To avoid repeating mistakes of the past, an alert citizenry today should take the trouble to learn how easy it can be for a powerful minority to manipulate information to win the support—or the indifference—of the majority towards its actions. People need to be sensitized to these methods if they are to guard adequately against such manipulation.

There are occasions when it is right to be alarmist about propaganda, but at the start of the twenty-first century a cold eye may be more appropriate. The art of mass persuasion is embedded in contemporary societies, those of liberal or neo-conservative democracies included. Public relations methods are intertwined with all major functions of modern life. During the 1930s, President Roosevelt pioneered the use of radio for gaining public support for his progressive programs through his so-called "fireside chats." Today, whether one deals with Exxon or Greenpeace, with multinational corporations or the coalition that disrupted the World Trade Organization meetings in Seattle in 1999, techniques of mass persuasion are involved. From the viewpoint of discourse analysis, there is little reason to speak of "propaganda" on only one side of a hotly contested issue when both sides are using techniques of persuasion to the hilt. We can sympathize with those charged with governing a country who see that a campaign of information dissemination is needed to forestall poorly grounded opposition to much-needed action. Only when there is full appreciation of the need and justification for some forms of public information can there be a properly measured response to the ubiquitous phenomenon of propaganda in today's world.

It may well be thought that with the arrival of the Internet the heyday of propaganda is over. We do not have to listen to some official party line about, say, a conflict in the Balkans. We can go to a Website operated by Serbs, Croatians, Albanians, etc. Search engines put us in touch with official, heterodox, or iconoclastic viewpoints as we choose. Although it is true that the Internet has provided us with a very different communications world, it is premature to suppose that the power of propaganda will be lessened. First, not everyone can afford to make full use of the resources offered by the Internet. Some lack the computer hardware, others cannot afford the monthly fee charged by a service provider. Those who are online may lack the time or the specialized knowledge to know or find out who is telling the truth about, for example, issues like global warming or genetically modified organisms. We can access many different points of view, but do we know the credentials of those expressing them?

The primary objectives of this book are to define what is meant by propaganda, to assist in understanding how it works, and to come to grips with ethical problems surrounding its use. The specific media may change, but principles of human nature have remained fairly constant over the millenia. We can learn from studying techniques used in ancient Greece and Rome. Plato, Aristotle, Cicero, and Quintilian, among others, catalogued and analyzed the rhetorical art. Also, because so much in the way of opinion-shaping goes on in areas other than war and revolution, it seems inadvisable to restrict the focus of this study to the most obvious and reprehensible uses of propaganda in politics. Advertising and public relations are two other areas of interest.

The definition of "propaganda" is not settled, though the use of this word is as current as ever. To insist on using and studying only what fits a narrow definition of the term is too exclusive. We want to study communication practices that mislead people, that get them to do things they would not do were they adequately informed. The extent to which the term "propaganda" can be defined to include all such cases is a matter for argument—the objective is not to hit upon a satisfactory definition for its own sake, but to understand and evaluate the overall phenomenon of mass persuasion, particularly the sort where a persuadee comes to feel, or should come to feel, deceived as a result of succumbing to a deceptive message.

This form of evaluation amounts to an ethics of persuasion and brings into play questions of means and ends, truth-telling, deception and integrity, and suchlike. The ethical questions lead into ethical-political matters, such as whether to have legal controls over deception in communication or to have laws which discourage a small minority from effectively controlling systems of communication on which the majority must rely for political awareness. These will be dealt with in due course. It should be acknowledged that much of the inspiration for this work derives from the powerful, penetrating, and wide-ranging work of Jacques Ellul, the "Bordeaux prophet" as he has been called. There will be many references to his work in what follows.

DEFINITION

There are many definitions, explicit and implicit, of the term "propaganda." In some ways the term has been discredited for serious analytical purposes, but it continues to be part of the arsenal in wars of words. It is common to identify an opponent's communications as propaganda, while maintaining that only one's own side is telling the truth. There is a strong association, in English-speaking countries, between the word "propaganda" and the ideas of lying or deception. This association may date from the time when a committee of (mainly) cardinals was convened by Pope Gregory xv in 1622, primarily to oversee missionary activity. It was called the *Congregatio de Propaganda Fide* (Congregation for the Propagation of the Faith), continuing a name given to meetings of Pope Gregory xiii with three cardinals in 1572–85 with a view to combating the Reformation.[2] Early usage of "propaganda" referred to the committee itself rather than to its activity. Later it came to be applied to the activity of spreading either faith or political doctrines.

In Latin countries, where "propaganda" means advertising, the word has no negative associations, although it is, of course, likely to be affected in time by one's perceptions of what is propagated. In more recent years it has been taken to mean, according to *Webster's Third International Dictionary* (1960), "dissemination of ideas, information or rumour for the purpose of helping or injuring an institution, a cause or a person." But this characterization of "propaganda" as neutral misses its negative connotation. Politicians and bureaucrats generally avoid using the term to describe their own activities, tending to reserve it for those of their opponents, although the difference may not be perceptible to an unbiased third party.

Lenin and Goebbels did not mind applying the term "propaganda" to describe their attempts to mould opinion. The Allies in both world wars characterized such opinion-forming activity by the enemy as propaganda and treated it as largely composed of lies, while their own information dissemination was treated as the truth. Exceptions exist: Winston Churchill's information officer, Brendan Bracken, among other officials, openly avowed his work as propaganda and defended the use of "good propaganda" against "bad propaganda." That strategy can work under the right circumstances, where attention is focused on the question of definition. Otherwise, it is wiser to accept that in public consciousness there will be, for the most part, a connotation of deception or manipulation in English language usage.

Kinds of Definition

DESCRIPTIVE DEFINITION

Before embarking on the task of examining and evaluating different definitions of propaganda, it is worth reflecting first on the nature of definition itself. Sometimes we do not know the meaning of a word, and we go to the dictionary to look it up, or we ask someone whom we have found knowledgeable about such things. Take, for example, the word "biometrics." In the *Oxford English Dictionary* the term is defined as statistical methods applied to biological subjects. This is a *lexical* definition, what dictionaries offer. But dictionaries do not always keep up with trends in language. In current usage, the term popularly refers to identification of individuals through such methods as digitized fingerprints, retinal scans, and facial recognition technology. In the event that a lexicon is not sufficient, we might speak of a *reportive* definition, as one that reports usage, or a *descriptive* definition. In both cases we are describing what a word means. It is a feature of both lexical and reportive definitions that they can be true or false.

STIPULATIVE DEFINITION

Different from descriptive definitions are those in which a person does not lay claim to describing or reporting how others use a particular word, but rather announces or *stipulates* that this is how he or she will be using it. Anyone can stipulate any meaning for a term. Although clearly useful in science, stipulations can also be confusing and misleading. When a word such as "pacifism" is stipulated to apply to certain behaviour in rats, it is easy to suppose that experiments with these rats tell us something about pacifism in general. Yet, they do no such thing, unless there is independent evidence to link the stipulated behaviour to what we would recognize as pacifism in our human behaviour, since that is what the word in its ordinary application is all about. To take another example, a sociologist, seeking some objective measurement of poverty, might stipulate that "poor" meant "not having a computer." One is in danger of confusing the stipulated meaning with the ordinary accepted meaning and of forgetting that some quite wealthy people might decide by choice not to have a computer.

Although stipulative definitions are not true or false, they may be good or bad, advisable or inadvisable, helpful or confusing. They may also be deliberately used for the purpose of confusing people and for furthering propaganda aims. For example, a government might stipulate that people who have been unemployed for such and such a length of time are no longer to be considered in the labour market and therefore are not to be classed among the "unemployed." It is not difficult to see how a government could "improve" its unemployment record by altering the stipulated criteria in the definition of unemployment. It would be easy to "eliminate" poverty by defining poverty at such a low income level that in order to be poor you would have to be starving to death (and thereby soon removing yet another statistic on the poor side of the ledger).

Sometimes words are defined in ways that are neither purely reportive, nor merely stipulative, but seek either to give greater coherence to existing usage or to give us greater insight into the nature of objects referred to by a term. One name often given to this form of definition is *rational reconstruction*. Another is "real definition." As an example of the latter, the definition of a human being as a "rational animal" attempts (successfully or unsuccessfully) to pick out what is "really" or "essentially" human. One who emphasizes the subjective contribution to what we see as reality is more likely to prefer the former term.

PERSUASIVE DEFINITION

Worthy of special attention in the context of trying to define "propaganda" is what Charles Stevenson, in his influential *Ethics and Language,* called "persuasive definition." When hotly disputed matters are at stake, people often make use of definitions that tend to favour their side of a given argument. We need to recognize that language has uses other than mere description: it can exhort, evaluate, threaten, and express emotions. As Stevenson analyzes persuasive definition, it involves taking a word with a high emotive content and altering its descriptive content "usually by giving it greater precision within the boundaries of its customary vagueness," but *without* making "any substantial change to the term's emotive meaning." This definition is used, consciously or unconsciously, "to secure, by this interplay between emotive and descriptive meaning, a redirection of people's attitudes."[3] Not surprisingly, then, a term such as "democratic" which has a favourable emotive sense today, is likely to be defined differently in an ideological defence of socialism from the way it would be defined by a defender of capitalist ideology.

The socialist is likely to lean towards definitions that stress equality in some form, while the capitalist is more likely to emphasize freedom, such as the freedom to engage in commercial contracts without government interference.

Although Stevenson defines "persuasive definition" in such a way as to have the "emotive meaning" kept relatively constant, it is not difficult to see how this notion might usefully be extended. Consider Oscar Wilde's characterization of fox-hunting as "the unspeakable in full pursuit of the uneatable."[4] If we treat it, light-heartedly perhaps, as a definition, it is condemnatory and has persuasive power; yet, far from altering the descriptive content while keeping the emotive side relatively fixed, it purports to keep the facts of foxhunting in full view, while supplying an emotive, ethically judgmental colouration of those facts with the word "unspeakable." If the occasion demands it, we might wish to speak of "persuasive definition in Stevenson's sense" as against "persuasive definition in a larger sense."

In any case, the expression "persuasive definition" is a very useful one. It has particular relevance to the definition of propaganda itself, since, as already remarked, propaganda has for the most part a negative connotation in English. Therefore, we need to be alert to the possibility of someone wanting to define propaganda in such a way that his or her activity of persuasion does not constitute propaganda itself; in other words, the act of defining propaganda can become itself an effort to engage *in* propaganda.

In the present context we are trying to understand rather than persuade, to discover how the term is, in fact, used. What we find are two broad categories of definitions: *negative* and *neutral*. Rather exceptionally, there also exists, as already noted, a few people who speak of propaganda favourably. What follows is a brief review of some definitions representative of the term.

Negative Definitions

The characteristics to be found in propaganda as negatively defined are such things as lack of concern for truth, failure to respect the autonomy of those with whom one communicates, promotion of self-serving ends, seeking control over others, etc. As an historical note, it may be observed that the *Encyclopedia Britannica* carried the word as an entry for the first time following World War I.

The following are some examples of definitions with a negative import.

1. Chalmers Mitchell, in the twelfth edition of *Encyclopedia Britannica*: The first characteristic of propaganda is that its objective is always "to promote the interests of those who contrive it, rather than to benefit those to whom it is addressed." Those who engage in it "may genuinely believe that success will be an advantage to those whom they address, but the stimulus to their action is their own cause." The second characteristic is its indifference to the truth. "Truth is valuable only so far as it is effective. The whole truth would generally be superfluous and almost always misleading."

2. Harold Lasswell, one of the most notable propaganda analysts of the twentieth century: "Propaganda is concerned with the management of opinions and attitudes by the direct manipulation of social suggestion rather than by altering other conditions in the environment of the organism."[5] What gives this definition its negative connotation are the words "manipulation" and "suggestion," which together give the impression that the propagandee is being made into a tool, an unwitting servant, of the propagandist.

3. Leonard Doob: "Propaganda can be called the attempt to affect the personalities and to control the behaviour of individuals toward ends considered unscientific or of doubtful value in a society at a given time."[6] Here the aspect of control over others signals something negative, particularly when the ends are of doubtful value or are "unscientific," a bad word in modern western culture. His definition introduces an element of relativity, which makes it difficult to apply with any precision. Suppose we deal with the advocacy of phrenology—the study of the shape of the skull as a clue to character and intelligence—thought to be scientific in the nineteenth century. Do we call this propaganda? As soon as we ask the question, we realize that the definition presents a problem: do we judge whether something is propaganda from our present-day viewpoint, regardless of how it was considered in an earlier period? Should we take that view, we would have to allow that people can be involved in propaganda without realizing it. By contrast, some might wish to restrict the term to cases where conscious manipulation is involved.

4. The element of power and control is central to Jacques Ellul's definition of propaganda as well. For him, propaganda is, somewhat loosely translated, a "means of gaining power by the psychological manipulation of groups or masses, or of using this power with the support of the masses." ("Moyen pour conquérir le pouvoir grâce à l'appui de groupes ou de masses psychologiquement manipulés, ou pour utiliser ce pouvoir en s'appuyant sur les masses.")[7]

5. Bertrand Russell's definition starts out in a somewhat neutral fashion, but becomes negative toward the end as he characterizes propaganda as a one-sided approach to truth. "Propaganda may be defined as any attempt by means of persuasion, to enlist human beings in the service of one party to any dispute. It is thus distinguished … from instruction by its motive, which is not the dissemination of knowledge but the generating of some kind of party feeling." Information given, he writes, may be accurate, but even then "it will consist of such information as tends in a given direction, to the exclusion of such information as has a contrary tendency." The reference to "party feeling" also points to a force of divisiveness in a community.[8]

6. Bruce L. Smith gives a somewhat more qualified, but more detailed negatively oriented definition. "Propaganda is the more or less systematic effort to manipulate other people's beliefs, attitudes, or actions by means of symbols (words, gestures, banners, monuments, music, clothing, insignia, hairstyles, designs on coins

and postage stamps, and so forth). A relatively heavy emphasis on deliberateness and manipulativeness distinguishes propaganda from casual conversation or the free and easy exchange of ideas."[9]

7. Alex Carey, who focuses attention on corporate propaganda and its negative impact on individual liberty produces a definition similar to Russell's. "By 'propaganda' I refer to communications where the form and content is selected with the single-minded purpose of bringing some target audience to adopt attitudes and beliefs chosen in advance by the sponsors of the communications. 'Propaganda' so defined is to be contrasted with 'education.' Here, at least ideally, the purpose is to encourage critical enquiry and to open minds to arguments for and against any particular conclusion, rather than close them to the possibility of any conclusion but one."[10]

8. Interestingly in the light of Carey's definition, Edward Bernays, who as one of the founders of public relations in America was deeply involved in promotion of corporate interests, defines propaganda relativistically, as did Doob. "The only difference between 'propaganda' and 'education,' really, is the point of view. The advocacy of what we believe in is education. The advocacy of what we do not believe is propaganda."[11] Unless we are deliberately seeking a challenge to our opinions, most of us tend to view with disfavour the propagation of what we do not believe in, at least where important interests are concerned.

Before leaving this sampling of negatively oriented definitions of propaganda a few comments are in order. Jacques Ellul's definition is useful for distinguishing between disinterested spreading of a faith as distinct from deliberately seeking power through dissemination of beliefs. For Ellul, Peter the Hermit and the Inquisition both were involved in propaganda, whereas the monks of Cluny were not. Ellul thus makes his focus, in defining propaganda, on the *ends* sought, rather than the *means*. This definition has enough plausibility to make it a useful tool for analysis, but it cannot be taken to capture what people generally understand by the term, since there are clear divisions of opinion on the matter. Some argue that Ellul presents a persuasive definition, but in order to substantiate this charge, they have to show that there is an agreed-upon descriptive meaning for the term; that may be difficult to prove. As we can see by contrasting the definitions above with those of neutral definitions below, the term "propaganda" is subject to deeply divided understandings.

Neutral Definitions

These definitions are neutral in the sense of not prejudging the moral standing of propaganda. One who accepts a neutral definition is free to condemn propaganda, but not simply by virtue of its *being* propaganda. The condemnation would have to be related to the ends served by the propaganda or the use of some unacceptable means.

9. *Webster's Third International New Dictionary* 1966: Propaganda is "dissemination of ideas, information or rumor for the purpose of helping or injuring an institution, a cause or person." This definition would cover the case of a hospital's fundraising board providing information about its operations in order to solicit donations or increased government revenues—hardly anything sinister.

10. Richard Taylor's definition is clearly neutral, but it also tackles the different question of whether propaganda by definition must be successful. "Propaganda is the attempt to influence the public opinions of an audience through the transmission of ideas and values. The use of the word 'attempt' implies both that the purpose of the activity *is* important and that the result is *not*. Propaganda can fail, and be seen to have failed."[12]

11. Vernon McKenzie states that the "real sense of propaganda is the spreading of information whether it be true or false, good or bad—literally 'spreading the faith.'"[13]

Favourable Definitions

Some practitioners of propaganda are eloquent about the potential of propaganda for good and so must be counted among those who view it at least as a neutral term, possibly even a favourable one.

12. Brendan Bracken, Minister of Information for Britain during World War II: "[P]ropaganda ... is a perfectly respectable name, attached to one of the most profoundly religious institutions in the world. It is really too respectable a veneer to put upon a thing like the Ministry of Information. I do not mind the use of the word 'propaganda.' In fact, I welcome it. There is nothing wrong with the name except that it connotes to certain minds something that they do not really understand."[14]

13. John Grierson, documentary filmmaker and founder of the National Film Board of Canada (NFB): "There are some of us who believe that propaganda is the part of democratic education which the educators forgot.... We believe that education has concentrated so much on people knowing things that it has not sufficiently taught them to feel things.... It has given them the three Rs but has not sufficiently given them that fourth R which is Rooted Belief.... We can, by propaganda, widen the horizons of the schoolroom and give to every individual each in his place and work, a living conception of the community which he has the privilege to serve. We can take his imagination beyond the boundaries of his community to discover the destiny of his country. We can light up his life with a sense of active citizenship. We can give him a sense of greater reality in the present and a vision of the future."[15]

A Proposed Definition

In the light of these different definitions, it is clear that one feature, common to all, should be present in any definition of propaganda: it is an organized and deliberate attempt to influence many people, directly or indirectly. The root idea, from the Latin *propagare*, to propagate, is inseparably tied to the use of this word. From this it follows, given that the masses are generally not patient enough to listen to sophisticated and complicated arguments, that some simplifying of a message will be necessary. The inducements of music and attractive visuals may be used to affect belief. It follows, then, that propaganda is likely to involve deceptions of some sort—for example, by facts selected so as to give an incomplete picture, one shaping the sort of belief that the propagandist desires. These may be harmless deceptions, and they may correspond in fact with what a reasonable person would conclude on being fully informed, but that judgment is one the propagandist makes, since the target audience is not given the fuller picture from which they might make such an evaluation themselves. Here we are speaking of well-intentioned propaganda. There is also, of course, propaganda consisting of lies, where anything that the propagandist can get away with will be used if it helps the objective. Thirdly, propaganda tends to involve, by definition, psychological influences, which bypass rational determination of belief on the part of message receivers. (I refer to conscious or subconscious message reception, rather than some purely physiological mechanism, such as electro-shock therapy, sometimes called "brainwashing.") This does not mean avoidance of rational arguments; rather, it means that at some point in a chain of reasoning a hidden, misleading, or otherwise unexamined presupposition will affect the outcome in a way not consciously assessed by the propagandee. Thus, the use of repetition of emotively charged words, slogans, coins, monuments, and other imagery influences people through prestige and contagion, leading to irrational or not fully rational acceptance of another's power over them. All of us are influenced by such factors. The propagandist simply harnesses them in a deliberate campaign to affect beliefs and attitudes.

With these features in mind, I propose the following definition, which aims at simplifying the foregoing, but regrettably remains somewhat cumbersome.

> PROPAGANDA = (def.) The organized attempt through communication to affect belief or action or inculcate attitudes in a large audience in ways that circumvent or suppress an individual's adequately informed, rational, reflective judgment.

This definition is not meant to exclude as propaganda those methods of influencing others which anticipate that the propagandees will make use of their own reason and informed judgment to act in some way which the propagandist desires.[16] What is crucial is that the propagandist sets the stage to provide some false or unexamined premise in the picture of reality affecting a propagandee's action. The word "manipulation" would be convenient for this idea, but there are definitional problems arising in connection with that word itself.[17]

The definition I have given may seem to rule out, unjustifiably, Communist propaganda organized through group discussions by social animators. However, it would include this kind of case if it could be shown that the agitators (as they were called) excluded from consideration any relevant evidence that tended toward an unwanted conclusion, or if rewards and punishments put constraints on the supposedly "free discussion." There is also the matter of "reflexology," which is explained in Chapter 3 below.

Our proposed definition might be criticized on the ground that it includes too much. Let us say that a newspaper announcement of a public land-irrigating project is timed to link profitably to the newspaper proprietor's own previously purchased land in the area.[18] Public opinion might be affected in an organized way for one person's profit; thus, it qualifies as propaganda on my definition, even though it would not ordinarily be classified as such. We tend to think of propaganda more in terms of ideology or political power, but the commercial world carries with it some ideological baggage that can sometimes—as with the case of Amway (short for the American Way)—be very prominent, at other times out of sight but present in some degree.[19] For instance, I would include the massive promotion of the McDonald's fast-food chain in the US and Canada under my definition of propaganda. An advertising executive boasted some years ago that in America McDonald (the clown) had "a recognition factor among children second only to Santa Claus."[20] More recently, Naomi Klein has shown how many items are marketed through a "branding" process, which tries to associate the product, through its logo, with a lifestyle or worldview, so that the buyer is buying an identity along with the product.[21] It seems worthwhile to include such pervasive forms of influence under the rubric "propaganda," although usage shows some resistance to doing so.

The question of the definition of propaganda continues to be an open one, given the existence of such diversity in interpretation of the concept. Some suggest giving up use of the term in serious discussions, so as to avoid misunderstanding. For the purposes of this book, it should be sufficient to have the rough parameters for the understanding of the concept provided by this discussion.[22]

TWO MAJOR PROPAGANDA THEORISTS: GEORGE ORWELL AND JACQUES ELLUL

Many writers have been preoccupied with the question of individual freedom and the domination of the crowd; for instance, we can name Sören Kierkegaard, Friedrich Nietzsche, Ortega y Gasset, G.K. Chesterton, Gabriel Marcel, Albert Camus, Elias Canetti, Karl Jaspers, and Jean-Paul Sartre. Martin Heidegger deserves to be mentioned for his *Being and Time*, but he cannot escape ignominy for his support for Nazism in 1933. The list is easily expanded if we think of playwrights such as Henrik Ibsen and Arthur Miller, or sociologists such as Gustav Le Bon, Wilhelm

Reich, and Sergei Chakotin. Another powerful voice raised in defence of individual autonomy is that of Noam Chomsky, about whom more will be said later.

Two outstanding writers will serve, in the rest of this chapter, as an introduction to the general phenomenon, as distinct from the definition, of propaganda— George Orwell and Jacques Ellul. Both were gravely concerned about the future of the individual in mass-mediated society, and both played an effective role in rallying forces to oppose the threat of monolithic culture. People from both left and right have claimed Orwell as defending their side. Ellul's fate has been that of the prophet more welcomed elsewhere than in his own land: in France, he was far too independent a thinker to gain a strong and steady following. In polarized politics one must declare allegiance to one or other of different rival camps, with no ambiguity: Ellul was all for depolarization.

There are many similarities between Orwell and Ellul, but perhaps one difference is the Biblical roots of Ellul's thinking and his committed Christian involvement. Orwell's orientation is more secular. Both thinkers sought to expose the forces at work integrating an individual into a larger system and frustrating an individual's self-development and freedom. My hope for this book is that it will be perceived as a continuation of their efforts in that regard.

George Orwell

George Orwell, whose birth name was Eric Blair, was born in India in 1903 and educated at Eton, later serving in Burma with the Indian Imperial Police. An early work of his, *Burmese Days,* recounts his disgust with the cultural chauvinism of the English ruling class, their philistinism, and lack of interest in the culture they were dominating. He also wrote about the psychological pressure a crowd can impose on a person in his essay "Shooting an Elephant." Orwell fought with a splinter group on the Republican side against the fascists in the Spanish Civil War. His testament to that period, *Homage to Catalonia,* is filled with references to propaganda.

Orwell's best-known works, *Animal Farm* and *Nineteen Eighty-Four,* have left a powerful imprint on modern consciousness. From the former come memorable, pointed, and oft-quoted (adapted) phrases, such as "some ... are more equal than others" and "four legs good, two legs bad"; from the latter come expressions like "newspeak," "Big Brother," and "doublethink." A flourishing publication, *Quarterly Review of Doublespeak,* has carried on his work of exposing misuse of language for propagandist purposes by tracking attempts by corporations or government to use language to mislead people. For instance, a directive to those working in the US Environmental Protection Agency said that they should not speak of "acid rain" but refer instead to "poorly buffered precipitation." The Pentagon once referred to its purchase of "wooden interdental stimulators" instead of "toothpicks" (possibly to justify a higher price?). As William Lutz, author of *Doublespeak* points out, people today are not fired or laid off; they are subject to "restructuring," "downsizing," "workforce readjustments," or "negative employee retention."[23] The slogan "War is peace" does not seem far removed from the thinking involved in naming the MX intercontinental ballistic missile "Peacekeeper." In Orwell's *Nineteen Eighty-Four*, strict controls prevent deviation from the Party line; in today's world, economic and political structures help to accomplish many of the same results. A deception perpetrated on the public by some official source accomplishes, as we often see, a given objective. It is later found to be a deception, but the mass media are no longer interested in publicizing the truth, partly because the correction arrives too late to undo the damage caused, partly because exposure of the deception would also incriminate the media as negligent or dupes. It is not in the interest of the media to injure their own credibility by such exposure. Examples of this kind of thing can be found regularly by tuning in to alternative media such as *Extra!* published by FAIR (Fairness and Accuracy in Reporting); its Website is <http://www.fair.org.>

Orwell can be credited with a particularly strong and lasting battle for liberty on the language front. Other writers and thinkers of his time were aware of the enslaving effects of propagandistic language, but none brought this awareness so effectively and passionately to public attention. Orwell is distinguished by his attention to propaganda not only in the political realm, but also in connection with advertising and commerce, as in his *Keep the Aspidistra Flying*. He exposed propaganda wherever it occurred, whether on the left or right of the political spectrum. "One of the dreariest effects of this war," he wrote of the Spanish Civil War, "has been to teach me that the Left-wing press is every bit as spurious and dishonest as that of the Right."[24] After an interview with Harry Pollitt, the General Secretary of the British Communist Party, he judged that Pollitt had "evidently decided I was politically unreliable."[25]

Orwell could put up with some distortions in detail in order to make a truthful overall point, but not the use of distortions of objective reality for pragmatic purposes. He was inclined to accept at first the tactical arguments of the Communists against his own POUM militia—POUM stands for *Partido Obrero de Unificación Marxista*, the United Marxist Workers' Party; it was called Trotskyist by the Communists—but he parted from Communists and left-oriented intellectuals who made truth totally subservient to practical necessity. He fiercely and bitterly resented misleading expressions, such as "objectively Fascist" applied to the POUM, especially when made by people in comfortable surroundings many hundreds of miles from scenes of suffering and death.

Orwell recognized the need for use of political force, including suppression of opinion in extreme circumstances, but he refused to accept the perversion of judgment about literary merit. "To say 'x is a gifted writer, but he is a political enemy and I shall do my best to silence him,' is harmless enough," Orwell wrote. "Even if you end by silencing him with a tommy-gun you are not really sinning against the intellect. The deadly sin is to say 'x is a political enemy: therefore he is a bad writer.'"[26] Orwell respected certain limits, fixed by demands for nothing other than truth itself, in the pursuit of political goals, however important and justified they might be. This is a contrast to Frantz Fanon's "In every age, among the people, truth is the property of the national cause.... In [the] colonialist context there is no truthful behavior: and the good is quite simply that which is evil for 'them.'" Jean-Paul Sartre comes to a similar conclusion to Fanon regarding the truth in "A Plea for Intellectuals."[27]

It is clear that the Spanish Civil War, and the misreporting of it, profoundly shaped Orwell's attitude to truth. His later popular writings dramatize and powerfully express the deep antipathy he developed to distortions of truth in a time of war. One feature that makes the deceptions he has in mind different from ordinary lies is that they operate through presupposition rather than direct contradiction of fact:

> I saw great battles reported where there had been no fighting, and complete silence where hundreds of men had been killed. I saw troops who had fought bravely denounced as cowards and traitors, and others who had never seen a shot hailed as the heroes of imaginary victories; and I saw newspapers in London retailing these lies and eager intellectuals building emotional superstructures over events that had never happened. I saw, in fact, history being written not in terms of what happened but of what ought to have happened according to various "party lines."

He is surprisingly contemporary in his worries about truth. What is peculiar to our age, he wrote, "is the abandonment of the idea that history *could* be truthfully written. In the past people deliberately lied, or they unconsciously coloured what they wrote, or they struggled after the truth, well knowing that they must make many mistakes; but in each case they believed that 'facts' existed and were more or less discoverable." But totalitarianism destroys the notion that there could be a body of neutral fact. Nazi theory denies that "the truth" exists, he wrote:

> There is, for instance, no such thing as "Science." There is only "German Science," "Jewish Science," etc. The implied objective of this line of thought is a nightmare world in which the Leader, or some ruling clique, controls not only the future but *the past*. If the Leader says of such and such an event, "It never happened"—well, it never happened.[28]

"NINETEEN EIGHTY-FOUR"

As a satire, Orwell's *Nineteen Eighty-Four* has been successful at highlighting many tendencies in modern political life. In 1993 the Liberal Party in Canada was elected on a platform that included a commitment to get rid of a general sales tax on goods and services. In the run-up to this election, Liberal Leader Jean Chrétien stated unequivocally that he would scrap the tax if elected.[29] When the tax was not abolished, Liberals claimed that there was never any such commitment, it was misunderstood, there was only a commitment to "harmonize" federal and provincial sales taxes, etc. US President George Bush (senior) made the expression "Read my lips, no new taxes" famous when he abandoned in June 1990 his campaign promise at the Republican convention in August 1988 to hold the line on taxes.[30]

In *Nineteen Eighty-Four*, the political leaders of Oceania, one of three political groups in its world, have figured out how to control a population for an indefinitely long period of time: it is only necessary to foment hatred and to eliminate memories and independent thinking. War is necessary to limit the abundance of goods, since otherwise people would have sufficient time and leisure to ask themselves why they allow a privileged elite to rule over them. The population is taught the language of Newspeak, designed to narrow the range of thought.[31] In Newspeak every concept is expressed "by exactly *one* word, with its meaning rigidly defined and all its subsidiary meanings rubbed out and forgotten." As alliances shift, people might ask themselves whether the enemy, who was previously their ally, can be all that bad. To avoid that, records must be effaced and rewritten to show, for example, that a previous ally never was an ally and that any enemy always was an enemy. Names given to government functions are not politically neutral, but shape the thinking of people in a desired way. For example, the government institution dealing with falsification of records is called the Ministry of Truth, or "Minitrue" in shortened Newspeak. The Ministry of Peace, or Minipax, is the ministry concerned with war.

Devices keep people under regular surveillance. Called "Big Brother," these collectively are considered to be the guardian of the people, watching them constantly for their own good. The protagonist of the novel, Winston Smith, has the problem that, as a worker in Minitrue involved in changing records, he sees things as they are, not as they are supposed to be. This is very dangerous, because the Thought Police are always on the alert for any thinking that might undermine the state. To survive, Winston must engage in Doublethink:

> To know and not to know, to be conscious of complete truthfulness while telling carefully constructed lies, to hold simultaneously two opinions which cancelled out, knowing them to be contradictory and believing both of them; to use logic against logic, to repudiate morality while laying claim to it, to believe that democracy was impossible and that the Party was the guardian of democracy; to forget whatever it was necessary to forget, then to draw it back into memory again at the moment when it was needed, and then promptly to forget it again; and above all, to apply the same process to the process itself. That was the ultimate subtlety: consciously to induce unconsciousness, and then, once again, to become unconscious of the act of hypnosis you had just performed. Even to understand the word "doublethink" involved the use of doublethink.[32]

Winston cannot efface memories that conflict with Party demands of the moment. O'Brien, the Party's inquisitor, tries to straighten out Winston's thinking. First he notes that the past does not exist in some place as a world of solid objects. Winston has to admit that the past lies in records. Since the Party controls the records, the

Party also controls the past. O'Brien quotes the reasoning of Emmanuel Goldstein, the founder of the society: "Whatever the Party holds to be truth, *is* truth."[33]

The Party is kept in power by judicious reconstruction of the records to give full support to whatever policy it favours at a given time. A Party slogan is: "Who controls the past controls the future." Another, "Ignorance is strength," means that, by effacing inconvenient memories, it is possible to be devoted all the more strongly to the cause of the moment. That is why doublethink is so important. As Goldstein wrote: "*Doublethink* lies at the very heart of Ingsoc [short for English Socialism, the name of the ruling party], since the essential act of the Party is to use conscious deception while retaining the firmness of purpose that goes with complete honesty."

ESSAYS

Orwell's nostalgic love of things rural, which is evident in *Nineteen Eighty-Four* as well as in his choice of living in seclusion on a Scottish island, combines with other features of his thinking to impress some with a view of him as a Tory anarchist. But to be passionately anti-Stalin and to be apprehensive about the possibility of socialism heading in that direction is not the same as to be anti-socialist. There was an egalitarian streak in Orwell, which emerged in his support of the working class, even though his relatively privileged upbringing led him to recoil against the living habits of many sections of the class whose interests he championed. Like Camus, Orwell was motivated by an ethic of solidarity with the human race, leading him to choose for a while a life of poverty in London and Paris, about which he wrote knowledgeably. Orwell had his baggage of prejudices, against Roman Catholics (Irish in particular) and gays, for example. G.K. Chesterton, who was not Irish, excited his great antipathy, perhaps because Chesterton was so adept at using words in defence of causes Orwell opposed and in ways that Orwell objected to, as explained in his essay "Notes on Nationalism." Curiously, Chesterton and Orwell both opposed modern technology, were attracted to the traditional English way of life and the countryside, and were passionate lovers of words, genuine insight, and novel forms of expression. Both hated jargon, especially the use of acronyms divorced from the etymologies of words. They both revered language as a revealer of historical continuity. Both were at one time propagandists for the state, Chesterton in World War I and Orwell in radio broadcasts to India in World War II. One of Orwell's earliest writings appeared in a publication by Chesterton. Entitled "A Farthing Newspaper," the article dealt with corporate influence on public opinion through the news media, a concern which Chesterton shared.[34]

Orwell's essays provide penetrating insights into the nature and power of propaganda. One of his earliest, "Boys' Weeklies," describes the way imperialist ideology was instilled in young minds through adventure stories and comic books, such as *Gem* and *Magnet*. One of the offensive things he notes is the stereotyping of other nationalities, usually in uncomplimentary ways, with frequent use of derogatory epithets, such as "Froggies" and "Dagoes." The working class was also treated in comic fashion or as semi-villains: "As for class-friction, trade unionism, strikes, slumps, unemployment, Fascism and civil war—not a mention. Somewhere or other in the thirty years' issue of the two papers you might perhaps find the word 'socialism,' but you would have to look a long time for it." A little later, he observes that the clock in these weekly magazines stopped at 1910, when "Britannia rules the waves, and no one has heard of slumps, booms, unemployment, dictatorships, purges or concentration camps." The impact of the boys' weekly magazines was a transmission of values appropriate to capitalist, imperialist Britain to an extent greater than people might suspect. Orwell writes:

> Here is the stuff that is read somewhere between the ages of twelve and eighteen by a very large proportion, perhaps an actual majority, of English boys, including many who will never read anything else except newspapers; and along with it they are absorbing a set of beliefs which would be regarded as hopelessly out of date in the Central Office of the Conservative Party. *All the better because it is done indirectly,* there is being pumped into them the conviction that the major problems of our time do not exist, that there is nothing wrong with *laissez-faire* capitalism, that foreigners are unimportant comics and that the British Empire is a sort of charity-concern which will last for ever. Considering who owns these papers, it is difficult to believe that this is unintentional.[35]

I have put the comment "All the better because it is done indirectly" in italics because Orwell here touches on themes central to our concerns: the most effective propaganda is not recognized as such, and its message is often best presented obliquely.

In his essay, "Notes on Nationalism," Orwell describes a certain form of closed-mindedness that has an affinity with propaganda. He uses a persuasive definition for the word nationalism (as he recognizes and states at the outset), including within its scope such things as Communism, "political Catholicism," and the more amorphous concepts of anti-Semitism, Trotskyism, and pacifism. In this, he has usefully spelled out a recognizable and significant phenomenon that deserves to have a name, even though calling it nationalism is confusing. In his definition, it involves obsession, instability, and indifference to reality. It is a mentality, he says, that excludes or deforms the truth. (Perhaps a better word for what he is describing would be "fanaticism.") It assumes that human beings can be classified in the same way we classify insects and that millions of people can be confidently labelled "good" or "bad." Depending on what form of nationalism a person adopts, certain facts will be found unpalatable and therefore not acceptable. For example, the pro-Soviet finds it hard to admit the truth of the Stalin-induced famine in the Ukraine in 1933. The anti-Semite finds unbelievable the fact that six million Jews were systematically murdered by gas, bullets, or other means by the Nazis during World War II.

Nationalism, for Orwell, is the "habit of identifying oneself with a single nation or other unit, placing it beyond good and evil and recognizing no other duty than that of advancing its interests." He distinguishes nationalism in this sense from patriotism. Patriotism involves devotion to a place and way of life, but in

Orwell's view it lacks the "wish to force others to adopt this." Nationalism, by contrast, is "inseparable from the desire for power." The nationalist becomes so preoccupied with advancing the unit to which devotion is given that objective treatment of things affecting their basic value is impossible. Literature opposing a particular person's nationalism is treated as bad literature regardless of its literary merit. Inconsistencies coexist in the nationalist mind, as portrayed by Orwell. The nationalist "spends part of his time in a fantasy world in which things happen as they should—in which, for example, the Spanish Armada was a success or the Russian revolution was crushed in 1918—and he will transfer fragments of this world to the history books whenever possible."[36]

One of Orwell's most frequently cited essays concerning propaganda is "Politics and the English Language." Just as many of his works lament the perversion of language in the service of political or commercial ends, here his aim is to rescue good English for its own sake and for the sake of clear thinking. Fighting propaganda means fighting mental laziness. "Modern English, especially written English, is full of bad habits which spread by imitation and which can be avoided if one is willing to take the necessary trouble. If one gets rid of these habits one can think more clearly, and to think clearly is a necessary first step towards political regeneration: so that the fight against bad English is not frivolous and is not the exclusive concern of professional writers." An example of lazy thinking is the misuse of metaphors, turning them into clichés which no longer have evocative power. For instance, the expression "toe the line" conveys the idea that everyone must stand with their toes touching a given line; writing this as "tow the line" shows a failure to grasp the sense of the original imagery. A second source of fuzzy thinking is the elimination of simple verbs in favour of extended phrases. Everyone understands the word "kill" and its negative connotations. This truth is obscured by using phrases such as "terminate with extreme prejudice" (meaning to assassinate) or the Gulf War's "collateral damage." Pretentious diction, meaningless words, and use of double or triple negatives are also denounced in Orwell's essay.

Orwell saw the political speechmaking of his own time as a defence of the indefensible, in which euphemisms, question-begging, and "sheer cloudy vagueness" played a large part. "Defenceless villages are bombarded from the air, the inhabitants driven out into the countryside, the cattle machine-gunned, the huts set on fire with incendiary bullets: this is called *pacification*."[37] The extraordinary thing about this observation is that exactly the same word for exactly the same kind of activity was used in the Vietnam War many years later. Euphemisms still abound in bureaucratic tracts; the Central Intelligence Agency's manual, *Psychological Operations in Guerilla Warfare*, uses the word "neutralize" in a context where "kill" is a synonym by inference. The manual was designed for CIA operatives in Nicaragua during the early 1980s, and members of the Armed Propaganda Teams, as they were called, were told, "It is possible to neutralize carefully selected and planned targets, such as court judges, police and state security officials, etc. For psychological purposes, it is necessary to take extreme precautions, and it is absolutely necessary to gather together the population affected, so that they will be present, take part in the act, and formulate accusations against the oppressor."[38] Orwell's rules for clarity include the elimination of any nonfunctional word; the use of the active voice instead of the passive wherever possible (further attention to "deleted agent of the passive" is provided in Chapter 4 below); and the replacement of foreign phrases, scientific words, or jargon if an everyday English equivalent is possible.

Jacques Ellul

There is probably no other thinker who has thought as deeply about propaganda in all its dimensions and ramifications as Jacques Ellul. What sets him apart from other analysts is his rare if not unique combination of expertise in history, sociology, law, and political science, along with careful study of biblical and Marxist writings. He lived through some of the century's most pervasive propaganda periods, from the call to arms from Spain in the late 1930s, to the phoney war, through the years of Nazi occupation, to the rise of liberation movements, such as the FLN in Algeria, to the Cold War. At the end of World War II, he had a brief experience as a holder of political power in the Bordeaux city administration. He came to have a profound distrust for the notion that political solutions can be found for human problems and wrote *The Political Illusion*[39] as a testament to the constraints he saw likely to confront an idealized approach to world betterment. His study of propaganda, *Propagandes*, translated as *Propaganda*, appeared originally in 1962, the year when French rule in Algeria ended. He wrote a special study of FLN (*Front de Libération Nationale*) propaganda intended for a second edition of his book, but it never appeared in that form.[40]

Some have viewed Ellul as a Calvinist and a pessimist, but his works belie any attempt to categorize him as a fatalist. From printed interviews and by reading widely among his writings, it becomes clear that he is far from adopting a position of hopelessness concerning political involvement. He does believe that human nature is thoroughly flawed and that it is a pervasive human characteristic to be swayed by illusions. Opportunists can exploit this tendency; others may be as much dupes as dupers. Ellul's message is not to remove oneself from political action and to "cultivate one's garden." It is, rather, to free oneself of illusions. These may be packaged by an official propaganda arm of a state, or of some movement, or by commercial interests. In every case the illusions challenge an individual's search for, and affirmation of, his or her unique identity.

Ellul's studies of the history of institutions gave him an extraordinarily rich background for the understanding of today's power structures.[41] When he writes about technological society, he does so from a perspective incorporating many social changes based on numerous scientific and technological advances over three millenia. For instance, his study of recruitment by the French Army in the sixteenth and seventeenth centuries gives him insights into the techniques of persuasion or control on matters of life-and-death significance.

With that background, Ellul sounds the alarm against one of the most threatening illusions he sees facing the world since the 1950s: the faith that human ingenuity, in the form of technology, is going to solve all our problems. The faith allows that new gadgetry may create problems, but these can be solved by more refined inventions. Against this faith and ahead of his time, Ellul warns in *The Technological Society* (1964) that human beings are losing their control over technology. He presents the frightening notion that technology has developed a pattern of "self-augmentation" (*auto-croissance*), which continues whether this growth benefits society or not. Ellul is not concerned with science fiction, but is looking at social realities, recognizing that scientists and technicians have livelihoods to make, and noting ordinary human propensities, such as the desire to have influence and to turn a profit. His description of the scientist's dilemma in wanting to be cautious before allowing a new discovery to be marketed, yet not wanting to thwart the companies funding his or her research, has contemporary relevance. The recent case of Dr. Nancy Olivieri in Toronto is a highly-publicized example of a researcher refusing to be silent about possible dangers relating to a particular drug use. When, in 1998, her research found unexpected risks associated with a drug manufactured by her corporate sponsor, Apotex, Inc., the company threatened her with legal action should she disclose the risks to patients at the Hospital for Sick Children or publish her findings. The Canadian Association of University Teachers came to her defence, and in October 2001 a Committee of Inquiry issued a report on the case, warning that tougher measures are needed to protect patients' rights and to ensure that clinical drug trials are free from the influence of drug manufacturers.[42]

What Ellul writes about technique is fundamentally connected to his thoughts about propaganda:

> Technique has become autonomous; it has fashioned an omnivorous world which obeys its own laws and which has renounced tradition. Technique no longer rests on tradition, but rather on previous technical procedures; and its evolution is too rapid, too upsetting, to integrate the older traditions.[43]

In other words, propaganda is itself a technique, resulting partly from the application of the social sciences, including psychology, to technology. It is a technique used to promote acceptance of other techniques. Viewing the technological system as a whole, we see that maximal efficiency—defined, for example, as maximal return on investment over a given period of time—may no longer involve adapting products to human wants, practices, and capacities. It may instead require adaptation of human beings to the requirements of the system. If the reader is involved with an institution of any size, he or she may be familiar with the scenario wherein perfectly workable routines, which have performed satisfactorily, are replaced by a new system that appears to accomplish the same tasks more efficiently, but does not. Certain important things are lost in the process, such as continuity and the ability to make adequate comparisons with past practice. Another common result is that the range of discretion is reduced, and equitable concerns are de-emphasized in favour of mechanistically arrived-at results. For instance, in the healthcare profession, more and more reliance is being placed on gadgetry and monitoring rather than on human contact between patient and caregiver. But if the frenetic pace of modern life is too upsetting to some individuals, the system itself does not have to slow down. What we see is the development and marketing of mood-enhancing drugs to enable people to cope. As Ellul points out, one branch of technology makes up for deficiencies in another, but the technological system as a whole keeps growing.

Propaganda plays a key role in all of this. At each stage various interests work to minimize the prospective harms and inconveniences and to maximize prospective benefits appearing in the assessment of some new technique. Each specialized contribution to the technological system is promoted in connection with the narrow contribution it can make, without any overall assessment of where the system as a whole may be heading—for example, to an unsustainable ecology, to pill-popping zombies, or whatnot. Publicly funded bodies, designed to look at the long-range, overall impact of technological developments on society, might be expected to provide a counterweight to specialized interests, but the experience in Canada has been that they have a precarious existence and are easily targeted when the government is looking for ways to cut back on spending. For instance, cutbacks put pressures on universities to accept funding from private sources, which may dampen the enthusiasm for speaking out on matters that might adversely affect those same sources.[44]

Ellul's analysis of propaganda comes from a concrete source: his experience in working on such local projects as the preservation of the fishing life in southwestern France in the 1950s. His opponents worked for a bureaucracy with the impressive name of the "Interdepartmental Mission for the Amelioration of Aquitaine." It involved three things he detested: technocracy, the bureaucratic attitude, and capitalist power. The technocrats chose a place for tourist development, without consideration for the actual terrain. If flaws in their studies were pointed out, the technocrats claimed the studies were outdated. Maps were drawn not to scale, but to fit the preconceived plan; for instance, what appeared on their maps as a hairline backroad was, in a reality, a major expressway. Administrative secrecy was the rule.

Ellul feels that people have to be educated to deal with this kind of circumstance, that universities should not turn out good technicians who will make capable executives who are also nonentities. Instead, he thinks students should learn, along with the appropriate knowledge of their field of study, an understanding of people and a fundamentally critical approach to their discipline, their lives, and the world. Then, the justificatory ideologies and powers of any kind can be questioned, not in order to destroy them, but to allow each person to exercise freedom. Social transformation begins with business executives, since it is no good separating the expertise which gets things done from the criticism of society in which Marxists, for example, engage. You need both expertise and criticism. In

Ellul's view, Marx is important, because he wanted to reintegrate the totality of the human being in a scientific study of economy and society.

Ellul makes clear that his goal is not to seek to eliminate technology, but to recapture a space for human spontaneity, openness, and understanding of what is happening in the world. He has been credited with inventing the phrase "Think globally, act locally." In order to act effectively, people must understand the influences operating on their consciousnesses, influences often generated from sources that seek to benefit their own, private interests, which have little to do with the public good. One might be tempted to demonize external forces, but Ellul focuses not just on the purveyors of propaganda, but on the willingness of the population generally to accept it.

Ellul sees the modern individual as hungry for a sense of meaning for his or her existence. The decline of church, village, and family influences has tended to atomize human existence, cutting people off from bonds that automatically provided a sense of identity. Under these circumstances, with individuals thrown together in a mass, there is a fertile field for propaganda. Lacking the determination and energy required to make sense of the world, the modern individual is all too willing to have meanings supplied to him or her through the mass media. Or else they opt out of any serious thinking. In an interview with Claude Steiner and Charles Rappelye, Ellul says, "Today, the greatest threat is that propaganda is seeking not to attract people, but to weaken their interest in society. I am astonished by the enormous number of TV game shows, football games, computer games. They encourage people to play: 'Let yourselves be entertained, amuse yourselves, do not concern yourselves with politics, it's not worth the trouble.'"[45]

PROPAGANDA ANALYSIS

One of Ellul's main contributions to the study of propaganda is his expansion of the horizons under which it is commonly viewed as a highly organized, top-down, politically motivated strategy for controlling a population. This needs to be supplemented by other categories and related considerations. The study of propaganda needs to take into account the way a targeted group is conditioned to make it more receptive to the propagandist's message. Ellul calls this "pre-propaganda." No direct propaganda can be effective, he writes, without pre-propaganda, which creates images, ambiguities, and stereotypes, apparently without any particular purpose. The essential objective is to prepare a person for a particular action and to do so without delay. It does not have a precise ideological objective. "It proceeds by psychological manipulations, by character modifications, by the creation of feelings or stereotypes useful when the time comes." Besides altering stereotypes, a propagandist may seek to build up useful myths in the minds of a population, which would also count as pre-propaganda. Ellul explains what he means by "myth":

> By "myth" we mean an all-encompassing, activating image: a sort of vision of desirable objectives that have lost their material, practical character and have become strongly coloured, overwhelming, all-encompassing, and which dis-

place from the conscious all that is not related to it. Such an image pushes man to action precisely because it includes all that he feels is good, just, and true. Without giving a metaphysical analysis of the myth, we will mention the great myths that have been created by various propagandas: the myth of race, of the proletariat, of the Führer, of Communist society, of productivity. Eventually the myth takes possession of a man's mind so completely that his life is consecrated to it. But that effect can be created only by slow, patient work by all the methods of propaganda, not by any immediate propaganda operation.[46]

Elsewhere Ellul refers to other governing myths, which he identifies as work, happiness, the nation, youth, and the hero. His thesis is that when one or other or all of these myths take hold of a population's consciousness, they pervade all thinking. The obvious case is the racist myth in Hitler's Germany, but Ellul claims that other myths can also take root and dominate our outlook on life. Take the notion of work. A non-mythological attitude is that work is something most of us have to do to provide a livelihood. It would be better if we had the leisure to do creative things, but life is not so kind to everyone, and work in the sense of something necessary but disagreeable is the lot of many or most people. But work is mythologized when it is treated as something especially meritorious, as if the "worker" were some being superior to others. The mythologized notion of work is convenient for the unscrupulous capitalist, since it provides the psychological conditions for an exploited class to accept atrocious working conditions willingly, even enthusiastically. Ellul is not contradicting St. Benedict's idea that work, carried out in the right spirit for love of God, can be good for the soul. What he treats as myth is the idea that work is good in and of itself, conferring nobility and superiority on the working class over other classes in society. Ellul thinks that work took on a mythical nature in the nineteenth century, when people were needed for degrading labour in factories. As myth, one could perhaps view it as a capitalist tool, which was turned against its originators by the labour movement.

Each of Ellul's proposed "myths" could be the subject of extensive discussion, but there is one area in which his arguments can be juxtaposed with those of Orwell. Ellul says that one of the "four great collective sociological presuppositions in the modern world" is the myth of happiness, and that "A propaganda that stresses virtue over happiness and presents man's future as one dominated by austerity and contemplation would have no audience at all."[47] Orwell, by contrast, writes in his review of *Mein Kampf* that "however they may be as economic theories, Fascism and Nazism are psychologically far sounder than any hedonistic conception of life." Obviously, he is not writing in approval of these doctrines, having put his life on the line in opposition to them; instead, he is remarking on the psychological appeal of these ideas to the masses:

Whereas Socialism, and even capitalism in a more grudging way, have said to people "I offer you a good time," Hitler has said to them "I offer you struggle, danger and death," and as a result a whole nation flings itself at his feet.[48]

Here, Orwell and Ellul are in contradiction. Ellul may have qualified his statement to allow for the special circumstances of Nazi Germany; Orwell, himself, amended his own statement by concluding "Perhaps later on they will get sick of it [the struggle, etc.] and change their minds, as at the end of the last war." Alternatively, one could argue that Nazi propaganda was presenting its own version of happiness, interpreted as living a supremely Germanic existence, with Hitler the apotheosis of the German spirit.

Pre-propaganda in the form either of myths or stereotypes may be less easy to detect, because it is "softer," in the sense of less galvanizing, but, once it has settled into a public's consciousness, it will be much more difficult to counteract the subsequent propaganda. Therefore, it is important to expose and resist pre-propaganda before it is utilized for nefarious purposes.

There is much common ground between Orwell, Ellul, and Noam Chomsky concerning their perception of propaganda, even though their politics, at least in the case of Ellul and Chomsky, differ considerably. Like Ellul, Chomsky sees propaganda as not necessarily controlled by the state. In *Chronicles of Dissent* he said of the US: "We're not a society which has a Ministry of Truth which produces doctrine which everyone then must obey at a severe cost if you don't. Our system works much differently and much more effectively. It is a privatized system of propaganda, including the media, the journals of opinion and in general including the broad participation of the articulate intelligentsia, the educated part of the population." In apparent partial agreement with Ellul, Chomsky saw the media and educational structures as set up in a way "to design, propagate and create a system of doctrines and beliefs which will undermine independent thought and prevent understanding and analysis of institutional structures and their functions."[49]

CATEGORIES OF PROPAGANDA

Ellul's notion of pre-propaganda has contributed greatly to propaganda theory. So also has his much-used and discussed analysis of the different categories of propaganda. It is important to understand and appreciate these categories even though they make it difficult to maintain a tight, consistent grasp on the definition of propaganda.

Ellul groups propaganda into four different pairs of contrasting kinds. As presented here, the first of each pair represents the kind that would normally spring to mind when people think about propaganda. The second represents Ellul's extended notion, which terms as propaganda things not ordinarily viewed as such.

1. *Political* versus *sociological* propaganda. *Political* propaganda is carried out by a definite body—for example, a government, a political party, an administration, a pressure group—for definite goals. The methods are quite deliberate and calculated; goals are clearly distinguished and quite precise. By contrast, *sociological* propaganda is diffuse, based on a general climate of opinion operating imperceptibly without the appearance of propaganda. It is the sum of the ways in which society tries to inte-

grate the maximum number of people into itself, to unify its members' behaviour according to pattern, and to spread its style of life abroad. It creates new habits and new standards of judgment and choice that appear to have been spontaneously adopted. American films of the 1950s, with their stay-at-home mothers and businessman fathers, are an example of this kind of propaganda.

Sociological propaganda does not fit our usual definition of the term, which includes the idea of an "organized attempt" to persuade. Ellul, himself, writes, "one hesitates to call all this propaganda,"[50] but he has a reason for wanting to extend the definition to cover these cases: it is to draw attention to the fact that the effects *on us* of these influences are similar to those of propaganda in the usual sense. Sociological propaganda, like its political counterpart, imparts myths and standards of good and bad behaviour. A person's environment is changed at the deepest level by sociological propaganda. It acts gently, introducing an ethic in benign form, penetrating very slowly, and ending by creating a fully established personality. It is more like pre-propaganda than propaganda, inasmuch as it does not lead, by itself alone, to concerted mass action. Rather, it provides the basis for organized propaganda. For example, in the US, the "American way of life" is the backdrop for much propaganda. Once one accepts the American way of life as superior, it becomes a criterion of good and evil; things that are un-American become evil. Thus, it provided the rationale for McCarthyism in the 1950s and supported Monroe Doctrine foreign policy, permitting invasions of Central American countries. A good example of this kind of jingoism, American style, is "Red Nightmare," a Cold War propaganda film made in the 1950s, supported by the US Department of Defence, and directed by Jack Warner. Good things like family life, democratic meetings, involvement with schools, etc., are treated as if they were peculiarly American rather than common to many other liberal democracies. Because of the source of its funding, "Red Nightmare" can be considered to belong in the top-down category, but its ideas and images form the subtext of many Hollywood movies not so funded.

2. *Agitation* versus *integration* propaganda. *Agitation* propaganda is the most visible kind. It is usually revolutionary, but it can be used by a government to whip up its people to some very high level of sacrifice—to go to war or increase productivity, etc. It cannot be kept up for very long. The usual form of agitation, subversive propaganda, is easy to make. Hatred of a particular enemy is fomented; liberty, bread, and fulfilment are offered as inducements. This propaganda feeds on itself and does not require the continued use of the mass media.

By contrast, *integration* propaganda is a propaganda of conformity aimed at getting the individual to participate in society in every way, stabilizing the social body, and unifying and reinforcing it. It seeks a total moulding of the person in depth. Intellectuals are particularly susceptible to this form of propaganda. It is difficult to develop when a nation has been whipped up by agitation propaganda. Mao Zedong solved this problem by simultaneously subjecting his people to stereotypes, slogans, and interpretations that integrated them well into the group.

3. *Vertical* versus *horizontal* propaganda. *Vertical* propaganda is what people normally think of as classic propaganda; it occurs in a top to bottom direction, from the leader to the people—Nazi propaganda is one example. The leader is a technician, a political or religious head who acts from a position of authority. Such propaganda is conceived in secret enclaves and uses all the technical methods of mass communication. The masses undergoing this propaganda are seized, manipulated, and become committed. In a sense, they are like hypnotic subjects. They become depersonalized, acting from conditioned reflex. They do not act spontaneously, though they may believe they do. They are mechanized, dominated, and passive.

By contrast, *horizontal* propaganda is made within the masses, not top to bottom. The group leader acts as animator, letting individuals condition each other, but the person who enters the group does so on the basis of information, data, and reasoning that are distorted. Horizontal propaganda needs a huge organization of people. The groups must be small—about 15 to 20. It is a characteristic of horizontal propaganda that it is not distinguished from education by the participants. This is how Mao could proceed from subversive to integration propaganda.

4. *Irrational* versus *rational* propaganda.[51] Once again, *irrational* propaganda represents what we denote by propaganda in its familiar sense—emotive appeals, myths, symbols, and so on, which are used to influence people. What is novel is Ellul's characterization of some forms of *rational* communication as propaganda. Despite appearances, rational and irrational propaganda have much in common. Rational propaganda has the appearance of genuine scientific truth, but is often mystification. Citations of facts and figures leave the impression of great rationality, but often the hearer is unable or unwilling to analyze the figures and is persuaded by the appearance of rationality rather than by coming to grips with factual reality. The individual affected is often convinced by an emotional feeling, treating science in effect as myth. As people become progressively more educated, propaganda becomes more rational and factual in form. It is not clear whether rational persuasion ceases to be propaganda when there is a genuine, rational appraisal of the information offered. Ellul writes that the use of facts, statistics, and economic ideas is still propaganda because it "uses these *facts* to *demonstrate, rationally* the superiority of a given system [the Soviet one in his example] and to demand everybody's support."[52] His form of words suggests that genuinely rational persuasion can still be propaganda, but the example points to the opposite. Ellul did not believe for a moment that the system in the Soviet Union was superior. Therefore, any facts used to prove that it was would have to be insufficient and misleading, if not downright false.

Ellul's categories provide a refreshing, inspirational base from which to approach the understanding of propaganda. They throw into confusion any attempt to give a precise definition for the term, but that is not necessarily a shortcoming, since, as we have seen, there are already deep divisions in the way the word is understood. Ellul's aim is to concentrate on the phenomenon and the effects of propaganda, and for this purpose the widening of the concept of propaganda has a useful function. As we develop our understanding of propaganda in the following chapters, it will be useful to keep these categories in mind, even though we will not always refer specifically to them. What most people typically think of as propaganda is political, agitative, vertical, and irrational. Yet, if Ellul is right, we have every reason to be concerned also about sociological, integrative, horizontal, and supposedly rational propaganda.

PLAN OF THE BOOK

In the following chapters, we will view propaganda first from a historical perspective and then from an analytical standpoint. For lack of space, the historical section is not a complete survey, but a chronological examination signalling new, or what I feel to be particularly striking, developments of propaganda in history. Succeeding chapters will examine propaganda, rhetoric, and persuasion from an ethical standpoint. We live in a time when complex ethical questions are easily subordinated to the demands of efficiency, profit-maximization, and maintenance or furthering of political power. Each of these demands has its own ethical component, but is far from the whole ethical story. What is needed is a look at wider ramifications of persuasive devices designed by some body or groups to support or advance a particular concern. Government information, corporate public relations (PR), and advertising figure prominently, but the relevant list is much broader.

It is not difficult to show that the negative associations attached to propaganda are often richly deserved. This book aims to expand awareness of the most pernicious forms of propaganda and to draw attention to social and legal controls over it. It seems indisputable that propaganda has contributed mightily to some of the worst evils of our time, but is there any form of control over it that will not require compromising with the ideal of self-reliance and self-development? And if compromise is necessary, to what extent? The Internet has brought with it added complexities related to the technical difficulties—some would say impossibility—related to control of that medium. The question of control occupies the final section of this book.

NOTES

1   The idea that advertising and public relations learned a lot from World War I activities is only part of the truth. The other part is that some of the techniques were well established in advertising and that there was indebtedness in the other direction. The famous Alfred Leete poster, "Britons: Kitchener wants you!" appears to have taken its cue from a noted BCV cigarette advertisement a few years earlier. See Nicholas Hiley, "'Kitchener wants you' and 'Daddy, what did YOU do in the Great War?': The Myth of British Recruiting Posters," *Imperial War Museum Review* II (1997): 40-58, at 53.

2   Jacques Ellul, *Histoire de la propagande* (Paris: Presses Universitaires de France, 1967).

3   Charles Stevenson, *Ethics and Language* (Yale University Press, 1944) 210.

4   Oscar Wilde, *A Woman of No Importance*, ed. Ian Small (London: A&E Black, 1993) Act I:19.

5   Harold Lasswell, *Propaganda Technique in the World War* (London: Kegan Paul, Trench and Tubner 1927; New York: Alfred Knopf, 1927) 4.

6   Leonard Doob, *Public Opinion and Propaganda*, 2nd ed. (Hamden, CT: Archon 240).

7   Jacques Ellul, "propagande," *Larousse, La Grande Encyclopédie* (1975) 9888.

8   Bertrand Russell, *Education and the Social Order* (London: George Allen and Unwin, 1967; originally published 1932) 126. On "party feeling," see Richard Whately's remarks in Chapter 5.

9   Bruce L. Smith, "Propaganda," *Encyclopedia Britannica Macropedia* (Chicago: Encyclopedia Britannica, Inc., 1985).

10 Alex Carey, *Taking the Risk Out of Democracy: Corporate Propaganda versus Freedom and Liberty* (Champaign, IL: University of Illinois Press, 1997) 20.

11 Edward Bernays, *Crystallizing Public Opinion* (New York: Boni and Liveright, 1923) 212.

12 Richard Taylor, *Film Propaganda: Soviet Russia and Nazi Germany* (London: Croom Helm, 1979) 28.

13 Vernon McKenzie, *Through Turbulent Years* (London: Geoffrey Bles, 1938).

14 Brendan Bracken, British *Parliamentary Debates*, Fifth Series, Volume 401: 926.

15 See Forsyth Hardy, *Grierson on Documentary* (1966, 1946; New York: Praeger, 1971) 246.

16 For this point I am indebted to P. King, who commented on an exploratory paper dealing with this issue at the Ockham Society, Oxford University, 7 March 1988.

17 See Joel Rudinow, "Manipulation," *Ethics* 88 (1978): 338-47.

18 David Halberstam describes a case like this in *The Powers That Be* (New York: Alfred Knopf, 1979) 115-16. See also Upton Sinclair, *The Brass Check* (Passadena, CA: n.p., 1920).

19 See Steve Butterfield, *Amway: The Cult of Free Enterprise* (Montreal and Buffalo: Black Rose Books, 1986). "The test of all 'truth' in Amway is whether it strengthens the business and increases PV [point value]" (84).

20 The speech is recorded in the movie, *Have I Ever Lied to You Before* (National Film Board of Canada, 1976), which is about Jerry Goodis.

21 Naomi Klein, *No Logo* (Toronto: Alfred A. Knopf, 2000) *passim*.

22 The interested reader is referred to Barry Allen, "A Note on the Definition of 'Propaganda,'" *The Canadian Journal of Rhetorical Studies* 3 (September, 1993).

23 William Lutz, *Doublespeak* (New York: HarperPerennial, 1990) 127-28.

24 George Orwell, *Homage to Catalonia* (1938; Harmondsworth: Penguin Books, 1962) 64.

25 See Sonia Orwell and Ian Angus, eds., *The Collected Essays, Journalism and Letters of George Orwell*, Vol. 1 (Harmondsworth: Penguin Books, 1970) 352. For identification of Pollitt's position, see Bernard Crick, *George Orwell: A Life* (Harmondsworth: Penguin, 1980) 314.

26 George Orwell, *The Collected Essays, Journalism and Letters of George Orwell*, Vol.2, ed. Sonia Orwell and Ian Angus (1968; Harmondsworth: Penguin, 1970) 336.

27 Frantz Fanon, *The Wretched of the Earth* (New York: Grove Press, 1963) 50; Jean Paul Sartre, "A Plea for Intellectuals," *Between Existentialism and Marxism* (New York: Morrow Quill Paperbacks) 228-285; see, especially, 261.

28 Orwell, *Homage to Catalonia* 234, 236. It is worth noting that the original publication date of this text was 1938.

29 "Chrétien would scrap GST," *The Globe and Mail* (29 October 1990): 1.

30 *The New York Times* (19 August 1988): A14.

31 George Orwell, *Nineteen Eighty-Four* (Harmondsworth: Penguin, 1949) 45.

32 Orwell, *Nineteen Eighty-Four* 31-32.

33 Orwell, *Nineteen Eighty-Four* 200.

34 George Orwell, "A Farthing Newspaper," *G.K.'s Weekly* (29 December 1928).

35 George Orwell, "Boys' Weeklies," *Collected Essays* (London: Mercury Books, 1961)110, 114
(emphasis added). I am reminded of the pseudoscientific displays in occupied France during
World War II, in which were labelled parts of a face "the Jewish nose," "the Jewish eye,"
etc., precisely with the harmful effect alluded to by Orwell (on page 101), of treating a
human being as an insect.

36 George Orwell, "Notes on Nationalism" (London: Mercury Books, 1961) 265-87, 275.

37 George Orwell, "Politics and the English Language," *Collected Essays* (London: Mercury
Books, 1961) 337-51.

38 See *The New York Times*, "Excerpts From Primer for Insurgents" (17 October 1984). *Soldier
of Fortune* Magazine (February 1985), republishing the manual, comments that "There is no
specific direction to indicate that the term means kill, kidnap or simply relocate. Adherence
to the basic philosophies presented would indicate the first choice would be the last one
made by a guerilla leader concerned with his image among the people" (95-1A). But if "kill"
is not a central part of the thinking, why the need for such extreme precautions?

39 Jacques Ellul, *The Political Illusion* (1967; New York: Random House, Vintage Books, 1972).
Originally published as *L'Illusion politique* (Paris: Robert Laffont, 1965).

40 Jacques Ellul, *Propaganda: The Formation of Men's Attitudes*, trans. Konrad Kellen (New York:
Random House, Vintage Books, 1973). Ellul gave me permission to publish a translation of
this second text, which appeared as *FLN Propaganda in France During the Algerian War*
(Ottawa: By Books, 1982).

41 Jacques Ellul, *Histoire des Institutions* (Paris: Presses Universitaires de France, 1961).

42 The issued is covered in the CAUT *Bulletin On Line* 48,9, found at
<http://www.caut.ca/english/bulletin>.

43 Jacques Ellul, *The Technological Society* (New York: Random House, Vintage Books, 1964)
10, 14.

44 See Neil Tudiver, *Universities for Sale* (Toronto: James Lorimer, 1999).

45 Claude Steiner and Charles Rappelye, "Interview with Jacques Ellul," *Propaganda Review*
(Summer 1988): 32.

46 Ellul, *Propaganda* 31; 31-32.

47 Ellul, *Propaganda* 40.

48 Orwell, *Collected Essays*, Vol. 2, 29.

49 Noam Chomsky, *Chronicles of Dissent* (Vancouver: New Star Books, 1992) 5.

50 Ellul, *Propaganda* 64.

51 In order to preserve symmetry, I have reversed the order in which Ellul presented these two
categories of propaganda.

52 Ellul, *Propaganda* 84.

TWO

HISTORY OF PROPAGANDA

INTRODUCTION

When we consider propaganda as the attempt to shape the thoughts and feelings of others, in ways conforming to the aims of the communicator, we find a vast array of different examples throughout history. For any brief summary, there are problems of selection. Which of the many candidates for our attention merits inclusion and why? Insofar as we think of propaganda as involving a relatively deliberate intention to influence a given public, many examples that at first present themselves for our consideration become problematic. Oliver Thomson's *Easily Led: A History of Propaganda*[1] gives a wide and useful range of historical examples. However, they have not been filtered to leave only cases where deliberate opinion-shaping was a proven guiding motive. Although the more inclusive approach to studies of propaganda can be justified, we will follow a more restricted strategy.

First and foremost are those instances of propaganda recognized as such by ancient theoretical treatments of rhetoric. These take on special significance by virtue of their impact on theorists and practitioners of persuasion down through the ages. Second are historical events deemed to be especially useful as a way of illustrating forms of persuasion used today or that are especially relevant in some way to current controversies about opinion formation. Major developments in political propaganda from ancient times through the Middle Ages and the Napoleonic Era to the wars and revolutions of the first half of the twentieth century will be briefly surveyed in what follows.

ATHENS

Pisistratus

The ancient Greek tyrant Pisistratus (sixth century B.C.E.) pioneered two powerful techniques for influencing public opinion. The first, as described by Herodotus, was what today would be called "victim hegemony"—the description of oneself or one's group as the victim of unjust behaviour on the part of others so as to gain public support and, hence, power. Pisistratus wounded himself and his mules, making it seem as though enemies had set upon him with murderous intent. He asked the Athenian people for personal guards, which they gave him out of respect for his military successes in earlier battles. He then used this guard to take control of the Acropolis. Two centuries later, Aristotle noted in his *Rhetoric* that the use of a vivid example can be a powerful means of persuasion. As an illustration, he considered what might happen if a politician of his own time were to ask for a bodyguard: people would be reminded of what happened in the case of Pisistratus when such a request was granted.

A similar principle has been used many times in the course of history: one country will invent, exaggerate, or provoke an incident involving insult or violence to some of its citizens. The resulting wave of indignation will be used to support a pre-planned war effort against the offending nation. Hitler's invasion of Poland was presented as a response to injustice. American support for the Vietnam War followed what was presented as an unprovoked torpedo attack on US vessels in international waters off the coast of North Vietnam.

Pisistratus's second technique was to persuade the public to believe that he was under the protection of a god. Pisistratus had been expelled from Athens when his enemies became united against him. He took the opportunity of later divisions among them to make an alliance with one of his former opponents. On his return to the city, he was accompanied by a tall and beautiful woman dressed in a full set of armour and mounted on a chariot. He presented her to the people of Athens as the goddess Athena. Herodotus observed that the city-dwellers were so taken in that they actually prayed to her. This, too, is a commonly used method of garnering public support. In one way or another, the would-be ruler in a believing society tries to indicate that the deity or deities favours him or her. It is a commonplace that in war "God is on our side" is met with "Gott mit uns" by the other. This continues to be true today in the "war against terrorism," in which claims on one side to be engaging in a Jihad, or Holy War, are met by appeals to "just war" principles in what initially was dubbed a "crusade" in pursuit of "infinite justice."

Pericles

One of the models for oratorical persuasion down through the centuries is that used by Pericles at the end of the first year of the Peloponnesian War in 431 B.C.E. His speech honoured Athenians killed in battle while also strengthening the resolve of survivors to continue to fight. Political leaders for good and evil causes have made use of the techniques found in this text; for instance, Abraham Lincoln used it in his Gettysburg Address. They include a large component of what Ellul called "propaganda of integration," which gives the audience a sense of belonging to a special group or nation.

It does not much matter that the speech attributed to Pericles is partly a reconstruction and partly an invention of the historian Thucydides, who recorded it.[2] What matters is the reasons for its power. Beginning by praising the past and lauding the present for its superiority over the institutions of its neighbours through the practice of democracy in government, Pericles extols the virtues of Athenian society: Athenians are law-abiding, even towards unwritten laws; they enjoy recreation and have good taste; they are open to whatever foreign goods may benefit them, and the city is open to the world. They regularly fight and win battles, without relying on allies, as the Spartans do. People are public-spirited: "[W]e do not say that a man who takes no interest in politics is a man who minds his own business; we say that he has no business here at all." Athenians make friends by doing good to others, rather than by receiving benefits. Because Athenians are superior to the rest of the world, in defending Athens, soldiers die for something of great value. They have a vision of Athens' greatness and put the communal good above their private welfare. They are honourable, and their survivors must emulate their conduct to be worthy of the same honour. If a soldier is brave and remains alive, he will always have to contend with jealous people, but for those who die there is sincere and unchallenged honour. And if a soldier leaves children behind, the state will look after them.

Without much adaptation, the same inspiriting ideas have been used to bolster the war efforts of modern nations. Remembrance Day ceremonies in honour of those who died in World War I strengthened the resolve of nations fighting World War II and later wars, provoking some opposition to the ceremonies themselves. From a present-day perspective, Pericles's speech is likely to be seen as a two-sided affair. It promotes worthwhile things such as respect for law, equality, and dignity, but it also exalts Athenian society over others, providing an excuse for colonization and spreading contempt for those who do not belong to it.

Pericles's speech presents Athens, past and present, through rose-coloured glasses. Oliver Thomson comments that "propaganda usually chooses to flatter— it tells its audience that it is racially or ethnically superior, religiously superior, militarily superior; the master race, God's chosen people, the invincible."[3] It matters little that the Athenians boasted about their democracy. Down to the present day the luminous image of democracy has often served as a pretext for the most undemocratic actions. As we learn from Jeffrey Keshen's study of propaganda and censorship in Canada during World War I, the illusion of general equality often obscured a deeply imbedded tendency toward nativism, or the treatment as inferior of those newcomers to Canada who harboured "customs, beliefs or racial backgrounds preventing easy assimilation into white Anglo-Protestant society."[4]

The power of this kind of funeral oration lies with the special connection it makes between living and dead, time and eternity. The more the dead are honoured, the more the living can look forward to being honoured in similar fashion when it comes their turn to die. It is no surprise that Goebbels made such a showing of Nazi funerals or that funerals have been the occasion for political statements by established powers and terrorist organizations alike.

Plato

Plato's distinctive contributions in relation to rhetoric and persuasion are most commonly associated with his philosophical analyses of these practices, rather than in his practice of the art itself. Three of his dialogues—the *Gorgias*, the *Phaedrus*, and the *Menexenus*—deal centrally with questions of rhetoric. Plato presents Socrates as a seeker after truth in opposition to the sophists, rhetoricians concerned only with appearances rather than reality; hucksters, who sell the ability to convince others of what is not the case—rather as some modern lawyers can convince a jury that a defendant who is guilty is not guilty. But the simple dichotomy between the truth-seeking Socrates and the truth-contemptuous sophists does not work. For one thing, Socrates transparently engages in some of the techniques he ascribes to the sophists. Secondly, he endorses the use of deception on very special occasions, and he quite generally accepts the use of myth for imparting truths established on more rational grounds.

In the *Gorgias*, Plato articulates one important principle of rhetoric: basing persuasive arguments on the preexisting beliefs of the audience.[5] A frontal attack on another's entrenched belief is likely to meet with rejection. The artful rhetorician packages ideas to make them palatable, like sugarcoating a bitter pill. The *Phaedrus* describes how persuasion can be achieved through a succession of individually barely perceptible conceptual shifts.[6] An interlocutor accepts an idea and is made to accept another idea almost indiscernible from it. Having made successive concessions of this sort, the interlocutor is brought to a point where the final result is recognizably very different from the starting point and would never have been conceded at the beginning. In both cases, Socrates expresses unhappiness about the fact that persuading someone to believe what is false may thus be achieved, although he makes skilful use of such rhetoric himself.

Plato's most profound insight is that, to have the most lasting persuasive effect on matters of the greatest moral significance, the ordinary rules of rhetoric may not suffice. On the surface Socrates contributed to his martyrdom by breaking a rule of rhetoric. Instead of recognizing and placating the prejudices against him held among the juror-judges, which he would certainly have been capable of doing, he antagonized them by suggesting that he should be rewarded for his gadfly work by getting free maintenance at the state's expense. This provoked them into calling for the death penalty. At a deeper level, Plato says that persuading an audience of certain fundamental and important truths as distinct from getting immediate assent and applause may require the force of personal witness, paying the price for such witness with one's life.[7]

The *Menexenus*, whether genuinely written by Plato or not, is clearly written with Pericles's funeral oration in mind and provides analytical insights into that form of rhetoric. Socrates tells us how he gets very moved by such speeches at the time they are given, how they puff up his pride, allowing him to imagine himself "a greater and nobler and finer man than I was before," and how they cause him to experience a sudden consciousness of triumph over foreigners.[8] In this work, Plato gives us a vivid, detailed example of a form of discourse often exploited through history for the purpose of promoting racism or nationalism. We may choose to take the use of a funeral oration today for a warning, or we may see it as open to adaptations that would allow for spirit-building and community pride, while eschewing the racial superiority message. We will have more to say about Plato in Chapter 4.

Aristotle

Aristotle's *Rhetoric*, as the name suggests, goes into greater detail on principles of rhetoric than Plato's work does. It provides us with insights so basic for an understanding of persuasion, whether rhetoric or propaganda, that it will be worthwhile to summarize his main contributions. These are in the form of both general observations and specific injunctions. Aristotle writes that persuasion is based on three things: the *ethos*, or personal character of the speaker; the *pathos*, or getting the audience into the right kind of emotional receptivity; and the *logos*, or the argument itself, carried out by abbreviated syllogisms, or something like deductive syllogisms, and by the use of example. Of the three he places greatest stress on the *ethos* for persuading audiences, and, at least regarding general audiences, he may be right.[9] What *ethos* amounts to is credibility, something different from facility with words. It may be, Aristotle says, that people ought to pay more attention to argument than they do, but he is aware that we must treat audiences as we find them, and the fact is that how a person projects herself does make a difference to her credibility. To persuade an audience you need a spokesperson whom people can trust, to whom they can relate. The Nazi propaganda machine made full use of this principle, as we shall see. The Soviet Union made use of Vladimir Posner, who, having grown up in New York, spoke English like an American.[10] *Ethos* is also exploited in modern advertising, with the use of celebrity endorsements.

Aristotle's observations about *pathos* are as appropriate to propaganda today as they were to the rhetoric of his time. He recognizes that the judgments we make when we are pleased and friendly are not the same as those when we are pained and hostile. If an audience is angry with a person, they will not be receptive to even the best arguments that person may make.[11] This concentration on emotional impact is used in modern advertising, in ads that create or exploit such things as fear of offensive body odour or envy of another's more powerful car.

Thirdly, Aristotle considers the power of argument for affecting beliefs. A rhetorician should come across as knowledgeable on the facts used in argument, but should not assume too great a retentive power on the part of the audience. He recognizes that a crowd has a limited capacity for complicated logic and so accepts only two ways of arguing, either through what he calls "enthymemes" or through examples. Enthymemes are syllogisms, but they are often shortened versions of the normal syllogism.[12] Not surprisingly, he has little to tell a modern audience about statistical analysis. He recognizes the need for experience of the past, through examples, for predicting the future. A vivid example can have a persuasive power beyond its weight in systematic statistical analysis. Experience confirms this. In World War I, the sinking of the *Lusitania*, a passenger ship crowded with women and children, was often used to illustrate German brutality, with important rhetorical effect. After the shooting down of the passenger airliner KAL 007 by the Soviets in 1983, it was not difficult for the US Congress to pass a huge appropriations bill in support of MX missiles.[13]

Aristotle also divides rhetoric into three divisions, usefully distinguished because of some differences in the persuasive techniques appropriate to each. Political contexts aim to get some public policy accepted; the courtroom or forensic situation deals with proof of guilt or innocence; and ceremonial oratory eulogizes or censures some person or persons. In a general way political speechmaking looks to the future, forensic speaking to the past, and ceremonial (also called "epideictic") talk to the present. It is not difficult to see the likelihood of overlap between these different divisions.[14]

To get a proposed public policy accepted, the orator must convince the audience that it is a good, and that means linking it in their minds with what they already believe to be good. Since everyone values happiness as a good, one strategy is to show that the proposed course of action will bring happiness to people.

It is in connection with his insights into the power of emotion and the *ethos* of the speaker, that Aristotle may have the most to contribute to the modern-day theory of rhetoric. When he says that the character projected by the speaker "may almost be called the most effective means of persuasion he possesses," he reminds us of the way inarticulate but sincere voices can often prevail in public meetings against verbally slick speakers. He also recognizes the necessity to know one's audience. Different audiences will have different preconceptions and predispositions, which will affect the *logos* of the rhetoric, and different emotional sensibilities, which will affect the *pathos* of the appeal.[15]

Aristotle also understands the need for the speaker to develop a rapport with the audience, to come across as a friend in order to receive a favourable reaction to his message. For this purpose friendship is not close and personal, but a relationship of utility or affinity. A friend is one who wishes another's good, for their own sake, and wishes to bring that good about as far as possible. Friends share in each other's pleasure. People tend to be friends who like and dislike the same things and who have similar likings regarding other people. We tend to like virtuous people. We also like people who would like to become our friends. We are friendly toward those who are pleasant, who admire us, who are affable and not cantankerous, who can make and take a joke. We like those who aren't fault-finding and who praise our good qualities, especially when we are unsure about them. We don't like people who nurse grudges.[16] This makes very clear what some politicians know instinctively; namely, that it is most unwise to "lose one's cool" at a public meeting and to berate some opponent or questioner. Such a response projects enmity, not friendship.

Aristotle does not provide a short, handy list of rules of rhetoric; however, at the risk of giving the false impression that he did, we can summarize his main points.

1. Know your audience.
2. Know your subject-matter.
3. Simplify, so that the message is understood.
4. Repeat, so that the message is not forgotten.[17]
5. Maintain attention. Sometimes, raising of the voice or vigorous bodily gestures will be needed.[18]
6. Secure appropriate emotive appeal.
7. Maintain credibility.
8. Undermine the credibility of your opponent, but without appearing mean.
9. Stress your strong points, deflecting attention from your weak points.
10. Do the opposite towards your opponent, harping on his or her weak points, deflecting attention away from the strong ones.

Aristotle gives some very practical debating counsel as well, although sometimes it seems morally questionable. (Ethical considerations in general will be dealt with in Chapter 5.)

1. Don't say something nasty about your opponent if it makes you seem abusive or ill-bred. Quote someone else as having said it.
2. If a straightforward answer to an opponent's question is likely to seem evasive, it may be better to respond with another question instead. Ambiguous questions should be met by drawing reasonable distinctions, not by a curt answer.[19]
3. Always tailor the complexity of an argument to the capacity of a given audience to follow it.
4. If an opponent makes a mistake on a seemingly irrelevant matter, take note of it, because it will hurt his credibility in other matters.
5. Style is important. Pay attention to volume of sound, modulation of pitch, and rhythm of speech.
6. If you speak after another whose arguments have been well received, you may need to give a short answer to those arguments first, in order to put the audience into a state of mind receptive to your arguments.
7. If good examples are not available, maxims and sayings may be of some help, because they at least appear to represent some long-standing truth. Sometimes one maxim can be set off against another. So "birds of a feather flock together" can be met with "opposites attract, likes repel." Likewise "no smoke without fire" has as a counter "one swallow doesn't make a summer."

Aristotle's *Rhetoric* contains much more than has been indicated here. For instance, he includes valuable tips for the courtroom lawyer and witness. He knows the usefulness of distracting an audience on occasion. His study of the emotion of pity helps explain some of the difficulties in getting people to support charities for people in far-off lands.

ROME

Quintus Cicero

Insights into methods of persuasion during Roman elections have been handed down to us in a remarkable treatise purportedly drafted by Quintus Cicero, brother of the famous orator Marcus Tullius Cicero prior to the latter's campaign for consulship, which he won in 63 B.C. His *Handbook of Electioneering* can be compared with methods and principles in use today. The handbook lays down the strategy and techniques necessary for winning and makes the point that reticence is out of place during election campaigns.

One important theme concerns what might be called the propaganda of prestige. When we talk about political candidates today, the expression "credibility" is invoked. Candidates have to show that they have important sources of support, in people or money, otherwise they will not be taken seriously. Quintus's advice to his brother can be paraphrased as follows: Make the number and variety of your friends and powerful backers well known and make sure that important people think you are worthy of the position. Cultivate close contacts and recruit people of influence and power. If you have claims on others for past favours, collect them now; at the same time, let people know that you are prepared to give favours. Make it clear that you know whether those who owe you favours are repaying them or not. Although ingratiating yourself is usually considered a fault, in an election it is absolutely necessary. It is also a time when you can approach new people without losing face. Leading people will want you as a friend if you show you value them. So flatter people. Small-town people assume you are a friend if you simply remember their names. Let people, from the most powerful to the least powerful, know what you expect of them. Don't expect too much from the powerless.

Successful electioneering involves putting on a good show. The impression of a great deal of support must be created. Hence the door-to-door canvass should be carried out with many escorts and attendants. Court publicity to the full.

A candidate should be careful not to alienate anybody. If someone calls on you, appear to show great interest, even though some people call on all the different candidates. If you spot someone as a phoney, don't let the person know you see through them; that way, you keep open the possibility that they will change their mind, whereas you could never make a friend out of someone who thinks you hold them in contempt. The same applies to opponents. Get to know them. Some you can never win over, but others may have come to dislike you on the basis of misinformation. You should try to win them over by a kindness or indication of affection.

If you can't deliver on a promise, decline the promise gracefully, or better, *don't* decline. A good man will do the former, but a good candidate the latter. Of course you can't agree to do something ignoble, but if your reason for declining is a commitment to a more powerful person, people will come to hate you. They would rather you lie to them. Honesty may be the best policy, but it is not always the best politics.[20] A seasoned politician will refuse nobody, because it sometimes happens that what seems impossible at one time later becomes possible. If you refuse, you are certain to arouse antagonism. If you promise, it is uncertain whether anger will eventually be forthcoming; in any case, it is not immediate. Not all those who ask for favours will need them when the time comes.

Modern-day "dirty tricks" were not unknown in the ancient world. Quintus advises his brother to so arrange things if he can that "there should be scandalous talk, in character, about the crimes, lusts, and briberies of your competitors." Noticeably absent is any requirement that such talk be limited by rigorous concern for truth.

Finally, Quintus urges his brother to appear upbeat by saying to himself every day: "I am new, I seek the consulship and this is Rome." He should prepare himself against the many snares, intrigues, and vices of all sorts in this kind of election; great skill is needed to escape resentment, gossip, or treacherous attack.[21]

Quintus's thoughts boil down to the following: If you are aloof from the messy dealings of electioneering, you won't get elected. It's important to appear to be uncorrupted, but you need to get the right support one way or another and that will involve putting yourself out for people, making deals, etc . A similar understanding of election campaigning appears in the work of Niccolo Machiavelli, who wrote in the fifteenth and sixteenth centuries and that of Max Weber in the twentieth century, especially his essay, "Politics as a Vocation."[22] The ethical problems arising from these putative requirements for successful electioneering are a matter for Chapter 4.

Augustus

Between Julius Caesar and his grandnephew Octavian, later renamed Augustus Caesar, Rome underwent the transformation from republic to empire. Both Caesars were skilled propagandists and self-advertisers, but the former's propaganda was deficient in one respect at least: it failed to win the support of powerful senators, who assassinated him. Augustus was more cunning and was prepared to make use of the trappings of established power systems, while gathering real power to himself.[23] He played up the connection with his grand-uncle to the hilt, helped by the fact that Julius had adopted him as his son in his will. Since Julius Caesar was considered to have been divine, Augustus encouraged the idea that he was the "son of a god."

Propaganda can be carried out by verbal and nonverbal means, or by means that give extension to ordinary forms of verbal communication. Under Augustus coins bearing his image and favourable things relating to him were produced. Scholars differ on the question of whether different minters struck these coins spontaneously or as the result of a direct order from the top; it could be that nominally independent people curried favour with what they saw as a new power source.[24] It would be surprising if the production of such coinage were without any encouragement on Augustus's part, since the appearance of his image and his exploits on coins gave him an aura of money and power in the minds of the people. In this respect it is worth recalling Jesus's famous response to the question of whether Jews should pay tribute to Caesar: "Render unto Caesar what is Caesar's, and to God what is God's."[25]

Augustus managed to preserve the appearance of respecting older institutions while increasing his own relative power. The legend "S.P.Q.R.," displayed on his coinage, stands for "The Roman Senate and People" (one still sees these letters on the sewer caps of modern Rome). He also made use of monuments, both for prestige on their own account and for the inscriptions they would carry, such as the honorific title "Pater Patriae" ("Father of his Country"), or his equestrian statue in the Forum Augustum, or the self-congratulatory list of his achievements in the inscription of the *Res Gestae*, a replicated monument reaching many people. The monuments were praised by the poets, thus adding to Augustus's presence in Rome.[26] Strong administration following the civil war preceding his rule brought loyalty from the people. For the lower orders who did not respect the law, the imperial administration made use of terror-inspiring punishments, such as crucifixion. This kind of punishment, like the burning at the stake during the Inquisition, makes a deep impression on those who witness it. The rationale for such cruelty was—and is—not so much retribution as the making unthinkable the doing of certain proscribed acts.[27]

THE EARLY CHRISTIAN ERA

A movement such as Christianity can be seen either in its own religious terms, or as one movement among many, competing for adherents among the world's population. When the ancient deities were replaced by Christianity in Rome and its empire, the practice of seeking or confirming political power through divine favour did not cease. Coronation of king or emperor by the Church reinforced the idea of political authority as coming from God.[28] The Emperor Constantine (274-337 C.E.) experienced a heavenly vision, witnessed by many soldiers, of "a sign of the cross," along with the inscription in the noonday sky of the words "By this sign, you will conquer" (*in hoc signo vinces*). The sign in Greek superimposed the letter *chi* (X) on the letter *rho* (P). Not only were these the initial letters of "Christ," but the *chi-rho* symbol was known by pagans to stand for *chreston* (meaning useful) and was used to mark important passages in a text.[29] This existing use enhanced the religious message. The *chi-rho* became a widespread symbol for Christianity, first appearing as a badge on the emperor's helmet in 315 C.E. Other vivid Christian symbols helped propagate the message of this faith. The drawing of a fish had multiple meanings: Saint Peter was asked by Jesus to be come a fisher of men; there was the miracle of the loaves and fishes; and in Greek the expression *Iesus Christos Theos* appears in acronym as *ichthus*, meaning "fish."

As might be expected, when Christianity became politically powerful what was religiously praiseworthy translated into political points. The discovery and canonization of new saints resulted in an increase in prestige for the regions that claimed them. Not surprisingly, many false tales and forgeries were spread during the medieval period, as different areas vied for a higher quotient of sanctity. However, this was also a time when storytelling was an accepted method of conveying truths of a general nature, and literal historical detail was "subservient to the great aims and purposes" of the hagiographical genre of literature, which is "altogether different from history," in the words of one medieval scholar. Thus, these historical falsehoods were not necessarily spread with a view to deception, still less with a cynical view to manipulating minds for the sake of obtaining power.[30]

One of the most outstanding forgeries of the medieval period, and perhaps the one with the greatest propaganda impact, was the so-called Donation of Constantine. This document handed over the Emperor Constantine's lands and imperial powers to Pope Sylvester and the Church. While the document was alleged to have been written in the fourth century, careful scholarship has located it as likely produced in the eighth century. Its effect was to increase the temporal involvement of the Church and the power of the Holy See. Had it been forged with these ends in view, one could say the project was very successful. However, at least one medieval historian thinks the forgery might have been done by a minor cleric of the Lateran basilica as "a hagiographical propaganda tract, based on the *Via Silvestri*, in favour of his own basilica."[31] If so, there is a lesson here on how falsehoods can get out of hand.

FROM THE MIDDLE AGES TO THE ENLIGHTENMENT

It is common today to invoke an early humanistic ideal of universities as centres of learning free from extraneous influences, such as the training of people for the work force. Yet, historians tell us that European universities evolved in answer to the increasing need to produce people capable of managing the increasingly complex worlds of church, government, law, medicine, and education when cathedral schools could no longer handle the demand for production of such skills.[32]

Jacques Ellul, in his *Histoire de la Propagande*, views the period following the twelfth century as one in which monarchical power was promoted by the Anglo-Norman princes, with the assistance of favourably written history, the political songs of wandering minstrels, and the recitation by pilgrims of heroic poems. But the main agents of propaganda in his mind were the legists, legal philosophers whose objective was to justify and explain the new centralized monarchy. While most jurists admitted the universality of imperial power, these legists affirmed the independence of what we may call the "national" powers of king and princes against the emperor. They were skilled in canon law to combat the Church and in feudal law to combat the lords. These were the people Ellul credits with building the centralized state, succeeding because of their knowledge of the popular mentality and of persuasive arguments. They wrote numerous memoranda to interested persons and made use of ceremonial public debates. Ellul also attributes their success to use of the *slogan*. They had a genius, he writes, for making up simple and easily retained formulae. Repeated many times, a slogan became looked upon as a kind of truth, accepted without any critical spirit.[33] Examples of such slogans were: *Princeps legibus solutus* ("The king is above the law") and "Tout justice émane du roi" ("All justice comes from the king"), both of which were invoked against the feudal system, and "Le roi de France est souverain en son royaume" ("The king of France is sovereign in his kingdom"), which was invoked against the emperor. Another slogan was "Que veut le roi, si veut la loi" which can be translated as "What the king wants is what the law wants," or, more pithily, "The king's will is law." The Christian view that all authority comes from God could be reconciled with this monarchical absolutism by treating the coronation of a king by the church as delegating divine authority.

When Machiavelli (1469-1527) stressed the importance of *appearances* in shaping public opinion, he based his theory to a large extent on the practices of the legists, Ellul tells us. Machiavelli proclaimed the principle that "to govern is to make believe" and carefully assessed likely public responses to different courses of action. These have earned him a preeminent place among modern propaganda theorists and advisors. By emphasizing the practical importance of appearances, Machiavelli set the stage for the conflict between normal ethical impulses to veracity and honesty and the more calculating kind of ethics that sees some valuable consequences as attainable only by curbing those virtuous impulses.

Edmund Spenser (1552-99), best known as a great Elizabethan poet and author of the *The Faerie Queene*, also wrote what amounts to a propaganda tract specifically encouraging the colonization of Ireland by the English. In *A View of the State of Ireland* he provides both a justification for doing so and a detailed plan of how it should be done.[34] Spenser's method of persuasion is a prototype for colonization generally. He stereotyped the Irish as an ignorant people living in dirty, inferior surroundings, held in thrall by a superstitious religion and laws that seem far from just to the English mind (although the punitive approach to crime favoured by the English has lost some ground since then to the restitutive approach he attributes to the Irish). He likened them to colts who have broken away from the discipline of English law, with the result that small privileged rebellious groups have subjected a majority of other Irish to their will. Spenser's solution was to deploy garrisons of English soldiers and import English farmers to make better use of the land to provide for general prosperity. English laws would replace existing custom, and the Anglican religion would displace Catholicism. As so often with colonial arguments, the objective was presented as that of bringing justice, order, education, proper food and shelter, and good living generally to the colonized people.

Many aspects of Spenser's account make it suitably characterized as propaganda: stereotyping, the omission of a voice expressing the viewpoint of the rebels themselves, and the lack of support for many factual claims. Finally, there is the uncritical supposition that the use of force will result in peace.

Louis XIV (1638-1715) used a number of notable techniques for bolstering his extraordinary power. He kept in touch with the general public through the use of gazetteers, who served the double function of spreading news that the king felt should be broadcast and of bringing him feedback, reporting reactions from the people. Today public opinion polls are used for much the same purpose, after some policy trial balloon has been flown. The propaganda of prestige was brought into play through grandiose buildings such as Versailles and the sumptuous life associated with royalty. Intricate court etiquette served to distinguish the favoured from the disfavoured.

The periodical press in Europe was subject to licensing and censorship during the seventeenth century, so that intellectuals came in time to distrust this form of publication. In the eighteenth century some critics of the established order, such as Voltaire, made effective use of pamphlets for promoting the ideals of what came to be known as the Enlightenment (a term suitable in itself for propaganda use).

THE FRENCH REVOLUTION AND ITS AFTERMATH

With the French Revolution in 1789 propaganda became more widespread than ever. The theory of revolution had as a central tenet the equality of human beings. Jean-Jacques Rousseau provided the intellectual groundwork for restructuring society by presenting a vision of the human being as innately good, but deformed by an existing repressive social system. Education was to emphasize free, unhampered choice, paradoxically in a controlled environment, so that the free choice would be exercised with a positive outcome. With that kind of educational philosophy, it is not surprising that he was also led to say that in political matters people might have to be "forced to be free." The conflict between the collective good and the individual good can ultimately undermine both, and some restriction on the pursuit of private interest may be necessary in each individual's own interest.[35]

There is a good case for claiming, as Ellul does, that the French Revolution brought a transformation in propaganda.[36] The social disruption brought about a need for propaganda, as well as a shift in the *intention* of the propagandist. The value of tradition was forced to yield to that of progress, rational thinking, and the suppression of hierarchies. Traditional morality was rejected, the Christian religion was questioned, and the values of "king" and "fidelity" were replaced by "*patrie*," "liberty," "equality," and the like, along with promotion of the value of happiness. In the middle of these upheavals, individuals felt themselves lost. They had to proceed rapidly to changes and adaptations so fundamental that they could not produce them alone. They needed guides, new values, and orientations. Propaganda allowed a person to recognize himself or herself and to act amid all these great changes. Problems were accentuated when the king was executed, as this had a traumatic effect on subconscious levels of the population's psyche. We have seen, in the case of Augustus's use of coinage, the importance of imagery on the public consciousness; the replacement of the king's portrait by the Goddess of Liberty on the official seal, following the establishment of the Republic, no doubt helped to fill a void.

In response to such needs, a *Bureau de l'esprit publique* was set up under the Ministry of the Interior. The assembly voted it a large sum of money to print propaganda materials. At the beginning of the revolution, Ellul notes, there were also "think-tank" clubs, such as the Jacobin Club, which served as instruments of propaganda. These clubs had branches throughout the country and, thus, were a means of getting opinion elsewhere in line with that in Paris. The most distinctive institutions of propaganda were the *Sociétés populaires*, which sprang up under the Convention. These organizations, which included the most active revolutionaries, had multiple roles, propaganda being among them. They were to be "arsenals of public opinion," disseminating the ideas of the Convention, controlling the opinions of bureaucrats, and launching campaigns against the Church. Widespread use of festivals, engravings, medals, ribbons, songs, posters, crockery, and even playing cards kept the revolutionary message in people's minds.[37] Symbols, such as the liberty tree, the pikestaff and liberty cap, the Bastille, and the *sans-cullottes* (trousers representing the ordinary, hardworking, unprivileged citizen), were easily recognizable as pointing to elimination of class differences stemming from feudal times. Jacques-Louis David put art in the service of revolutionary ideals; his painting, *Marat Assassinated*, is a notable example. Ellul describes some of the large-scale ceremonies as ritual gatherings for the purpose of creating a mass psychology; for instance, the *Fête de la Fédération*, on July 14, 1790, attracted 200,000 delegates from all parts of the country.

At this time, education also came under government instead of Church jurisdiction with the result that love of *la patrie* (fatherland) and republican convictions were inculcated at an early age. Teaching was not to be disinterested and objective, but done in such a way as to help future citizens become useful to their country. The army also became itself an instrument of propaganda, since it uprooted the young recruit from family and community ties and placed him in an environment where he would be more susceptible to the new ideas fostered by the government.

James Leith locates the height of propaganda as taking place under the Jacobins (also known as Montagnards) following their domination of the Convention in August 1793 and reaching a peak shortly after the spring of 1794. They eliminated the moderate press, took control of the theatre, and set up a National Institute of Music with a view to fostering military feelings among other things. David was made a "virtual dictator of the arts." A Committee of Public Instruction planned to produce primary school textbooks, which would associate republicanism with favourable ideas in their choice of grammatical examples. However, during their short reign of terror, the Jacobins lacked the time and resources to put into effect their plans for total propaganda in schools or elsewhere. In Leith's view, the

Jacobins were "moving toward that central control which we associate with modern propaganda," with propaganda functions carried out by different agencies: "At the centre the Committee of Public Safety, the Commission of Public Instruction (an executive body), the Committee of Public Instruction (a legislative organ), the Jacobin Club, and the Paris Commune all shared in initiating and directing propaganda, producing such confusion that some historians have habitually ascribed certain activities to the wrong agencies."[38]

Ellul notes another technique used by the revolutionaries to promote cohesion, that of naming official enemies of the people. Three things are effected by this technique: crystallization of public opinion, removal of a feeling of inferiority and injustice (revenge being a catharsis), and the possibility of compensating for certain difficulties, such as shortcomings in the state leadership. Hitler was later to exploit this technique against the Jews and Lenin against the Kulaks. Some care is needed in the selection of enemies, Ellul observes. They should be near enough at hand and relatively known, not too powerful, and sufficiently different from the people, but not entirely so. It helps if the chosen enemy is already suspect and little loved in the eyes of popular opinion. The choice of clergy, immigrants, Chouans (western insurgents) and Babouvists (followers of Babeuf, egalitarian communists) as official enemies satisfied these requirements. In the French Revolution Ellul's categories of integration propaganda, sociological propaganda, and horizontal propaganda had widespread application, to an extent not seen before. In Leith's analysis, propaganda fitting Ellul's other categories—agitation propaganda, political propaganda, and vertical propaganda—also advanced under the Jacobin terror.

Napoleon

Napoleon Bonaparte (1769-1821) understood with a kind of genius the nature and importance of public opinion and the means by which it might be shaped in order to be gain control over the masses. His absolute dominance over France and most of Europe was testimony to his ability to lead people. When he tells us how it is done, we listen, not because his totalitarian form of rule is attractive, but because knowledge of his technique helps in defending against them, and some of them might be applied for more benign purposes and policies than those he pursued.

Two aphorisms stand out regarding Napoleon's overall philosophy: "Government is nothing unless supported by opinion" and "The truth is not half so important as what people think to be true."[39] Like Aristotle and Plato, he understood the necessity of knowing one's audience and of shaping minds from a young age. Because, like St. Ignatius of Loyola, he knew the importance of reaching young people who "can hardly avoid accepting whatever version of the facts is presented to them," he exercised control over the school system. Students had to read Caesar's *Commentaries*, Pierre Corneille, and other texts supporting established order. They had to pledge allegiance to Napoleon, much as young Americans of my generation had to pledge allegiance to the flag. Certain army bulletins were regularly read in schools as well. He made use of the established religion. A catechism read: "What are the duties of Christians with respect to the princes who govern them, and what are in particular our duties to Napoleon I our Emperor?" The requisite answer was "...love, respect, obedience, fidelity, military service, tributes ordered for the preservation and defence of the Empire and of his throne... To honour and serve our Emperor is therefore to honour and serve God himself" (141).

Censorship was an important part of his method for controlling opinion. "I shall never allow the papers to say or do anything contrary to my interests," he said, and his actions bore out this claim. By decree he reduced the number of newspapers in Paris from 73 to 13; by 1811 there were only four remaining (44). Eliminating a newspaper was simple: the police instructed the post office to stop any copies in their system and directly blocked other forms of distribution in Paris. His official publication, the *Moniteur*, was distributed in schools as well as army camps. To downplay his own totalitarianism, he had the press report on censorship occurring in other nations, while ensuring that newspapers were full of his praise (52).

Napoleon also manipulated people by his control over awards, decorations, pensions, the arts, and so forth. "You lead people with toys and trinkets—decorations and the like," he said. Authors received prizes from him, and actors got pensions. After a decree of 1806, no theatre could be established without his authorization, the number of theatres was reduced from 33 to eight, and the remaining were regulated. Plays would be censored if they were felt to affect opinion adversely. During the Russian campaign, for example "all plays with passages favourable to Russia or its rulers were suspended" (147, 150).

The willingness of people to abide such totalitarian control was no doubt assisted by the benefits of his rule. Public works such as the Arc de Triomphe provided employment. He established the lycées—superior schools for students of high school age and slightly older—and supported the sciences and government administration with elite, post-secondary institutions. His military conquests brought prestige to France. He provided for old soldiers and widows and orphans of military men. Conspicuous pardons gave him a more human image. He encouraged free vaccination of all citizens (34).

Like Hitler years later, Napoleon promoted the identification of his own will with that of the country he led. He said: "Frenchmen, my will is that of the people; my rights are its own; my honour, my glory, my happiness can be none other than the honour, glory and happiness of France" (May 31, 1815) (173). Joey Smallwood, Premier of Newfoundland, although not in the same league, of course, also made use of the same technique.[40]

Napoleon knew something about the principle of orchestration. Those who study propaganda are aware that seemingly insignificant items can have cumulatively a powerful affect on people's thinking. Napoleon wrote that "Every day [propaganda] pieces of every type, of every style, tending to the same goal but addressing themselves to sundry sentiments and mind, must be published. It is thus that a whole nation is successfully put into a kind of intoxication" (180). True to his principle that what people believe true is more important than what is actually true, he exaggerated the strength of his forces by two or three times, and he greatly underestimated his military losses (189).

Finally, it is worth noting the technique Napoleon used of circulating rumours. There were three purposes for these, Holtman tells us: they could bolster public morale, as with rumours of peace; they could support military tactics; and they could give an indication as to whether public opinion was favourable to an idea or not (112-13).

It is not difficult to see that Napoleon introduced and developed propaganda on a grand scale. In turn, it is not surprising that Carl von Clausewitz, military leader of one of his conquered nations, should have absorbed some of these ideas and taught them to new recruits, ideas that were later to be used—ironically—against France herself.

Carl von Clausewitz

Carl von Clausewitz (1780-1831), director of the Berlin Military Academy, is renowned for having apparently stated, "War is a mere continuation of politics by other means." People often react with horror to this statement, because it implies a callousness about the brutality of war. In fact, von Clausewitz wished to ensure that war had a rational purpose and that waging it—and experiencing its horrors— was necessary only to achieve some important objective. In contrast to what he is reported to have said, his actual words were, "War is not merely a political act, but also a real political instrument, a continuation of political commerce, a carrying out of the same by other means."[41]

Von Clausewitz knew all too well that war creates passions, which can fuel combat beyond the point where anyone's interests are served. He felt that propaganda was a vital instrument in war, because it helped bring out the best in one's own troops and demoralized the enemy. Like Henry v at Harfleur, he looked favourably on the cheap victory. If war is glorified, it tends to eclipse the policies it is meant to serve. By stressing the subordination of the military to the political, von Clausewitz was promoting a humanitarian end, in relative terms.

His approach to war was coldly analytical: "*War…is an act of violence intended to compel our opponent to fulfill our will.*"[42] The stronger the enemy's feelings, the costlier the war is likely to be. Conversely, he believed, if one's own people don't feel strongly about the cause, success will be less likely. Sometimes feelings among one's own masses need stimulation, because "usually no innate hostile feeling" exists between individuals. However, once combat starts, it kindles a hostile feeling of itself. There is a natural desire to retaliate against those bent on harming us, even though they may only be following orders and have no personal animosity against us. That people do not aim their retaliation more selectively, giving priority to those giving the orders as distinct from the followers in the field, is just a fact of human nature. The legacy of hatred and ill-feeling that follows war, prolonging it unnecessarily, should be anticipated at the start and factored into the overall calculations. Otherwise, the war may turn out to be more costly than anticipated and not justifiable.

Von Clausewitz also took note of the value that neutral nations may have for the success of a war. It is important to present one's case to neutrals in such a way as to gain their sympathy, since they could affect the course of war by supporting in various ways one's own side or the other's. Therefore, he emphasized the value of propaganda for accomplishing a nation's objectives on three fronts: to one's enemy, to one's own side, and to neutral nations.

LATER NINETEENTH-CENTURY DEVELOPMENTS

Statistics

Given the widespread use of misleading statistics today, it is worth taking note of a particularly controversial census, the US sixth census of 1840. It recorded 17,456 "insane and idiots," with relatively similar proportions in the North and the South for the white population, but with a proportion 11 times higher for freed blacks than for those under slavery in the South. This led to the pro-slavery argument that slavery was far better for a black person than freedom, and the census was frequently cited for that purpose.

However, a contemporary physician, Dr. Edward Jarvis, a founder of the American Statistical Association in 1839 and a specialist in mental disorder, found minor discrepancies between the national statistics and those of the Overseers of the Poor in Massachusetts, the former reporting far fewer "insane and idiotic paupers" than the latter. More importantly, he found internal inconsistencies in the census, such as reports for many towns in the North where no black residents were listed, but nevertheless several black insane were said to exist. He concluded that "no reliance can be placed on what purport to be facts, respecting the prevalence of insanity among free Negroes [sic], set forth in that fallacious and self-condemning document, the Sixth Census of the United States."[43]

Co-opting the Press

During the American Civil War, US Secretary of War Edwin Stanton followed Napoleon's example by manipulating casualty figures, issuing daily bulletins, suspending newspapers, arresting editors, and enforcing censorship in other ways. By the 1860s the mass-circulation press was well-established, and the military exercised various means for co-opting correspondents, who were often denied adequate expenses by their editors. Edmund Stedman, of the *New York World*, defended his acceptance of $50 from an artillery officer on the ground of need. "Of course he expects me to keep a lookout for his guns hereafter, and I believe

I can do so with a clear conscience," he wrote to his wife. With hot competition between newspapers, reporters sought out any superior vantage point from which to observe the war. Tom Cook of the *New York Herald* wrote to his editor to suggest a deal with the Navy, whereby he would get a boat from them in return for a promise of more favourable coverage in the *Herald's* pages.[44]

Confederate propaganda was carried out by Henry Hotze, who furnished, according to his own account, news items and editorials to various London papers. He not only had seven paid writers on his payroll, but distributed boxes of cigars from Havana, whiskey, and other articles as inducements to the British press to report favourably on the Southern cause. On May 1, 1862, he began publishing a weekly periodical, called *The Index*, which, by appearing to be British, concealed its propaganda purpose.[45] The novel aspect of Hotze's technique was revealed in his private communications, in which he declared that the paper itself was not the primary vehicle of propaganda. Since those who worked on the *Index* as assistant editors were also contributors to major London newspapers, there was naturally a spill-over effect. As Burton Hendrick wrote: "The information and opinions they had absorbed as *Index* workers inevitably formed the groundwork of their contributions to leading London organs of opinion. Thus they received double payment. Hotze paid them as salaried workers on his staff; the London papers paid them for the same articles when warmed over for their editorial columns. This wider field was the important one...."[46] Hotze's method of tangential influence is worth remembering in the more recent context of payments by corporations to distinguished writers, seemingly with no direct interest in the content of the subsidized articles. In 1976, E.B. White, the children's book writer, essayist, and grammaticist, passionately denounced such practices, saying that "Buying and selling space in news columns could become a serious disease of the press."[47]

The mass-circulation press had grown so much in power and influence by the end of the nineteenth century that William Randolph Hearst was reported to have said to an artist correspondent in Cuba, who had complained about there being no war to depict, "You send pictures, I will furnish war." He proceeded to do just that, whipping up US hysteria against the Spanish, which led to the Spanish American War.[48]

With the Boer War came some of the earliest uses of newsreel cinema for war propaganda. The Boers were depicted as immoral; for instance, one scene showed them firing on a Red Cross tent while a brave British medical team tried to treat a wounded soldier. According to Phillip Knightley, "[t]he film was a fake shot with actors on Hampstead Heath, a suburb of London." The war also produced the first concentration camps, along with suppression of news connected with them. Crowded tents, disease, foul drinking water, heat, and suchlike brought a soaring death rate. About one-third of the interned adults and half the children died.[49]

Another aspect of propaganda during the Boer War was the harnessing of racial mythology to support the war effort. According to Knightley "the government did everything it could to mobilize public opinion for queen and country. This involved encouraging the racialism and jingoism, in their most virulent forms, and creating animosity against the enemy with the tireless ploy of the atrocity story." *The Times* carried phrases like "the common man of Empire," "the fundamental grit of the breed," and "the unanalysable qualities that have made the Empire."[50] Such propaganda involved techniques later applied on a vastly greater scale in World War I.

BRITISH PROPAGANDA IN WORLD WAR I

British propaganda in World War I was very extensive, effective, and well documented. It is not surprising that the word "propaganda" became an entry in the *Encyclopedia Britannica* for the first time in the twelfth edition, 1922, following the events of this period. Hitler and Goebbels later claimed with some justification that a significant part of their own propaganda technique was modelled on that of the British at this time. A wealth of different methods were developed, and they make for instructive study. They use, in different ways, principles of persuasion we have already discussed, but the introduction of new mass media in the form of pictorial magazines, radio, cinema, and telegraphic news services gave a whole new dimension to the speed and reach of propaganda as well as greater powers of orchestration. As we shall see, the British also emphasized a form of personal propaganda, getting the message to media–influential people.

The study of propaganda is a complex undertaking. It is not always easy, for example, to determine the extent to which propaganda activity is directed from above as distinct from spontaneously generated by individuals or groups below. For example, H.G. Wells was recruited to carry out propaganda, but he was already publishing materials suitable for propaganda purposes before any formal state-sponsored structure was organized. This distinction between political and sociological propaganda, in Ellul's terms, is only one of many different ways of categorizing the propaganda to be studied. Also to be considered is the target audience: propaganda directed at the British people themselves, allies, neutral nations, and the enemy. A third, quite different, grouping is by the media chosen to disseminate messages—books, periodicals, pictures, movies, telegraph, or personal contact. A fourth, overlapping approach concerns the nature of the message itself and the form of its appeal, such as the creation of anger and indignation by the use of atrocity stories. A fifth focal point relates to the development, over time, of the propaganda organization, in the case of Britain from its beginnings in Wellington House and the Foreign Office to the Department of Information under John Buchan and then to Lord Beaverbrook's Ministry of Information. Finally, propaganda can also be treated by examining single episodes, such as the use of the Bryce Report, the handling of the sinking of the *Lusitania*, and, most importantly, the "corpse utilization" atrocity story, singled out by numerous commentators as the most notorious of the whole propaganda war.

Wellington House

With important exceptions the bulk of British propaganda was carried out by an organization that worked at Wellington House under the direction of Charles F.G. Masterman; its first meeting was held September 2, 1914. His detailed reports, containing submissions from individual directors of propaganda targeted at individual countries or groups of countries, are very informative. An insider's overview of propaganda activities can also be found in the form of a published but unsigned report, "British Propaganda During the War 1914-1918" (hereinafter cited as the "BP Report"), a copy of which, marked "secret," is in the Sir Campbell Stuart collection in the Imperial War Museum (it is now in the public domain). Although the document conveys an element of self-justification, it provides much factual information, which can be usefully compared with other sources. Of course, people engaged in propaganda activities can be expected to be adept at self-promotion, and some discounting of self-congratulatory interpretations may be in order. For example, the BP Report describes the work of the Department of Information as "remarkably successful—largely owing to the honesty of the means it employed," whereas German propaganda was characterized by a "complete disregard for the truth and entire lack of scruple. The German Government spent on propaganda vastly greater sums than we."[51] Whatever the authors may have thought, "honesty" is hardly the right term to apply in connection with some of the materials disseminated by the department.

C.F.G. (Charles) Masterman (1874-1927), former literary editor of *The Daily News* and a Liberal member of Parliament, was already involved in what could be viewed as a kind of propaganda activity prior to the outbreak of war on August 3-4, 1914. As chairman of the National Insurance Commission, he worked in Wellington House, coordinating speakers in and outside government to travel the country persuading people of the value of the National Insurance Act, a progressive piece of legislation.[52] When Prime Minister Herbert Asquith called upon him to take on the propaganda work, he set up the organization conveniently in his own building. He brought together a distinguished group of writers and paid various publishing houses to publish their books.[53] His organization sought and obtained the cooperation of the publishers to not reveal that the government was subsidizing these works. One of the aims was to produce propaganda to counteract German propaganda and "to present the allied case and Great Britain's share in the war in the proper light" (BP 1).

An interesting aspect of the Wellington House operations, at least from the point of view of our study of propaganda, is the secrecy with which they were carried out. The ethos of the writers chosen to propagate the British side of the propaganda war was high, but it is a fair assumption that it would have been greatly reduced if the targeted audience had known these writers were representing a propaganda organization. The BP Report stated:

> The existence of a publishing establishment at Wellington House, and, a fortiori, the connexion of the Government with this establishment were carefully concealed. Except for official publications, none of the literature bore overt marks of its origin. Further, literature was placed on sale where possible, and when sent free was always sent informally, that is to say through and apparently from some person between whom and the recipient there was a definite link, and with a covering note from the person to whose private patriotism the sending of the literature seemed due. (BP 7)

Much of the distribution took place through British steamship companies, who absorbed the costs. Other business firms, patriotic organizations, religious societies, and the like also gave their help.

Six classes of literature were produced: official publications; speeches of ministers, the full texts of which were often translated into the language of target countries; pamphlets and books generated by Wellington House, either original material written on request or already existing work; pamphlets and books merely distributed by Wellington House; declarations of opinion by various classes of persons; and articles and interviews in the press (BP 5). Masterman gives a figure of 300 books and pamphlets distributed in 21 languages by September 1916.

Masterman's committee was designed to influence opinion in Allied and neutral nations, not to affect the enemy nor even, ostensibly at least, the home audience, although in the latter case substantial effects can be presumed. In the beginning pamphlets and press summaries were the main focus of activity. Later came the production of weekly, fortnightly, and monthly illustrated papers in English and foreign languages, as well as of films. From the first there was constant collaboration with the News Department of the Foreign Office under G.H. Mair. After January 1916, Wellington House activities were subsumed under the office of the Secretary of State for Foreign Affairs.

The scope of the British undertaking grew and, under the Department of Information, during 10 months of 1917, over 40 million items of all sorts (including pamphlets, pictures, postcards, and so on) were issued. Monthly and fortnightly journals (see below) in many languages were distributed throughout the world. Photographs were taken of the Navy, of troops in training, and of munitions-making. Artists added an aesthetic dimension, which had its own "propagandist value." Both photos and drawings were sent to newspapers all over the world, in the case of the former at the rate of 4,000 a week by September 1916 and more later on. Exhibitions in Britain and abroad were arranged for the materials. For rural districts in Russia, Italy, and other countries, lantern slides were prepared along with picture postcards. Other materials produced were "maps, diagrams, gramophone records, cigarette cards, model tanks for ashtrays, calendars showing German crimes and British victories, bookmarkers and blotting slips" (BP 6-7).

After January 1916, films such as "Britain Prepared," the "Battle of the Somme," and the "Battle of Arras," were successfully produced and distributed, and film came to be one of the main features of the Ministry of Information. The change in emphasis came with a feeling that Masterman's approach had been too soft and indirect and that what was needed was louder and bolder propaganda, "developing with special energy the most direct and effective known forms of publicity—personal propaganda, and propaganda by film, by wireless and by cable" (BP 7, 8).

Masterman clearly states that the important propaganda work of supplying current news items to daily newspapers of the world was not one of his responsibilities. This work was organized by G.H. Mair, at first under the Home Office, but always in conjunction with the News Department of the Foreign Office. Censorship for the different news organizations meant daily consultation with the Foreign Office to speed things up. Newspapers were generally very cooperative, but the Hearst newspapers "provided the exception" and underwent severe sanctions. According to the BP Report, the Hearst papers, despite a warning, printed material damaging to the British, which was generated in New York but which was presented as coming from London. As a result, the Foreign office "stopped supplying the Hearst newspapers with news, and arranged for a similar cessation of facilities from all other Government Departments, including the use of the British cables" (BP 2). In those days the telegraph was the source of the most up-to-date information. By carefully feeding countries around the world with a regular diet of material by telegraph, the British propaganda organization helped to ensure that its own side of the story reached audiences with the greatest speed. It is a matter of common experience that the person who tells his or her side of the story first has the better chance of influencing the recipient's perceptions.

Visits to the fleet, beginning October 1915, were regarded as an "immense success," the journalists writing "ecstatic accounts of it to their papers." Four to five months later correspondents were allowed to visit the lines in France, writing "enthusiastic accounts of what they saw." The War Office made it a policy to grant facilities to correspondents, giving them 12 hours notice before the Battle of the Somme, for example, so that they could arrive on time to witness the activities.

The Department of Information

In February 1917 a Department of Information was formed, under Colonel John Buchan, with a view to coordinating more closely the separate propaganda activities already described. It also became more aggressive, as the case of the "corpse factory story," discussed below, illustrates. Clerics generally had been targeted by Wellington House operations, but the BP Report specifically mentions that monthly letters were sent to "nearly every Catholic priest in the United States and Canada, and they were issued in French, Italian, Spanish, Portuguese, Dutch and German for distribution to leading Catholic priests and laymen in the countries concerned." Cinema production exceeded a million and a half feet, sent to 40 foreign countries. "The Battle of Arras" was considered particularly successful. About 400 press articles a week were sent to foreign newspapers. Copies of English newspapers were delivered daily to more than 300 newspapers in small American towns. A London letter was supplied weekly to 109 papers in the American midwest. In Russia, broadsheets were issued for distribution to soldiers and workmen at the rate of one million a day, despite the difficulties caused by the Russian Revolution.

Some activities were aimed simply at creating goodwill. For example in Spain "for some months about 200 free dinners a day were provided for poor women with babies, and a great many were without doubt kept by these meals from starving." Members of the embassy in Spain also met with many high-ranking clerics to discuss the war.

Hospitality operations flourished. Close to 500 visitors were taken in the last six months of 1917 to munition areas, military camps, the fleet, debates in Parliament, hospitals, schools, universities, Ireland, internment camps, etc. Visitors were constantly sent to three chateaux on the Western front, which were under the department's control. The large amount of space given by the French and Italian press to British military operations was attributed to this hospitality (BP 9–25).

The Ministry of Information

By the time propaganda activities became consolidated in March 1918 under the Ministry of Information, headed by Lord Beaverbrook, much experience had been gained. The BP Report records an even more aggressive stance and gives an interesting overview of the nature of propaganda, reflecting past and current activity:

> There are three types of propaganda: propaganda by the written word, including pamphlets, articles, cables and wireless; propaganda by picture, including cinemas, photographs and drawings; and propaganda by getting hold of the right man, telling him the facts, and then taking him to the places where he can see for himself that what you say is true. Personal propaganda of this kind is obviously the most convincing of the three, but it can be used only on a limited scale, and, though through showing one important editor the concrete evidence of this country's achievement you can reach hundreds of thousands of readers, for getting into more direct touch with large masses of men other means have to be found.

Pictures were useful for "conveying a fact or the summary of an argument to immense masses, educated and uneducated." Some subtle as well as crude means were used to affect opinion as well:

> The task of the Ministry of Information was therefore to direct the thought of most of the world. This task it performed sometimes through hints and indirect suggestion, more often with the brazen tongues of facts and statistics. In the way of propaganda by implication and nuance, it sent British musicians at times to strengthen the reputation of British music abroad; or it sent Union

Jacks to remote parts of France where they were rarely seen; or unofficially offered prizes in French schools for essays on the British Navy ... Such activities are, however, exceptional...

As an everyday concern the ministry communicated to the US the total number of British killed and wounded in the war to "point out to Americans the hard facts of what this country has done and suffered," and to hint at the "moral significance of these facts—the soul that lurks in the statistics."

One form of propaganda pioneered by the ministry was, as indicated, that of personal propaganda and hospitality. It deserves special attention, because of the widespread imitation of this method later in the century by Nazi Germany, South Africa, the Soviet Union, and the US Pentagon. The BP Report calls it one of the "greatest achievements" of the ministry. High-ranking military officials gave regular briefings to US and other "foreign and colonial" journalists who met regularly at the Overseas Press Centre, used mostly by Americans and "guests from the Dominions." Not just journalists but "the most influential men available" from all over the world were invited to stay for a month to six weeks. They were "shown absolutely everything they wished to see which was not put quite out of the question by military requirements." Often the guests would be shown around in groups of 20. American editors were most frequently targeted, with other guests being newspaper proprietors or sometimes professors or "men eminent in other ways." As might be expected, keeping so many guests happy for such a long period of time could be problematic, especially since some had "long-standing antipathies" to others in the group. With the application of "tact and patience" few hitches occurred. The great benefit came when the guests "went home and conducted on their own initiative among their own people propaganda of greater value than anything we could ever have done." Once again, the importance of *ethos* and its effect on credibility is illustrated.

An additional benefit from this form of hospitality was the securing of invitations from American organizations for British speakers to visit the US. "Some disabled officers went out in this way, primarily to support the Liberty Loan Campaigns. Afterwards, through the intervention of the Ministry, they were enabled to cooperate in Red Cross Drives and publicity campaigns of various sorts."

The ministry also helped entertain American troops, providing sports, bands, concert parties, and invitations to ceremonies such as investitures by the king. There were river trips between Maidenhead and Henley with lunch and tea on board. The work was professedly "not done from propagandist motives," although it "had a considerable propagandist value; for with the ordinary man from the purely propagandist standpoint it is more important to produce an atmosphere of personal kindliness and sympathy than almost anything else. Beyond this obvious hope that good-feeling would result, the Ministry had no axe to grind, and no surreptitious introduction of improving thoughts was made" (BP 14-18).

RADIO AND TELEGRAPH PROPAGANDA

In this age of instant Internet communication it may be difficult to envisage the importance for British propaganda at the time of the relatively primitive radio and telegraph services. With considerable efforts, the ministry was able to send out by radio 8,000 words every 24 hours to counteract enemy propaganda directed at neutral countries. The average person formed impressions "almost entirely by newspapers" and "unless a constant stream of official wireless and cable messages is sent out, foreign newspapers, for lack of anything better, will print faulty and misleading information." Against such misinformation it would be "idle to try by means of cinemas, pictures and literature to impress the magnitude of Britain's effort and achievement on the stony ground of a mind that has been accustomed to watch the Germans nobly and majestically advancing to victory day by day in the local paper."

The ministry was concerned that in countries with restricted information sources "the most preposterous enemy stories will obtain belief unless steps are taken to contradict them before they become old and venerable." Hence the importance of rapid communication: "Nor is it enough to oppose the uttered lie: one must disarm it by supplying accurate news in advance." The point is recognized in modern public relations, where it is referred to as a "preemptive strike," which, incidentally, can also be used to lessen the impact of damaging truthful information.

In pre-satellite days, messages by radio could not reach Australia directly, but many radio operators would pass on messages of their own accord "simply because they like operating." Radio was valued over cable because cable lines were often blocked, largely as a result of military needs. Radio messages were sent to Maine and then, by courtesy of the US government, were handed to the chief press agencies (BP 19).

PUBLICATIONS AND PRESS WORK

The ministry's focus shifted towards the production of articles for press consumption from the earlier method of pamphlet production. A great variety of different writers from many different walks of life were recruited for this purpose—soldiers and sailors, airmen, church leaders of every denomination, novelists, publicists, journalists, diplomats, civil servants, engineers, scientists, businessmen, etc. For example, about 236 articles were placed in French Swiss publications alone.

The strategy involved in these articles is fascinating for its use of more subtle forms of persuasion. The articles turned out by the Ministry

> concerned themselves with every conceivable subject—academic, scientific and aesthetic—casually suggesting, rather than introducing, their moral. The same effect was aimed at as in the Chinese "stop short" poem, where "only the words stop, but the sense goes on." The success of the articles was proved by the eagerness of papers all over the world to print them. (BP 21)

FILM

The power of movies to influence opinion was greatly appreciated by the ministry, and extensive efforts were made to utilize the medium. The BP Report estimates the size of weekly attendance at cinema theatres as 20 million, with about the same proportion of the population attending in other countries. What impressed the ministry was the wide range of appeal of this medium, wider "than any other medium of propaganda," speaking to small children and people from widely differing cultural backgrounds and sometimes, depending on the film, having as great an effect on mature and educated audiences. Moreover, the "fact that the cinema is incapable of argument is, from the point of view of promiscuous propaganda, an advantage." For example, it is easy to convey by pictures the operations on a huge scale of men and guns.

For propaganda to home audiences, the ministry invented an "entirely new species" of film, namely the "film-tag"—a short film, taking about two minutes to show, and embodying, usually in story form, "some useful moral such as 'Save Coal' or 'Buy War Loans.'" They were called "tags" because they were attached to resumés of the latest news. These were mainly designed for home audiences, and distribution was facilitated by three firms, which controlled topical, longer-length films. "Tags" were very popular with government departments concerned to get a message out to the public; each was seen by 10 million people.

A regular supply of films was sent out to "practically every country in the world," with titles such as "Repairing War's Ravages," "Woman's Land Army," and "London—Fact and Fiction," the latter refuting claims about which buildings had been destroyed in London by air-raids. Exhibitions of films were particularly well received in Italy, where audiences in one two-month period consisted of nearly 200,000 soldiers and sailors and 50,000 civilians (BP 22-23).

STILL PHOTOGRAPHY

Nowadays, television has stolen much of the attention formerly given to pictorial magazines, so an effort of imagination may be needed to envisage the power and influence exerted by these publications in the early part of the twentieth century. The Ministry of Information was very proud of its own *War Pictorial*, an illustrated monthly magazine, produced in colour by the latest processes. The BP Report claimed it was without doubt "one of the most important instruments of propaganda"(BP 25). The total of Spanish, Portuguese, French, Dutch-French (for Holland, Belgium, Dutch East Indies, etc.), Anglo-Dutch (for South Africa), and Greek distribution was about half a million per month, and "Banks, shops, professional men such as dentists, and so on were always glad to have it on their waiting-room tables or in other prominent places, knowing that it would offend none of their clients." The *War Pictorial* contained both photographs and drawings. Other illustrated publications produced for Oriental readers contained only photographs, for the curious reason that "the Oriental trusts the camera and mistrusts drawings."[54] Success of the fortnightly Chinese version, *Cheng Pao*, was claimed on the basis of "reliable testimony" that it had engendered among the

Chinese masses "such a respect for Allied aims that it became possible for the Chinese Government to declare war against Germany" (BP 27). Fortnightly journals were published in Arabic, Turkish, Persian, Hindustani, Chinese, Japanese, Spanish, Portuguese, Greek, Hindi, Bengali, Tamil, and Gujerati. By the end of 1916 over a million copies of all these papers put together were being circulated, and there was a continuous increase (BP 6,7).

Atrocity Propaganda

The aim of British propaganda was to persuade its various audiences that the cause of war against Germany was just, that the Allies were going to win, and that civilization depended on their winning. A key element of this propaganda was a constant harping on the theme of German barbarity. A never-ending series of reports relating to that theme were fed to the media, who seemed prepared to suspend their critical faculties, either out of a sense of contributing to the war effort or simply because these stories appealed to their readers. We know now that the thirst of the media for fresh atrocity stories was so great that journalists sometimes embellished or invented them.[55]

As with virtually all atrocity stories, an undisputed factual background provides fertile grounds for belief. On August 3, 1914, the Germans invaded neutral Belgium; as expected, some Belgian civilians resisted and were shot by the Germans. However, stories about this resistance emphasized wantonness on the part of the Germans, who allegedly engaged in mass killings, pointless burning of villages, raping, pillaging, and mass slaughter.

Published in spring 1915, the Bryce Report—the Report of the Committee on Alleged German Outrages—carried a high level of credibility among the general public. Viscount James Bryce, former British Ambassador to the US, was a greatly respected speaker and writer. His committee consisted of three prominent lawyers, an eminent historian, the editor of the prestigious *Edinburgh Review*, and the renowned jurisprudential theorist, Sir Frederick Pollock. The report discounts the idea that Belgian witnesses might have made up stories out of vindictiveness, saying that it was rare for them to describe what they had seen or suffered.[56] After the war, many of these stories were discredited, but at the time the report claimed that hearsay evidence was distrusted and used only after careful sifting. Nevertheless, the stories were sensational, and, as so often happens, they were very effective in producing the desired result, namely, a sense of revulsion against Germany that strengthened the resolve of the Allies and helped to bring about the support of neutral nations. Wellington House ensured the widest circulation for this report, and versions were printed which departed from the objective tone of the original. For example:

> It is the duty of every single Englishman who reads these records, and who is
> fit, to take his place in the King's army, to fight with all the resolution and courage

he may, that the stain, of which the following pages are only a slight record, may be wiped out, and the blood of innocent women and children avenged.

The report accused German soldiers of, among other things, decapitating babies, cutting off women's breasts (BR 25-26), publicly raping women in the marketplace (BR 48), bayoneting children and hoisting them in the air (BR 52), cutting off children's hands and ears while forcing parents to watch (BR 47), and nailing a child to a farmhouse door (BR 28). These acts impress the imagination, but the report itself placed more emphasis on the systematic killing of noncombatants, which it claimed to be the "gravest charge against the German Army" (BR 40, 42). The systematic killings were divided into two kinds—hostage-taking and reprisal killings. The latter it claimed were "altogether unprecedented." In its concluding statement, the report viewed the outrages, such as the large-scale murders, rapes, looting, house-burning, hostage-taking, and abuse of the Red Cross and white flags as "fully established by the evidence" and hoped that the disclosures would "rouse the conscience of mankind" (BR 60-61).

How much of the Bryce Report was true, and how much was founded on nothing more than lying or perhaps over-imaginative witnesses? Were the eminent members of the Bryce Committee deliberately setting out to authenticate what they knew were falsehoods? Or were they actually persuaded by the witnesses, so that they themselves wrote the report in good faith? The difficulty of establishing the truth in such matters can be seen when we subject to careful scrutiny what Phillip Knightley calls "the most popular atrocity story of all,"[57] namely, the corpse factory story of April 1917.

THE CORPSE FACTORY STORY
The story of the German corpse factory is worthy of detailed study for many reasons. It was successful, in the sense that it had a powerfully persuasive effect on many people around the world. It was cleverly presented to maximize credibility. A model for atrocity propaganda generally, the way it was handled illustrates the basic rules of propaganda. Arthur Ponsonby concluded his account of it in *Falsehood in Wartime* by quoting from an editorial that appeared in the Richmond, Virginia, *Times-Dispatch* on December 6, 1925: "In the next war, the propaganda must be more subtle and clever than the best the World War produced. These frank admissions of wholesale lying on the part of trusted Governments in the last war will not soon be forgotten."[58] The newspaper was wrong. Atrocity propaganda continues to fuel wars today, and the means used are often no more subtle than those that successfully raised hatred of the Hun to a new pitch in 1917.[59]

What was the story, why was it so effective, what basis was there for it, and how did it get disseminated?

Simply put, the story claimed that the Germans were boiling their own dead soldiers to extract from their bodies lubricating oil, fats, soap, glue, glycerine for explosives, bonemeal for animal feed, and fertilizer (the list tends to vary with different versions of the story). The story gained widespread currency in 1917 and was taken as particularly graphic evidence of German barbarity. It may well have had a key role in turning China against the Germans. It was not until December 2, 1925, that British Foreign Secretary Sir Austen Chamberlain referred to it as a "false report" in the House of Commons and expressed his hope that it "will not again be revived."[60]

However, the story was widely believed at the time. How did that happen? One obvious answer is that many people wanted to believe it. The war was well under way, with all its horrors and grief. To think that the enemy was the incarnation of evil helped the war effort, although conscientious people still scrutinized evidence of such perversity. The Northcliffe press, which published the *Times* and the mass-circulation *Daily Mail*, presented the story in a way to make the evidence in support of it seem overwhelming. They took an idea that until then lacked credible corroboration and anchored it in what appeared to be irrefutable eye-witness testimony. Two reports of corpse-rendering establishments in two different locations were utilized, one from a Berlin correspondent writing in his own newspaper, the other from a Belgian newspaper. Although the Berlin version makes no clear reference to human corpses, the Belgian report does so unambiguously. Both are dated April 10, 1917. Obviously, British propaganda could have no control over the date of the German newspaper, but it easily could have arranged that the damning Belgian report be backdated, to make it appear as though it were independent corroboration, while, at the same time, it twisted the interpretation of that report. Masterman's Third Report states: "At first our relations were mainly with the Bureau Documentaire Belge, a special propaganda department attached to the Minister [*sic*] de la Guerre at Havre [*sic*] and under the direction of M. Passelecq, but subsequently the Belgian propaganda work, so far as concerns its connection with this country, was put wholly in the hands of the Belgian Relief Committee in London.... [T]here is a constant interchange of views and information of every sort relating to actual or potential propaganda in the interests of Belgium."[61]

No published account that I have seen focuses on the issue of confusion created by juxtaposition of the two different reports. Phillip Knightley, in *The First Casualty*, says that the Belgian newspapers picked up the story from the Berlin newspaper, but the latter contained only 59 words of passing reference, as distinct from a detailed description of over 500 words in the Belgian account. He supposes that the story was an invention by war correspondents who mistranslated a German word.[62] Mistranslation did play a role, but the plot is much thicker and more complicated. There are varying accounts, some of which are very different, though not always inconsistent, with each other.

1. *Charteris's Story.* For ease of exposition let us first consider the relatively uncomplicated—but, in part at least, demonstrably false—version of events told by Brigadier-General John Charteris, who had been Chief of Army Intelligence in 1917, to a dinner meeting of the National Arts Club in New York City on October 19, 1925. According to a report of his speech in the *New York Times* the next day, General Charteris himself concocted the story to influence China against

Germany by transposing the word "cadaver" from a picture showing a train taking dead horses to a rendering plant, so that fat and other things needed for fertilizer and munitions might be obtained from them, to one showing a train taking dead Germans to the rear for burial. Six weeks later, a letter in the popular British hunting and fishing magazine, *The Field*, quoted the horrible details.

Thus, according to this version, the story was destined only for China and was circulated in England and thence around the world only by chance. Following the publication of the letter in *The Field*, there developed a controversy in the *Times* about the meaning of the German word *Kadaver*. An indignant Englishman wrote that the story must be a fake, because the German language uses the word *Kadaver* for carcass (of an animal) and another word, *die Leiche*, to refer to a human corpse. Therefore, it would be linguistically wrong, as a matter of ordinary German usage, to infer that Germans taking something marked *Kadaver* to a rendering factory were taking human bodies. However, an English physician who had studied in Austria wrote to say that *Kadaver* in Austria and Bavaria can mean the same as cadaver in English. "The controversy raged until all England thought it must be true, and the German newspapers printed indignant denials," the *New York Times* account continued. When the matter came up in the House of Commons, Charteris answered that, from what he knew of the German mentality, he was prepared to believe anything. Now, eight years after the event, he claimed that this was the only time during the war when he actually dodged the truth.[63] What he meant was that it was the only time he lied to the British people, at least in Parliament. In fact, a further deception had been in the works, according to his own account:

> The matter might have gone even further, for an ingenious person in his office offered to write a diary of a German soldier [substantiating the corpse factory story] … It was planned to place this forged diary in the clothing of a dead German soldier and have it discovered by a war correspondent who had a passion for German diaries. General Charteris decided that the deception had gone far enough and that there might be an error in the diary which would have led to the exposure of its falsity. Such a result would have imperilled all the British propaganda, he said, and he did not think it worth while, but the diary is now in the war museum in London.

Charteris chose to tell his story in order to cultivate friendship with the US by extending confidences; revealing secrets announces a spirit of trust and the hope that such trust will be reciprocated. Alternatively, or in addition, it is possible that Charteris was feeling in a particularly relaxed mood and hit upon a path of self-aggrandizement by embellishing the truth.

What is false about Charteris's story? Certain facts are easily established. There was, indeed, discussion in the London *Times* about the terminology of the word *Kadaver*, but there is no evidence of it stemming from any letter or column appearing in *The Field*; in a search through the pages of *The Field* from January to April 1917, I was unable to find any such letter. The widespread attention paid to the story began on April 17, 1917, when both Lord Northcliffe's papers, the *Times* and the *Daily Mail*, reported a passage that had appeared on April 10 in the Berlin *Lokal-Anzeiger* (*Local-Advertiser*), an official German government newspaper. According to the Northcliffe press, this passage gave authoritative confirmation of the existence of a corpse utilization factory, in corroboration of the Belgian story. The *Lokal-Anzeiger* reporter, Karl Rosner, wrote that he detected a smell like burning lime when he was travelling through Evergnicourt, north of Reims. According to the translation that appeared in the *Times*, he wrote, "We are passing the great Corpse exploitation Establishment (*Kadaververwertungsanstalt*) of this Army Group. The fat that is won here is turned into lubricating oils, and everything else is ground down in the bones mill into a powder, which is used for mixing with pigs' food and as manure." Subsequent letters in the *Times* disputing the translation of *Kadaver* made no reference to *The Field*.

What could be true about Charteris's story? The general's claim that a fake diary was invented, but not used because of the risk attached to detection, seems plausible enough, even though efforts to locate such a diary in the Imperial War Museum have not been successful. That he sent the picture with its false caption to China might be believed if we can confirm the existence of a story in the *North China News* of February 26, 1917 or the *North China Herald* of March 3, 1917 (see below). It has been argued that, in early 1917, Charteris was at army headquarters behind the lines in France and could not have been engaging in this sort of world-scale propaganda, but his diaries reveal he occasionally travelled back to London.

In sum, there is propaganda associated both with the story that was given and with the giving of the story. When it was revealed, the chicanery involved astounded many British and Americans who had believed it. Because of this, many people did not believe the stories about Jews being incinerated in huge ovens, when they began to leak out of Germany during World War II. An Israeli scholar, Shimon Rubinstein, researched the story more recently and came up with the surprising conclusion (not shared by the present writer) that, despite the many unfounded and deceptive statements affirming the existence of the corpse establishments, the possibility that they existed has not been definitely eliminated. Among other things, Rubinstein looks at the propaganda surrounding Charteris's telling of the story. Admitting that the British had engaged in slanders against the Germans would have helped improve relationships between the two countries in accordance with the spirit of the Treaty of Locarno. This viewpoint is reinforced by an account in the *New York Times* which links the signing of the Locarno treaties to just such an admission by the British ("London Counsels Patience by Reich," December 2, 1925). Rubinstein observes that Charteris's revelation would have been more helpful, though, had it come prior to the signing of the Versailles treaty, rather than in 1925 when Hitler was able to use the exposure of British deceptions for his own nefarious purposes.[64]

2. *The Northcliffe Press.* As already mentioned, the real source for the story is to be found in the pages of the Northcliffe press. The London *Times* and the *Daily Mail* ran almost identical articles on April 17, 1917, of what purported to be a vivid,

gruesome eyewitness account of one of the corpse-rendering establishments. The story is reported as coming from the French-language Belgian paper, *L'Indépendance Belge*, dated April 10, 1917, which in turn sources it in the daily *La Belgique* without giving a date. Following so closely the previous day's report of the passage in the *Lokal-Anzeiger* (mentioned above) it carries an air of authenticity. The paper reproduces the German reporter's extract again, as a prelude to the eyewitness account. Both newspapers present the story under the headings "Germans and their dead," "Revolting treatment," and "Science and the Barbarian Spirit," and both include specific details on the management of the company responsible for operating the factory, as well as on the transportation, handling, and processing of the corpses into material to be used in the war effort or in agriculture. The report concludes with a description of the workers as virtual prisoners, unable to talk about the awful job they are doing.

No mention is made of how the eyewitness got close enough to the factory to provide the intricate details. Secondly, while the German reporter's story supposedly provided corroboration, he located the factory quite far from its location in the Belgian report. The reader was encouraged by the Northcliffe press to confuse the German and Belgian stories, and, indeed, the *New York Times* three days later reported, "The French press is greatly stirred over an article, taken from the Berlin *Lokal-Anzeiger* and reproduced by the *Indépendance Belge*, about a German factory for extracting chemical products from the corpses of German soldiers."[65] That the scheme was deliberate propaganda seems inescapable, given Lord Northcliffe's intimate involvement with the official British propaganda organization.

To fully appreciate the propaganda value of this story it is worth taking note of the list of seven requirements for successful propaganda set out by A.J. Mackenzie in his book *Propaganda Boom*, published in 1938.[66] The first is repetition. The argument about the meaning of *Kadaver* provided an excuse to carry the story day after day. The detailed description derived from the Belgian newspaper was sure to provoke letters in response, which it did. The second is colour, the need to grab the imagination rather than simply stating the bald facts of an atrocity. The supposed eyewitness provides this colourful detail. Third, propaganda should always contain a kernel of truth. In this case, the Germans were boiling down animals for oils, pig food, and the like; this was well-established by the German reporter. Fourth, propaganda should be built around a slogan. The "corpse factory" story lent itself to numerous slogans, such as "The Germans are ghouls," found as part of a banner headline in the *War Illustrated*.[67] Fifth, propaganda should be directed towards a specific objective, in this case, to increase hatred of the Germans, encourage recruitment, and raise morale generally. Sixth, the motive of the propaganda should be concealed. Here the appearance of merely reporting on what others had said tended to obscure the propaganda motive. Seventh, timing is the key to propaganda success. The timing of the *Indépendence Belge* report so close to the *Lokal-Anzeiger* passage provided just the right impact, as described earlier.

Such was the mood of the time that even a respected scientific journal did its part, wittingly or unwittingly, to further British propaganda aims. In its April 21,

1917 edition, *The Lancet*, a top British medical journal, provided a detailed, scientific description of the chemicals available from human bodies, noting, for example, that 1000 bodies would yield approximately 400 pounds of glycerine to make soap. "The dividends of the enterprising company known as the *Kadaververwertungsanstalt* (Corpse Utilization Establishment) may, according to this calculation, be quite satisfactory to the directors and shareholders, enabling them to face criticism with complacency."[68] This kind of article greatly benefits propaganda, because of its scientific factualism; it presupposes that human corpses were rendered for fats and explained the economics of doing so. When falsehoods are communicated as presuppositions, the communicatee is less likely to be on guard against the deceptions than if they were presented as assertions. It is not surprising that the *Lancet* item also appeared in the *Times*.

3. *Conclusion.* The "corpse factory" story had tremendous impact on opinion around the world. The seeming authoritativeness attached to its supposed derivation from a German reporter for a German government newspaper, combined with the luridness of the Belgian newspaper's account gave it force. By sourcing the story in a Belgian paper which supposedly reproduced it from another Belgian daily newspaper, British propaganda made authentication difficult. The *Frankfurter Zeitung* condemned the propaganda in a front-page editorial entitled "Moral Insanity," April 29, 1917, saying that the hatred fomented by such atrocity stories would cause the war to last a long time. Not only that, one might add, but hatred produces a hateful response, and the propaganda of one war can sow the seeds for a further one. When Hitler wrote about the British making use of the "big lie," he might well have been thinking of this kind of atrocity story. A Nazi propaganda booklet, *Britische Propaganda*, by Hans Bühr, published in 1940, devotes two full pages to the story and the official admission of its untruth.

The atrocity story continues to be used to foment war and revolution today. There are still missing pieces to the jigsaw puzzle about the "corpse factory," but its intricacies make it an excellent focal point for any discussion of the ethics of propaganda.[69]

LENINIST PROPAGANDA

Bolshevik propaganda theory did not begin with Lenin, but he successfully linked theory with practice both in achieving and maintaining power. Earlier theorists of propaganda contributing to Lenin's views included Peter Tkachev, Georgi Plekhanov, and A. Kremer.[70] Their problem was how to build a revolutionary movement among disparate classes and interests: the industrial workers (each with their separate trades and shops), the peasantry, and the intelligentsia and sympathetic elements of the bourgeoisie. Workers were in danger of accepting the path of trade unionism and incremental improvements in working conditions. The peasantry already practised a communal existence to a large extent and lacked the education to understand the benefits of joining a total revolutionary movement. One group of intellectuals, called Narodniks, saw little commonality with industrial workers in the fight of the intelligentsia and the peasants for social justice. Plekhanov, on the contrary, came to believe that "The workers' party alone is capable of solving all the contradictions which now condemn our intelligentsia to theoretical and political impotence." He felt that the hope of revolution was to be found in joining together the interests of peasantry and industrial workers through a philosophy of socialism, the propagation of which was being facilitated in areas where village communes were breaking up as a consequence of industry becoming more developed. His idea was that "the forces which are being freed by the disintegration of the village commune in some places in Russia can safeguard it against total disintegration in other places."[71]

Plekhanov and Tkachev have both been credited with defining the distinction between propaganda and agitation, which is built into Lenin's theory. The social-democratic theory of revolution, in all its Marxist economic trappings, is complicated and needs careful explaining to the few individuals who can understand it. However, since revolution requires enlistment of the masses, the latter's support has to be obtained through agitation, which involves focusing on concrete injustices and wrongdoings and bringing home to selective audiences that these injustices are not unavoidable facts of life, but the result of an oppressive system, which can be overthrown. Kremer makes the point that agitation must derive from an intimate knowledge of conditions prevailing in factories. Agitators need to "catch the pulse of the proletarians and attune their appeals to the keenly felt grievances and immediate needs of the workers in the mass."[72] By reaching out in this way to the masses, revolutionaries make it difficult for a government to control the revolutionary activity.

In What Is to Be Done? Lenin further developed the idea of agitation-propaganda, or agitprop as it has come to be known. A conscious vanguard of the proletariat must engage in political education to develop in the people a sense of commonality of interest between all kinds of different workers normally concerned only about benefits to their narrow group. The agitator identifies the most striking concern of his audience—for example, the death through starvation of a group of the unemployed—and, building on this well-known fact, puts all his efforts into getting across a *single idea*: that of the absurd contradiction between the simultaneous increase in riches and of poverty. He will then *incite* discontent and mass indignation against this crying injustice, leaving to the propagandist the task of providing a more complete explanation of this contradiction. Consequently, the propagandist operates chiefly by means of the *printed* word; the agitator by means of the *spoken* word.

Lenin employed the idea of revelations, the only way capable, he said, of arousing a political consciousness among the masses. This meant exposing what was wrong with society, which, in turn, involved agitators reaching into *all* sectors of society. This idea was not totally new. St. Paul, after all, considered it necessary to "become all things to all men," Aristotle had stressed the need to tailor arguments to the preconceptions of an audience, and Quintilian, following Aristotle, had noted the potential of emotion-arousing examples. But with Lenin these principles became applied to mass persuasion not through individual rhetoric, but through an organized campaign involving an army of agitators at all levels. The task, he wrote, must be to utilize every manifestation of discontent and to make the most backward worker understand or *feel* that the student, the sectarian, the peasant, and the writer are exposed to the harms and arbitrary acts of the same dark force which oppresses and weighs on him at each step of his whole life. Having felt that, he will irresistibly react on his own initiative. Today he will create an uproar against the censors, tomorrow he will demonstrate against the governor for putting down a peasant revolt. What is needed are vivid public charges of wrongdoing, catching people red-handed, and stigmatizing them everywhere and before the whole world.[73] This he thought would be much more effective than any "appeal." The daily newspaper *Pravda* was founded April 22, 1912, and, after a rocky start, eventually earned Lenin's approval, carrying out powerful agitational work on a nationwide scale, inciting industrial workers and peasants alike.[74]

Following the Bolshevik victory, Lenin had to deal with the problem that shortages and injustices could no longer be blamed on the Czarist autocracy. In Ellul's terms, agitation propaganda had to yield to integration propaganda. In August 1919 Lenin signed a decree nationalizing all cinema enterprises. The propaganda value of a film such as Eisenstein's classic *Battleship Potemkin* lay in reminding people how terrible things were under Czarist Russia, so as to deflect attention from shortcomings under Communism. Lenin is reported to have said "of all the arts, for us cinema is the most important," and Stalin claimed it was the "greatest means of mass agitation." Despite this, Trotsky was to lament that the Party leadership, nearly six years after the revolution, had not "taken possession of the cinema."[75]

Given that such a large proportion of the Soviet peasantry was illiterate, a great effort was made to encourage reading. Village reading rooms were set up, and a literacy train crossed the country. Peter Kenez reminds us that, at that time, trains were seen as symbols of the new age of technology.[76] (This, incidentally, gives us reason to reflect on how space-age imagery is used today—to sell vacuum cleaners designed like space vehicles, for example.) Posters by talented artists such as D.S. Moor were distributed widely to enlist public support for an officially sanctioned cause. The pictures conveyed a message even when the words could not be read. Lenin made clear that his reasons for emphasizing literacy had an ulterior motive: "As long as there is such a thing in the country as illiteracy, it is rather hard to talk about political education. To overcome illiteracy is not a political task, it is a condition without which one cannot even talk about politics."[77] As Ellul has commented, contrary to some deeply-embedded ideas of progress, literacy is not an unmixed blessing.[78] Kenez points out that someone recruited to head a branch of the youth group Komsomol, for instance, might not fully agree with Party doctrine: "But as the person was carrying out propaganda on behalf of the new regime, he or she was won over. The propagandists usually were the first to become victims of their own propaganda. There is no better method of convincing someone than by asking him or her to convince others." Kenez thinks it is "indisputable that the Bolshevik regime was the first to not merely set itself propaganda goals but also through political education to aim to create a new humanity suitable for living in a new society. No previous state had similar ambitions, and no leaders had paid comparable attention to the issues of persuasion."[79] This claim may be challenged by considering the educational reforms instituted in revolutionary and Napoleonic France.

Bekhterev and Reflexology

Peter Kenez thinks that people were not rationally persuaded under Leninist propaganda, but that they succumbed to it all the same. The constant repetition of slogans, for example, gradually brought on a "proper consciousness." Expressions like "we will storm the bastions of illiteracy" were repeated so often the words were emptied of meaning. His analysis is interesting in the light of the work of Vladimir Mikhailovic Bekhterev, a Russian psychiatrist, neurologist, and, as he called himself, "reflexologist." He was also head of the Military Medical Academy in St. Petersburg. Bekhterev was the author of *Suggestion and Its Role in Social Life*, published in 1908, and *The Subject Matter and Goals of Social Psychology*, in 1911. His writings left their imprint on both Soviet and Nazi forms of persuasion and on the methods of recruitment used by some cults today. Bekhterev's theory, to which he gave the name "reflexology," explained how three objective conditions affect the suggestibility of crowds. First, there is "confinement to the same position for long periods of time, which, besides restricting active movement, leads to physical exhaustion"; in other words, "the more stationary the target, the greater the fatigue, the less the resistance, in both the personal and the general sphere, to the attempt to influence and the more vivid the ultimate psychic event." Secondly, there is "prolonged concentration on the same subject (usually on the leader and his speech) [which] undermines the ability to concentrate." This works because "the more prolonged the required attention of the target, the greater the loss of control of conscious attention and the less the possible resistance through mustering counter-arguments to the influence attempt." Thirdly, there are "the leader's demagogical methods, accompanied by appropriate gestures and facial expressions [which] determine the uniformity of the mood, which in turn defines the direction of the active attention of the crowd, since a rise in mood is associated with readiness for action."[80]

One notable case where principles of reflexology were clearly at work, whether or not with full consciousness of Bekhterev's principles, were the Nazi Party rallies.

NAZI PROPAGANDA

Given the extent of British World War I and Soviet propaganda before World War II, it might seem difficult to surpass either. Adolf Hitler and Josef Goebbels, who studied the propaganda of both, provided the world with mass manipulation and multi-layered propaganda in a variety and scale never before seen. All the mass media of communication—radio, newspapers, cinema, theatre, books, magazines, etc.—came under Nazi control in 1933. The educational system, the Hitler Youth, the displays of posters and uniforms, Nazi Party rallies, and the existence of loud-speakers in public places which broadcast martial and patriotic music and speeches in the streets—all contributed to a saturation of propaganda in everyday existence. For those who were recalcitrant, there were the death camps. Behind all this orchestration was a calculated plan, based on an understanding of the behaviour of the masses and their susceptibility to simple ideas repeated endlessly. Nazi propagandists knew about organization and about telling a simple story that would appeal to pride among the German people after the humiliation of Versailles.

To understand Nazi propaganda, we need first to look at Hitler's theory, which was published in *Mein Kampf* ("My Struggle") in 1925 and 1927. It is filled with the spirit of what Nietzsche called *ressentiment*, a deep-seated resentment, and it seems to have resonated well with the spirit of the times. It is also worth studying the tactics Goebbels used to bring the Nazi Party into power. Finally, some particular propaganda tactics used in World War II deserve attention.

Propaganda and Mein Kampf

Hitler devoted two chapters of *Mein Kampf* to propaganda, which clearly fascinated him. He was not the first to see that human beings in a mass can act like lemmings, but he was perhaps unparalled in the strength of his determination to understand and orchestrate such behaviour. His success should give liberals and democrats a powerful reason for analyzing his theory with a view to finding what might be done to prevent mass consciousness from being similarly hijacked in future.

THE "BIG LIE."

Hitler's theory of the "big lie" is not found in either of his two chapters on propaganda, for reasons that are not difficult to fathom. Had he suggested that his own side was making use of the "big lie," he would have damaged his future credibility. In discussing the causes of Germany's downfall in World War I in Chapter X of *Mein Kampf*,[81] he singles out the "Jews and their Marxist fighting organization" for blaming General Erich Ludendorff for losing the war. This was one example of what he called the big lie, another being the English and American pinning of the entire war-guilt on the Germans. Still today, unscrupulous politicians run mud-slinging election campaigns on the basis of the principle "*semper aliquid haeret*" ("always something sticks"), the same principle the Nazi propaganda machine used on a grand scale.

The value of knowing about the "big lie" theory is that once the principle is understood, the knowledge can be used to expose this technique, and thus disarm it, or cause the propaganda to boomerang.

APPEALING TO THE MASSES

The real art of propaganda consisted of "understanding the emotional ideas of the great masses and finding, through a psychologically correct form, the way to the attention and thence to the heart of the broad masses" (MK 180). Hitler thought the English and Americans had produced more psychologically sound propaganda in World War I than his own side. By thinking of the enemy as barbarous and thereby convinced of the justice of their cause, their soldiers had fewer qualms about killing and more acceptance of risks entailed in the fighting.

Propaganda, then, does not work through half-measures. "It does not have multiple shadings; it has a positive and a negative; love or hate, right or wrong, truth or lie, never half this way and half that way, never partially, or that kind of thing" (MK 183). It is a means to the end of convincing a target group. The masses are "slow-moving, and they always require a certain time before they are ready even to notice a thing, and only after the simplest ideas are repeated thousands of times will the masses finally remember them" (MK 185). In this connection, a change in tactic is needed, one that could accommodate change; hence, the need for a sufficiently flexible central doctrine. Propaganda must be designed so that it always says the same thing. "For instance, a slogan must be presented from different angles, but the end of all remarks must always and immutably be the slogan itself. Only in this way can the propaganda have a unified and complete effect" (MK 185).

In Chapter XI of the second volume of *Mein Kampf*, Hitler paid careful attention to the relationship between propaganda and Party organization. The number of supporters of the movement could not be too great, he wrote, but the number of members had to be kept manageably small. Supporters were those who declared their agreement with the Party's aims, while members were those who fought for them (MK, 581-2). The future of the movement would be conditioned by the militancy, exclusivity, rigidity, and fanaticism (MK 582, 337) with which its adherents presented it as the only right one. He saw it as important to have a geopolitical centre, as in the case of Rome and Mecca (MK 347). For Hitler the chosen centre was Nuremberg.

Propaganda was so important for Hitler that he saw the accomplishment of his Nazi goals in two stages. The first task of propaganda, he said, is winning people for the organization; the first task of the organization is winning people for propaganda. The second task of propaganda is to destroy existing conditions to achieve acceptance of the new doctrine. The second task of the organization is the fight for power, to achieve the final success of the doctrine. In saying this, Hitler drew on his experience as propagandist for the Nazis in 1921. He noted that the skills of a theoretician were not at all the same as those needed for a good organizer. The latter had to be a shrewd judge of human psychology, knowing the strengths and weakness of different people. The great danger he saw was the dilution of the membership by unrestricted entry of mere supporters to the position of Party workers (MK 584-5).

Hitler himself understood the emotional make-up of his audiences, and he manipulated them with powerful metaphors and imagery. For example, he made use of the symbols of fire and wind to convey the idea of burning away the old and bringing in the new. As Elias Cannetti has pointed out, the symbol of fire is also one of friendliness, when it is in the hearth. Flags, he pointed out, are important for making the wind visible. The symbol of the swastika represents power: it is the waterwheel driven by a current. Wind gathers things up in a storm and drives them where it is headed. In his speech "Art and Politics," given in 1934, Hitler provided the groundwork for genocide with his metaphorical linkage of Jews to disease and pestilence.[82] We can learn from this to take seriously the impact of words on consciousness and action and not to ignore incitement when it occurs.

THE ROAD TO POWER

Goebbels, who was later to take charge of Nazi propaganda, also knew and understood principles of propaganda and had insight into the moods of audiences, perhaps through his academic study of the theatre.[83] Starting out with very little money, the Party attracted attention through violent confrontations. Blood-red posters announced forthcoming meetings, with striking lettering and provocative titles. On May 5, 1927, a few months after their office had been set up in the city, the police banned the Nazis from Greater Berlin, and later Goebbels was banned from speaking in the whole of Prussia. A poster was produced, showing a gagged Goebbels, proclaiming that he alone among millions of Germans was not allowed to speak. He went to places where members of the Reichstag would be speaking, since no meeting where they were present could be banned. He was charged and fined, but such incidents were publicized to gain sympathy for the Party. Goebbels launched a newspaper, Der Angriff ("Attack") on July 4, 1927, and with it relentlessly ridiculed Bernhard Weiss, the Jewish Deputy Chief of Police in Berlin, until he came to be seen as a joke. Police court hearings were welcomed by Goebbels, who used them as media events, where he could show off his sarcastic wit. The ban was called off shortly before the Reichstag election in May 1928; 12 Nazi Party members were elected, Goebbels among them.

Despite their calls for free speech, the Nazis showed no such spirit of toleration for messages of which they did not approve. To discourage people from seeing the movie "All Quiet on the Western Front," SA troops (Sturm-Abteilungen, Storm Troopers, founded in 1921) bought tickets to screenings, at which they let off stink bombs and released white mice. Eventually the government banned the showing of that movie as likely to cause more rioting. When Goebbels was arraigned following the smashing of windows of Jewish-owned shops in 1930, he refused to testify, simply haranguing the court. He was fined only 200 marks, an indication, perhaps, of the fear that his paramilitary force was beginning to instil.

Goebbels appears to have worshipped Hitler, and he worked at deifying him for the general public, spreading legends about him living an Olympian existence in Berchtesgaden, being a crack shot, etc. Leni Riefenstahl's film, *Triumph of the Will*, assisted this aim: it shows Hitler descending from the clouds in an aircraft for the start of the 1934 Nuremberg rally. The film also shows how the appearance of immortality in the new Germany was given to deceased Party faithful. Beginning in 1932 many funerals of SA or SS (*Schutzstaffel*, "Protection Squad") men were exploited to serve as inspiration to others. Tens of thousands of people showed up for these events, and aircraft displaying Swastika flags circled overhead in a display of strength. In one instance, Goebbels created a hero: Horst Wessel was the author of a political verse, published in *Der Angriff*, that went well with a tune popular among Communist youth. When he died in 1930, his lyrics and the tune became the "Horst Wessel Lied (song)," which the Nazi Party adopted as its anthem, to be sung at all rallies.

Goebbels cleverly exploited the new media of communication. He entertained large crowds with recorded discs of Chancellor Brüning's speeches, which he switched on and off, interspersing witty responses, and "scoring emphatically on all his points, which he had prepared carefully in advance."[84] Another technique successfully used at election time was to concentrate forces in small, winnable areas such as Lippe-Detmold, with a population of only 150,000, thereby making gains and creating an image of momentum.

TOTALITARIAN POWER

In 1933 the Nazi Party securely grasped the reins of power, riding a wave of indignation following the February Reichstag fire—possibly, if not probably, engineered by Goebbels himself, although accounts are divided.[85] Of one thing we can be sure: Goebbels would certainly have been aware of the huge propaganda coup to be made with this event and was, in fact, delighted when it happened. Victor Klemperer, an astute observer of goings-on in Germany at the time, observed: "I cannot imagine that anyone really believes in Communist perpetrators instead of paid [Nazi] work."[86]

News accounts of activities before the event show a pattern of Nazi power-plays, especially following the appointment of Hitler as Chancellor of Germany on January 30, with the help of former Chancellor Franz von Papen. After a meeting with President von Hindenburg, Hitler issued a proclamation that the coalition cabinet he was to lead was not "truly representative of Hitlerism,"[87] since it limited his power. On February 6 Hindenburg issued a decree restricting freedom of the press, to great applause from the Nazis. Newspapers or periodicals were to be suppressed for, among other more immediate threats to the state, "holding up to contempt the organs or institutions or leading officials of the government." Simultaneously, Hitler broadcast a campaign speech over radio, which he, as Chancellor, now controlled; it was recorded on a phonograph record so that no one could miss it.[88] A few days later he gave another speech in the Sportpalast (Sports Palace) announcing that there were only one of two possible outcomes of the election: "the German nation or Marxism." The presentation of two exclusive alter-natives, with the phraseology favouring one of them, is a powerful propaganda device. It helps to polarize opinion, and, when that happens, the shrill cries of the opposing forces drown out any voices of moderation. US President George W. Bush used the same device when he stated to nations of the world, in his "Address to a Joint Session of Congress and the American People" on September 20, 2001, "Either you are with us or you are with the terrorists." (A nation might be against terrorism but not necessarily supportive of the means chosen by the US, includ-ing suspension of certain vital civil liberties, to combat terrorism.)

The Reichstag elections took place March 5. The Nazis took 43.9 per cent of the votes, other nationalists combining with them to make a bare majority. Goebbels became Minister for Propaganda and Public Enlightenment just over a week later.

Now that they were firmly in control, the Nazis extended and consolidated power on a breathtaking scale. Recognizing the radio as a powerful means of pro-paganda, they fostered the manufacture of inexpensive sets, and by 1938 nearly 10 million were in use. In October 1933 a Journalists' Law required all journal-ists to get a licence issued from Goebbels's office. A journalist had to show "qualifications which fit him for the task of spiritual influence in the sphere of pub-licity."[89] This approval, of course, was determined by party members. Jews were barred from any form of journalism, with rare exceptions. Newspapers purchased by the Party reached a circulation eventually of 8 million combined. A prestigious paper such as the *Frankfurter Zeitung* tended to be left alone to indicate to the wider world that there was sill freedom of expression in Germany. In February 1934 a Censorship Committee was formed to judge every film produced in the coun-try. Finally, the Reich Chamber of Culture, on September 22, 1933, took charge of all cultural activities. To engage in a cultural occupation without being a member of the Chamber meant making oneself liable to a fine of 100,000 marks.

Censorship was virtually complete. When the *Vossische Zeitung* printed the heading, "The Stock Exchange Is Weak," Goebbels's ministry replied, "The Stock Exchange is not weak" and suspended publication of the offending newspaper for three weeks. Another paper, the *Grüne Post* printed a satirical note about Goebbels and was banned. Goebbels sought and obtained the ability to orchestrate what appeared in the press. In March 1933 he issued a decree announcing that all shares of the RRG, the German Broadcasting Company, had been acquired by the Propaganda Ministry, and Eugen Hadamowsky was put in charge. Hadamowsky announced that "All major officials with anti-National Socialist credentials have been dismissed, though only one has behaved like a gentleman and hanged him-self."[90] Programming began with a purely propagandist diet of march music, the "Horst Wessel Lied," Wagner, etc., until listeners got tired, after which Goebbels sought a greater proportion of entertainment value to keep them tuned in.

Writers, publishers, booksellers, and anyone involved in any way in the liter-ary profession had to belong to the Reich Chamber of Literature, the president of which was Hanns Johst, author of the phrase (in one of his plays) "When I hear the word 'culture', I feel for the safety catch of my revolver."[91] A decree of April

25, 1935, empowered the Chamber of Literature to draw up a blacklist of all books and authors detrimental to government policy.[92] On August 1, 1934, the president of the Chamber of Fine Arts was given the power to prosecute people for neglecting to "give priority to [their] professional responsibility to the nation and the Reich." Art exhibitions were subject to supervision. Theatre was also given close attention as a means of propaganda. Goebbels paid special attention to film, insisting that it be good entertainment, that it not "degenerate into a medium of intellectual and pseudo-intellectual experiments."[93] Plots were to be simple and to repeat themes of anti-Semitism, American decadence, and the German Folkish attachment to home and hearth, woods and meadows. Attention also was paid to architecture as propaganda, and buildings were required to be grandiose and impressive—tall columns in long rows and huge arenas. Schools were not neglected, and texts showed pictures of Hitler Youth, with their future military vocations (air, sea, land).

GERMAN WAR PROPAGANDA

In the so-called "phoney war," which lasted from September 1939 to the Blitzkrieg in May 1940, the Goebbels' propaganda machine cleverly exploited the boredom and disruption of family life affecting new conscripts in the French Army. Messages of peace were broadcast, undermining any desire of the French to fight and capitalizing on memories of the loss of life and the horrors of World War 1. Goebbels managed to persuade an excellent native French speaker to broadcast to France. Known to the French as Ferdonnet, "le traître de Stuttgart," the speaker popularized such slogans as "*On ne mourra pas pour Danzig*" (Danzig is not worth dying for) and "England will fight Germany down to the last Frenchman," to exploit French distrust of its ally. In fact, while the real Paul Ferdonnet wrote the scripts, another person with a better voice actually read them.[94] After the war began, Ferdonnet broadcast that British soldiers were giving tips to people to tell them which women had husbands at the front, so they could make out with such women.[95] Posters showed British soldiers barring the French from escaping to Dunkirk.

Nazi propaganda directed to the rest of the world, particularly the United States, has been scrutinized by Edmund L. Taylor in *The Strategy of Terror*. Taking his information from French intelligence, he remarked that the real aim of Nazi propaganda was not to convert outsiders to their cause, but to "demoralize the enemy, to destroy the cohesion, discipline and collective morale of hostile social groups." Their aim was to sow seeds of doubt, undermining confidence in authority. "I had just discovered for myself, in Czechoslovakia and in Austria just before the Anschluss, the Nazi trick of defying and ridiculing authority, to destroy its prestige." Fomenting anti-Semitism abroad was done for a similar reason, Taylor suggests: not because it was likely to be adopted, but because it would "get the Gentiles fighting among themselves over the Jewish question."[96]

In that context, the propaganda of William Joyce ("Lord Haw-Haw") in his radio broadcasts to Britain may have been more successful than has been acknowledged. Born in New York of an Irish, naturalized American father, he studied in

England and became a follower of Sir Oswald Mosley and his Fascist organization. Moving to Berlin, he was an obvious choice for radio propaganda to Britain. Joyce lampooned the British upper class with humorous stories about tax-evaders and profiteers and warned about air raids before they happened, thus demonstrating his insider knowledge to make listeners trust him.[97]

Taylor observed that utilization of the foreign press was a major art of government propaganda of the time, and that foreign correspondents were the principal carriers of it. Nazi propaganda disguised itself by appearing in the newspapers of neutral countries, such as Sweden. Newspapers such as the Stockholm *Tidningen* and the afternoon newspaper, the *Aftonbladet*, were often quoted by the American press. Both newspapers were owned by Thorsten Krueger, a fanatic Nazi. An example of propaganda carried out this way was an *Aftonbladet* story picked up by the *New York Times* and United Press correspondents in Stockholm. It reported that a British expeditionary force had landed in Archangel. As Sidney Freifeld, a news analyst for the Canadian government in New York during World War II and later a Canadian ambassador, notes, this might seem at first sight to be contrary to Axis interests, but millions of people in England, Canada, the US, and other countries had been eagerly waiting for the landing of British troops on the continent in order to divert Nazi pressure from the Eastern front.[98] The effect of this story was to raise false hopes, which were subsequently dashed, and to encourage pessimism about British initiative. The British denied the story. The Canadian Department of National Defence unwisely stated that there "has been no confirmation that any Canadians are included in the expedition to Archangel." Upon this the United Press issued the report: "Tacit acknowledgement that Britain might have sent an expeditionary force to Archangel was given today by a military spokesman here, but official defense sources discouraged any conclusion that Canadians might have formed a part of the force." This United Press report shows two things: first, how wishes influence interpretations; and secondly, how one can unintentionally launder a false news item. The press should have shown itself far more sceptical about reports coming from Nazi newspapers.

Goebbels's propaganda also produced stories linking Jews with lice, and these stories actually were carried by the wire services. Freifeld noted that Louis Lochner, chief for many years of the Associated Press bureau in Berlin, reported information derived from a map he saw in a military office where he was conducting an interview. The map indicated where Germany might invade Britain, but the newspaperman did not make the reasonable assumption that this was a setup to deceive his readers into thinking such an invasion was being planned. The US media could have—and should have—shown more of the same kind scepticism used to reject commercial press agentry at home. Against Goebbels their guard all too often dropped.[99]

Two other sources throw light on Goebbels's war propaganda tactics. First are the official British fortnightly summaries. For example, during the Blitzkrieg in early May 1940, the theme of military operations was most prominent. This was followed by British weakness, German strength, and finally British brutality.

"The invasion of the Low Countries was preceded by a very great volume of propaganda asserting that the Allies were about to extend the war to southeastern Europe. It appears that such a propaganda feint generally precedes every German surprise move."[100] As Napoleon once noted, victory is very powerful propaganda.

The second source is R.G. Nobécourt, who wrote a detailed account of German propaganda in occupied France.[101] Among the many materials he studied was a propaganda manual which appeared in 1943. The main points of the manual were:

1. In the pure state truth is difficult to handle. Truthful items may create a wrong impression. Packaging is important.
2. An established opinion can only be modified progressively. Do not present a thesis ready-made, but rather offer propositions that leave one reflecting and that suggest a route leading unconsciously to the desired conclusion. (This is reminiscent of the reference to the "stop-short" Chinese poem in British World War I propaganda. See above, page 68.)
3. Present the idea in accessible form. Typography, image, and figures with an impartial air are often striking and prove things to people. (In more recent jargon, "figures do not lie, but liars can figure.")
4. Orchestration must be rigorous. Unity of propaganda plays the same role as naval artillery.
5. The law of repetition applies. As Goebbels said, "Repetition ends by transforming into faith a simple tendency without the individual being aware of this work."

Nobécourt remarked how seemingly insignificant facts, astutely chosen and edited, cumulatively have an insidious, unstoppable effect on consciousness. "Facts bring their own interpretation," and not because they are false. The malice lies in their form, in the discretion with which they are handled. They *suggest* more than they *articulate* the desired conclusion. Multiplied, they soften the mind, which drinks in the content. As stated in the propaganda manual, "the telegram of two lines is of more psychological importance than the editorial signed by a powerful name." The perfidiousness of this kind of propaganda consisted in its lying while all of the time not lying. One cannot fight against it. Examples of the proliferation of minor details to underline a major message are numerous. Propaganda Abteilung, the German propaganda detachment, reported on January 22, 1943, that, since Roosevelt took power, crimes committed by young people in the US had risen 18 per cent for robberies, 23 per cent for sex crimes, and 30 per cent for intemperance. These statistics were reinforced by a story from Inter-France *Confidentiel* on March 6, 1944, that more than two million US recruits were sent home for lack of military suitability, as a result of illness, alcoholism, etc. Besides the promulgation of these small facts, there was suppression of such minor news items that might have a negative impact. So, the Propaganda Abteilung advised on February 26, 1943, that the press not give attention to agreements between the haute couture industry and the authorities, since activities of this kind were not indispensable to war.

CONCLUSION

This historical overview introduced numerous techniques of persuasion and the principles behind their operation. The twentieth century brought more systematic harnessing of an even greater array of communications media for purposes of national power and prestige, war, and advancement of private corporate interests. From history we know that the aims of freedom and happiness, spread by propaganda, are often accompanied by repression and abuse of power. This is good reason for viewing with suspicion new political, economic, or technological systems that are presented by those with the power to get their message across as saving humankind.

The foregoing has provided a small, but, I hope, salient and instructive, selection of war and revolutionary propaganda from Grecian times to the twentieth century. In what we have treated, we see over and over again how successful propaganda relies on surreptitious presentation of its message. We also find that totalitarian propaganda involves not so much adding to the theory of rhetoric and propaganda as it does putting knowledge of such principles into effect in all-encompassing ways, based on thorough control over all the media of mass communication. The job of the propagandist is, as always, that of knowing the audience and who and what the audience will find credible, then adapting the message accordingly. Sometimes a message will not be acceptable without the kind of pre-propaganda described by Ellul in Chapter 1. I believe that the most penetrating and lasting propaganda will touch on the most basic existential questions about human existence and on a target audience's deepest commitments and highest aspirations. This point will be revisited when we consider commercially oriented propaganda in the form of advertising, branding, and public relations in Chapter 5.

NOTES

1 Oliver Thomson, *Easily Led: A History of Propaganda* (Phoenix Mill, England: Sutton 1999).

2 Thucydides, *The Peloponnesian War*, trans. Rex Warner (Harmondsworth: Penguin Books, 1954). Usefully reprinted and analyzed in James A. Murphy and Richard A. Katula, et al., *A Synoptic History of Classical Rhetoric* (Davis, CA.: Hermagoras Press), 217-24. A translation can also be found online at <http://www.wsu.edu:8000/~dee/GREECE/PERICLES.HTM.> Quotations below are from this source.

3 Thomson 328.

4 Jeffrey A. Keshen, *Propaganda and Censorship During Canada's Great War* (Edmonton: University of Alberta Press, 1996) 5, and *passim*.

5   Plato, "Gorgias," *The Collected Dialogues of Plato*, ed. Edith Hamilton and Huntington Cairns, trans. W.D. Woodhead (New York: Pantheon Books, 1961) 521e-522c. Unless otherwise mentioned all references to Plato will be to this edition.

6   Plato, "Phaedrus," *The Collected Dialogues of Plato*, ed. Edith Hamilton and Huntington Cairns, trans. R. Hackforth (New York: Pantheon Books, 1961) 261e-262a.

7   See further, on this point, Quintilian, *Institutio Oratoria*, Book XI, I, trans. H.E. Butler (Cambridge, MA: Harvard University Press, 1979) 8-13; and Cicero, *De Oratore*, I, LIV, trans. H. Rackham and E.W. Sutton (Cambridge, MA: Harvard University Press, 1988) 232-33.

8   Plato, "Menexenus," *The Collected Dialogues of Plato*, ed. Edith Hamilton and Huntington Cairns, trans. Benjamin Jowett (New York: Pantheon Books, 1961) 235a-c; 245d.

9   Aristotle, "Rhetoric," *The Basic Works of Aristotle*, ed. Richard McKeon, trans. W. Rhys Roberts (New York: Random House, 1941) 1356a; and 1377b 25-33 to 1378a 1-5.

10 See Philip Taubman, "Soviet Union's Chief Spokesman on American TV," *The New York Times* (30 December 1985).

11 Aristotle, *Rhetoric*, 1380b 7-11.

12 Aristotle, *Rhetoric* 1357a 1-15; 1357a 16-23.

13 R.W. Johnson, "A Conspiracy Theory for the Downing of KAL 007," *Manchester Guardian Weekly* (25 December 1983).

14 Aristotle, *Rhetoric*, 1357b 36-1358b 20.

15 Aristotle, *Rhetoric* 1356a 1-14; 1389a-1390b.

16 Aristotle, *Rhetoric* 1380b35-36 to 1381a1-2; 1381a8ff and 1381b1.

17 Aristotle, *Rhetoric*, 1419b 27-30.

18 "Choose therefore any point in the speech where such an appeal is needed, and then say... 'I will tell you that whose like you have never yet heard for terror, or for wonder.' This is what Prodicus called 'slipping in a bit of the fifty-drachma show-lecture for the audience whenever they begin to nod.' It is plain that such introductions are addressed not to ideal hearers, but to hearers as we find them." Aristotle, *Rhetoric* 1415b 13-17.

19 Aristotle, *Rhetoric* 1419a 20-21.

20 For this phrasing, I thank Christine Marlin.

21 Quintus Cicero (?), "Handbook of Electioneering," *Cicero XXVIII*, trans. W. Glynn Williams, M. Cary, and Mary Henderson (Cambridge, MA: Harvard University Press, The Loeb Classical Library) 739-91, 787.

22 Max Weber, "Politics as a Vocation," From *Max Weber: Essays in Sociology*, trans. and ed. H.H. Gerth and C. Wright Mills (New York: Oxford University Press, 1946, 1958) 77-128.

23 Colin Wells, *The Roman Empire* (London: Fontana Books) 54.

24 Barbara Levick is one scholar who has cautioned against the assumption that Augustus deliberately set out to shape public opinion with the design of different coins. The mint-masters might have been concerned to present to him a design that he would find pleasing, not a design calculated to manipulate public opinion in his favour. She does, however, allow that the coins might be viewed as "publicity" for the emperor. See her "Propaganda and the Imperial Coinage," *Antichthon* 16 (1982): 104-16. For an account of the increase in portrayals of Augustus on coinage, see F. Millar, "State and Subject: The Impact of Monarchy," *Caesar Augustus: Seven Aspects*, ed. F. Millar and E Segal (Oxford: The Clarendon Press, 1985) 44.

25 Matthew 22: 17-22; Mark 12: 14-18; Luke 20: 21-26. The image referred to in the Gospel would likely have been that of Augustus's successor, Tiberius, but the point remains the same.

26 Here I am indebted to S. Harrison, "Augustus, the Poets and the Monuments," a paper read to the Corpus Christi Classical Seminar, 18 November 1987, at Oxford, and to a personal communication.

27 See M. Hengel, *Crucifixion* (London: SCM Press; Philadelphia: Fortress Press, 1977).

28 See A.K. McHardy, "Religious Ritual and Political Persuasion: The Case of England in the Hundred Years War," *International Journal of Moral and Social Studies* 3,1: 95-110.

29 Robin Lane Fox, *Pagans and Christians* (London: Penguin, 1988) 613-17.

30 P. Meyvaert, "Medieval Forgers and Modern Scholars: Tests of Ingenuity," *Bibliologia* 3, ed. P. Ganz (Turnhout: Brepols, 1983) 91-92. "Obviously many medieval forgeries are what we would call pious frauds, concocted for what seemed the best motives at the time. Viewed in this kindly and indulgent way, there is little or no harm in them, and their authors can be absolved from criminal intent" (84).

31 Meyvaert 92.

32 My source for these remarks is A.B. Cobban, *The Medieval Universities: Their Development and Organization* (London: Methuen 1975) 8-9.

33 Jacques Ellul, *Histoire de la propagande*.

34 Edmund Spenser, *A View of the State of Ireland*, ed. Andrew Hadfield and Willy Maley (Oxford: Blackwell Publishers, 1997) 58.

35 "[I]t may be necessary to compel a man to be free..." Jean-Jacques Rousseau, "The Social Contract or Principles of Political Right," *Social Contract*, intro. Sir Ernest Barker, trans. Gerard Hopkins (Oxford: Oxford University Press, 1947) 261.

36 Ellul, *Histoire de la propagande*.

37 See on this and the following, Lynn Hunt, "Engraving the Republic: Prints and Propaganda in the French Revolution," *History Today* (30 October 1980): 11-17.

38 James A. Leith, *Media and Revolution* (Toronto: Hunter Rose Company for CBC Publications, 1968) 82.

39 Robert B. Holtman, *Napoleonic Propaganda* (Baton Rouge, LA.: Louisiana State University Press, 1950) opening quotations; references below are taken from this work and will be indicated in the text by bracketed numbers.

40 See Robert Paine, "'Presence' and 'Reality', and a Smallwood Speech," *Propaganda and the Ethics of Rhetoric, The Canadian Journal of Rhetorical Studies* 3 (1993): 57-73. I am also indebted to him for insights into metonymy, discussed earlier.

41 Anatol Rapoport, ed., *Clausewitz on War* (Harmondsworth: Penguin Books, 1968) 119.

42 Rapoport 101.

43 Louis Ruchames, ed., *Racial Thought in America*. Vol. I of *From the Puritan to Abraham Lincoln* (Amherst: University of Massachusetts Press, 1969) 388-89.

44 Philip Knightley, *The First Casualty* (London: André Deutsch), 23, 23-24.

45 Ephraim Douglass Adams, *Great Britain and the American Civil War*, Vol. II (Gloucester, MA: Peter Smith, 1957) 154. See also Knightley 34.

46 Burton J. Hendrick, "Propaganda of the Confederacy," *A Psychological Warfare Casebook*, ed. William E. Daugherty (Baltimore: Johns Hopkins, 1958) 83.

47 E.B. White took issue with *Esquire's* publication of a 23-page article by Harrison Salisbury in February 1976. Xerox sponsored the article, but gave the magazine and author "full editorial control." Salisbury was paid $40,000, plus $15,000 in expenses, and Esquire received $115,000 in advertising. White wrote a letter to the *Ellsworth* (Maine) *American* and subsequently directly to Xerox, complaining that "Buying and selling space in news columns could become a serious disease of the press. If it reached epidemic proportions, it could destroy the press ... I want to read what the editor and publisher have managed to dig up on their own—and paid for out of the till." Xerox agreed with his arguments and aborted two other projects along the same lines See "Xerox, please copy!" *The Boston Globe* (5 July 1976): 33.

48 Knightley 55-56. As Upton Sinclair tells the story, Hearst admitted and was proud of his role in causing the war. Sinclair, *The Brass Check.*

49 Knightley 75.

50 Knightley 72.

51 *British Propaganda during the War 1914-1918* (n.d.), 11. This 60-page document has no named publisher and is marked "secret," though I have seen it openly displayed in the Reading Room of the Imperial War Museum. I first came across it in the papers of Sir Campbell Stuart in the IWM. It was written by Ministry of Information insiders at the war's end, as a record of their and their predecessors' activities. Hereafter cited in the text as the BP Report. Further quotations from this work come from this source and will be indicated by bracketed reference (BP and page number) in the text.

Masterman's own reports were titled "Work Conducted for the Government at Wellington House." The Third Report, the most interesting, has been assigned the reference number 49/3 (41) 01 [Foreign Office News Department]. In comparing divergent spellings between the reports, reference will be to pages in this document.

52 See M.L. Sanders and Philip M. Taylor, *British Propaganda During the First World War, 1914-18* (London and Basingstoke: Macmillan, 1982) 39; and Gary S. Messinger, *British Propaganda and the State in the First World War* (Manchester and New York: Manchester University Press, 1992) 28.

53 The writers Masterman gathered together at Wellington House included William Archer, Sir J.M. Barrie, Arnold Bennett, A.C. Benson, Mgr. R.H. Benson, Robert Bridges, Hall Caine, G.K. Chesterton, Sir Arthur Conan Doyle, John Galsworthy, Thomas Hardy, Anthony Hope Hawkins, Maurice Hewlett. W.J. Locke, E.V. Lucas, J.W. Mackail, John Masefield, A.E.W. Mason, Professor Gilbert Murray, Henry Newbolt, Sir Gilbert Parker MP, Sir Owen Seaman, G.M. Trevelyan, H.G. Wells, and Israel Zangwill. Rudyard Kipling and Sir Arthur Quiller Couch were unable to attend the first meeting of September 2, 1914, but expressed willingness to help. In addition to these names, Masterman credits the following, in his Third Report of September 1916, as assisting in Wellington House work: Lord Bryce, Lord Cromer, Lord Revelstoke, Hume Williams, Professor J.H. Morgan, Archibald Hurd, J.M. Robertson, Alfred Noyes, H.W. Massingham, G.W. Prothero, and the Dutch cartoonist Raemaekers. See Peter Buitenhuis, *The Great War of Words* (Vancouver: University of British Columbia Press, 1987) 15-16.

54 At least as regards the Japanese, there appears to be no foundation for this assumption. Non-photographic depictions were widely used in propaganda by the Japanese to their home audiences. I owe this point to Jacob Kovalio, Department of History, Carleton University.

55 Knightley 106-07. Captain F.W. Wilson's invention of the baby of Courbeck Loo is a prize example. Wilson, a reporter for the Daily Mail on assignment in Brussels, was unable to find evidence of German atrocities, so he invented the pathetic story of a baby rescued from the Hun amid burning buildings. The story caught the public imagination, with people donating clothing for the baby. To avoid embarrassment he reported the baby died of a contagious disease, thereby explaining the absence of a public burial.

56 Report of the Committee on Alleged German Outrages, as Presided over by The Right Hon. Viscount Bryce, O.M. (London: HMSO, 1915) 5. Hereafter, cited as Bryce Report. Further quotations from this work come from this source and will be indicated by bracketed reference (BR and page number) in the text.

57 Knightley, 105.

58 Arthur Ponsonby, *Falsehood in Wartime* (London: George Allen and Unwin, 1928) 113.

59 In December, 1990, in what turned out to be a prelude to US involvement in the Gulf War, Amnesty International was widely reported as confirming that Iraqi soldiers had entered hospitals following the invasion of Kuwait City and had removed incubators for shipment to Iraq, leaving 320 babies to die. This horror story was later discredited, with Amnesty International itself issuing a retraction. See Chapter 5, pp. 194ff.

60 Austen Chamberlain, *House of Commons Debates*, 2 December 1925, 2233.

61 Charles F.G. Masterman, " Introduction," Third Report 88.

62 Knightley, 105.

63 *New York Times*, 20 October 1925.

64 Shimon Rubinstein, *German Atrocity or British Propaganda, The Seventieth Anniversary of a Scandal: German Corpse Utilization Establishments in the First World War* (Jerusalem: Academon, 1987). I came across this interesting work in the Imperial War Museum after I had already covered much of the same ground. In addition to close textual analysis he provides a useful study of the political forces surrounding both the 1917 and 1925 parliamentary questions and answers.

65 *New York Times*, 20 April 1917.

66 A.J. Mackenzie, *Propaganda Boom* (London: John Gifford, 1938) 50-71.

67 *War Illustrated*, 19 May 1917.

68 "The Chemicalising of Corpses," *The Lancet*, 21 April 1917: 635.28. New York Times, 22 November 1925: VIII, 14.

69 There is much more that can be discussed. See Rubenstein for a fuller treatment.

70 See Albert L. Weeks, *The First Bolshevik* (New York: New York University Press, 1968) 88-89; Georghi Plekhanov, *Selected Philosophical Works*, Vol. 1 (Moscow: Progress Publishers, 1974) 339-49; Samuel Baron, *Plekhanov* (Stanford, CA: Stanford University Press, 1963), 148f.

71 Plekhanov 344; 345.

72 Baron 149.

73 For this and other passages I am translating from the French version of the text, *Que faire?* (Pékin: Éditions du Peuple, 1972) 82-83, 85, 88.

74 See on this Carter Elwood, "Lenin and *Pravda*, 1912-1914," *Slavic Review* 31 (June 1972); *History of the Communist Party of the Soviet Union (Bolsheviks)* (Moscow: International Publishers, Inc., 1939) 145ff. Online at <http://gate.cruzio.com/~marx2mao/Other/HCPSU39ii.html#c5s1>.

75 Richard Taylor gives his reference as G. Boltyanskii, *Lenin i kino* (Moscow, 1925) 16-17 in *Film Propaganda* 44; also *Film Propaganda* 29, 51.

76 See Peter Kenez, *The Birth of the Propaganda State: Soviet Methods of Mass Mobilization 1917-1929* (New York: Cambridge University Press, 1985) 60, 113.

77 Kenez 72.

78 Ellul, *Propaganda* 110.

79 Kenez 85, 4.

80 I am indebted for this material to Lloyd Strickland, and to an unpublished paper which he co-authored with Tzvetanka Dobreva-Marinova, titled "Bekhterev's Conception of Mental Phenomena, Activity, and Persuasibility," presented to the International Society of Political Psychology, Annual Scientific Meeting, 1995. The direct quotations in the context of Strickland's reporting are taken from Bekhterev's *Kollektivnaia reflexologia* (St. Petersburg: Kolos, 1921); in the context of his interpretation they refer to the text of the unpublished paper itself (11-12).

81 See Adolf Hitler, *Mein Kampf*, trans.Ralph Manheim (Boston: Houghton Miflin, 1943, 1971). Page references will be to this text, but some of the wording not in direct quotes is from the Alvin Johnson and John Chamberlain edition (New York: Reynal and Hitchcock, 1939). Further quotations from this work come from this source and will be indicated by bracketed reference (MK and page number) in the text.

82 See Elias Canetti, *Crowds and Power* (Harmondsworth: Penguin Books, 1960) 21, 88-93, 100-101 and *passim*. I am indebted to Professor Jutta Goheen of the Department of German at Carleton University for drawing my attention to Hitler's speech and the relevant powerful metaphors.

83 These and other details in this section are taken mostly from Roger Manvell and Heinrich Fraenkel, *Doctor Goebbels: His Life and Death* (New York: Simon and Schuster, 1960).

84 *The New York Times*, 16 April 1932. The technique can be hilarious. In the early 1980s Don Harron, sometimes asked questions of Prime Minister Trudeau on air for the Canadian Broadcasting Corporation; he then played some recorded excerpt, which, out of context, made an incongruous impression. Harron meant only to amuse, but Goebbels wanted to score political points; at any rate, it gave him and his Party a higher profile with the international press coverage it attracted.

85 Contrast the account by Helmut Heiber, *Goebbels* (New York: Hawthorn Books, 1972) 217-218, with that of Manvell and Fraenkel, who have no doubt it was a plot hatched by Goebbels; see Manvell and Fraenkel , 120-21. Viktor Reimann, *Goebbels* (Garden City, NY: Doubleday, 1976) 162, has doubts about the postwar Nuremberg trial testimony of Hans Gisevius, which fingered Goebbels as the mastermind behind the fire. Reiman says, "There was a general tendency during the Nuremberg trial to unload as much as possible on the dead Goebbels."

86 Victor Klemperer, *I Will Bear Witness*, 1933-1941 (New York: Modern Library, 1999) 5.

87 *New York Times*, 31 January 1933: 1.

88 *New York Times*, 7 February 1933.

89 The following account is taken largely from Derrick Sington and Arthur Weidenfeld, *The Goebbels Experiment* (New Haven: Yale University Press, 1943).

90 Sington and Weidenfeld 141.

91 The translation given is by Sington and Weidenfeld 230. Hanns Johst (1890-1978) has a character say this in his play "Schlageter," first performed in 1933. The actual words are "Wenn ich Kultur höre, entsichere ich meinen Browning."

92 Sington and Weidenfeld 231.

93 Sington and Weidenfeld 211.

94 See <www.histoire.org>.

95 See John Harris, *Dunkirk: The Storms of War* (Newton Abbot: David, 1980) 13.

96 Edmond Taylor, *The Strategy of Terror*, rev. ed. (1940; Boston: Houghton Miflin, 1942) 63, 64.

97 J.A. Cole, *Lord Haw-Haw* (London: Faber and Faber, 1964) 155. Biographical information has also been derived from this book.

98 Sidney Freifeld, "The War of Nerves in the News," *Contemporary Jewish Record* (February 1942): 2-31. See 24-25 for the Lochner reference. A shorter version appeared in *Public Opinion Quarterly* (Summer 1942), under the title "Nazi Press Agentry and the American Press," 221-235. Quotations below are taken from this source.

99 Freifeld.

100 Department of Publicity in Enemy Countries, "Analysis of German Propaganda, May 1-16, 1940" (27 May 1940) (C 6592/18/18), 1. The document is included in the Sir Campbell Stuart papers, Imperial War Museum, London.

101 R.G. Nobécourt, Les secrets de la propagande en France occupée (Paris: Fayard, 1962).

THREE

PROPAGANDA TECHNIQUE
An Analysis

If we keep in mind the notion of propaganda as a systematic, motivated attempt to influence the thinking and behaviour of others through means that impede or circumvent a propagandee's ability to appreciate the nature of this influence, then we have a basis for analyzing different techniques of propaganda. These can be separated in various categories. We can distinguish verbal from non-verbal forms of propaganda. We can focus on those techniques that appeal in some way to *ethos*, roughly translatable as good character and credibility; others that are designed to affect *pathos*, or feeling; and still others devoted to persuasion by *logos*, or argument. We can also take note of large-scale strategies, which combine a whole range of techniques. Or we can choose to look at individual devices or facilitators, not enough by themselves to produce successful propaganda, but contributing to the larger end. Logic books often contain a selection of "informal fallacies." These deal with illogicalities in reasoning, logical traps into which even well-intentioned people sometimes fall. At least some of these errors can be exploited for propaganda purposes, and it is useful therefore to be aware of them. It should be borne in mind, though, that those who use such techniques run the risk of exposure, resulting in a boomerang effect. Exposure as a propagandist is fatal to the would-be persuader. As Richard Crossman noted, "The art of the propagandist is never to be thought a propagandist, but to seem to be a bluff, simple, honorable enemy who would never think of descending to the level of propaganda."[1] One common way of avoiding such exposure is to operate on the level of ambiguity, to suggest and encourage desired beliefs and behaviour, perhaps with mood-affecting music or pictures, while all the time making no demonstrably false assertions.

Propaganda analysis that exposes types of ambiguity and the ways in which attention is captured and directed by the propagandist performs a useful service by alerting us to possible manipulation by others. But the same knowledge can assist those who wish to engage in propaganda or persuasion more generally; hence, the need for an ethical assessment of the activity (we will deal with this issue in Chapter 4). Ideally, from a moral point of view, one expects that persuasion should always be carried out by transparent, non-devious presentation of truthful claims. But in the world we inhabit, message recipients often come with prejudices and attitudes that may preclude successful communication in the form of artless transparency. Between outright mendacious manipulation and artless transparency there is a wide range of communicative behaviour awaiting examination.

OVERVIEW

We begin by looking at propaganda from a broad perspective. There are certain things people want. Propaganda, when it is not simply appealing to reflex or herd instinct, presents its goals in a form or guise that appears to satisfy one or more of those preexisting wants. At the most abstract level, people want happiness, so the art of persuasion will show them, sometimes only implicitly, that a proposed program, ideology, way of life, commercial object, or whatever will contribute to their happiness. Religious beliefs may postpone happiness to another life after death, but happiness is still the ultimate goal. For example, an Arabic language document, some pages of which were reportedly found in a suitcase of a September 11 hijacker, Mohamed Atta, advised hijackers "You're doing a job which is loved by God, and you will end your day in heavens where you will join the virgins."[2] The word "happiness" may suggest a state of blissed-out withdrawal from the world or a total immersion in a sensual Valhalla, neither of which everybody wants. Some people are happy bearing the burdens of life, taking care of others regardless of their own desires, knowing that they are at least bringing happiness in some sense to these others. To avoid being sidetracked into a full-fledged philosophical discussion of happiness, let us think here of happiness tautologically in terms of what people ultimately seek. People tend to be concerned in a general way about better living conditions. For example, they do not want the environment destroyed or to find traffic at a standstill on their way to work. The propagandist will argue or suggest that whatever it is he or she is pushing will prevent destruction of the environment, help to reduce traffic congestion, or whatever else relates to the special concerns of the audience. The formula is simple, and the complexity comes only in knowing, first, what it is that a given audience holds near and dear to their hearts and, secondly, how to present this in such a way as to be believed.

Knowing the mind of an audience comes in modern times largely through opinion polls. Money gives a great advantage to a modern propagandist, since polls are not cheap. Even so, polls have their limitations, and people can change their minds. But, assuming that the preexisting beliefs and attitudes of an audience are known, the problem becomes one of convincing people that the program, measure, person, political party, commercial object, or whatever the propagandist is pushing, is desirable. This is where a great number of different methods and considerations come into play.

Attention

Whether we deal with legitimate persuasion or ethically dubious propaganda, the first problem has always been to secure the attention of an audience. Merely putting something in someone's field of vision does not ensure getting their attention. We tend to filter out of our perceptive field what does not interest us. If it does not pertain to our interests we are likely to ignore it, unless it suddenly barks or screams or hits us over the head. It is interesting how advertisements on some Internet provider pages are sometimes so jumbled that we don't notice them until they start to move; then we find our attention drawn to them, even against our will. Since those who wish to get our attention for propaganda purposes want to secure our compliance, they will not use irritating means. Much ingenuity has been exercised in the past to find an acceptable way of gaining and holding people's attention. George Orwell, when he was only 11, once stood on his head near a fence bordering a neighbour's garden where three children were playing cricket. One of them asked, politely but with curiosity, why he was standing on his head. The young Orwell replied, "You are noticed more if you stand on your head than if you are right way up."[3] Orwell knew something about gaining attention, which is to present novelty. We may recall that the rise to power of the Nazis in Germany during the 1920s and early 1930s was assisted by Goebbels's clever, attention-getting posters, such as one in blood-red ink, announcing that "The Kaiser of America Speaks in Berlin,"[4] and through the use of violence. It seems an unfortunate truth that the unscrupulous have an easier time getting press coverage.

However, attention is affected by more than just the unusual. Pictures of scantily clad, beautiful women and men are hardly unusual today, yet they are still eye-catching. We notice things that already preoccupy us in some way or other. Our own name will jump out at us from a list. Our professional concerns will cause our attention to fasten on key words related to our work as we scan a newspaper. Skilful advertising depends partly on knowing what kinds of things will capture the attention of the relevant market audience, without causing offence in doing so.

Totalitarian states exact the attention of people by force. In a free society, the right of a person to choose what messages to see and hear will place limits on the right of others to communicate with him or her. In democratic states today, attention is often sought by producing good visuals for television. People of the Cree First Nation brought war canoes to Central Park in New York, successfully getting press attention for their cause of opposition to further Hydro-Quebec damming of their lands. More recently, anti-tobacco campaigners dressed up in costumes to look like cigarettes, in imitation of the cartoon-character drawn by Doonesbury. Such public relations gimmicks are risky, because the desire of the media for good pictures is counterbalanced by their resentment against being used. In the "Who is using whom?" assessment, it is hard to predict the outcome. Either way familiarity could breed unconcern. Fresh stratagems need to be thought up from time to time. Even a sympathetic editor is likely to recoil from repeat performances.

Emotional Appeals

In a general way, propaganda and persuasion rely to a large extent on emotional levers. Wartime propaganda fuels hatred and anger against an enemy by turning the enemy into a non-human creature, unworthy of rights or respect in the eyes of propagandees. Or it appeals to fear of the consequence of inaction. Recruitment propaganda often appeals to the sense of belonging, to the fear of being left out and not counting as a somebody in one's peer group. Beer and tobacco commercials stress the sense of group-membership, of acceptance in fun-loving crowds when drinking or smoking.

There are many different kinds of emotional appeals, all linked to reigning ideas of what is thought right or admirable at a given time. Emulation, greed, envy, and the like are sometimes stimulated by messages and signs that invite the reader, viewer, or hearer to be like some successful person portrayed in them: "You, too, can be thin, healthy, if...."; "You, too, can be a responsible parent, if...."; "You want to have beautiful skin? Here's how...." Of course, there may be rational grounds for linking a given product with some featured admirable quality, but typically the emotional appeal works independently. Perhaps the deepest anxiety in all of us relates to death and the afterlife, and it is not surprising that religions offering palliation of such anxieties can also convince people to part with a large part of their possessions to support their ministries. If the religion is too successful in answering these anxieties, a hell-fire sermon may be useful for restoring them. A religion which confronts and answers our deepest anxieties is at least doing the job asked of it. In modern times we see language or music previously reserved for the holy and sacred applied to mundane products pushed by the advertiser. The success of this seemingly contradictory effort remains to be seen.

One use of emotion is to distract people from evaluating evidence. There is an old joke about advice given to a novice trial lawyer: "If the law is on your side, pound it into the judge. If the facts are on your side, pound it into the jury. If neither the law nor the facts are on your side, pound it into the table." It helps, in a lawsuit for damages, if the victim appears before the court bandaged up and looking to be in a pitiable state. If a newspaper supports a politician, it publishes pleasant pictures, perhaps showing the politician surrounded by smiling children. If it chooses to undermine a politician, it prints pictures showing an unsmiling face, surrounded by angry people.

Credibility

As indicated, emotion can sometimes distract an audience from raising questions about the authority and believability of a given message or spokesperson, but moods change from day to day, and a more concrete grounding for belief-acceptance may be needed over time. Repetition can help, but some further anchor is usually needed. The best anchor is reason, but not everyone can follow and appreciate the intricate arguments surrounding, say, risks from mishaps in a nuclear reactor. Since the public cannot always follow the arguments, it looks instead to the credentials of the person or group making them. This leads to what is perhaps the most important concern of propagandists, public relations consultants, and the like: namely, how to impart credibility.

In modern times, the credibility of honest science is very high. That is why a lot of money is spent on studies to show scientifically whatever it is that the persuader wishes the public to believe. But the public can be deceived in two ways. First, the scientists themselves may be corrupted, ignoring those things that count against the wishes of the funding group and reporting only those things that tend to support them. Secondly, the scientists may be perfectly honest, but the public may come to believe that the results have an authority they do not in fact have. For example, a few years ago the Canadian gold-mining company, Bre-X, had its Indonesian ore-samples analyzed by a prestigious, reputable firm, which found a very high concentration of gold in them. The analyzing company noted that the samples were supplied by Bre-X, but this fact received insufficient attention. Later, it was revealed that the samples were "salted" (i.e., had gold artificially added to them to make them appear richer than they were). The stock of Bre-X soared, only to drop precipitously when the worthlessness of the samples came to light.

In a general way, a major goal of the propagandist is to seek some kind of authoritative backing for the belief he or she is propagating. Different devices (to be looked at later) can be used to achieve that aim.

Analogy and Scope

The propagandist seeks in general to link the project, person, ideology, party, or whatever to some thing or things that are viewed favourably and unlike some thing or things that are viewed unfavourably. Words and pictures are both well suited for this activity. Certain favourable buzz-words are applied to features of the relevant project, etc., or unfavourable buzz-words get applied to things the propagandist wants the public to reject. Cultural icons are readily exploitable for propaganda purposes. Of course, icons can be toppled, and words can lose their buzz over time.

Different words have different breadths of meaning, and these differences can be exploited for persuasive purposes. A heinous action may be made to appear innocent by choosing a word or expression that is applicable, but that has broader connotations. "I merely told the truth about x's past," may disguise the simple fact that the destruction of x's reputation was involved. Where there is a blameless accidental killing, as in the case of some car accidents, the blamelessness can be disguised, sometimes intentionally, by the deliberate omission of the qualifier, "accidentally."

Morally Evaluative Language

Words can also be used to convey a moral attitude or a whole moral framework, which will affect the understanding or appreciation of a given idea, activity, person, group, etc. Whether we view a protest action as striking a blow for justice, as distinct from engaging in a despicable, cowardly terrorist act, that maims innocent victims, will depend partly on the individual facts of the episode referred to (the maimings might have been accidental), but also on one's overall moral assessment of the justification for the protest and of the risk involved. The events of September 11, 2001, have rightly been condemned in world opinion, but it serves neither clarity of thinking nor future world peace to treat them as if they had no connection with previous US military actions in the Middle East (direct or indirect) and innocent victims of this involvement. It tends to be a feature of warlike situations that opponents' actions are viewed in the blackest possible light, with morally-loaded language reflecting that interpretation, while one's own, or one's allies' actions are treated in the most favourable light.

DEVICES INVOLVING LANGUAGE MANIPULATION

Some Examples from Bolinger

Many forms of manipulation make artful use of language. The Harvard linguist Dwight Bolinger, drawing on the work of others, has provided some interesting examples, to which he has given useful names.[5]

The first is what he calls, following Julia Stanley, *deleted agent of the passive*. In this we rephrase a sentence from active to passive voice and delete the subject of the first sentence. Instead of "Jane kicked the ball," the sentence is written "the ball was kicked." Instead of "Willy broke the window at 5 p.m.," we get "The window was broken at 5 p.m." As can be seen, it is a useful device for obscuring responsibility, and it is, not surprisingly, a favoured language for boardroom minutes where the aim is to avoid divisiveness or public recriminations. Equally, it is language frowned on by editors who are looking for directness and transparency in writing. Stanley's example reproduced in Bolinger's text is illuminating. Suppose Shanks and Shaughnessey dispute a medical bill. Shanks says that Shaughnessey sewed him up after an operation, leaving sponges and a scalpel inside. Shaughnessey says that that is a dirty lie. Depending on whom an editor favours, the headline might read: "Shanks charged with slander," or "Shaughnessey charged with malpractice." The other person's name does not appear in the headline, and the reader is primed to put the focus of guilt on the named person rather than on the namer.

Secondly, and rather similar to the first, there is what Bolinger calls, following Donald Smith, *experiencer deletion*. Experiencing verbs are those such as believes, knows, feels, senses, touches, and so on. If we say, for example, "it is believed that over 10,000 people appeared at the demonstration," and leave out the relevant fact

that the belief was held only by some wishful-thinker in the sponsoring organization, who did not attend the meeting and who notoriously exaggerates the numbers, we give a false impression. Stanley makes a similar point, using a different
terminology. The sentence, "In the fifth century the known world was limited to
Europe and small parts of Asia and Africa," obscures, as she points out, the fact that
large parts of the world, outside the stated geographical limits, were known to many
people who happened not to live within the limits indicated.[6] It is not difficult to
think of other examples of deceptions using this form of language. Of course, the
experiencer deletion can be replaced by an equally misleading substitute. For
example, a foreign correspondent reporter may write, "Seasoned observers here
feel that..." when the reference is only to a taxi driver, himself, or other journalists holed up in some hotel bar, with no real access to what is going on outside.

Thirdly, there is what Bolinger calls the *deletion of a qualifying performative*.
People with some expertise in a particular field of knowledge may be called on
by the media to express their views to the public. Wanting to be helpful, they may
say things like, "Well, I haven't looked into the matter, but my guess would
be...." It is a case of deleted qualifying performative if the report gives the rest
of the sentence without including the first part. The media prefers to present readers with uncomplicated facts, but the interests of truth demand the inclusion of
qualifiers, since otherwise readers or listeners will be led to misjudge the strength
of the speaker's support for the claim, whatever it was. Performatives such as "I
think ..." or "I feel..." are included precisely in order to signal to the listener that
the speaker is giving only limited endorsement to what follows. To omit these
qualifiers can mislead people, in some cases seriously and unfairly. Bolinger makes
a Cold War example. Someone in authority says, "America is lagging behind Russia
in arms production." It makes a difference whether that statement is founded on
good intelligence, or whether the speaker is making a guess, or attributing the view
to someone else who happens to be uninformed.[7]

Finally, Bolinger views the act of *naming* along with "favorable or unfavorable
overtone" in the terms selected as "the favorite device of the propagandist and
the ultimate refinement in the art of lying."[8] Here we are reminded of Orwell's
Nineteen Eighty-Four and the naming of the ministry where lies are continually rein-
vented as the "Ministry of Truth." Among examples Bolinger takes from Henry
Steele Commager are the use of terms such as "surgical strikes" for precision
bombing (often not so precise, nor so healthy), "pacification centers" to apply to
concentration camps, "incontinent ordnance" for bombs that miss their target, and
"friendly fire," which kills innocent civilians by mistake.[9] A government may choose
to title legislation that drastically cuts back on funding for education, as "An Act
for the Improvement of Education," treating as a truth what is, at best, only
debatably so. A great deal of effort and expense is often required to counteract
impressions so formed.

Name-calling in general is a powerful force for influencing opinion because names
are easily remembered. Words like "Uncle Tom," "demagogue," "racist," "sexist,"
"traitor," and the like carry powerful emotional overtones, but they also cause per-

ceptions of the individual so named to be warped. It is sometimes said of such powerful terms that a person is "guilty if charged," such is the tendency of people to believe that there's "no smoke without fire," and that denials are only to be expected and not to be believed without further evidence. Names can have a powerful revealing effect, causing people to become aware of some truth. But, used in propaganda, names invite us to form our opinions without reviewing the evidence and, thus, to overlook those aspects of the truth the propagandist prefers to see concealed. In our own day we find words like "Communist," "leftist," "liberal," "extreme rightist," "bigot," "neo-con," and so on used pejoratively, often without a clear idea as to the meaning of the term so applied.

Bolinger usefully investigates how names or descriptions can exploit hidden associations in our language. The two words "baseless" and "groundless" have the same literal meaning, but he feels that the former term is the stronger of the two, because of the association with the term "base" as something mean and unworthy.[10] (Never mind that "baseless" should mean "less base." The association is unconscious and so logic does not play a part.)

Sometimes it seems impossible to discuss controversial issues without slipping into tendentious language. In the abortion debate, one side speaks of "pro-abortion," the other of "pro-choice." Both terms have an element of truth and falsity. To say that someone who opposes criminal laws prohibiting abortion is "pro-abortion" misses the distinction between those who favour abortion and those who do not, but who believe that a criminal prohibition will do more harm than good. To say that someone who opposes criminal prohibitions for abortion is "pro-choice" obscures the fact that the nature of the choice involves the destruction of the beginning of a human life. It concentrates only on the abstract notion of free choosing, avoiding the particularities of the choice. The names given to opposing participants in the debate are highly loaded, yet it seems difficult to find terms that avoid tendentiousness without being awkwardly long.

Examples from the Institute for Propaganda Analysis

A compact, frequently reproduced list of "tricks of the trade" was furnished in 1939 by the New York-based Institute for Propaganda Analysis. In addition to name-calling, there are six common tricks, examined below.

1. *Glittering Generality*. This is defined as "associating something with a 'virtue word' ... to make us accept and approve the thing without examining the evidence." Glittering generalities *"mean different things to different people; they can be used in different ways."*[11] A prime example of such a word is "democracy," which in our day has a virtuous connotation. But what exactly does it mean? To some people, it may be treated as supportive of the status quo in a given society, while others may see it as requiring change, in the form, say, of a reform of election financing practices. The ambiguity of the term is such that Nazis and Soviet Communists both felt they

could claim it for their own system of governance, despite the fact that many in the West saw these systems, with reason, as the antithesis of democracy.

The expression "free speech" is another glittering generality, which can be used to deny free speech to others. *The Fine Art of Propaganda* was aimed at combatting the influence of popular radio speeches by a fiery priest, Father Charles E. Coughlin of Detroit. In one talk given January 1, 1939, Father Coughlin stated "[Americans] are seldom advised that the free speech of the Communist or the free speech of the Nazi may not be used to destroy the free speech of the American" (FAP 51). The effect of his address was to call for the denial of free speech for Communists and Nazis, while all the time making use of the glittering generality of "free speech." Use of glittering generalities can give power to individuals who exploit them. Senator Joe McCarthy used the House Un-American Activities Committee hearings to appeal to a particular concept of what constitutes "American" as a way of bullying Americans of a more socialist political standpoint than his own.

2. *Transfer.* The Institute defines this term as follows: "Transfer carries the authority, sanction, and prestige of something respected and revered over to something else in order to make the latter acceptable" (FAP 70). It observed how Father Coughlin's radio speeches opened with churchlike music, giving the impression he represented the Catholic Church in the views he broadcast. "By Transfer he attempts to carry the authority, sanction and prestige of something respected and revered by millions (the Roman Catholic Church) over to something else (his own economic, political, and even racial views) that he wishes to make thus more acceptable to us" (FAP 69).

Transfer is a very common device. A younger, aspiring politician has a photograph taken with a senior political icon in order to share the latter's prestige. Photographing a politician against the background of a revered institution, such as Parliament, can have the same effect. Having the flag as background is a frequent form of transfer. Always, the aim is to be seen in the company of persons, places, or things that will resonate well in the minds of voters. If public transportation is in favour, then it helps to be seen riding a bus, whether or not the party platform endorses increasing public subsidies for mass transit.

There are legitimate and illegitimate uses of transfer. It is legitimate when transfer is used to represent fairly what a candidate stands for. It is illegitimate when this or any other propaganda device is used unfairly, to pretend that the candidate favours something which he or she does not (FAP 73). Among the irritants at election time are publicity-seeking candidates who try to take credit, through photo-opportunities, for projects with which they had nothing to do or even may have opposed. The reverse of this is taking photographs of opponents in the presence of people who have earned the hatred and contempt of the community and then publicizing the pictures to suggest an affinity between the candidates and the others. Of course, the technique of photomontage can produce the same effect with very little effort, but it risks a boomerang from detection.

3. *Testimonial*. In the Institute's definition, "*Testimonial* consists in having some respected or hated person say that a given idea or program or product or person is good or bad" (FAP 75). This appeal to authority encourages us to accept ideas without subjecting them to critical examination. To avoid being duped by such appeals, we should ask ourselves who or what is quoted in the testimonial; what reason there is for regarding the person, organization, etc., appealed to as authoritative; and, finally, what merits attach to the idea, etc., apart from the testimonials.

Deception occurs when the supposed authority never said what is attributed to him, her, or it; when the views of the authority are distorted; or when the authority is untrustworthy. A popular film star may lack the expertise to speak competently on scientific, economic, or complicated political issues, or a famous scientist may pronounce on something outside his or her field, without the lack of competence being communicated to the audience. Father Coughlin in certain instances made anti-Semitic statements based on information provided by a Nazi propaganda sheet, *World-Service*, but he cited official government documents as his sources. The latter either did not contain the information attributed to them or acknowledged a lack of adequate evidence for the very claims he made on air (FAP 76-84).

In the early debates on abortion in the 1960s, anti-abortion activists complained that the number of alleged illegal abortions in Canada—35,000 in Toronto alone and 100,000 for the country as a whole—was greatly exaggerated by those seeking liberalization of the laws. The Toronto figure was attributed to the former head of the abortion squad of the Morality Department of the Metropolitan Police Department, Detective Sergeant William Quennell, who included statistics for natural miscarriages and abortions as well as criminal abortions in this figure.[12] Information not properly sourced may undergo a "laundering" effect in this way. A few years ago the Regional Medical Health Officer in Ottawa-Carleton provided an exact figure for the number of area lung cancer deaths caused by secondhand smoke. This might appear to the uninitiated as a very reliable figure, but he could have obtained that kind of information only by appealing to worldwide research into the matter, which would give an estimate of the number of such people per 100,000 population who die each year in the country or countries where the research was done. He would then have taken the number of such cancer deaths per 100,000 of population, divided the area population by 100,000, and multiplied by the number. This kind of result is very unreliable. However, being the local medical authority, his estimate took on a much more solid appearance, as if there had been an exact number of death certificates listing "secondhand smoke" as the cause of death.[13]

Science gets its credibility by appearing to be objective, giving us results from nature and not what individuals or corporations wish to be the case. Yet, individual scientists have been known to skew results in the hope of getting fame or further funding. The crafty consultant, we are sometimes told by insiders, will insist on maintaining his or her integrity, but will be interested, at the start of contracted research, to know what the sponsoring party would like the investigation to reveal. This can affect what aspects of the investigation are trumpeted and what will be effectively suppressed. When industries are the sole funding sources for the safety of their products, the public has reason to be apprehensive about the level of detachment connected with the research. Scientific testimony, to be fully credible, needs to be assessed in the light of potential biases. The issue is of great concern in the light of recent cut-backs in funding for universities and research institutions.

The importance of adequate scrutiny of sources can hardly be overestimated. Again and again the public is misled by appeals to people or institutions who *seem* to have the requisite authority, but who do not.

4. *Plain Folks.* This device is defined as "the method by which a speaker attempts to convince the audience that he and his ideas are good because they are 'of the people', the 'plain folks'" (FAP 92-93). In practice, it is put into action by presenting oneself to the public as a homey type, "just like you"; for North American politicians, it may involve such things as showing devotion to little children and pets, attending church services, pitching hay, and going fishing. Aristotle understood the reasons for such a device: people will vote for a friend, someone who values the same kinds of things they do, not for an enemy. A candidate for election who is seen taking part in the same day-to-day activities as the general public will be more likely to be trusted than someone who appears to be aloof. The number of people who actually talk directly to a state, provincial, or national politician is relatively small. However, people like to vote for someone who "speaks their language," with whom they feel they would be comfortable communicating. What is missing from the "one of us" characterization is a careful enumeration of policies, which the electorate should try to discover.

5. *Card-stacking.* This is defined as "the selection and use of facts and falsehoods, illustrations or distractions, and logical or illogical statements in order to give the best or the worst possible case for an idea, program, person or product" (FAP 95).

Card-stacking covers a very large area, including many or all misuses of statistics, polls, and the like, which we deal with separately below. It seems an especially appropriate term when applied to the mass media selection of experts to quote or to engage in debate on major issues of the day. The complaint is often heard that radical viewpoints are left out of political reporting and that, with only a few non-threatening exceptions, speakers are chosen because they support the existing power structure. Alternatively, voices on the right will often complain that reporters are on the whole more "liberal" than the mainstream population. By choosing an appropriate mix of speakers, one can ensure that a given viewpoint will be likely to emerge as strongest in debate. It is card-stacking to ignore or under-represent important positions on issues with a view to preordaining that one's own favoured view will be dominant.

What is true of choosing speakers or experts is true also of scholarly sources. It is card-stacking to select as evidence only those writings that agree with certain of one's preconceptions and to ignore contrary opinions, no matter how well argued they may be. It is to be expected that there will often be disagreement about what constitutes a fair selection of opinions or evidence, but opposing ideological factions can reach agreement on the matter.

6. *Band Wagon.* This is the attempt to persuade based on the premise that "everybody—at least all of *us*—is doing it." The idea is that the group addressed should therefore accept the propagandist's program, follow the crowd, and "jump on the bandwagon" (FAP 105).

Mass rallies and demonstrations give people the sense of overwhelming support for the party, program, cause, etc., on whose behalf the rally is being held. This will help undecided people to join, on the grounds that the movement is unstoppable and that it is better to share in the benefits of joining than to be left out. The propagandist employs for this purpose "symbols, colours, music, movement, all the dramatic arts. He gets us to write letters, send telegrams [e-mails today] to contribute to his 'cause.'" To combat this form of propaganda, the Institute recommends asking, first, precisely, what is the program that the propagandist wants us to accept? Second, what is the evidence for and against the program? And third, does the program serve the interests of one's group? One might also question the motives of others who show up to a rally. Has free beer, pizza, or other benefit been promised? Are they going because they like the music, the colour, and the excitement, rather than because they have a strong commitment to the cause?

Rallies have a legitimate role to play in a democracy. People who pay to support election campaigns have an interest in getting a fair estimate of the chances a given candidate might have of winning. It becomes propaganda when efforts are made to artificially boost the numbers by extraneous inducements or hinted threats of some kind.

Use of a term like "American," when addressing an American audience is often calculated to promote bandwagon effects. To say that Communism is un-American is to promote a herd mentality, "us" versus "them." Such an appeal is insidious, because there is no single set of characteristics that defines an American as American, or a Canadian as a Canadian, and so on with other nationalities. Every society has its dissenters, people who disagree with the majority view. There is no good reason to define them as not belonging to the given nationality merely because they do not share the prevalent views. The defence the Institute offers against this propaganda, as with the other devices is simple: "Don't let yourself be stampeded, beware of your own prejudices, suspend your judgment until more sides of the issue are presented, and analyse them" (FAP 134).

Some Examples from Eleanor MacLean

There are many other ways in which language can be used to manipulate an audience. One obvious way is simply to lie. However, once caught in a lie, the liar loses credibility. Therefore, propagandists are reluctant to lie unless there are special circumstances, such as the likelihood of achieving some desired goal before the lie gets detected, or some way of arguing that a lie was not involved (this is called "plausible deniability"). Eleanor Maclean, in her 1981 book *Between the Lines*,[14] compiled a list of such deceptive practices involving language. I will illustrate her list with real-life examples where some device has been used. Ideally, every device should come with a citation of its use. If it is claimed that such-and-such a device is commonly used in deceptive persuasion, then why should it be difficult to provide an example? One problem is this: it is difficult to know the intention of the writer or speaker who supposedly has made use of a deception. In using a real-life example, the principle of charity requires us to assume that some honest mistake is involved. To circumvent this problem I will give real-life examples, but treat them as possibly hypothetical. The examples would be well-suited to propaganda purposes, whether or not the individual mentioned intended to deceive a given audience.

1. *Bold Assertions*. Sometimes dubious claims are presented with expressions like "unquestionably," or "undeniably," or "as everyone knows." The exaggerated claim helps to deflect attention away from weakness. A particularly striking example of bold assertion occurred in a letter to a Toronto newspaper, in which the writer, attached to the Center for International Affairs at Harvard University, wrote: "Despite intensive efforts by Chileans of the left, the international media and a US Congressional investigation to establish a connection between the coup [that overthrew Allende] and the US government, not one shred of evidence of such a link has ever been uncovered."[15] But a lengthy study by a US Senate Committee established that the US spent approximately $7 million in covert action to support opposition groups in Chile; that the CIA spent $1.5 million in support of *El Mercurio*, the country's largest newspaper; and that "[a]ccording to CIA documents, these efforts played a significant role in setting the stage for the military coup of September 11, 1973."[16]

2. *Selective Omission*. One common device for deceiving an audience is the omission of certain facts or circumstances connected with an event, so that the hearer forms a false impression. The device has been around so long that it has a pair of Latin names for it, namely *suppressio veri* with *suggestio falsi*: "suppression of the (or a, or an aspect of) truth, with suggestion of the false." For example, take the case of a politician who has to vote on a bill combining very popular measures along with some unacceptable ones. It is selective omission to report that the politician voted against the popular measures without mentioning that the bill also contained the other, unacceptable features.

A notable example of truth suppression occurred immediately prior to the Falklands invasion by the British in 1982. Sir Frank Cooper, Undersecretary of Defence, was asked by the press whether there was going to be a D-Day style invasion on the Falklands; he denied this. The next day there was a massed landing of troops. In response to an outcry against such deception, he gave testimony before a Defence Committee of Inquiry established by the British Parliament. He said, "We did not tell a lie—but we did not tell the whole truth." He explained that in denying that there was going to be a D-Day style invasion, he had in mind a landing where there is opposition. The forces landing at San Carlos were "unopposed." This led to the following exchange between Dr. Gilbert, MP, and Cooper:

DR. GILBERT: There is a legal phrase with which you are no doubt familiar: *suppressio veri* and *suggestio falsi*—suppression of the truth and the suggestion of what is false, in the course of which you do not tell a single lie. Would that be a fair assessment of the role of your Department in this crisis?

COOPER: No, I think that is rather an obnoxious suggestion, if I may say so.

DR. GILBERT: You have admitted to *suppressio veri*.

COOPER: I would rather speak in English.

DR. GILBERT: Suppression of the truth.

COOPER: No.

DR. GILBERT: I beg your pardon?

COOPER: I find those questions both obnoxious, and I do not accept them.

DR. GILBERT: But you have admitted to it already, have you not, suppression of the truth?

COOPER: No, I have not admitted to that, and I am not going to admit to it.[17]

Cooper's instincts were probably right. He no doubt sensed that the Latin terms were terms of opprobrium, and he wanted to be sure that it was understood that he was morally justified in omitting to clarify what he meant in issuing the denial to the press. Once he had made that case, the acceptance of a technical term for what he had done became easier for him, and he went on to concede Dr. Gilbert's point.

3. *Quoting Out of Context.* It is possible to make someone appear to hold views that they do not in fact hold, by reproducing only a part of what a person said (selective quotation) or by quoting out of context so that such things as ironic intent are not conveyed.

Here is an example of quoting out of context, taken from a subcommittee meeting of the Canadian Senate. Brian McKenna, of Galafilm Inc., had made a documentary, *The Valour and the Horror*, which questioned the wisdom of World War II blanket bombing raids, such as that on Dresden. Because the film portrayed some of the air command leaders in an unfavourable light, veterans objected to it, complaining of inaccuracies. In the subcommittee hearing, McKenna's patriotism came under attack. Senator John Sylvain accused him of unpatriotism, since he had written in an article published in his college newspaper, "It would appear that those Canadians who died defending what these symbols represent were fools." McKenna replied that he had written the article years earlier and could not remember exactly what he had said and why he had said it. Sylvain read aloud the article, about a prank played by some American students, who hoisted the American flag on a Montreal campus flagpole, on a day when the news came that the centennial flame on Parliament Hill had been snuffed out by the cold. The article concluded, "It would appear that those Canadians who died defending what these symbols represent were fools. The torch they threw us was extinguished long before the flame froze over on Parliament Hill. Patriotism seems to have disappeared from the Canadian vocabulary." McKenna replied:

> Obviously, that is written with sarcasm and irony, outraged that an American flag could fly over the campus and no one would notice it.... I can supply this committee, after the hearings cease, with all the articles I wrote during that period on this issue. You will see that the entire record supports what I am telling you now.[18]

In this case, clarification of the context took away what otherwise seemed to be a damaging statement by McKenna. Without the clarification, the media covering the hearings would have had a juicy item to report, and McKenna would have had to fight to restore a tarnished reputation. With the clarification, there was no news item, or at least none that most newspapers had space to handle. To explain what appeared to be an attempt to deceive by quoting out of context would take a lot of ink, and most readers would not have had the inclination to sort out the details.

4. *Twisting and Distortion.* Distortion can be achieved by selective quotation, as we have just seen, but it can also occur by omitting some of the circumstances in which something is said. In 1983, a magazine article about Mary-Lou Finlay, a popular CBC radio personality, reported her as saying she did not know how much money her senior co-host, Barbara Frum, made. In a letter to the *Ottawa Citizen*, Finlay protested that the way the interview was reported made her seem interested and possibly jealous of Frum. What really occurred, she said, was that the interviewer had asked her if this were so. "Why should I be jealous?," Finlay answered. The interviewer suggested, "She makes more money than you, doesn't she?" To which Finlay responded, "I don't know, I've never asked her." To illustrate how the mis-reporting occurred, she retold an apocryphal tale about Pope John Paul II's first visit to New York. When asked whether he was going to visit any night clubs, he replied with disdain and affected ignorance, "*Are* there any nightclubs in New

York?" The story that appeared began "The Pope's first words on visiting New York were ... (you guessed it)"[19]

5. *Meshing Fact with Opinion.* Sometimes a controversial opinion can be concealed behind claims that appear to be purely factual. MacLean gives the example: "Southern Africa is being overrun by Communists." One value judgment involves the definition of the term "Communist," if it is not intended here to be limited to card-carrying Communist Party members. A second value judgment enters with the verb "overrun," which signifies that the speaker thinks there are too many of the designated group in the area. We need to attend to what the verb connotes—implies in addition to its literal meaning—and the nouns denote—their literal meaning.[20] The description of a certain country as "overpopulated" may conceal the problem of food shortages caused by market manipulations and corruption, or it may reflect negative racial attitudes towards people in that country. Likewise, the statement that there is a "problem" with some ethnic group may reflect a bias. Hitler's "Jewish problem" was a "Nazi problem" to Jews and many others.

Logical Fallacies

Since the time of Plato and Aristotle philosophers have had an interest in taking note of common fallacies in reasoning. A reason for doing so is to avoid making such mistakes. But these fallacies can also be exploited by the unscrupulous to deceive an audience. What follows is a list of language-linked fallacies, many of which date back to Aristotle and earlier. Sometimes an alleged "fallacy" has legitimate use; it is important to sort this out from the illegitimate.

1. *The Ad Hominem Argument.* This Latin expression literally means "to the person." It is a fallacy to reject what a person says or supports merely because the person can be shown to have a bad character. A good policy does not become bad merely because a bad person advocates it. The supposition that it does is sometimes called the *genetic fallacy*. Likewise, a good person may advocate a bad policy. To avoid fallacious reasoning we need to examine the case for or against a policy on its own merits, not on the character of the person supporting it.

Attention to the character of the speaker is not always fallacious, for instance, when the issue is one of trust. Indeed, as we have already seen, the establishment of one's credibility and the undermining of an opponent's is a vital component of successful rhetoric.

It is also not fallacious, in attacking a person's support for a given measure, to point out that the same person had presented diametrically opposed arguments on a previous occasion, where a similar measure affected his interests negatively. It is reasonable to ask for sincerity and consistency in a person, at least to the point of calling for reasons explaining sudden reversals. To advance only those arguments that suit one's interests, with no genuine concern for the general welfare, is called *special pleading*, and, when exposed, it tends to discredit the person making the argument. Still, even a special pleader may have a good case, and the matter should not end with the exposure of inconsistency in the person making the case.

2. *False Cause.* It is a fallacy to think that merely because one occurrence follows another, the first causes the second. The real cause of hard times following upon the election of a new governing party may lie with the financial mess left behind by the previous government. The attribution of causality cannot be established merely by the temporal sequence. It is sometimes called the fallacy of *post hoc, ergo propter hoc* ("after the thing, therefore because of the thing"). It comes into play when an action appears to have a causal connection to a result; for instance, a politician takes credit for prosperity, which resulted from no policy or action of his or her own, but because good weather caused a bumper harvest or because a major trading partner has an especially strong economy. An apocryphal medical story concerns the cure for warts: the latest and least-tried cure turns out to be the most successful, because it is tried last of all the remedies, by which time the wart has dropped off spontaneously. Once the cure gets a reputation for success, and is tried first of all the remedies, it rapidly loses its reputation.

In making statistical correlations, we need to be on our guard against assuming a causal connection between two statistically correlated happenings, because the connection may reflect a more fundamental cause. Suppose we find that, among octogenarians, fewer smokers have Alzheimer's disease than nonsmokers. We cannot assume without more evidence that cigarette smoking helps prevent Alzheimer's, because the population of people in their 80s has proportionately fewer smokers, since a higher proportion of these have died as a consequence of smoking. A possible alternative hypothesis is that those who have the genetic constitution to resist death from lung cancer might also have a superior constitution for resisting Alzheimer's or other diseases. (Here my aim is to call attention to the complexity of the issue, not to decide it one way or the other.)

3. *Hasty Generalization.* The prejudiced mind requires little evidence to draw conclusions about how a whole class of people behave on the basis of having seen a very small sample. A person has a bad experience with a lawyer and makes the blanket accusation that all lawyers are crooked.

4. *Ignoring the Question.* It is a time-honoured device, used by officials pursued by the media with some damaging accusation, to deflect the questioning by giving the answer to some different issue, ignoring the actual question altogether. Canadian Prime Minister Jean Chrétien, when asked about the use of pepper spray by the Royal Canadian Mounted Police (RCMP) in British Columbia against a crowd protesting the visit of Indonesian head of state General Suharto, responded that he, Chrétien, used pepper on his plate.[21]

5. *Ignoring the Logical Force and Direction of an Argument.* It is possible, such is the nature of human irrationality, to sway people by producing excellent premises for an argument, developing fine lines of argument based on those premises, and then producing a totally irrelevant conclusion. An argument to the effect that a given crime is heinous and needs to be punished does not answer the question whether a given accused in fact committed such a crime. Building up emotional indignation can result in easier bridging of this logical gap. It has been well said that just as iron is more malleable at white heat, so people are more manipulable when their passions are aroused. There is also an element of appeal to authority. If a person displays clever reasoning abilities through most of the argument, it builds confidence in what the person says and lowers the level of alertness for possible slips in logic.

6. *Begging the Question.* Fanatics especially are prone to this form of fallacy. They are so imbued with their own set of beliefs that they have difficulty putting themselves in the mindset of someone who does not accept them. Thus, they will argue against an opponent in a way that presupposes what is at issue between them. A frequently-used example of question-begging is that of the theist arguing against the atheist that God must exist, because the Bible asserts that God exists, and the Bible must be true because it is divinely inspired. The belief that it is divinely inspired presupposes what is contested, namely, that God exists. The example can be turned around. It is no less circular for the atheist to reject the possibility of the Bible being divinely inspired because God does not exist, when that is the very point at issue. It is important to be clear that circularity is not necessarily fallacious in itself. There is a question-begging circularity only when a link in the circle is advanced in a way that purports to ground some contested item, while all along presupposing what is contested.

7. *False Analogy.* Our learning is constantly a matter of drawing analogies between various events, circumstances, or things. Likewise, when we try to convince others that some course of action is good or bad, we commonly appeal to similarities and dissimilarities with other courses of action that have already been experienced. If it is a matter of going to war or not going to war, arguments will be advanced linking the situation to other experiences in the past by analogy. "Munich" has become symbolic of any attempt at peace that involves appeasement of a dictator bent on conquest. "Vietnam" for North Americans has become a symbol for getting involved in a costly war in a faraway territory, where guerilla warfare makes advanced weaponry largely ineffective. Much debate on such questions is taken up with the extent to which a new challenge resembles the circumstances of older challenges, and whether the same or a different policy would be better in the light of past experience.

It is always possible to find some kind of similarity between two different events, sets of circumstances, or things. False analogy is the fallacy of placing undue weight on some similarity or set of similarities while ignoring more important differences.

The argument that because more horses would have won the battle in a previous war, therefore more horses are needed for a new war, is a false analogy, because in the meantime machine guns and tanks may have made the horses useless.

There are important rhetorical pitfalls attending the use of analogy. The persuader who wants to press an analogy for one purpose must take care that the same analogy will not lend itself to even better use for an opposite purpose. A noted demographer once tried to argue that the French language was not at risk in Quebec, because the language was surviving very well as things were. However, he took an analogy that backfired in a most unpleasant way. He argued that in science, if you want to test for some effect, you test under conditions where that effect is most likely to be found; if the effect is not there, you have some assurance that it's not likely to be anywhere else either. So, if you are testing for pollution, you "give all possible chances to the pollutant element to exert its undesirable influence." Therefore, in testing for the diminishing of use of the French language, you should test it in a place close to where a lot of English is spoken, to see if there is an effect from this proximity. The demographer's argument favoured federalism, since he noted that French in the Hull area, across the river from English-speaking Ottawa, was surviving well. However, the media seized indignantly on the comparison between English and pollution, either choosing not to see, or simply missing the more abstract point he was trying to make.[22]

8. *Amphiboly*. Language is full of sentence constructions that can be parsed differently to get different meanings. The word "amphiboly" applies to cases of ambiguity stemming from the construction of a whole phrase or sentence rather than an individual term. Headlines often provide amusing ambiguity in this way, as the following examples taken from the Internet indicate: "Squad Helps Dog Bite Victim," "Miners Refuse to Work after Death," "Deer Kill 17,000," "Include Your Children when Baking Cookies," "Enraged Cow Injures Farmer With Ax," "Juvenile Court to Try Shooting Defendant," "Kids make Nutritious Snacks," and so on. A constant source of jokes is the amphiboly in "Drink Canada Dry."

Propaganda enters the picture when amphiboly is deliberately exploited to induce people to understand the meaning in one (false) way, while answering the charge of lying by pointing to another (true) meaning.

9. *Accident*. The fallacy of accident, noted by Aristotle, involves taking something that is nonessential and treating it as essential. If a person is insulted by not being invited to a dinner, it is fallacious to think that the particular insult can be removed by the person buying herself an equivalently delicious meal somewhere else. The insult is tied to the fact of not being invited, not to the contents of the dinner. Gun control opponents sometimes argue that murder is not essentially connected with guns, because people who want to kill can do so with knives or other methods. It is chance, they say, that someone chooses a gun for the purpose, so that limiting the availability of guns will not stop such murders. If they are right, the view that guns are responsible for murders is an example of the fal-

lacy of accident. However, as long as at least a proportion of people who kill by guns in fact would not have done so if guns were less freely available, with the result that fewer people overall would be murdered, there is no fallacy of accident. Instead, there is a material connection between the availability of guns and the number of murders.

Misleading Imputations of Intention

One major opportunity for misleading a public arises from the ambiguity and imprecision in our language as it relates to action descriptions, in particular to the mental state accompanying actions. To take one example, the verb "to kill" and cognates such as "killing" can be used in the case of an intentional killing (murder, with some possible exceptions) and for an accidental killing. To say nothing more than "A killed B," when the killing was accidental, will leave open, in the mind of the hearer, the possibility that the killing was intentional. Particularly if the accidental killing was not associated with negligence, the failure to modify "killed" with the word "accidentally" is likely to create a false impression. The propagandist may want to discredit some enemy, and one way of doing this is to exploit this kind of ambiguity.

Let us first look at some actual examples. Once again, it is worth repeating the cautionary remark that false or misleading impressions are not always conveyed wittingly. One example comes from the *Globe and Mail* of January 26, 1984; the front-page headline stated, "Nazis fled after war with help of Vatican, US document reveals." The headline suggests, without clearly asserting, that the Vatican knowingly helped Nazis escape, even though there was no good evidence in the story itself that the relevant knowledge was present. On the contrary, the story quoted Reverend Antonio Weber, who headed Opera San Rafaele, the Vatican's organization for emigration aid during World War II, as saying that his office helped many people, including about 20,000 Jews fleeing Hitler, without knowing their real identities in many cases. "We didn't know if they were or weren't war criminals," Father Weber is quoted as saying, "Even if these war criminals came with their real names, who knew at the time they were war criminals?" Now common sense tells us that under the circumstances it is very likely the Vatican would have assisted some Nazis, without knowing they were Nazis. The important question is that of knowledge, and the story provided no good evidence on that point. So the headline creates an unfavourable impression of the Vatican that the story itself does not warrant.[23]

On May 24, 1984, the same newspaper boxed a headline on the summary column of page one: "Pope Fouls Up Bar Mitzvah." The story concerned the change of plans for a bar mitzvah, necessitated by the large crowds anticipated in the area of a synagogue because of the pope's visit. Obviously, the pope intended no such problem by his visit, even though it was a foreseeable outcome that many changes in plans would have to be made in the light of anticipated crowds.

To fix on one such plan, treating it in isolation from the general set of problems, and describing the pope's relation to it by the somewhat intention-imputing verb "to foul up," encourages the belief that the pope is disposed malevolently towards bar mitzvahs—if not in general, then this one in particular. Stated explicitly, the idea is absurd, but the essence of a very effective way of affecting beliefs and attitudes is that this be done by suggestion rather than statement.[24]

Different verbal expressions fit into different places on a continuum between the intention-imputing and the intention-silent or intention-disclaiming. For example, "Karen defaulted, so that Judy lost," does not imply, although it may suggest, that Karen intended to ensure Judy's loss. To avoid any such suggestion, the sentence could be written: "Karen defaulted without intending that Judy should lose." If there were such an intention, we can make this clear by saying, "Karen defaulted with the aim of bringing about Judy's losing, and she succeeded." In between we have verbal expressions of greater or lesser intention-imputation and with greater or lesser definiteness. To say "Karen helped Judy lose," suggests to some extent the presence of the intention to bring about the stated consequence. The suggestion seems to me stronger (not every reader may feel this way) when we use such verbal expressions as "brought about" Judy's loss or "ensured" Judy's defeat. It seems strongest when we use a term such as "engineered." One hardly "engineers" a defeat without intending that result. The exception might be of the following sort: Karen engineers a complicated course of action for another purpose, which happens to result in Judy's defeat, although Judy's defeat was no part of the plan. One might be tempted to say, misleadingly, "Karen engineered Judy's loss."

Let us call verbal expressions that impute intention to a doer more definitely, or to a higher degree, in relation to some consequence, "intention-promoting." The use of intention-promoting words can raise the level of alleged culpability from inadvertence to negligence, recklessness, or maximum culpability. "A caused B's death" is less intention-promoting than "A killed B," and both are less intention-promoting than "A murdered B."

A skilled rhetorician can make use of verbs and adverbs with the desired ambiguity or indefiniteness to conceal or reveal as much as she or he wants to conceal or reveal. It is worth adding a word to make clear that intention not only as to consequences, but also as to circumstances, may play an important part in the ambiguities of action description.

Schopenhauer felt that each fallacy or misleading device should be given a name. The expression "referential translucency" can serve here, but it needs explaining. Use of this term presupposes a well-known distinction made by the late logician and philosopher, W.V.O. Quine, between referential opacity and referential transparency.[25] For the benefit of those with the requisite interest and patience, I will explain the terminology; others may prefer to skip the explanation and leave the expression alone.

Verbal expressions such as "pass by" are, in the sense to be explained, referentially transparent. You happen to pass by on the street an old school acquaintance, Phil. He happens to have won the lottery, but you don't know this. It would still be true, though, that when you pass Phil by, you pass by the winner of the lottery. The case is called "transparent" because all kinds of information about Phil can be added to the statement about your passing Phil without it being any less true that you passed him by. If Phil has authored a book, then it's true that you passed by the author of that book, even though you might not know he was an author of anything, and so on.

Opaque contexts are different, because they are defined, for our purposes, as involving a linkage with some person or persons' state of mind.[26] The verb "know" obviously has such a linkage. In this case—and in all of what are called "intentional contexts"—we find that we cannot do the same kind substitution of other descriptive truths and still be assured of the truth of what we say. From "You know Phil," we cannot deduce, "You know the winner of the lottery" (in the sense of "You know who won the lottery"), even though it is true that Phil won the lottery. To take another example: one can know that Voltaire (Arouet's pen name) wrote *Candide*, without knowing that Arouet wrote *Candide*, so that it would be false to infer that because one knows that Voltaire wrote *Candide* and because Voltaire and Arouet are the same person, that it follows, therefore, that one knows that Arouet wrote *Candide*.

Not all contexts are clearly referentially transparent or opaque. Some verbs are ambiguous or indefinite as to the extent of intentionality implied. As earlier noted, the word "help" is such a verb. When we say "Jones helped bring about the Progressive Party's defeat," we may think of this *either* as a case where Jones acted with the *intention* of bringing about that defeat, *or* as a case where Jones may have intended nothing of the kind, perhaps may have been working to avoid the defeat, but working in ways that, as things turned out, were counterproductive. The verb "help" in this context is what I choose to call neither clearly opaque nor clearly transparent. Extending the metaphor of luminescence, we have our convenient term, "referential translucency," to signal the field exploitable for propaganda purposes, in the ways described.

During the Spanish Civil War, the POUM (*Partido Obrero de Unificación Marxista*) and the Anarchists were accused by the Communists of dividing and weakening the opponents of Franco. There was a case to be made that division among the left did indeed help Franco, but it was a very different accusation, and a very damning one, to suggest that they might have intentionally helped him. As it turns out, some Communists apparently did make the unjust, overt accusation that the POUM was supported by Franco and Hitler, but others played around with the ambiguities of intention in the language they used.[27]

The term "referential translucency" arises in the context of some communicator reporting on another person's action or mental state with regard to some consequences, circumstances, etc. In a courtroom setting a lawyer can make use of this ambiguity in the form of questions, so that a witness is led into the role of communicating about his or her previous acts and mental states in ways that distort the truth. The witness will *seem* to be specially qualified to describe those things, but befuddlement about intentionality can easily lead the witness to say either something untrue but desired by an opponent's lawyer, or something demonstrably false which can be pointed out to discredit the testimony.

The Rhetorical Use of "Or"

The word "or" provides an opportunity for suggesting certain things without actually asserting them. This possibility occurs because of the logical rule of addition. If I say something true, such as "Nunavut is part of Canada," then add a sentence formed by forming a disjunct with any other statement, the combined statement is still literally true. So, with certain qualifications to be described, "'Nunavut is part of Canada' or 'The Moon is made of green cheese'" is literally true. Put in symbolic form, with letters representing statements, if "A" is true, then "A or B" will also be true. The statement asserting "A or B" can be defended by appealing to the truth of "A." Meanwhile, the suggestion of "B" is made with no risk of being proven wrong. Qualifications are needed, because as Paul Grice has pointed out, there are tacit rules of conversational discourse that need to be added to traditional rules of logic.[28] Exposure of such violations can reveal culpable deceptions, which, in some cases, are tantamount to lying. The appropriate place for exploring such culpability or lack of it is in the next chapter. Meanwhile, we may note that it is often difficult or impossible to determine whether the speaker is disingenuous or is engaged in legitimate speculation in making suggestions with the use of "or." My purpose here is to show that, because of the difficulty of being caught out in an intentional deception, use of this device can be a fairly safe way of carrying out propaganda.

For the same reason, provable examples where the word "or" was used with the intention of creating false impressions are hard to come by; however, there are cases where we can reasonably speculate about such a possibility. Consider a Reuters news report published in the *Ottawa Citizen* in 1982. The headline read, "Soviets okayed assassination attempt on pope: US diplomat." Former US Ambassador to Poland, Richard Davies, was quoted as saying "They (the Russians) authorized *or at least did nothing to stop an effort to assassinate him*. They would like to get rid of this inconvenient priest" (italics added).[29] The part of the statement that says the Russians did nothing to stop an effort to assassinate the pope is highly plausible. It is consistent, in fact, with their knowing nothing about the assassination attempt. Since that disjunct is true, the disjunctive statement is also true. The reader gets the impression that there is a good chance that the Russians authorized the assassination, without the speaker actually have made that claim. Not having *made* that claim, the speaker cannot be shown to have *falsely* made that claim. In one sense, "or" is a precautionary device, but it can be used recklessly as well. We do not know the mind of Ambassador Davies, but we do know that the headline writer wrote something that was not adequately supported by the quotation, and that the phrasing of the quotation is such as to encourage just such a misapprehension.

The defence against intentional misleading of people through the device described is to expose what is happening. People should be accountable for what they suggest without adequate foundation as well as for what they actually state. Grice's work is very valuable in this regard.

My suspicious nature has been spurred, perhaps unjustifiably, on more than one occasion by certain commercial labels involving "or" and "and/or" (the latter making clear that the disjunctions are inclusive, that is to say, "one or the other, or both," as distinct from "one, or the other, but not both"). A package says, "contains real cream and/or milk and/or skim milk powder." This statement is true if there is only skim milk powder in it. Is this a gimmick to make people think the contents grander than they in fact are? At least Canada's marketing lawmakers have issued regulations about the use of "and/or" in packaging. The statement "may contain sugar and/or dextrose" indicates that, when a sweetening agent is used as an ingredient, it may be sugar or dextrose or a mixture of each that is used, "[t]he probability being that more sugar than dextrose will be used during the twelve months" from the time the label is applied. Ingredients must, according to the regulation, be listed "in descending order of the proportion in which they will be used."[30]

NON-VERBAL TECHNIQUES

The Numbers Game: Polls and Statistics.

In modern times sound policy-making must often come to grips with numbers. The problem is to know whether numbers cited by various experts are accurate and whether they are numbers relevant to determining policy. There is an old story about a drunken man looking at night for a lost $20 bill under a lamppost. He explains that, although he lost it elsewhere, he is looking in this spot because "the light is better." Among the many forms of propaganda in existence, there are those of the experts who try to show us that "the light is better" in the area of their particular expertise and that social progress can only take place with input from their particular discipline. The ordinary citizen would be helpless against domination by the experts were it not for the existence of experts on different sides of various political divides. It is often possible to enlist credible support to challenge technical opinion conscripted in the service of a dominant class. It is also important for an alert citizenry to know of some common pitfalls in the use of polls and statistics.

OPINION POLLS
Since the western world presupposes that democracy is a superior system, arguments for a given policy or measure generally gain strength if one can show that the proposals have the support of the people; hence, the importance in today's world of opinion polls. But it is easy to be fooled by opinion polls. Indeed, even the pollsters, or those commissioning the polls, can be misled. For example, they may misjudge the latent strength of feeling on an issue that has not been widely

discussed. When something becomes an issue, and various interest groups speak out, the reaction may produce opinion different, or more intensely felt, than what existed before the controversy. An example of this occurred some years ago when William Davis was premier of Ontario. Polls indicated no great objection to fully funding all years of secondary school for the separate school (Roman Catholic) system. By the time it came to implementation, a very strong challenge had built up, with a considerable cost to his popularity.

Polls can deceive in many ways. Some deceptions relate to polling methodology; others affect the people polled, by implanting certain ideas in their minds under the guise of seeking their opinions. Phoney polls of this sort have been called "ruse polls" or "push polls" when they are designed to push voters for or against a candidate. On June 27, 1996, the *New York Times* reported that a group called the American Association of Political Consultants complained that "campaigns hire companies to make thousands of calls spreading negative and sometimes false information about an opponent while posing as pollsters." They objected also to telephone calls that failed to clearly and accurately identify the sponsor of the call.[31] An example of a "push poll" reportedly conducted by the Ontario government in 1996 was denounced by the Ontario Secondary School Teachers Federation. One question the poll asked was, "Since teachers have had it so good for so long, should they not be asked to suffer a little?" The poll was conducted to determine public opinion about the decision to cut up to $1 billion out of education spending. The wording of the question was reconstructed from teachers who had been polled and who called the federation to complain. OSSTF president Earl Manners was quoted as saying of the Conservative government, "They are now engaging in a propaganda strategy to sway public opinion regarding the actions they intend to take in the education sector."[32]

Hugh Winsor pinpointed a commercial example of a "push question" in a poll. Eurocopter Canada was trying to sell the French-made Cougar helicopter to the Canadian military for use in Canadian search and rescue efforts. Pollster Angus Reid added the following question to its regular October omnibus poll: "If the government buys its competitor's product, the Cormorant/EH101, would it be breaking the promise it made during the 1993 election campaign?" Winsor adds, "Surprise, surprise, 71 per cent said Yes."[33]

Some social activist organizations solicit opinions about matters concerning which opinion is likely to be a foregone conclusion. Such a poll does not intend to learn anything from respondents, but hopes to encourage awareness and indignation in relation to the problems noted by the questions. People who work in marketing are not happy with this pseudo-polling, because they believe it will encourage resistance to answering their own information-seeking polls.

The ways in which polls can and do mislead can be divided into groups:

1. the problem of randomness in sampling procedure;
2. effects resulting from who it is that does the polling;

3. mathematically determinable ranges of error, built into the theory of polling, and reports which ignore those ranges;
4. bias or incompetence in the wording of the questions and their contexts;
5. lying respondents;
6. dishonest survey collectors;
7. biased or incompetent interpretation of answers;
8. fluctuation of opinion;
9. deliberate attempts to skew the results in some way; and
10. the use of totally unscientific "polls," carried out simply to persuade, not to determine public opinion.

1. *Randomness.* The theory behind polling is that one can get an idea of the composition of a whole population by examining a small sample taken from this population and examining it. Provided the sample is absolutely random and is reasonably large (a few hundreds, at least, for a population in the millions), one has a fair chance that the composition of the sample will be closely matched with that of the population as a whole. Randomness is obviously a requirement. It takes little effort to see how misleading a sample taken entirely, say, from Montreal, with its high proportion of French speakers, would be for inferring the proportion of French speakers in the population of Canada as a whole.

A famous example of error through biased (nonrandom) sampling occurred during the 1936 election in the US. The *Literary Digest* mailed a survey to names taken from directories of automobile owners and telephone subscribers. On the strength of the two million responses, a prediction was made that the new president would be Alf Landon, who would win 370 electoral votes, while Franklin Delano Roosevelt would win only 161. In fact, Roosevelt won the election handily, and the discredited magazine folded shortly after. The sampling was taken from a higher proportion of the wealthier part of the population, but Roosevelt was supported by the not-so-wealthy, whose opinion was not measured adequately in the polling. Today telephones are so widely distributed that there is no longer the same bias toward the rich. Omitting unlisted numbers through use of telephone directories could be a source of bias, but such numbers can be reached by random dialing. It is well known that biases against stay-at-homes are created when polling is done on the streets, and that owners of vicious dogs chained near the front entrance to a house are less likely to be represented in a door-to-door poll. People who do not want to answer questions do not get represented. Michael Wheeler reports a pollster's estimate that upwards of 20 per cent of those polled refuse to answer.[34]

2. *Interviewer effects.* Biases can also be created by whoever it is that does the polling. Studies have indicated that when African-Americans ask the questions, African-American respondents are prepared to speak their minds more freely about racism than they would to white pollsters.[35] Since interviewers for Gallup (a major polling firm) are almost all women, this may produce a bias regarding opinions expressed

to them on women's issues. Opinion polls taken prior to the 1980 referendum on Quebec independence tended to overestimate support for the *Oui* side, in favour of secession. Some speculated that badges for the pollster, the Institut Québécois d'Opinion Publique, resembled something official, suggesting a tie-in to the ruling independent party, the Parti Québécois. This may have caused respondents to be more reticent to proclaim their support for federalism and the *Non* side. As the *Ottawa Citizen* reported, "The poll showed the *Oui* forces with 40.4 per cent of the vote compared to 36.5 per cent for the *Non* side but there was a steep 23.1 per cent who were undecided or would not say how they would vote."[36] The outcome showed that the undecideds were overwhelmingly supporters of the *Non*.

How pollsters divide up the undecideds can make an important difference to the assessment of public opinion. Barry Kiefl, director of research for the Canadian Broadcasting Corporation (CBC) noted that, "Some pollsters assume the undecided will split the same way as decided voters, others weight some of the undecided by the direction in which they are 'leaning' or according to the party they voted for in an election. Some polls exclude those who indicate they're unlikely to vote, others include all eligible voters." Kiefl pointed out that the procedures can "completely alter results, especially in a campaign during which there have been major shifts in opinion."[37]

3. *Mathematical Limitations.* To get a useful glimpse (actual polling theory is much more complicated) of what is involved in polling theory, we might compare it to a huge urn containing hundreds of thousands of black and white balls and nothing else. Assuming we don't know how many of each there are, how sound an estimate could we get of the composition as a whole, if we took samples? If we took 100 balls, and found that 45 were white and 55 were black, what is the probability that the composition of the contents of the whole urn are in exactly that proportion? If we already know the composition of the urn, we can consider what happens when we take samples, and what chances there will be of a match between the composition of the sample and that of the urn as a whole.

Obviously, the larger the sample, the greater likelihood of exact matching. But if we can be content with rough matching, we can get a close approximation with a relatively small sample. Suppose, to make things simple, that the composition of the urn is half white balls and half black balls. What would happen if we took a sample of two and guessed that this represented exactly the composition of the urn as a whole? Assuming that the balls are well stirred, and that each ball is picked at random, there will be an exactly even chance of picking either a white ball or a black ball first. The same holds true for the second pick. The result is one of four different, but equally likely, outcomes: WW, WB, BW, BB. In two of these cases (WB and BW) there is complete and exact matching, but in the other two the prediction would be 50 per cent wrong. In other words, one predicts that the whole urn is white, because one took out two white balls, or black if two black balls were picked. If three balls are taken, the sequences become equally probable: WWW, WBW, BWW, BBW or WWB, WBB, BWB, BBB. Out of the eight equiprobable results, two are completely wrong by a margin of 50 per cent. Of the other six, none is an exact match, since the prediction based on them is one-third of one colour and two-thirds of the other. The error in the prediction amounts then to 50 per cent less 33 1/3 per cent, or 16 2/3 per cent for one set of balls, and 66 2/3 per cent less 50 per cent, or 16 2/3 per cent for the other set. Being out by 16 2/3 per cent six times out of eight is still far off the mark, but it is better than being out by 50 per cent. If we take a sample of four, the equiprobable out-comes are sixteen or 2^4. A sample size of N would number 2^N, and it is easy, although tedious, to calculate the likely compositions of increasingly large samples in the way already done. Thus, two variables need to be taken into account. First, there is the proximity of equiprobable outcomes to the known composition, and, sec-ondly, there is the proportion of equiprobable outcomes that meet this degree of proximity. So, in the sample of three, 16 2/3 per cent measures the closeness, but "six times out of eight" measures, equally importantly, the proportion in which these outcomes are to be found among the total outcomes in the sample.

For this reason, polling results must always take account of those two variables. By convention, "19 times out of 20" has been treated as an acceptably close fre-quency and so is not always stated. A Gallup poll comes with statements like the following: "The study in Canada was conducted with a random sample of 741 adults in mid-September, with personal interviews in homes across the nation. A sample of this size produces results accurate within a 4 percentage point margin of error, 19 out of 20 times."[38] The larger the sample, the smaller the range of error. Curiously, the mathematical outcome of the analysis indicates that, when we deal with large populations, the important variable is sample size. The same sample size gives roughly the same range of error whether we deal with Canada or the US, which has a population ten times greater. To make this result intuitively plausi-ble, some compare the operation with taking samples from different pots of soup. We sample a soup by taking a spoonful or two; provided the soup is well stirred, it doesn't make much difference to the accuracy of our tasting whether the spoon-ful is from a small pot or a large vat.

Polling theory is much more complex, but we are now able to understand the potential for deception. For one thing, a given poll could be the one-in-20 "rogue poll" that is way off the mark. Using the urn analogy, with such a poll, you could be unlucky enough to pull out a succession of white balls every time, until there are none left. Secondly, the poll gives us information about the probabil-ity of something being within a certain range; it does not get more specific than that. So, if one poll tells us that 36 per cent of Canadians favour Jean Chrétien as prime minister, and another poll later tells us that 38 per cent favour him as prime minister, and the range of error of the poll is plus or minus four percentage points, we cannot assume that his popularity has increased. The range of error in the first case takes us from 32 per cent to 40 per cent and in the second case from 34 per cent to 42 per cent. Quite possibly the first poll was measuring a true figure of 40 per cent, and the second poll was measuring a true figure of 34 per cent, both figures being within the stated ranges. In other words, a real drop in support might have appeared as an increase in support. That is why, when newspapers trumpet a supposed increase in support, when the "increase" is within the range of sampling error, readers should take the trumpeting with a grain of salt.

Another important observation is the increasing unreliability of polls when subsets of populations are considered. A 1990 Globe and CBC poll of 2,259 respondents spread evenly across Canada (except for the Northwest Territories and the Yukon) gave a stated range of error of plus or minus 2.2 percentage points. But if we then start talking about Quebec, we refer to the sample from that province alone, which of course is smaller than the total sample for Canada including Quebec. This will entail a considerable increase in the range of error as a result. As worked out by the pollsters, the relevant range became 4.3 percentage points for Quebec, 4.4 percentage points for Ontario, 4.8 percentage points for the Prairies, 4.9 percentage points for British Columbia and 4.8 percentage points for Atlantic Canada.[39]

Newspapers do not always spell out the change in error range and, thus, can mislead the public as to the true state of opinion. The exclusion of the Yukon and the Northwest Territories, perhaps explainable by cost factors, skews the overall results very slightly, but more importantly makes for blindness as to possible significant differences of opinion in those areas.

Just before the October 30, 1995, referendum on Quebec sovereignty a mass rally was held in Montreal to express support from the rest of Canada for a "No" vote. Those who were at the rally felt that it boosted support against sovereignty, but newspaper reports claimed differently, on the ground that surveys of Quebec opinion before and after the rally showed a drop of one percentage point. As pollster Michael Marzolini pointed out, the surveys were of only 400 Quebecers, thus giving a margin of error of five percentage points. Also, no question had been asked about the rally. His own firm, Pollara, which he identified as the Liberal Party's polling firm, asked strictly about the rally and, in his own words, "found that the rally actually won over almost 10 per cent of voters to the federalist side, based on a sample of 1,000 Quebecers."[40]

4. *Wording and Context of the Question.* Of all the ways in which opinion polls can be used to shape public opinion, perhaps the most important is the wording of the question. "Are you in favour of nuclear power and the reduction of coal-fired, polluting, ecologically harmful power stations?" can be expected to elicit a more favourable response to the nuclear industry than a question such as "Do you favour nuclear power despite its high cost, the problems of nuclear waste disposal, and the remote possibility of meltdown?" A report on the poll might emphasize that people were "for" or "against" nuclear power, without spelling out the full question. In any responsible report on a poll, therefore, the full question should always be given. Readers should be given the opportunity to test how they might have responded to the question and for what reasons. Journalistic integrity requires that the wording and the methodology be presented for the readers' inspection, even if only at the end of a story.

The semantic impact of sentences that appear closely synonymous often elicit very different answers from respondents in ways that seem inconsistent. Part of the explanation may have to do with the context of the question and with the kinds of sentences with which it is contrasted. For example, the Legal Research Institute at the University of Manitoba found respondents from Montreal, Toronto, and Winnipeg answered in the proportion of roughly 93 per cent in the affirmative to the question "I must always obey the law." Yet, four questions later, the very same respondents answered affirmatively in the proportion of about 47 per cent to the question "There are situations when it is right not to obey the law."[41] That means 40 per cent are upholding both sides of a contradictory pair of sentences. Anyone who felt "I must always obey the law" would have to deny that "There are situations when it is right not to obey the law," for how can one be obligated to do the opposite of what it is right to do?

A clue to the resolution of the seeming inconsistency comes from the context of the two questions. The first was contrasted with "It is all right to break the law as long as you don't get caught" (answered affirmatively only by 7 per cent). The second question was contrasted with "Disobedience of the law can never be tolerated" (answered affirmatively by roughly 52 per cent). Since the respondent was told to indicate the statement which "best represents your opinion," it becomes apparent that an obvious source of the seeming inconsistency lies with the degree of aversion to the contrasting statements, and the affirmative claims do not necessarily represent a view with which they fully agree. The import of an answer to a survey question cannot be fully appreciated without seeing the question in context. To see how misleading this form of survey could become, consider the following extreme: "Which best represents your opinion? 'The tooth fairy exists' or 'Democratic Party rule will be best for the United States.'" People may have aversions to the Democratic Party, but if the only alternative is belief in the tooth fairy, most people would find they had to accept the second alternative, joking aside. It should not be difficult to construct question pairs where the "push" is subtler and not so obviously manipulative.

Pollster Louis Harris helped improve the perception of President Richard Nixon's standing in public opinion in the early 1970s. Instead of asking whether Nixon should be impeached, Harris's question was whether respondents wanted Nixon "impeached and removed from office." As Michael Wheeler comments, "Impeachment and removal, of course, are two quite different things. In essence, Harris was asking not whether Nixon should simply be tried, but whether he should be tried and hanged!"[42] Clearly, fewer people would give an affirmative answer to "impeached and removed from office," than they would to "impeached" alone.

An important rule, emphasized by Wheeler, for interpreting the significance of poll results, is "to read the questions to see if you yourself would be comfortable giving agree/disagree answers. If you would not, then you must discount the results of the poll, no matter how conclusive the statistics seem."[43]

Polls have become part of the weaponry of policy justification, so it is not surprising that, where politically contested ground is involved, appeals are made to different pollsters with their sometimes divergent results. For example, in October 1997, an Angus Reid poll said that the majority of Canadians wanted the government to cut both taxes and the national debt. However, a poll taken about the same time by Ekos said that three-quarters of Canadians were deeply concerned about the growing gap between rich and poor and wanted the government to start spending again on social programs. As critics pointed out at the time, the discrepancy comes in part from the superficiality of the context in which questions are presented. Everyone wants more benefits and wants to pay less to get them, so that serious policy can hardly be formulated on the basis of slapdash responses saying one thing or the other. Frank Graves, president of Ekos, was quoted in the same story as saying, "Some polls are being used as part of a commando operation for one ideological point of view."[44]

5. *Lying Respondents.* Wheeler notes that a Harris memorandum prepared for interviewers stated, "It's been brought to our attention that almost all of our surveys are showing the population to be more educated than what the census says it actually is ... we feel respondents are exaggerating the amount of schooling they've had."[45] Obviously, if respondents lie, polls cannot be all that reliable.

6. *Dishonesty in Gathering the Information.* Some poll-taking involves simply filling in with pencil marks a few pages of coded blank spaces. Poll-takers are also often paid by the number of questionnaires filled out. It is easy to cheat by filling in sheets without doing interviews, although checkups might make this a risky process. Still, checkups are not all that strong a guarantee of integrity in practice. Michael Wheeler gives an example:

> In 1968 the *New York Times* commissioned Gallup to do an intensive survey of attitudes of Harlem residents. The information was collected, tabulated, and submitted to the *Times* for publication. An editor was so pleased with the poll that he decided to play it up by sending a reporter and a photographer to get a story about some of those who had supposedly been interviewed. At seven of the twenty-three addresses Gallup had given them, the newsmen could not even find a dwelling! Moreover, five other people who had allegedly been polled could not be traced—the addresses existed but apparently the people did not. Not even all the remaining interviews were legitimate. In one case the *Times* reporter learned that the interviewer had talked to four people playing cards and incorporated all their answers into one interview.[46]

7. *Biased or Incompetent Interpretation of Responses.* There are many ways in which failure to take account of polling theory and of limitations built into any sampling procedure can lead to misinformed conclusions based on polls. There may be a deliberate attempt to deceive, but there may also be errors stemming, not from malevolence, but from wishful thinking or sheer ignorance.

Katimavik, a youth group in Canada, received public funding under the Liberal Trudeau government, but had its funds cut off after the Mulroney Conservatives came to power in 1984. One of the reasons the group got bad press was their supposed use of illegal drugs. However, as a letter-writer to the *Ottawa Citizen* pointed out, the interpretation of a poll concerning drug use was very biased:

> One of the questions we had to answer was: "Are you aware of anyone having taken drugs during the period as participants in the program? It is from answers to this question that the report concluded that "55 per cent reported taking drugs."
>
> The real conclusion of this question, assuming the result is reliable, should have been "Fifty-five per cent of the participants are aware of the fact that at least one person has taken drugs." When our group responded to this question, we all answered Yes as there was, in fact, a participant who did take drugs. He was kicked out in the third week of the program.[47]

Sometimes a newspaper favouring a certain policy position will give prominence to a poll supporting that position, ignoring both methodological weaknesses of that poll and other polls supporting a contrary view. The *Globe and Mail*, for example, gave front-page coverage to a poll commissioned by the Canadian Abortion Rights Action League (CARAL). The story sought to interpret the results of the poll by interviewing Norma Scarborough, president of CARAL, the very group that commissioned it. It would have been fairer to get opinions from polling experts or from those not sharing Scarborough's preconceptions to supplement her views. When I wrote to the same newspaper to complain that it appeared to have ignored a 1983 Gallup poll indicating that 72 per cent of Canadians are against abortion on demand, I was not contradicted.[48]

8. *Fluctuation of Opinion.* It is a common observation that public opinion can be greatly affected by events that have a vivid effect on the public imagination. A particularly gruesome child-murder turned public attitudes against the sex industry flourishing on Yonge Street in Toronto in the 1970s. News items, editorial opinion, letters, and columns can have a powerful effect as well.[49] Pollsters themselves emphasize that they are giving only a "snapshot" of opinion at a given time. Politicians who rely on favourable polls as a basis for calling an election may find out that voters' opinions change, particularly if they feel that the election was called earlier than necessary, merely in order to ride a tide of favourable opinion. This resentment can be aroused, fed, and exploited by opposition parties, as former Ontario Premier David Peterson found when he lost the election he called in 1990.[50]

9. *Deliberate Attempts to Manipulate Polls.* Since opinion has been shown to be affected by prominent events, the idea of manufacturing such events has occurred to power-holders and power-seekers. Michael Wheeler describes Charles Colson's successful efforts to improve President Richard Nixon's standings in the polls, one

of which included giving a prominent pollster a lucrative contract, whereupon negative polls gave way to positive ones from that pollster.

Another tactic involved rigging a special newspaper poll on the Vietnam War by buying up thousands of papers and flooding the editors with questionnaires filled out in favour of Nixon's policies. Wheeler also reports that during the 1968 campaign, Nixon had a source within the Gallup organization who provided advance word on when the surveys were going to be taken. "This allowed Nixon to time his activities so that they would have the maximum impact on Gallup's polls."[51]

Wheeler also reveals the large part that discretion can play in tabulating answers to questions. Suppose the question asks whether there is an energy shortage immediately or looming in the future, and the respondent replies, "Well, I think the gas crisis was manufactured by the companies." When the answer is tabulated in the "no energy shortage" category, it may be misleading, because recognition that an immediate gas crisis is manufactured is not the same as saying that there are no longer-term energy shortages.[52]

10. *Bogus (Unscientific) Polls.* It is possible to produce all manner of unscientific polls, sometimes for amusement. For example, "hamburger polls" judge the popularity of a politician, political issue, or some other topic by the number of different kinds of hamburgers purchased. Unscientific polls can also be carried out and publicized with a serious intent to influence public opinion.

Conrad Black describes his own publication of a makeshift poll prior to the October 1973 Quebec election. His paper, *L'Avenir de Sept-Iles*, supported the Liberal party against the Parti Québécois. As Black wrote in his autobiography, *A Life in Progress*:

> Our reporting was fairly balanced for most of the campaign, but we did an editorial sandbag on the PQ, complete with publication of a poll indicating a Liberal victory. There was no indication of the number of people sampled so the fact that I consulted only seven people (including myself) never came to light.[53]

STATISTICS

Since 1954 Darrell Huff's *How to Lie with Statistics*[54] has provided guidance to some of the basic forms of deception through the use of statistics. His book, recently reissued, is still useful for spotting such techniques today. What follows is a selection of his observations; his hypothetical examples are supplemented with a few real-life examples. Huff identifies four ways in which statistics can be used deceptively.

1. *The Well-Chosen Average.* When we use the word "average," we can mean different things. Perhaps the most common meaning is specifically referred to as the "mean," defined in the following way. Suppose we are thinking of "average" income for workers in a plant. We divide the total amount of salaries by the total amount of workers, giving us the figure for what one "average" worker makes—

the "mean" salary. In practice, of course, things are not that simple. Do you include part-time workers and workers on disability pay, sick leave, etc.? There are many ways of fiddling figures.

Huff's point is that there are two other thoughts to keep in mind about the notion of "average." One is the idea of "median," defined as the midpoint in a range of things we are considering. In the case of workers' salaries, we would ask: what is the salary of that worker who stands at the midpoint when workers are ranged by salaries from highest to lowest? There is also the notion of "mode," which in this case refers to the income level at which more income earners are grouped than any other level. Suppose we draw boxes to represent workers earning up to $10,000, between $10,000 and $20,000, between $20,000 and $30,000, and so on. The box or category in which the greatest number of workers appears would be the "mode."

Where there is so-called "normal" distribution, the average of mean, median, and mode fall in the same place on a graph. It so happens that the height of human beings follows "normal" distribution, meaning that we have the greatest number of people in the middle of a bell-shaped curve that tapers off gradually at two ends of the graph representing the tall and the short. But not every curve is bell-shaped, and it may well happen that representation of "average" will vary significantly according to whether we present the mean, the median, or the mode. Suppose one person in a company earns $50,000,000 a year through salary and stock benefits, while the other 99 workers get $50,505.05 each. The "average" salary could then be represented as $55 million (rounded) divided by 100, or $550,000. That would conceal the fact that all but one earned a little over $50,000. A false picture is given by using the mean, whereas the median gives a more representative "average." If a corporation is talking to shareholders, the median figure might be the one to emphasize, while in labour negotiations management would prefer the mean figure to show how well-off workers are. Of course, the figures chosen here make it obvious how deception might occur, and no one would likely be fooled. However, with more complex sets of figures, a similar bias might not be so easily detectable.

Talk about "average income" of a community can be very unclear. Are children and retired people included in the mean figure or only salaried people? Are all sources of revenue taken into account? What about court settlements? When there is talk of "family income" the meaning becomes obscured by lack of precision as to what constitutes a "family."

2. *The Semi-Attached Figure.* To understand the state of a country or corporation, it is important to know on what various figures are based. If more people are killed in plane crashes than, say, 50 years ago, it does not follow that flying is less safe, because the number of planes flying—and having accidents—has increased. The relevant base is the number of fatalities per passenger mile.

When there is a lot of talk about increased employment, caution is needed before assuming that the population as a whole is doing better. Are casual, part-time, and non-benefit-paying jobs included in the employment statistics? Is there a greater proportion of these "McJobs" than earlier? We need to answer these questions first, in order to learn whether things are better than before. Also, it would be easy for governments to simply re-categorize a percentage of the population who have been out of a job for a stipulated length of time as no longer being in the labour force. If they are not in the labour force, they are not counted as unemployed, but they still do not have a job. Care is needed to verify that no such manipulation of the base for computing unemployment has taken place.

In Canada much work is seasonal, and so a better indication of whether employment opportunities are better or worse over time is to present the "seasonally adjusted" figure of those employed. Likewise, when salary figures over a period of years are compared, the relevant figure is more likely to be the salaries in constant dollars, which is to say, dollars adjusted for inflation. When government spending on health is concerned, the relevant figure may not only be that of constant dollars, but also the amount of money spent on an age-factored population, since it is well known that health costs increase for an elderly population. For education expenses, a relevant figure, in addition to the global budget, is the amount provided for per student.

When it comes to university enrolment figures, those universities with a large number of part-time students will be misrepresented if comparisons are made counting only full-time students. The same university may have a hard time keeping track of enrolment growth over time. One way of including the part-time component is to count full-time course equivalents, so that four or five courses taken by different part-time students in a given year would equal one full-time course equivalent.

In considering a statistical base, one must ask: will this base provide the right kind of figures to reflect adequately, for purposes at hand, the situation in the country, corporation, institution, etc.? Of course, there are many interests that create pressures to give something less than an adequate picture. In labour negotiations, it helps management to present a financial picture of the company that makes finances appear precarious. When presenting a report to investors, it helps to raise capital if a rosy picture is presented. Different accounting procedures (for example, whether estimated capital expenses are amortized slowly or rapidly, conservatively or optimistically) can alter the picture presented to respective audiences.

3. *The One-Dimensional Figure.* Pictorial representations of increases or decreases can be misleading if what is true in one dimension is presented pictorially in a way that suggests a two-dimensional or even three-dimensional situation. So, if moneybags are used to indicate an increase of 100 per cent or double, it is misleading to present one moneybag as having twice the height of the other moneybag, since you would in that way get the representation of the *volume* increase following from such a doubling. But doubling the linear measurement of an area gives an *area* increase, which is the square of the linear amount; for the volume, the increase is to cube the linear increase. In other words, the impression cre-

ated by the volume representation is 2^3 or eight times the actual increase. The same is true, but in the other direction, of representing a linear decrease by a half, as a volume decrease. An example of just such a misleading impression was published in the *Ottawa Citizen* on December 10, 1989, when student enrolment figures were in question.

4. *The "Gee Whiz" Graph.* A graph can be presented in a way to make it seem as if little change is occurring or, on the contrary, that big changes are happening. To get the first effect, the graph starts at zero; to get the second, it begins at a base number close to where the increase takes place. A revenue increase of $5 million, plotted over a 12-month period, will look small if the starting revenue was $100 million, and the graph starts at zero and ends at $120 million. On the other hand, if the graph starts at $95 million and ends at $110 million, the climb will look much steeper and healthier.

The picture of an institution can be put in a very different perspective by choosing the base year for comparison with present happenings. If a particularly bad year in the past is chosen, the current situation can look good by comparison. On the other hand, if a particularly good year is chosen, the reverse can appear to be the case. To avoid false impressions, the whole situation should be set out, but institutional managers have a strong desire to project figures in a way that minimizes their errors and maximizes their successes. It is reasonable to suppose that the more alert the general public becomes to possibilities for misrepresentation, the more risky such misrepresentation will become, with the result that there will be a disincentive to engaging in the practice.

As well as the deceptions pinpointed by Huff, there are other ways in which statistics can be manipulated.

1. *Fabrication of Data.* One notorious scientific fraud of the twentieth century attempted to link intelligence to social class and heredity. Sir Cyril Burt, considered an eminent psychologist in Britain at the time, influenced government policy with his findings. In a famous paper, "Intelligence and Social Mobility," he argued that the class system was an economic result reflecting genetic ability. Professor D.D. Dorfman of Iowa pointed out that the figures in one of Burt's studies, which compared the intelligence of 40,000 pairs of fathers and sons, matched a normal distribution so closely as to be statistically most improbable, particularly so since other studies involving Intelligence Quotients (IQ's) have produced asymmetric, non-normal distributions. In other words, the overwhelming probability is that Burt concocted his figures.[55] (In its more precise sense "normal distribution" means a distribution according to a mathematical formula devised by the mathematician K.F. Gauss, resulting in a bell-shaped curve on a graph. Exact replication of this formula in nature is unlikely, although approximations are common.)

2. *Misinterpretation of the Significance of Bell Curve Differences at the Extremities.* John Allen Paulos has drawn attention to features of bell-curve distribution that could mislead people on the alert for examples of discrimination. He notes that if two groups, A and B, are such that one group varies slightly from the other, say in having a mean height of 5'8" in one group and 5'7" in the other, then the two normal curves drawn to represent height distribution among members of each group will show a little difference in the middle of the curve, where the bulk of both populations are to be found, but differences will be accentuated at the outer edges of the curve. Perhaps 90 per cent of those over 6'2" will be found in the group with the slight height increase over the other.[56] Similarly, we should not be surprised if, where tests are done to establish job promotion potential, a group that performs only slightly worse than another may find that significant differences are to be found at the upper levels in the corporation, because of the nature of normal distribution curves. However, complaints about racial or other bias may still be well founded. The point is that finding disproportionate numbers of one group at the top level does not of itself prove discrimination.

3. *Psychological Availability Errors.* Paulos also draws attention to psychological literature showing how our evaluations of people based on ambiguous news items can be affected by words prominent in our thinking prior to examining the news items. For example, people asked to memorize a collection of words including "adventurous," "self-confident," "independent," and "persistent" were more likely to give a positive evaluation of a young person described in the news items, than were another group who had been asked to memorize "reckless," "conceited," "aloof," and "stubborn." The prominence given in the media to the killing of a police officer gives people the idea that police work is riskier than construction work, but the opposite is the case.

When certain judgments come readily to mind because we are primed to make them, having some fresh reminder of a particular way of viewing things, then we are under the "availability" influence. Paulos refers to a poll where 80 per cent of the respondents said that laws should be passed to eliminate all possibilities of special interests. The wording was altered to: "Should laws be passed to prohibit interest groups from contributing to campaigns, or do groups have a right to contribute to the candidate they support?" Only 40 per cent said yes. Presumably the presence of an opposing view in the question meant that this other perspective was more available to the respondent. "When and in what company a story breaks ... greatly influences our perception of it," Paulos observes, "and this is largely a matter of luck." In the next chapter some examples of the manipulative use of this feature of our perception will be described. For the moment, it is worth taking note of Paulos's recipe for avoiding or reducing these influences on our thinking: we should actively strive to search for interpretations or associations that undermine the prevailing one.

Paulos mentions two related ideas. The first is the "halo effect," or the tendency to upgrade our evaluation of a person or group in all categories if we are particularly impressed by one category. The other is the notion of "anchoring effects." If people are asked to make an estimate when they have no real knowledge—say, about the population of Turkey—how they will answer depends on what number is first suggested to them. "Of those who were first presented with the figure of 5 million, the average estimate was 17 million; of those first presented with a figure of 65 million, the average estimate was 35 million."[57]

A more difficult concept to understand is what Paulos calls "conditional probability,"[58] yet it is very important to do so if we are to have an adequate understanding of certain forms of risk. Risk can sometimes be exaggerated for propaganda purposes. As one saying has it: "funding follows fear." The saying is used to debunk activist groups, but it is also true that sales of some services or products (e.g., pharmaceuticals) can also be increased by fear.

Suppose, Paulos says, there is a test for a disease which is 99 per cent accurate; if you have the disease, the test will give a positive result 99 per cent of the time, and if you don't have it, it will be negative 99 per cent of the time. Consider, then, a case where a disease has a general frequency of only 0.1 percent, or one person in 1000. What will happen if 100,000 people are given the test? Statistically, there should be 100 people who have the disease, but what will the tests show?

Of the 100 people who have the disease, one will be shown not to have it, and the other 99 will be shown to have it. But of the other 99,900 people, 1 per cent, or 999 will be shown (falsely) to have the disease. The total number of people shown to have the disease will be 99 + 999 or 1,098. So, if you tested positive, there is still only a fairly small chance—99/1,098, or a bit over 9 per cent—that you have the disease, despite the fact that the positive test is 99 per cent accurate for those who have the disease.

CONCLUSION

The fallacies and devices discussed in this section are not all equally suitable for persuasive purposes, nor are they anywhere near a complete list. Some rhetorical and other persuasive techniques have been, and will be, discussed elsewhere (see, for example, Chapter 5) and are left out here merely to avoid repetition.

NOTES

1   Richard Crossman, "The Creed of a Modern Propagandist," *A Psychological Warfare Casebook*, ed. William Daugherty (Baltimore, MD: Johns Hopkins Press, 1958) 38.

2   Associated Press, Washington, 29 September 2001.

3   This anecdote was told by Jacintha Buddicom, "The Young Eric," *The World of George Orwell*, ed. Miriam Gross (London: Weidenfeld and Nicolson, 1971) 2, and is cited in Crick.

4   Manvell and Fraenkel.

5   Dwight Bolinger, "Truth is a Linguistic Question," *Language* 49, 3 (1973): 543f, crediting Julia Stanley for the first example and Donald Smith for the idea of experiencer deletion.

6   Stanley uses the different terminology of "passive adjective" to make the same point.

7   Bolinger 543. My ordering of Bolinger's points differs from his own. He puts the missing performative first.

8   Bolinger 545.

9   From Henry Steele Commager, "The Defeat of America," *New York Review of Books*, 5 October, 1972: 7-13.

10   Bolinger 547.

11   Not always with attribution. The source is Alfred McClung Lee and Elizabeth Briant Lee, eds., *The Fine Art of Propaganda: A Study of Father Coughlin's Speeches* (New York: Harcourt Brace and Company, 1939). Further references to this work are taken from this source and will be indicated by bracketed FAP and page number in the text.

12   In a brief to the House of Commons Standing Committee on Health and Welfare, the Association for the Modernization of Canadian Abortion Laws (AMCAL) stated: "Detective Sergeant Wm. Quennell, former head of the Abortion Squad of the Morality Department of the Metropolitan Toronto Police Department, has estimated that 300 women die each year in Canada as a result of illegal abortions, of which about 35,000 are believed to be performed in metropolitan Toronto alone each year." See, Standing Committee on Health and Welfare, *Minutes of Proceedings and Evidence* (2 November 1967) 139. Quennell, himself, in a private letter in my possession, attributed his figure to a newspaper report, which appeared in 1966 and which included natural as well as illegal abortions. The ambiguity of the word "abortion" (induced versus natural) caused much confusion in these early debates, so that figures tended to fluctuate. The figure of 100,000 yearly illegal abortions in Canada is attributed to AMCAL by Zena Cherry in a *Globe and Mail* article (in AMCAL's brief the figure of 300,000 is mentioned in the Minutes at page 143). Cherry also gives 8,000 a year as the estimate of illegal abortions in Toronto per year. See "AMCAL campaigns for end to abortion's barbarisms, " *Globe and Mail*, 22 March 1968: 9.

13   Dr. Robert Cushman, Medical Officer of Health, Regional Municipality of Ottawa-Carleton, in a letter to the *Ottawa Citizen* ("Second-hand smoke kills 100 each year," March 24, 1998).

14   Eleanor MacLean, *Between the Lines: How to detect bias and propaganda in the news and everyday life* (Montreal: Black Rose Books, 1981).

15   Lawrence E. Harrison, "Chile," letter, *Globe and Mail*, 20 September 1995.

16   See US Senate, *Covert Action in Chile, 1963-1973*, Staff Report of the Select Committee to Study Governmental Operations with Respect to Intelligence Activities (Washington, DC: US Government Printing Office, 1975) especially pages 27 and 29. I made these points in a letter to the *Globe and Mail*, published 27 September 1995.

17   UK Parliament, Defence Committee of Inquiry, *Minutes of Evidence taken before the Defence Committee*, 21 July 1982.

18   Senate of Canada, Standing Committee on Social Affairs, Science and Technology, *Minutes of the Proceedings on the Subcommittee on Veterans Affairs*, Seventh Proceedings, 6 November 1992: 79-81.

19   Mary-Lou Finlay, letter, *Ottawa Citizen*, 5 May 1983.

20 MacLean 35.

21 "Nov. 25 [1997]: Police and APEC protesters clash. The RCMP arrest 42 demonstrators after using pepper-spray to control the crowd. Prime Minister Jean Chretien jokes that 'for me, pepper, I put it on my plate.'" Julie Grenier and Owen Wood, "The APEC Summit, Timeline 1997-2001," CBC News OnLine, August 2001.

22 "Purity at Any Cost," editorial, *Globe and Mail*, 16 August 1982; and "Prof. Henripin responds," letter, *Globe and Mail*, 20 August 1982.

23 *Globe and Mail*, 26 January 1984: 1. In making this point, I am aware that new allegations and controversy have arisen over the extent of Vatican awareness, and I make no judgement on the matter here. I refer simply to the facts as presented in the story at the time.

24 *Globe and Mail*, 24 May 1984. It seems unlikely that the *Globe and Mail* was deliberately trying to stir up antagonism between Catholics and Jews. However, given enough examples, one can make a good case for at least the operation of some kind of unconscious bias. The media always have a temptation to widen their circle of readers or viewers by presenting items in a way that will strike a note of alarm.

25 W.V.O. Quine, "Reference and Modality," *From a Logical Point of View* (Cambridge, MA: Harvard University Press, 1961) 139-59.

26 Quine also uses the expression for modalities (necessary, possible, etc.), which do not concern us here.

27 Orwell, *Homage to Catalonia* 63.

28 Paul Grice, "Presupposition and Conversational Implicature," *Radical Pragmatics*, ed. Peter Cole (New York: Academic Press, 1981).

29 *Ottawa Citizen*, 30 October 1987.

30 *Marketing Law Reporting Service*, vol. 3 (Cobourg, ON: Business Law Reporting Ltd, 1984). I would also like to thank C.G. Sheppard and R.W. Lally of Consumer and Corporate Affairs Canada for helpful information.

31 *New York Times*, 27 June 1996: A6.

32 *Ottawa Citizen*, 10 February 1996: A14.

33 Hugh Winsor, "The Power Game," *Globe and Mail*, 14 November 1997: A6.

34 Michael Wheeler, *Lies, Damn Lies and Statistics* (New York: Dell, 1976) 82-86; 104. See also Darrell Huff, *How to Lie with Statistics* (New York: Norton, 1954) for this and many other examples of polling bias.

35 See Herbert H. Hyman, et al. "Interviewing in Social Research," *A Research Project of the National Opinion Research Center* (Chicago, IL: University of Chicago Press, 1954) 159ff.

36 *Ottawa Citizen*, 20 May 1980.

37 Barry Kiefl, letter, *Globe and Mail*, 11 September 1984.

38 I quote from a survey release-dated January 3, 1973. These surveys are sent to libraries and the media. I viewed this particular one in Carleton's MacOdrum Library.

39 *Globe and Mail*, 29 October 1990: A7.

40 Michael Marzolini, chairman of Pollara, Inc., in an article published in *The Hill Times* (Ottawa), November 10, 1997.

41 Robert J. Moore, "Reflections of Canadians on the Law and the Legal System: Legal Research Institute Survey of Respondents in Montreal, Toronto and Winnipeg," *Law in a*

Cynical Society? Opinion and Law in the 1980s, ed. Dale Gibson and Janet Baldwin (Calgary and Vancouver: Carswell Legal Publications Western Division, 1985) 73.

42 Wheeler 22.

43 Wheeler 109.

44 Chris Cobb, "Perils of polling: Is there no right answer?," *Ottawa Citizen*, 15 November 1997.

45 Wheeler 116.

46 Wheeler 111.

47 Jimmy Edwards, letter, *Ottawa Citizen*, 31 March 1986.

48 "Decision On Abortion Should Be Patient's Canadian Poll Finds," *Globe and Mail*, 23 September, 1982; Randal Marlin, "Abortion polls," letter, *Globe and Mail*, 22 April 22 1985.

49 See Randal Marlin, *The David Levine Affair* (Halifax, NS: Fernwood, 1998) for documentation of the rise and decline of the furor in the media against the hiring in Ottawa of David Levine, former Parti Québécois (separatist) candidate, as Chief Executive Officer of the newly amalgamated Ottawa Hospital in 1998.

50 Georgette Gagnon and Dan Rath, *Not Without Cause* (Toronto: HarperCollins, HarperPerrenial Edition, 1992) 252-255.

51 Wheeler 24.

52 Wheeler 107.

53 Conrad Black, *A Life in Progress* (Toronto: Key Porter Books, 1993) 125.

54 Huff. All further quotations are taken from this edition.

55 *The New Statesman*, 24 November 1978. Reference for Dorfman's work is given in the article to the *Journal of the American Association for the Advancement of Science* 201: 4362. See also Boyce Rensburger, "Briton's Classic IQ Data Now Viewed as Fraudulent," *New York Times*, 28 November 1976, which adds to the list of Burt's probable frauds and includes sceptical questions by scientists as to whether two collaborators, cited in his articles, ever existed.

56 John Allen Paulos, *A Mathematician Reads the Newspaper* (New York: Basic Books, 1995) 60-62.

57 Paulos, 14ff, 17.

58 Paulos, 135-37.

FOUR
ETHICS AND PROPAGANDA

WHAT IS ETHICS?

In today's world, with its many conflicting attitudes and moral outlooks, scepticism about the possibility of arriving at universal moral judgments is widespread. Disagreement on some fundamental issues exists even in seemingly peaceful, harmonious societies. However, whatever theoretical scepticism may exist, there is still the necessity to work out rules for living together in society. Among other things, ethics is a systematic study aimed at discerning which rules and forms of thought and behaviour will contribute to a better existence and which will not. So described, there is an element of circularity in this definition of ethics, since "better" already presupposes the existence of some difference between good and bad. That should not be a problem, though, because the study of ethics may revise our understanding of what is better. Everyone starts with their own preferences, in the light of which a notion of "better" operates, whether or not the person is conscious of this. Even a moral sceptic who claims to deny the existence of morality will express moral indignation at gross violations of rights, especially if that person is a victim of such transgression.

Ethics is also about lifestyles, happiness, and individual roads to self-improvement and perfection. For present purposes, the social aspect is more important, because propaganda is an activity that, by its nature, involves many others. What we are looking for is an ethical evaluation of propaganda or propaganda-like activities. To do this, we begin with a general outline of some dominant ethical ideas, as found in the history of ethics. Secondly, since propaganda has often been tied by definition to some form of manipulation, a discussion of the whole question of the ethics of lying will be undertaken, with a view to providing an anchor point from which to approach the other issues. Thirdly, the question of communications that are not lies, but that share some of the same propensities of lies, will be evaluated from an ethical point of view.

ETHICAL THEORIES

Ethical theory in the broadest sense is sometimes divided into meta-ethics and normative ethics. The main preoccupation of meta-ethics is the analysis of ethical concepts and the language used in discussions of ethical matters, along with the justification of ethical theories. Normative ethics involves the investigation of moral questions, with a view to providing answers from whatever ethical theory seems appropriate. It would seem that meta-ethics cannot be sharply distinguished from normative ethics, since a thorough investigation of normative ethical questions is bound to lead to raising questions deemed more suitable to meta-ethics: applying a certain theory to solve an ethical dilemma requires justifying the use of that theory and not another. Also, the language in which normative ethical answers are provided may contain words like "ought to" and "have a right to" that need clarification.

Extreme moral scepticism is theoretically difficult to refute, but it is also self-stultifying. To have a fruitful discussion of ethics, a measure of decency and goodwill must be presupposed, along with a certain openness to the possibility of improving one's own perspective by listening to challenges that others may bring to it.

Religion features prominently in many people's thinking about ethics. The major religions come with ethical codes, and some people accept them in fairly broad detail, although the exact interpretation of the Bible, Koran, or Torah is subject to much dispute. Whatever the source, religion or otherwise, of one's ethical prescriptions, there is always a twofold problem. First, does the set of prescriptions seem right? Second, are the prescriptions self-consistent? Suppose one of the prescriptions is to love one another and, therefore, not to judge other people, while another is to put to death someone who commits a consensual sexual act. Can the two prescriptions be viewed as consistent, from a modern perspective?[1] If not, how can the apparently contradictory injunctions be resolved?

Religion is often the source for deontological theories, meaning theories that do not make obligation depend on some consequence-based criteria, but upon some recognized authority. For many religious believers, the wrongness of eating certain foods, or eating them at certain times, is accepted as such because God has indicated this either directly through revelation or indirectly through a prophet. This is different from believing that rightness and wrongness of actions are to be determined only in the light of the anticipatable consequences of those actions. Theories of the latter kind—such as ethical egoism and utilitarianism—have been given the name consequentialism. The ethical theory of Kant combines rationality with deontology and is sufficiently influential to have earned the name Kantianism. To the theories so far mentioned, which deal with actions, there are also theories relating to individual self-improvement and perfectionist views.

To argue in detail for or against any of these theories is a matter for a book on ethical theory as such. Since we are dealing with applied ethics, only a brief outline of their strengths and weaknesses will be given. In our arguments relating to the ethics of propaganda, we should be aware of the different areas of likely agreement or disagreement between the different theories. Where their differences produce converging results, we have reason to be more confident in those results. When they differ, we will need to provide supplementary argument to indicate why we favour the outcome from one theory rather than another, or why we prefer to treat such an outcome simply as an unsettled question in ethics. We do not have to suppose that every question in ethics must have a definite, problem-disposing answer. We want our discussions of ethics to give us solutions to problems, but they can be illuminating and satisfying even if they do not have such a result.

The value of deontological theory is that it accords with the feeling or intuition of "seeing" that something is right or wrong in cases where consequentialist theory seems to yield contrary and unsatisfactory results. The idea that it might be right, under certain conditions, to execute an innocent person—perhaps because that would appease a large mob and prevent large-scale violence—has seemed to many people utterly abhorrent and morally corrupt. Yet, the situation can be described in a way that seems to require the pure consequentialist to accept the action as morally right. This is only one of many scenarios that lead philosophers to make room for the existence of bindingness not related to consequential considerations.

Kantian theory in particular is a form of deontology based on rationality. Kant thought that rightness or wrongness was determinable in the light of a certain test of rationality, presented in two forms. The first was the principle of universalizability: if you want to know whether an action is right or wrong, first ask what the underlying justificatory "maxim" behind the action is. For example, if you are tempted to steal, you might ask yourself what is implied by telling yourself that it is right to steal. One such answer is, "It is right to enrich myself, in whatever way I feel like, whenever I feel the urge to do so." Now ask whether that "maxim" can be universalized. As a rational being, you must recognize that others are rational beings similar to yourself. If you reason that you have a right to enrich yourself in that way, so may they, because, insofar as you are claiming rationality for your action, so may they. But can you accept that others have a right to steal from you? Clearly not. So the universalizability test reveals that the maxim was inspired by self-seeking inclination and not by rationality. It fails the test, and the action of stealing is deemed immoral. The second form of the test concerns whether our action shows respect for other people as ends in themselves rather than simply as a means to ends of our own. If we steal another's goods, we are not valuing that person for his or her own sake, but are treating them solely as a means to our gratification, ignoring their needs and wants. Judicial murder—the murder of an innocent person for expediency—treats the victim solely as a means to the ends of others and not as an end in himself. It is irrational to treat ourselves as worthy ends while denying such worthiness to others who possess the relevant attributes for worthiness. Kant thought the relevant attribute was rationality, but we may call the relevant fact that of being human.

Ethical egoism is the theory that enlightened selfishness is the right basis for determining morality. A major advantage to arguing from this stance is that a frequent rejoinder to claims about ethical obligations, "Why should I be moral?," is not difficult to answer. If you can show that something is to a person's advantage, they have an attractive reason for doing that thing. Normally, we think of selfishness as the antithesis of morality. "You are being selfish!" is usually said reprovingly, not approvingly. Hence, the key word for defence of this is "enlightened." The ethical egoist does not barge in ahead of others, or grab the largest slice of cake, because that kind of selfishness brings the rebuke of others, who are likely to exact some kind of sanction. Quite apart from that, it is possible to develop sensibilities that enable one to experience pleasure in the happiness of others. It is not difficult to see that egoism, so interpreted, appears to be no great threat to morality, despite the negative associations with the word "selfish."

Utilitarianism is a very popular theory, especially in relation to public planning policy. The idea of this theory is, first, that the morality of actions is determinable in the light of the amount of happiness and unhappiness that they create, taking into account all the people affected, and counting them all equally. If one contemplates a range of possible actions at any given time, the right one is that which will maximize overall happiness (one word for this is "optimific," but it has an awkward sound). There are many questions about utilitarianism. Is pleasure to be identified with happiness, as Bentham thought? If so, should we alter our understanding of pleasure, or of happiness, or both, and in what way? What happens to individual human rights if our sole guide is the overall net benefit? Consider such cases as that of Robin Hood, who stole from the rich to benefit the poor; it seems the net benefit to the poor is greater than the lack of benefit to the rich. Another, more macabre case posits three children who will die if they don't get a new lung, kidney, and heart respectively and soon. There is a seriously ill person with brain damage, but healthy organs otherwise. Should that person be killed to save the lives of the others? The utilitarian is asked whether an affirmative answer is acceptable to the theory. If it is, the theory seems subversive of law and order. Of course, the utilitarian could respond by saying, "law and order are very important for the common good, and a utilitarian cannot countenance acts that would undermine the system and produce chaos." Whatever the problems of detail, utilitarianism has a very strong attractive force overall, and in a secular or multicultural society its principles form a large part of the reasoning for policy decisions. The question is whether utilitarianism nevertheless leaves out an important part of the moral story. If it does, then in regularly appealing to the principle of utilitarianism, the policy-maker risks blindness as to its deficiencies.

Over two millennia ago Plato supplied us with a model for reasoning about ethics. In his *Republic*, the question "What is justice?" was discussed, and one of the answers supplied was that justice is repaying one's debts. However, Socrates asked whether one should give back a deadly weapon borrowed from a friend, when the friend came for it drunk, intending to kill someone. The answer, in the negative, showed that that principle of justice has at least one exception and, therefore, cannot be relied on always to give the correct answer. The collision between intuitions about a particular case and principles that seem otherwise sound is a common experience in moral thinking. We have to find a way to balance those intuitions against principles, which will need some kind of reformulation. The goal is to bring the two into what the contemporary philosopher John Rawls called "reflective equilibrium."[2]

Ethics is also concerned with character. If we suppose that utilitarianism is correct, we may find that the best course of action, so determined, could involve a politician having to break a promise. Assurances given at election time may later appear to him or her to be contrary to the public interest. We may find ourselves judging the actions of the politician favourably, but still dislike the character of a person who is readily able to abandon personal commitments.

THE MORALITY OF LYING

In the history of morality, lying has generally been viewed with disfavour. St. Augustine, St. Thomas Aquinas, and Kant all argued that lying is immoral, with no exceptions, although with varying degrees of turpitude depending on the lie. Yet, there are many other philosophers who argue that lying may be the right and even the morally obligatory course of action to take under exceptional circumstances. Some believe that lies are wrong only to those to whom truth is "owed," and they maintain that not everybody is entitled to the truth from another person. More recently, David Nyberg argued that lying is part of everyday experience and that it is frequently, and not just exceptionally, the right thing to do. Nyberg does not question lying generally, but concentrates on how to separate harmful and immoral lies from those that are harmless and beneficial. By talking about lying in general, he thinks, we lose the right perspective on those lies that are especially harmful. He prefers a "bottom-up" approach to the question of lying, that is to say, an approach that is generated by consideration of real-life experiences and seeks to formulate rules out of those experiences.[3] This is different from a "top-down" model, which seeks to find general principles first and then apply them to individual cases. Sisella Bok is among those philosophers who allow for the moral justification of lies in very exceptional circumstances. Her book, *Lying: Moral Choice in Public and Private Life*,[4] serves as a foil for Nyberg, since it continues the practice of earlier moralists of arguing from general principle down to individual cases.

Even if we disagree with the earlier moralists, it is valuable to start with their insights. It is sometimes more instructive to take a theory that is rejected, showing why it was rejected, than ignoring it altogether.

St. Augustine

St. Augustine (354–430) might be taken as the originator, in the Western world, of a certain tradition which, despite recognizing that in special circumstances there can be very strong moral reasons in favour of lying, and despite sympathy for the plight of people caught in such special circumstances, still refuses to accept and teach categorically that it is ever morally right to do so. He approves of some actions that might be thought by others to be lies, but does so only if, in his view, some essential feature of a lie is lacking. Truth to him is so vital that he is unwilling to have truck with even well-motivated lies, but he does not roundly condemn them either. Augustine is quite at ease with the idea that human beings might have to sin in a small way from time to time.

Augustine inclines toward a narrow definition of the lie. It is not enough for a person to say something false, knowing it to be false; the person must do so with the intention to deceive, or there is no lie. Augustine does not give an example, but an obvious case is the ironic rejoinder to an improbable statement, "Yes, and pigs fly." More problematic is the case in which a politician says, "I will not seek the nomination," knowing that people will judge by the very fact of the pronouncement that he will seek it. This is not a lie, on Augustine's account, because what the candidate says engenders true belief, and the candidate knows this.[5] For a similar reason, stories made up for jocular purposes are not lies, nor are fictional writings. "No one has been so illiterate as to think that similar fables of Aesop, related for the same purpose, ought to be called lies."[6] Although narrow in one sense, Augustine's view of what constitutes a lie is broader in another, for he also holds that a person can lie not only by words but by any outward manifestation contrary to what he or she believes.

Augustine presents us with a nice puzzle about lies and truth-telling. Suppose you know that down one fork in the road there are bandits, while there are no bandits along the other fork. You tell someone who never believes what you say that bandits lie in wait down the fork where you know there are none. You do this so that the person, disbelieving you, will take the safe road and not come to harm. Do you lie? Do you do something wrong? You surely do not do any wrong; indeed, if you told the truth the person would end up in great harm. Do you lie? Not if lying includes the intention to deceive. Now consider the case where, out of malice, you tell the person that there are no bandits down the road where there are no bandits, knowing that the person will take the dangerous road and come to grief, and wanting this to happen. Should this be considered a lie? Do you do something wrong? Clearly, Augustine says, you do something wrong. However, if we strictly hold to the definition of a lie as the saying of what one knows to be false in order to deceive, then there is no lie here either, because you are not saying what you know to be false, even though you speak the truth only to deceive.[7]

We will certainly avoid lies, Augustine writes, if we say what is true and deserving of belief, if there is a need to express the truth, and if we want to convince people of what we say. The inclusion of the idea of a "need to express the truth" is an important moral consideration, and, interestingly, it is reflected in the Anglo-American law of libel, in the existence of "qualified privilege" for people to say publicly things that are in the public interest to know. Certain defences against a libel suit are open to those with qualified privilege, but are denied to those who defame merely out of a desire to gossip or increase circulation of a scandal sheet.

There is still no lie, in Augustine's view, either if we merely say something false believing it to be true, or if we hold something to be true which we don't know to be true but don't know to be false either, or if we believe what is not worthy of belief, or if we express an opinion without a need to do so. In other words, there are factors that can seriously taint what we say with immorality, but that do not amount to lying. One of the great scholarly sins is to present as true something for which there is no evidence. At least with a lie, there will be some means of showing the statement false. When a totally unsupported claim is made in an area where no evidence exists for or against the claim, it is annoyingly unrefutable in the straightforward way of demonstrating its falseness. By detaching in this way the question of ignorant and deceptive communications from that of full-blown lies, Augustine has done a useful service. It helps to show that, to be morally wrong, deceptive communication does not have to involve what are, strictly speaking, lies.

Augustine distinguished different kinds of lies, from those that cause harm for no good reason to those that harm no one and have certain benefits, such as avoiding harm and injustice. Lying to cause harm or lying for the love of doing so and being reckless about ensuing harms are both obviously wrong.

Perhaps the most influential ethical idea attributed to Augustine (although it would be rash to credit him with complete originality, especially as he himself appeals to Judaic texts) is what has come to be known as the principle that the end does not justify the means. In this, Augustine combats the view that it is all right to lie for the purpose of discovering heretics and bringing them to account. The whole purpose of bringing heretics to account, he says, is to free the world from error. But how can one suitably proceed against lies by lying? The weight of scripture goes against lying in any form: "Thou wilt destroy all that speak a lie" (Psalm 5:7), "Thou shalt not bear false witness" (Exodus 20:16), "The mouth that belieth, killeth the soul" (Wisdom—"The Book of Wisdom" or "The Wisdom of Solomon, Apocrypha"—1:11) and St. Paul's "Wherefore put away lying, and speak the truth" (Ephesians 4:25). Besides this appeal to authority, Augustine gives a version of the slippery slope argument: once you start to do evil to avoid evil, then evil will no longer be measured by the norm of truth, but according to one's own desire and habit.[8]

Augustine teaches that a dogmatic, doctrinal defence of lying to do good cannot be sustained. It can never be right to lie, but it is right to be motivated to avoid harm, so that lies designed to avoid suffering, injustice, and death deserve less censure. For teachers especially, the unreserved championing of lies in special circumstances has a tendency to taint their own profession. "This much I know, that even he who teaches that we ought to lie wants to appear to be teaching the truth."[9] Appealing to 1 John 2:21, "The truth cannot give birth to a lie," Augustine claims that the teacher will be wrong to teach that it is sometimes right to lie. Augustine implies, although this is not spelled out, that if the teacher shows any compromising attitude to a lie, anything the teacher says becomes suspect. How can one be sure that the teacher does not see himself or herself in one of those situations where a lie is called for in the name of some public greater good?

St. Thomas Aquinas

Thomas Aquinas (1225-74) does not add much, in terms of fundamentals, to the position of Augustine. Schoolboys of an earlier generation were taught Aquinas's distinction between lies that are officious (in the older sense meaning "eager to serve or please others"), that is to say, done for a good purpose; those that are jocose, where the lack of intention to deceive removes an essential component of a lie properly considered; and those that are malicious. Like Augustine, Aquinas holds that the greater the good intended, the more the sinfulness of lying is diminished. He locates the wrongfulness of the most serious lies in their violation of obligations to God and of charity towards our neighbour. Teaching people falsehoods about science or moral conduct is injurious to them, but telling falsehoods about things not affecting them is not a serious (mortal) sin.[10]

Immanuel Kant

Immanuel Kant (1724-1804) shares with Augustine an uncompromising view about the wrongfulness of lying, although he locates the wrongness formally, in the violation of the principle of universalizability. If you lie, and take as a maxim that lying is all right to get out of a tough spot, then universalizing this maxim implies that anyone in a tough spot can lie to get out of it. If this were the practice, lies would no longer be believed, and the lying enterprise would in that way be self-defeating.[11] Truth-telling is a formal duty, for Kant, and so admits of no exceptions. Like Augustine, he considers the case of lying to save the life of an innocent person and refuses to be moved by the fact that death will follow the truth-telling. If you tell the truth and misfortune comes through another's act, the other person is responsible, not you, because you are fulfilling the duty to tell the truth. On the other hand, if you lie and unexpected misfortune follows, you bear some of the responsibility, because the causal chain will have gone through your wrongful act. Kant says (though not very convincingly to many people):

> After you have honestly answered the murderer's question as to whether his intended victim is at home, it may be that he has slipped out so that he does not come in the way of the murderer, and thus that the murder may not be committed. But if you had lied and said he was not at home when he had really gone out without your knowing it, and if the murderer had then met him as he went away and murdered him, you might justly be accused as the cause of his death. For if you had told the truth as far as you knew it, perhaps the murderer might have been apprehended by the neighbours while he searched the house and thus the deed might have been prevented.[12]

Here some belief in providence—the idea that an all-powerful God governs happenings in the world and can work things to punish wrongdoing—seems to be presupposed.

We can approach the morality of lying from the point of view of Kant's other version of his categorical imperative, the imperative that tells you what ought to be done categorically, not merely hypothetically—"do this if you want to obtain that." In this case, we ask whether lying is a violation of the principle calling for respect of others as ends in themselves. Kant does not see any difference resulting, but one might argue that, if another person is bent on taking the life of an innocent person, and the lie, and only the lie, would deflect him from his intention, then telling the lie would be more respecting of others as ends in themselves than would be truth-telling. The reason for this is twofold. First, we respect others as ends in themselves when we help to deflect them from a path of wickedness and do not contribute anything to help them along such a path. Second, we respect the potential victim as an end in herself if we act so as to prevent her demise.

Grotius

Moving from absolutists against lying to those who allow exceptions, we now consider the Dutch jurisprudential thinker, Hugo the Great, known from his Latinized surname as Grotius (1583-1645). Grotius grounded the wrongness of lying in the violation of the right of another to the truth. This right stems from liberty of judgment. If I do not know the truth about some matter, and if I am fed falsehoods, my judgment will not be sound. However, that right can be removed under three sets of circumstances. First, the person with whom we speak may expressly waive the right. (We sometimes play games in which lies are an accepted part.) Second, the right may be waived by tacit consent, or consent assumed on reasonable grounds. Third, it might be outweighed by another more compelling right.[13]

In so grounding the wrongness of lying, Grotius explicitly condones the telling of fictions to children or insane persons when this is for their own good, because they don't have the same liberty of judgment as sane adults. He also argues that the intended audience in any conversation has a right to the truth, but eavesdroppers do not. If I make use of fictional devices that do not deceive my intended audience, I do not have to accept blame for misleading those who have no right to be listening.[14] A wartime ruse, in which a false message is sent to an ally in order to deceive an enemy, is not considered wrong for the same reason. The enemy is not owed the obligation of truth-telling.

Grotius also allows for tacit consent to justify passing on a false report that will help a wavering person win a battle. After winning, the person lied-to can be presumed to approve of this form of deception. Grotius sides with those who place good results above the value of truth in itself. He notes, though, that in the case of the wartime "salutary lie" the infringement on liberty of judgment does not last long, and the truth emerges soon after.

Grotius conceives of the state as having rights superior to individuals within the state, and so he supported Plato's use of the "noble lie" as set out in the *Republic*.[15] The rulers of the state are justified in lying to the public in such a way as to encourage a harmonious state, it being assumed that a strong and well-functioning state will benefit the general public. In short, lying in the interests of the lied-to, by leaders who know the best interests of the public better than they do themselves, is acceptable and right, in Plato's and Grotius's accounts. It is this view that is strongly resisted by democratic defenders of an open society, such as Karl Popper and Noam Chomsky.

Kant replies forcefully to the view that the morality of lying is grounded in the right of another to the truth. Rights can be waived, but the demands of truth are not subject to such easy dismissal, the exception of game contexts notwithstanding. He points out that, by lying, one contributes to the erosion of trust and thereby of law generally and, thus, commits a wrong to mankind generally.[16] Kant is not arguing consequentially, as if the empirical likelihood of anarchy were the deciding factor. He insists that truthfulness is an unconditional duty. Here there comes into play his idea that morality involves more than duties to individuals; social policies must also respect all persons in a "kingdom of ends." The duty to tell the truth is linked to the fundamental demands of reason, which all share alike. To depart from truth, for whatever reason, involves jeopardy to the whole enterprise of reason itself and so cannot be condoned.

Kant, Aquinas, and Augustine view truth as something so fundamental that it cannot be bartered for some good. As a constituent of reason, a fundamental aspect of what it is to be human, it cannot be treated as some bargaining chip subject to negotiation. And yet, the outcome of their view, which apparently requires revealing the location of the innocent hunted person when silence is impossible (because it would have the same effect), seems contrary to decent feeling.

Ethical Thought in Late Nineteenth-Century England

The question of the ethics of lying fascinated a circle of thinkers in England during the late nineteenth century. The circle included Sir James Fitzjames Stephen, his cousin Edward Dicey (older brother of Albert Venn Dicey), and Mark Pattison, the Master of Lincoln College, Oxford. These were thinkers who combined philosophical thinking at a fairly high level with journalistic, legal, and political concerns. Dicey's "The Ethics of Political Lying,"[17] while clearly politically motivated against Charles Stewart Parnell, the Irish MP and Home Rule advocate, contains some interesting philosophical ideas, which are in close proximity to commonsense thinking and acting and to the demands of everyday administration.

Dicey begins with Dr. Johnson's definition of a lie as a criminal falsehood, with the intention to deceive. He then observes, "we are all agreed that as a general rule it is an honest man's duty to tell the truth." He does not claim that this is an axiom that brooks no exceptions; indeed, he allows that we all at times have said "the thing that is not" with a view to deceiving and would do it again under the same circumstances without compunction. But our code does regard falsity as a thing to be condemned. For whatever reason, Dicey says, the business world has adopted a standard of veracity according to which "to tell a direct lie is recognized as an offence against the ordinary standard of commercial behaviour." The same is true of lawyers, who may hold briefs for a client, arguing strenuously even when convinced of the client's guilt, but counsel is forbidden to "express his own personal conviction, to pledge his own personal belief, as to his client's innocence." By the code of the medical profession, a doctor is not bound to tell the whole truth to his patients, "but he is not justified in making statements on the strength of his professional knowledge and experience which he knows to be untrue." Diplomats may make false statements, but they are not "entitled according to our British standard to strengthen their force by giving [their] personal guarantee of their being made in good faith." In games of chance, you can play a false card to deceive an opponent, but you are not allowed to score points you have not got or refuse to follow suit.

Having made these commonsense observations about the code of veracity, Dicey considers the view that in politics one is not expected to speak the truth, or at any rate that lying in political matters is more venial than elsewhere. If the justification for this view is the principle that good can come from evil, his answer is that this is casuistry and "a dogma against which all Protestant divines and moralists have steadily set their face." If the justification is that lying is common practice in politics, this is false in fact. The code of party politics may be lax, but it "does not sanction the employment of the *lie direct*" (emphasis added).

This is a most interesting idea and deserves to be compared with modern-day viewpoints. There are some who claim that the public does not mind politicians lying, as long as the lies are not contrary to their own particular interests. Here we have the claim that the code in politics allows for all kinds of obfuscations and evasions, but that the direct lie is unacceptable. Dicey elaborates:

> In all other things, as I have endeavoured to show, the line is drawn at a distinct misstatement of fact, to which the utterer demands credence, in virtue of his hearers' belief in his own good faith and loyalty. In politics, as I contend, a like rule holds good also. No doubt the distinction between lying that is permissible and lying that is prohibited is of a very arbitrary and artificial kind. As a question of abstract morality it might be difficult to show that the *suppressio veri*, and still more the *suggestio falsi*, constitute a less heinous offence than the lie pure and simple. But practically the distinction in question is intelligible enough.... We are quite prepared to accept any number of conventional falsehoods.... But we still act on the assumption, that when a man commits himself to a positive statement of fact on his own authority, he does not make that statement knowing it to be false and with intent to

deceive.... Any one who offends against this convention is justly regarded as an offender against our social code, and anything which tends to upset the authority of this code is a public misfortune.

Dicey's observations come from first-hand experience with the world of business, in which he had some involvement early in life. In any case, the view that there is a line between acceptable hyperbole and over-optimism, on the one hand, and outright violation of trust on the other, accords well with some recent pronouncements on political ethics. The *New York Times* expressed its view that William Waldegrave and Sir Nicholas Lyell, two MPs under John Major, should resign following the revelation that they deliberately misled Parliament by relaxing rules governing arms sales to Iraq, which permitted the sale of previously prohibited sophisticated equipment, "some of which later turned up in Iraq's nuclear weapons program." Waldegrave "repeatedly told Parliament there had been no change. Sir Nicholas improperly pressed his Cabinet colleagues to issue gag orders to block disclosure of the loosened guidelines in a court case."[18]

With the rise of utilitarian philosophy, the absolutist stance has come increasingly under attack. Henry Sidgwick, a late nineteenth-century British philosopher, argued that, if it is sometimes permissible to kill in self-defence, surely it should be permissible to lie instead of killing. It may in general be permissible to prevent a "palpable invasion of our rights," he thought.[19] Obviously, truth-telling is enormously beneficial on the whole, and there are good utilitarian arguments to support this as a general practice. But we have already seen examples where occasional exceptions could avoid some grave wrong to an innocent victim. The idea that admitting such rare exceptions would bring down the whole edifice of trust seems ludicrous. And yet, from the very rare exceptions, what is to stop one from arguing to less rare exceptions and finally treating truth-telling as something that might be rejected routinely? Contemporary debate no longer treats that slippery slope as obviously abhorrent.

Contemporary Discussion: Bok and Nyberg

SISSELA BOK

Sissela Bok has resisted the slippery slope, while not totally embracing an absolutist position. She might be regarded as holding to an "almost absolutist" position. Her arguments are partly utilitarian and partly Kantian, involving questions of respect for others. Bok defines a lie as "any intentionally deceptive message which is stated." She argues that the wrongness of lying comes from the following:

1. There is a societal need for a minimum of trust. Lies tend to erode this. As she writes, "The aggregate harm from a large number of marginally harmful instances may ... be highly undesirable in the end—for liars, those deceived, and honesty and trust more generally."[20]

2. When you give false information you tend to restrict the freedom of choice of others. You are violating the principle of treating them with the respect due to beings which are ends in themselves. If we want to be moral, we should consider how we would judge the lie, not just from the point of view of the liar, but also from the point of view of the person lied to, and from the point of view of the general public.

> Liars usually weigh only the immediate harm to others from the lie against the benefits they want to achieve. The flaw in such an outlook is that it ignores or underestimates two additional kinds of harm—the harm that lying does to the liars themselves and the harm done to the general level of trust and co-operation. Both are cumulative; both are hard to reverse.[21]

Lying involves loss of integrity, a kind of double-entry bookkeeping: one column for those to whom one lies, another for one's own accounting. Such a person will need, as the Romans observed, a good memory. The loss of integrity is something regrettable on its own account, because with that loss goes some of our sense of well-being. Those who lose a sense of integrity are in constant danger of revealing this loss to others in their speech and actions. Thus, they are in constant danger of forfeiting one of life's great assets, the sense others have that they are trustworthy individuals.

3. The liar wants to be believed, but lying undermines the foundation for credibility. There is an element of self-contradiction and a violation of the universalizability principle.

4. As with Augustine, Bok sees that lying in one matter begets lying in others. A point she stresses is how prone we are, once we accept the possibility of exceptions to the truth-telling principle, to make exceptions that are grounded in our self-interest and not some general benevolence. Lying can easily become a habit.

In order to compensate for the biases in our estimation of the goods and harms to come from a contemplated lie, Bok gives us the following practical test for what is acceptable:

> As we consider different kinds of lies, we must ask, first, whether there are alternative forms of action which will resolve the difficulty without the use of the lie; second, what might be the moral reasons brought forward to excuse the lie, and what reasons can be raised as counter-arguments. Third, as a test of these two steps, we must ask what a public of reasonable persons might say about such lies.[22]

The same test can usefully be applied to evaluate the ethics of propaganda.

DAVID NYBERG

As mentioned earlier, David Nyberg's approach is bottom-up, meaning that he first considers real-life practices and the forms of deception encountered there, then moves from practices we accept or reject to arrive at a suitable encompassing theory. He thinks that starting out by treating lies in their generality gives us a false over-simplification. If, on the other hand, we focus on particular cases, we will not lose the ability to perceive the telling details, which so often make a difference to the ethical evaluation of a course of action. Nyberg approvingly quotes George Steiner, "the human capacity to utter falsehood, to lie, to negate what is the case, stands at the heart of speech...." Nyberg goes on to say, "Deception is not merely to be tolerated as an occasionally prudent aberration in a world of truth telling: it is rather an essential component of our ability to organize and shape the world."[23] The general upshot of his argument is that lies are so built into the fabric of our ordinary dealings that we should cease to agonize over moral questions about lying, as such, and concentrate instead on damaging, reprehensible lies. If we spend our time dealing with the generality of lying, we are less likely to marshall our condemnatory forces where they are most appropriate.

Much of Nyberg's treatment of deception relates to cases where we simply remain silent about what we are thinking. There is no question but that in our everyday dealings with others we have good reasons to keep in check what we may be thinking. Imagine if people were governed by the principle of speaking frankly, in the sense of always saying what is on their mind. You stop a complete stranger in the street and say, "You look remarkably ugly!" "Well, and you have terrible breath." "That may be, but your clothes show no taste whatever." It is not difficult to imagine such insults escalating into a street fight. Still, there is a difference to be kept in mind between not volunteering to communicate some truth when there is no need to do so and gratuitously saying what one thinks. St. Augustine, for all his absolutism against lying, was clearly not in favour of vol-unteering every truth one possessed. Some of Nyberg's defence of lying trades, I believe, on amalgamating that question with the distinct question of whether to express truthful thoughts when there is no specific obligation to do so. For exam-ple, we are meant to sympathize with Mrs. Ramsay in Virginia Woolf's *To the Lighthouse*. The children in the story look forward to a boat trip, and she holds out hope, despite impending bad weather. But Mr. Ramsay sees the barometer falling and "snaps out irascibly that there is no chance of going."

> She, on the other hand, still hopes the wind might change and doesn't want to disappoint the children prematurely, so she is unwilling to tell them the trip is canceled. She tells the children simply that it might be fine tomorrow, and for their sake, she hopes it will be. He curses her for "flying in the face of facts," is enraged by the "extraordinary irrationality of her remark," and accuses her of telling lies.

Mrs. Ramsay's response was astonishment at such lack of consideration for the children's feelings. Nyberg analyzes the situation: "Her passion was for clarity, relationships, and a caring morality. His was for simplicity, rules, and a principled morality. His mind was arranged more like a piano keyboard, hers like a painter's palette."[24] Since the section in which this appears in Nyberg's book is called "Lying to the Children," we are meant to conclude that, in some sense, Mrs. Ramsay was lying, and that it was right for her to do so.

If we take "lying" to mean, "say what one knows to be false, with the intention of deceiving," then Mrs. Ramsay could well be acquitted of lying, since she does not know for certain that the weather will be bad and the trip cancelled. On the other hand, she is not giving a fair account of the likelihood of this happening, so she is involved in some suppression of truth. A proper moral assessment of this kind of case must go beyond the context of strict lying and into the territory of withholding information.

Nyberg gives other examples where statements of falsehoods are involved in some way, where "lies" may be too harsh a description and where most people probably would agree that they are condonable. We are confronted in our modern world with endless cases of form-filling. The correct description of matters in one's personal life may be unclear and debatable. Marital status, job situation, place of residence, state of health, and so on may involve uncertainties, the nature of which the form provider may not have a right to know or, indeed, any direct interest in knowing. It is understandable that one intelligent approach to form-filling is to ask oneself why the information is needed and to provide whatever is the most helpful interpretation of one's situation consistent with an honest assessment of that need.

Here is an analogous example. Suppose your name is misspelled on an identity card, and you want to retrieve it from the athletic club after you finish playing squash. The attendant asks for your name. You can either pronounce the name as misspelled, or you can give your true name and expect a delay in getting your card back. Or you can explain that although your name is so-and-so, it was misspelled on the card, and the attendant should look for such-and-such. Meanwhile, the people in the line-up are getting impatient. It saves time and trouble if you pronounce the name as misspelled. Is it lying to do so? There are different ways of analyzing such a case. Nyberg says that it is better to resign ourselves to lying in this way from time to time. Augustine and followers tells us either to say the truth, with the resulting inconvenience to others and ourselves, or to find a way in which the false statement of name would not properly be considered a lie.

There is a moral tradition called casuistry, which arose precisely to deal with the problems caused by applying rigorous moral principle to practical situations. The word "casuistry" comes from "casus" meaning "case"; it means meshing principle and practice on a case-by-case basis. It was given a bad name by Blaise Pascal, especially, who attacked the Jesuits in the seventeenth century for what he saw as their moral laxity. In fact, however, the seeking of consistency following case-by-case studies is admirable and is the method of the English Common Law. There are many good things to be said about casuistry, and Albert Jonson

and Stephen Toulmin have said them in *The Abuse of Casuistry*. What brought casuistry in disrepute was the use of highly contrived distinctions to rationalize some
convenient evasion of moral or legal duties. Sometimes the distinctions were
useful and justifiable, but at other times they could be stretched beyond what
common sense could accept. One useful device was that of mental reservation combined with equivocation. Faced with the dilemma of telling the truth and violating trust or telling a lie, one solution proposed by casuists was to use equivocal
language. A priest, asked whether he knows something he in fact does know, but
only through hearing a confession, has an ethical dilemma. He is under the
strictest obligation not to reveal what he has heard in confession. On the other
hand, he is obliged either to not answer or to tell the truth. Saying he cannot answer
might suggest that he knows. The casuist defended a simple, "No," with the
unstated mental reservation, "I don't know with a knowledge communicable to
anyone but God." If asked by a well-known and persistent cadger whether we
can lend him something, "I don't have any money" is a recognized and widely
acceptable response, even though we may have money in the pocket and in the
bank. The mental reservation is present according to which "I don't have any
money" means "I don't have money for you at this time."

However, the doctrine of mental reservation can be taken to extremes, as the
following case described by Jonson and Toulmin indicates. In 1585 the English
Parliament passed an act banishing all Jesuits and seminary priests, declaring it
treason for any Englishman ordained overseas to enter England. The penalty
was to be hanged, drawn, and quartered. The Dean of Durham wrote about the
testimony of a certain Father Ward:

> First, he swore he was no priest, that is, saith he (in a subsequent explanation),
> not Apollo's priest at Delphi. Second, he swore he was never across the sea,
> it's true he saith, for he was never across the Indian Seas. Third, he was never
> at or of the Seminaries. *Duplex est Seminarium, materiale et spirituale* [Seminaries
> are twofold, material and spiritual], he was never of the spiritual seminary. Forthly
> [sic], he never knew Mr. Hawksworth; it is true, saith he, *scientia scientifica* [in
> the way of scientific knowledge]. Fifthly, he never saw Mr. Hawksworth, true,
> he saith, *visione beatifica* [he didn't see him in a beatific vision].[25]

Johnson and Toulmin cite a medieval casuist, Raymond of Pennacourt, as suggesting a possible equivocation that might be used to protect an innocent person
hiding in one's house. Asked by the intended murderer whether he is in the
house, one might reply, "non est hic," which can mean either "he is not here"
or "he does not eat here." The word "est" is an alternate form of the Latin "edit"
= "he eats." The speaker hopes that the murderer interprets the words in the first
sense. But a lie is not involved (on this theory) because the second meaning is the
one the speaker intends.

The use of mental reservation opens the door to a basis for widespread distrust,
regardless of whether it technically provides an escape from lying. It may do as

much harm to confidence in human assurances. If we cannot interpret meaning in the ordinary way words are understood, but must constantly be on the lookout for hidden meanings, communication will become too complicated. David Hume combatted this tendency in his *Treatise of Human Nature*, Book III, in which he insisted that the obligation of a promise depended on the conventional meaning of words, not on some unorthodox interpretation placed on them by a hidden intention:

> The expression being once brought in as subservient to the will, soon becomes the principal part of the promise; nor will a man be less bound by his word, tho' he secretly give a different direction to his intention, and with-hold himself both from a resolution, and from willing an obligation.[26]

Insofar as we trace an obligation to tell the truth to the existence of a right on the part of the hearer to be told it, the use of deliberate equivocation, designed to mislead, does not seem to be in a category very different from straightforward lying. What it does, perhaps, is to make the deceiver a little less uncomfortable in the deception. Apart from that, the arguments that might justify this form of deception might be deployed equally well in defence of lying. Nyberg offers us a less complicated picture or, rather, a picture in which the complications are located in the factual realm rather than in the contrivance of mental reservation.

Mental reservation may be difficult to employ when a continuous set of deceptions must be maintained. Nyberg relates how, during the Nazi occupation, a Dutchwoman deceived her neighbours about an expected baby due to be born to a Jewish family who had taken refuge in her home. She concealed this by "progressively padding herself with layers of clothing, letting others believe she was pregnant. None were surprised when a new baby appeared in the house."[27] It can be assumed that, along with the padding, a suitable false story was told to the neighbours to keep them from asking questions about where the baby came from.

The need for invoking mental reservation can be avoided if we accept Nyberg's proposal for the definition of a lie. In Nyberg's view a lie has four parts: it is a statement, a belief in the mind of the statement-maker, an intention, and involves the character and rights of the person addressed. Just as Grotius had argued that the intending assassin has no right to the truth, Nyberg takes the position that, if we think the assassin has no right to expect us to tell the truth according to the "ordinary mutual trust obligations in conversation," then he is "no longer operating within the context in which truth telling and lying can be sensibly defined. The very ideas of true and false are inappropriate and irrelevant, and so lying does not enter as a possibility." The lie "cannot be committed when truth is irrelevant." Jokes and tall tales told around the campfire, etc. also are removed from the area in which "true" and "false" are appropriate. Hence, Nyberg defines lying as "making a statement (not too vague) you want somebody to believe, even though you don't (completely) believe it yourself, when the other person has a right to expect you to mean what you say."[28]

The proposal may work well with jokes, irony, and other cases where people know and expect some blarney. But in the joke situation, both parties know and understand that no serious underwriting of what is said is straightforwardly intended (of course, one can have serious things to say through jests). By contrast, does the assassin share with the respondent the sense that a new game is being played, in which what is said cannot be expected to be treated as true or false? Quite likely not. And if the respondent gives any cue that a special game is in progress, the assassin will be tipped off. If the respondent is not harbouring the victim, he might well want the assassin to believe him when he says so. If he is harbouring the victim, he will not want to let on that he is playing any game. On the contrary, he will want his lie to be believed. Either way, the attempt to remove the situation from the realm where true and false apply does not seem convincing, and we are led back to Grotius's view. Perhaps if the assassin knows in advance that the respondent is a Nybergian, then he knows that there is a game in progress, but in that case he will take no account of the respondent's answer.

Nyberg's proposal is that, in telling falsehoods in the context of entertainment or danger, the "burden of having to justify uttering falsehoods is lifted completely."[29] That burden is certainly lifted if communicator and communicatee are both in agreement. If they are not, the burden remains, although one way of discharging it is to say that the context is one in which the communicatee "ought to know" or can be "presumed to know" that the communicator does not feel bound by the ordinary norms of truth-telling. However, this in turn would need justification, so the burden does not disappear so easily.

DIRTY-HANDS ARGUMENTS

The "dirty-hands" problem deals with variations on the theme of lying to save lives or killing to prevent more numerous killings. Arthur Koestler put the case for selective use of violence well, at a general level, when he had one of his fictional characters say about people who are averse to vivisection that "if these people had their say, we would have no serums against cholera, typhoid, or diphtheria."[30] But real people, not lower animals, are the subject of discussion. What seems like a disease in the body politic to some may appear to others as a liberation movement, as Koestler himself illustrates so well in *Darkness at Noon*. The consequential reasoning portrayed here does not differ much in form from that which lay behind the execution of heretics. In a strongly Christian era, when attention was focused on eternal life, it was appalling to think that some souls would be led to eternal damnation through heresy. In the light of that thought, executing a few heretics from time to time was felt to be a small price to pay, especially since the heretics themselves might be converted in time to save their own souls. This observation is not meant as a *reductio* (*ad absurdam*—proving the falsity of an argument by showing its conclusion to be absurd) of Koestler's case for the selective use of violence, but only as a way of engendering caution against assuming that the way in which consequences are computed is the right one.

Among those who have had wise things to say about the "dirty hands" problem, Max Weber is one of the most profound. In his oft-cited "Politics as a Vocation," he introduces the important distinction between two kinds of ethics: the "ethics of conscience" or "ethics of ultimate ends" and the "ethics of responsibility." The first kind of ethics, epitomized by the Sermon on the Mount, is a call to imitate Jesus Christ or St. Francis by eschewing violence and by achieving one's ends through means other than compulsion. By contrast, the "ethics of responsibility" accepts the necessity of using violence to prevent the potential violence of others from being actualized against innocent people. The same goes for truthfulness. At the end of World War I, German politicians were all too ready to publish documents in the name of the duty of truthfulness, especially those that placed blame on their own country. One-sided confessions of guilt followed, without regard to consequences. The result was not the furthering of truth, but an unleashing of passion. The impossible demands of the Treaty of Versailles and the later hyper-inflation which resulted from insistence on some of its provisions paved the way for Hitler's rise. The ethics of conscience reveals the truth it happens to possess, without regard for the consequences of doing so. The believer in this ethic protests against injustice in the world by testifying to pure intentions; however, such acts can have only exemplary value and, in many cases, will have an outcome quite contrary to the good intentions of the believer. Weber says that it is fine to hold an austere ethics and, in doing so, to save one's soul, as long as one avoids political life; the ethics of conscience, or ultimate ends, is not suited to the practical world where rules must be enforced by the use of violence against offenders. It does not help solve crime or deter murderers and robbers for a civic magistrate to announce that victims or their relatives and friends should turn the other cheek and only do good by forgiving their enemy.[31]

By contrast, the ethics of responsibility allows one to exercise power with effective consequences for law and order. Party politics in modern democratic society means pandering to a wide variety of different groups and sympathizing with their often quite base motives, such as revenge, power, booty, and spoils, to maintain the necessary level of support. Some elect you because they expect spoils from your success; that means you have to be ready with a payoff. The effect of all this compromise and dubious dealing is likely to be corruption. As Weber says, the politician "lets himself in for the diabolic forces lurking in all violence."[32]

Having said that and having recognized that politics is a matter of the head over the heart, Weber cautions against "windbags" who are intoxicated with romantic notions about doing what is right regardless of the consequences. The politician who has his admiration and support is the one who, fully cognizant of the need for taking account of consequences, nevertheless is weighed down by the considerations that an ethic of conscience produces. "In so far as this is true, an ethic of ultimate ends and an ethic of responsibility are not absolute contrasts but rather supplements, which only in unison constitute a genuine man—a man who *can* have a 'calling for politics.'" Such a person will not crumble merely because the world is unwilling to embrace hard choices, through stupidity, small-mindedness, or the like; such a person retains some vision of what is right, which has motivated him or her from the beginning.[33]

In the end, Weber does not give us an answer to the "dirty hands" problem, although he canvasses in an enlightening manner the different dimensions it assumes, taking account of the character of those making decisions as well as the effects of these decisions on others. There is no simple ethical formula, such as the utilitarian for example, which can operate to lighten the conscience of the politician. Weber's world where both ethics are pertinent gives us politicians with troubled souls.

Michael Walzer has situated Weber's position between two extremes. The first is that of Machiavelli, whom he characterizes as exemplifying the ethic of responsibility untroubled with the ethic of conscience. The opposite is that presented by Camus, in such writings as *The Rebel*, or his play *The Just Assassins*,[34] in which there is nothing praiseworthy about undertaking violence against another, although to do so may be necessary to prevent further violence. If one judges that it is a duty to kill some other person, the ethic of solidarity requires that one lose one's own life in the process. Walzer sees in the spirit of this restriction a certain necessary brake on the potential injustice that an unreserved embracing of the ethic of consequences might engender. We should hold our politicians to act according to certain principles, and they should follow the rules—no dirty-dealing, protecting the rights of citizens, and so on. Cases, however, may arise where playing strictly according to the rules will allow evildoers to escape punishment or when rules have to be bent to protect the rest of us. If officials are caught breaking the rules, however, they have to be brought to account. Even if they were morally justified in doing what they did, we cannot openly and publicly allow this, because the consequence of doing so would likely encourage future rights-violations by the authorities. As Walzer notes, this makes the general public, which would adopt such a prosecution of well-intentioned public officials, a party to dirty-hands dealings. "[Hoederer] lies, manipulates, and kills, and we must make sure he pays the price. We won't be able to do that, however, without getting our own hands dirty, and then we must find some way of paying the price ourselves."[35] Fortunately for the general public, it has itself too thick a neck for hanging; its punishment is the loss of principled people from government service following application of this theory, with more cynical people taking their places, resulting in harm for the public.

Frank Knopfelmacher, an Australian psychology professor, deals with the dirty-hands problem in a way that resembles in one respect Nyberg's treatment of lying; that is, he demarcates an area where the ordinary rules governing not just lying but any aspect of morality do not apply. The rules of morality are only transactable within a relatively stable society in which institutions can flourish, so the first priority will be to establish those institutions, and that will require force of some kind. Here, the norm of pacifism is ultimately self-destructive, because absolute pacifism prevents the enforcement of the rules establishing the institutions. A key claim Knopfelmacher makes is: "If the moral norms were always absolutely valid, they would be nontransactable in practice because they would lead sooner or later to the destruction of the very social order through which alone they can be maintained, and which in itself has to be maintained by frequently immoral methods."[36] Whether or not he is right, his view seems to have the support of people in the highest reaches of some justice systems. Consider the following report on a US Supreme Court decision, which appeared in the *New York Times*:

> The Supreme Court ruled 6 to 3 today that the police may use deception to keep a defense lawyer away while they interrogate a criminal suspect. The Court upheld a Rhode Island murder conviction based on a confession obtained after the police did not inform the suspect that a lawyer retained by his sister was trying to reach him, and falsely told the lawyer that no interrogation was planned.

To rule otherwise, the court said, "would inhibit crime-fighting because lawyers would prevent guilty suspects from confessing."[37]

The task of the statesman, Knopfelmacher says, is essentially strategic: to establish and defend institutions. As a man of society, the politician obeys the Ten Commandments, but as a statesman he cannot do so because he may have to use violence, deception, and fraud in defence of the polity. Knopfelmacher distinguishes two sorts of acts: intra-institutional and meta-institutional. Intra-institutional acts are guided by the norms that define them morally in an absolute manner. "The norms proscribing killing, stealing, raping and cheating are absolutely valid, except for the trivial proviso that, at times, proscribed acts represent a lesser evil—a state of affairs statable both in deontological and utilitarian terms." On the other hand, meta-institutional acts are regulated by the ethic of responsibility, which safeguards the institutional structure within which the way of life unfolds itself. This does not mean that anything goes at the meta-institutional level, only that the ordinary rules of morality don't apply. "How far one can 'go' must be judged by the culturally well-formed ear. There are no rigid rules…. There are no meta-rules…." The objection that this lack of moral rule-determination might lead to totalitarian disregard for human rights is met by Knopfelmacher in the following way. A totalitarian such as Hitler turns the whole institutional structure into a pernicious social order. It is the ends that condemn the totalitarian, not the means; however, the totalitarian also permits any action that will promote the utopian vision. In Knopfelmacher's scenario, the meta-institutional ethical rule-holiday is subject to rule-governance regarding the morality to be protected.[38]

Knopfelmacher's theory is dangerous because of a human propensity to seek to increase one's power. Without meta-institutional rules governing their activity, officials may find it much too convenient to dispense with bothersome things like the rule of law. This in turn provokes resentment, reaction, and the need for more severe measures to keep "law and order." Eventually injustices may become so widespread that it becomes debatable whether the existing order deserves to be kept in being. Overthrow may in some circumstances be preferable.

ELITISM

Knopfelmacher's view promotes a certain elitism, allowing that some people at the top have to violate conventional norms for the good of everyone. Plato, expressing some embarrassment, also feels that the super-guardians of his state are entitled to deceive people into behaving in ways that are good for them. The idea of super-guardians is necessary, because Plato wants to convince the guardians themselves that they have a divine quality, which does not require earthly riches. He wants his guardians to live an austere existence, because their austerity will promote respect for authority and maintain the order of society. This order is based on a Phoenician myth of the time: the gods create some people from materials mingled with gold, others with silver, and still others with iron and brass. Character is fixed at birth and is usually, but not always, of the same kind as one's father's. Those with gold are fitted to be rulers, those with other metals are their helpers. Artisans and farmers are born with iron or brass in their genetic make-up. The guardians must carefully observe the newly born to determine which category they fit into and so which is their proper station in life.

For his ideal Republic, Plato also advocates eugenics, a "noble lie" that the guardians know and must keep secret from the people. Only the very best men and women should have children. In order to get the right people to breed, without causing others to be jealous, breeding takes place during festivals and sacrifices. People are chosen for breeding ostensibly by lottery, but in fact the alleged lottery is fixed. That way people can blame luck rather than the system. Young men who show excellence have more frequent intercourse with women. Inferior children are subject to clandestine euthanasia, while the children of superior people are raised in a communal crèche, and parents are kept from knowing which children are theirs.

Only the rulers, if anybody, have the right to lie, on Plato's account, and then only for the benefit of the state. For other people to lie would be to introduce "a practice as subversive and destructive of a state as it is of a ship."[39]

Plato's "noble lie" theory is not helped, for modern audiences, by the examples he chooses. Racist theory, which parallels his Phoenician parable, has been discredited by science and by its genocidal application by Hitler. However, the theory that an elite circle of governing people have the right, even the duty, to deceive the masses is a recurring phenomenon. In August 1985, secret arms deals were negotiated between the US and Iran, with proceeds going to fund CIA-backed rebel forces in Nicaragua. The deals were contrary to US policy, but those involved felt the deception was justified.[40] The British government deceived the public over the circumstances of the 1982 sinking of the *Belgrano*, which precipitated the Falklands/Malvinas War.[41] In the 1970s, senior officials of the RCMP felt that it was perfectly acceptable to withhold from the solicitor-general information about illegal activities in which they were engaged, such as barn-burning, letter-opening, and the theft of the Parti Québécois membership list. They believed that withholding information was not the same as lying, although the deception was as effective as if there had been a lie. A Commission of Inquiry into the RCMP activities produced the following interesting treatment of the subject in its report:

> When we speak of "truth," "candour" and being "forthcoming," we intend to convey that a Minister is entitled to expect a public servant to meet those standards not only when a Minister expressly asks a question, but even when silence will cause a Minister to be misled or to be ignorant of that which his position in responsible government should require him to know. It would therefore be unacceptable to attempt to prevent the Minister from learning of illegalities being committed by members of the Force, and it would also be unacceptable not to volunteer such information, if such be known.

In answering a question from the commission—"… are you stating openly and unequivocally that the Force had meant never to let the Solicitor General, whoever he was, know of practices or operations that were not authorized or provided for by law?"—an assistant commissioner of the force responded, "Yes, sir."[42]

In all of these cases, the holders of power decided that deception of the public was for the public's own good. The RCMP were combatting both legal and illegal attempts to promote the breakup of Canada and felt justified in taking unorthodox and illegal actions for that end. In the case of Iran-Contra, the Cold War opposition to Communism and the influence of the Soviet Union and Cuba justified the high-stakes game of deception in the eyes of the participants in the scandal. In the case of Britain and the Falklands, it was clearly important from the British military point of view to get the shooting war started quickly to avoid prolonged costly maintenance of armed forces so far from Britain.

Since rule of law is one of the cardinal tenets of what most people regard as an acceptable democracy, and since the principle of rule of law was violated in the cases described, one would think that strong disciplinary action was taken against those involved in the illegalities. But, despite revelations of their involvements, Oliver North ran for public office in the US with a lot of popular support despite his role in the Iran-Contra affair; Margaret Thatcher's Conservative government suffered no great lasting disgrace in Britain; and in Canada some of the illegal practices of the RCMP were legalized, although with numerous safeguards. It is true that violations of the rule of law have been strongly condemned, but the elitist view has a substantial body of acceptance, not just among the elite, but among the masses, who perhaps are not always enthusiastic about the responsibilities involved with participatory democracy.

MISLEADING WITHOUT ACTUALLY LYING

There are many ways of misleading people without actually lying. We have already encountered the use of equivocal language and the case of misleading by not saying things.

1. *Ignoring.* One powerful form of directing minds is the systematic non-attention by the mass media to things that deserve attention. In order to ensure the defeat of Upton Sinclair's candidacy for Governor of California in 1934, the *Los Angeles Times* ignored him and his radical political movement, not bothering to cover his public speaking engagements, and publishing a story claiming that he was un-Christian and attacked the Bible.[43] A wealth of recent examples is regularly provided by FAIR (Fairness and Accuracy in Reporting), such as Jim Naureckas's observation that a consortium of news outlets, including the *New York Times,* the *Washington Post,* Tribune Co. (*Newsday's* parent company), the *Wall Street Journal,* Associated Press, and CNN chose to downplay its own finding that if the Florida overvotes had properly been accounted for in the 2000 presidential election, Al Gore would have won. An overvote refers to such things as a voter punching the hole next to a candidate's name and writing in the same candidate's name. "Since the intent of the voter is clear, these are clearly valid votes under Florida law," wrote Naureckas.[44]

A Canadian philosopher, Hans Classen, has observed how important evaluations are communicated by subtle shifts of attention brought about by changes in phrasing:

> When Communist China decided to modify its relentlessly hostile attitude toward the United States the conciliatory gesture was made not to "The United States of America," but to "the people of the United States." One could argue that there is no logical difference between the two, that the United States of America embraces all the people of the United States, and that the people of the United States is what makes up the United States of America. But logic is not of the essence in such subtle propagandistic maneuverings. By suddenly discovering the "people" behind, or beneath, the official facade the formerly hostile government can create the illusion that it has not necessarily shifted its stance but has merely extended the hand of friendship to a whole new entity, an entity that had, so to speak, always been waiting there, dormant, yearning, basically uncorrupted, ready for the glad tidings.

Classen also observed that the CBC did not wait for official recognition of China to use the expression "the people of China" to refer to the mainland Chinese. However, it did not refer to "the people of Spain" or "the people of Portugal" but to "the Franco regime," or "the Salazar regime." Among Allied nations during World War II, "the German people" ceased to exist; Germans were always referred to as "Nazis."[45]

Sometimes the ignoring is unintentional, which can be worse than deliberate. To be noticed by an enemy indicates at least having some status. To be ignored indicates powerlessness—that one does not count or even appear in the other's perceptual horizon. English-speaking Canadians, when talking about newspaper monopolies, sometimes forget to take into account the existence of French-language newspapers, such as Ottawa's *Le Droit*. Black African men under colonial rule were often called "boys" and faced the insulting understanding that the "anybody" in the question "Is anybody here?" referred only to whites. Ignoring can take the form of excluding a whole class of individuals from the meaning of the term "person." First Nations people, slaves, those purged by the Soviet government, Jews, and women have all been designated at one time as nonpersons. Currently foetuses in the womb have been so regarded in the law of Canada and the US, and some philosophers would not view personhood as applicable to newborn humans.[46] Nations can be ignored by not recognizing their existence. Some Arabs would prefer not to speak of "Israel" but of the "Zionist entity." For a long time, the existence of "Palestine" was ignored.

Photographs of civilian damage during US bombing raids in Tripoli, Lebanon, Grenada, Iraq, and Afghanistan have been conspicuously absent in major US media, as tight control over journalistic activity came to be adopted by the military in the post-Vietnam era.

2. *Presupposing.* Paul Grice points out that it is a convention of language to provide a maximum of information available during the time of a given conversational space. This follows from his more general characterization of what he has termed the "co-operative principle," namely, the principle that in our communications it is tacitly presupposed that people will give as much information of the right kind and that is relevant and perspicacious as will be helpful to the person with whom we are communicating.[47] Of course, people do not always follow the cooperative principle, but its existence allows for misdirection. One should be able to upbraid people for violations of the principle, since such violations erode confidence in it and in the value of conversation accordingly. We do not say things we presume people know already. Paradoxically, when we do say things people are presumed to know, we can create confusion or suspicions. For example, one might begin a rumour by saying, "the Right Honourable Prime Minister is not a sheep-stealer." What does one know about the prime minister that would cause one to make such a statement? Does the prime minister steal other things? Has someone made an accusation of sheep-stealing? Thus, we do not omit, or we should try not to omit, to say things we think people will not know and which are important for understanding what we are trying to communicate. The denial falsely presupposes the existence of the rumour, making people alert to hear it. This kind of denial also stimulates "psychological availability," described earlier, and so conditions people to be receptive to the relevant rumour. J.J. MacIntosh has provided a fine example: "If I remark that I have not seen my bank manager

sober in the past three months, and it turns out that I have not seen her, drunk or sober, in the past three months, you have a right to feel I have misled you."[48]

3. *Associating.* One very subtle way in which to affect the attitudes of people towards a targeted individual or group is to associate the person with negative happenings or features. The connection may be as tenuous as contiguity of picture and unrelated story in a newspaper, which, when repeated, is bound to have some impact on our thinking and feeling. Fred Landis describes convincingly how the CIA-funded *El Mercurio* in Chile engaged in this tactic, by placing pictures of Salvador Allende's government ministers next to rape stories. The same tactic has been used by newspapers opposing left-wing leaders, including *La Prensa* of Nicaragua and the *Daily Gleaner* of Jamaica.[49]

One of the pioneers of this technique was US Senator Joe McCarthy, whose name is associated with the expression "guilt by association." He named Communists with whom some target individual was associated in one way or another, without dwelling on whether the association was significant or not. The mere repetition of the target name in the context of so many Communists helped to seal the impression that the target shared the same political persuasion. "If it walks like a duck, quacks like a duck, and associates with ducks, I assume it is a duck," was the reasoning this tactic encouraged.

Arthur Miller's play *The Crucible*, written with McCarthyism in mind, drew attention to the chilling effect this kind of attack could have. Anyone who spoke out against the use of this tactic found themselves targeted, and fear worked to dampen expression of revulsion, as some potential targets became more interested in avoiding damaging associations or drawing attention to their own possible vulnerability.[50] Of course, there are many different ways in which to make use of associations. Miller's play itself associates McCarthyism with early American witch-hunts. The ethical question revolves around whether the claimed associations are legitimate or not.

Repetition can create a certain association. In Canada when Progressive-Conservative Party leader Robert Stanfield was challenging Liberal leader Pierre Trudeau in an electoral contest, he was pictured on television fumbling a football pass. He had caught many passes, but the cameras picked up one instance where he missed it, and the repetition of this single event created the impression of a fumbler.

These are only a few of many examples where one can mislead without actually lying. It is time to examine the ethics of such practices.

THE ETHICS OF COMMUNICATION

Jürgen Habermas

Jürgen Habermas points out how the goal of truthful communication is not captured adequately when we focus our concerns only upon the literal correspondence between reality and what a person claims. We have seen how it is possible to mislead without saying anything literally false. Habermas takes his key from J.L. Austin's writings, in particular the notion of "performative utterance": certain words in certain contexts do not report some already existing truth; they make something true by the fact of their utterance. Typically, "I promise ..." is a performative utterance, because it does not report a preexisting promise; rather, the form of words institutes a promise under appropriate circumstances.[51]

Habermas posits certain rules as underlying communication.[52] All smoothly functioning language rests on a background consensus, formed from the mutual recognition of at least four different types of validity claims in our speech acts. (The expression "speech act" is used to designate the range of different utterances: statements, questions, commands, exclamations, etc.) These are:

1. the utterance is understandable;
2. its propositional content is true;
3. the speaker is sincere in uttering it; and
4. it is appropriate for the speaker to be performing the speech act.

Habermas thinks that a speaker is always accountable for these norms of meaningfulness, truthfulness, sincerity, and appropriateness. One way of violating these norms is to insulate oneself from criticism by developing an impermeable, self-contained language system that defeats attempts to communicate with a general audience. You either swallow the ideology whole, or you ignore piecemeal attempts to criticize the system because the terms of criticism do not mesh with its ideologically loaded terms. Talking an economist's language, with its tacit translation of words like "better" or "beneficial" into "richer" or "greater prosperity," etc., makes it difficult to figure in such things as cultural identity, integrity, social conscience, equality, etc.

Truth in the largest sense, Habermas thinks, will be linked with the intention to promote the good and true life. If we want to evaluate the truth of an utterance in this largest sense, we must make sure that all types of validity claims are satisfied. Instead of the notion of the simple truth, of correspondence between what is said about the way things are and the way things are in fact, he prefers to talk about discursive justification. Truth should be seen as "warranted assertability," meaning that at all times and in any place, if we enter into a discourse, a consensus can be realized under conditions that identify it as a justified consensus. Therefore, we should pay attention to such things as whether relevant voices are being heard or whether constraints are placed on the speech situation, so that only one particular viewpoint gets adequately expressed. Ideally, everyone should have the same chance to criticize and question, and there should be unlimited discussion free from any constraints of domination. Without that, truth claims are not fully legitimate, because they have not been adequately tested before potentially contrary observations. On Habermas's view, "truth" cannot be analyzed independently of "freedom" and "justice." He does not say that a speech act is true only under these circumstances, but the ideal speech situation should be treated as a critical standard against which every actually realized consensus can be called into question and tested.

Habermas's view brings out what appears morally objectionable about many forms of propaganda. Propaganda is often felt to be a constraint. In virtually all forms there is no genuine dialogue. Typically, the slogans of the propagandist are ubiquitous. Symbols, pictures, and the like insinuate without necessarily stating. These communications are very far from the ideal speech situation. The propagandist's message is not a case of warranted assertability. Habermas's theory is well-suited to furthering democracy, because it ultimately favours development of autonomy for everybody.

However, familiar Platonic objections can be raised. Truth about how to pilot a ship needs to be acted upon by a knowledgeable captain before a consensus can be expected to be achieved among an ignorant crew. With scientific knowledge, the truth may lie for a time with an expert few, rather than with the untutored many. A view presented under conditions of constraint on the audience may still be true, even though the mode of presentation (perhaps involving unwillingness to give equal time to popular and accepted theories, for example) might discredit the communicator in the light of Habermas's test for legitimacy. A view might still be true, even though held illegitimately according to the test.

Thus, there may be situations where one might reasonably require constraints on free expression, although acceptance of this fact could open the door to great abuses. Take, for example, the illegal pursuit of war against another country. Discussion might be silenced on the ground that the country is now at war, prejudging in that way the whole question of whether the country *should* be at war, a question very worthy of debate. Habermas provides us with a valuable linkage between the public discourse of governing officials, and the question of the legitimacy of such government, assessed in the light of the transparency or opaqueness of their discourse and of the opportunity for rebuttal.

Richard Whately

As the author of numerous editions of books on logic and rhetoric early in the nineteenth century, Richard Whately made important contributions to the ethics of rhetoric, notably concerning influences on the emotions.[53] He recognizes that in most people's minds the appeal to emotions is considered a dishonest device to manipulate them into accepting what they would not accept by reason alone.

However, like David Hume, Whately takes the view that reason alone does not provide the galvanizing force to get people to act. The intellectual recognition that some acts need to be carried out is not the same as a strong impetus to carry them out, any more than the conviction of a man blind from birth that a given coat is of a certain colour gives him the experience of that colour. You need emotions to persuade people to do things. Granted, orators do sometimes influence the will with improper appeals, but they also can misuse reason that way. Whately says it seems "commonly taken for granted that whenever the feelings are excited they are of course over-excited." But, he says, the reverse is at least as often the case. That is, people are often dispassionate and disinterested when they should be moved to action:

> The more generous feelings, such as Compassion, Gratitude, Devotion, nay, even rational and rightly-directed Self-Love, Hope, and Fear, are oftener defective than excessive; and that, even in the estimation of the parties themselves, if they are well-principled, judicious, reflective, and candid men.

He is surely right in his claim that appeals to emotions are not necessarily wrong, and may well be justified in a majority of cases. Along the way, he provides useful insights into the question of how to influence the emotions. The peculiar thing about the emotions is that they are not under our direct control. We cannot suddenly feel angry or fearful at will, any more than we can successfully will our hearts directly to beat faster. But we can control our emotions indirectly. If we want to make our hearts beat faster, we can climb stairs or run. Likewise, if we want to feel angry, we can think about some conspicuous injustices or stupidities resulting in the deaths of worthy individuals, perhaps from unnecessary contamination of the water supply. If we want to feel calm and benevolent, we might reflect on the lives of people who have borne suffering and injustice heroically, such as many of the saints. In Whately's words:

> So again, if a man of sense wishes to allay in himself any emotion, that of resentment for instance, though it is not under the direct control of the Will, he deliberately sets himself to reflect on the softening circumstances; such as the provocations the other party may suppose himself to have received; perhaps, his ignorance, or weakness, or disordered state of health:—he endeavours to imagine himself in the place of the offending party;—and above all, if he is a sincere Christian, he meditates on the parable of the debtor who, after having been himself forgiven, claimed payment with rigid severity from his fellow-servant; and on other similar lessons of scripture.

Whately understood well, with Quintilian, that people's emotions can be stirred not just by exhortation, but also by descriptions. It is one thing to say someone was wounded, but it is much more moving to describe the wound in detail. In today's world, we recognize that television pictures of starving children can be much more moving than the mere statement that so many children have been affected by a famine.

Having granted that appeal to emotions can be justified, Whately nevertheless identifies an important ethical problem connected with emotional appeals: people resent the implication that they are in some way so morally deficient that they need to have such things as feelings of compassion aroused. Even if a person admits that he or she is in need of some moral awakening, there is likely to be some negative feeling toward the orator: "The mind is sure to revolt from the humiliation of being thus moulded and fashioned, in respect to its feelings, at the pleasure of another; and is apt, perversely, to resist the influence of such a discipline." Of course, if the orator is trying to instill unsuitable motives for the benefit of a special interest, the resentment will be much greater. In any case, in both these situations, Whately claims that appeals to the emotions should not be identified plainly as such:

> The first and most important point to be observed in every address to any Passion, Sentiment, Feeling, etc. is ... that it should not be introduced as such, and plainly avowed; otherwise the effect will be, in great measure, if not entirely, lost.

The ethical problem that presents itself is the apparent necessity for some lack of candour. There is arguably something wrong with a method of persuasion that cannot pass the test of publicity. Or can it? If Whately is right, we might recognize, indeed, our propensity to feel resentment at having our emotions under the sway of the orator, even though we agree the job needs to be done. If that is so, we might give our moral assent in theory to this lack of candour, even though we might still feel resistance in an actual case in which we are the targets of the emotion-rousing acts. In that way, the publicity test would be satisfied on a theoretical basis. In sum, we could concur with the orator dissimulating about what he or she is doing when influencing our emotions is involved. That we should feel resentment when we find out about the dissimulation does not morally invalidate it, any more than resentment against getting a ticket for speeding nullifies our judgment that it is right for the traffic cop to give it to us. It has to be emphasized, though, that we are talking about the case where the emotion is rightly called forth. If our emotions are manipulated for the special interests of the orator, of which we don't approve, we have good reason to object morally to the methods used.

PARTY FEELING

Before leaving Whately, it is worth taking into account some very commendable and pertinent remarks he makes about civilized discourse in connection with what he calls "party feeling."[54] By this he means the tendency to identify strongly with a group—whether by religion, nation, family, political leanings, or whatever. It exists when there is an "us versus them" mentality. At the time he wrote, religion was the cause of acrimonious division, but the same remarks are applicable to political, linguistic, and ethnic loyalties today.

Whately observes that party feeling—the kind of feeling that we encourage with political rallies, national celebrations, sports, school teams, and the like—is bound up with our nature and makes important things such as government possible, but it has also been the cause of the "most gigantic wars." (Whately was writing in 1822, following Napoleon, but this is even truer about the two twentieth-century world wars.) It is necessary to come to terms with this feeling, he says. Carried to extremes it makes people lose their sense of proportion. What starts as a verbal, symbolic, or political action as a means to some legitimate goal can come to take precedence over the ends sought. Those engaged in the battle may come to prefer the power, the leadership, and the glory to finding acceptable solutions. This can lead to disaster.

Whately condemns not party feeling as such, but excess of it. He identifies four causes leading to this excess: the desire of taking the lead; the desire for some excitement or novelty; love of disputation; and pride, or what we might today call ego-gratification, bound up with triumph over an opponent. We can see these destructive forces at work today, in some of the triumphal sectarian marches that take place in Northern Ireland. The advice he gives to combat these generators of violence is intended to get people thinking about their own conduct, not to give them additional means for finding fault with others. However, peace-lovers might profitably encourage their political and other leaders to abide by these maxims.

1. *Regarding ourselves.* We should beware of mistaking the meaning of anyone and imputing to our opponents feelings which they do not really entertain. We should make due allowance for the intellectual failings opponents may have and the likelihood they might make inaccurate statements unintentionally and without necessarily being malevolent. We should not jump to the conclusion that those who differ from us merely in temperament and outlook are for that reason immoral.

2. *Regarding others.* We must be prepared to find our opponents liable to the same faults as ourselves, including bitterness. We should counteract, or at least avoid promoting, those faults. As a practical matter, we should guard against putting our case too simplistically, in a way easily rebutted. We should avoid inflaming the spirit of controversy by assuming the polemical style, where an instructive style, in the spirit of truth-seeking, would be more suitable. We should take a comprehensive view of any question, instead of being exclusively occupied in answering every quibble that may be brought forwards. The argument should be tailored to the ends either of convincing those who are opponents, or of warning others away from false beliefs. In other words, we should be thinking about the likely impact of what we say, and whether it is likely to accomplish our objective.

3. *Regarding the subject matter.* We should avoid thinking that we understand something merely by the fact that the name is familiar.

4. *Regarding language.* We need to guard against the ambiguity of terms. We should not judge rashly other people's doctrines from their phraseology, and we should not insist that they use the same terms as ourselves. We should avoid adhering too closely to expressions that have been made, or are likely to become, the cant language of a party. Such language has a tendency to engender "strifes about words." (This last piece of advice is especially appropriate to debates about abortion, where insistence on having an opponent adopt one's own terminology can prevent genuine dialogue from taking place.)

Whately recognizes the strength of the argument that "if bad men combine, good men must unite" and allows that reaction may sometimes be necessary. But he cautions that, if all the evils are laid at the door of our opponents, "we shall see no need for caution against these evils, in our own conduct." "If we are not charitable in interpreting the motives of others, we may find ourselves aggravating the very errors we oppose," he wrote.

Acrimonious debate and an increase in "party feeling" do not necessarily lead to violence, but they greatly increase the risk that a vicious spiral of violent activity will get underway. Whately's precepts deserve to be taken to heart by politicians and other opinion shapers.

ON THE ETHICS OF PROPAGANDA

Enough has been said to be able to draw from the foregoing at least a preliminary sketch of some ways in which propaganda should be assessed morally.

First, insofar as we see propaganda as aimed at provoking action of some sort, it must be evaluated in the light of such action. If the acts aim at conquest motivated by greed or adventure, the propaganda promoting this is wrong.

Secondly, even when the object sought is good—for example, the defeat of a tyrant—the means chosen may go beyond acceptable limits. Was it necessary to promote racism or ethnic hatred to defeat the Germans and Japanese? The Allied war effort in World War II spread stereotypes of Japanese soldiers as sneaky, slant-eyed, buck-toothed men desirous of rape, sadism, and other evils, and of the German as a monocle-wearing, steely individual, capable of torture. Such stereotypes are likely to interfere with the civilized conduct of war (if there can be such a thing, Geneva Convention notwithstanding) and with the goal of peace. We have already seen how the atrocity propaganda in World War I built up hatreds that made the punitive provisions of the Treaty of Versailles so hard to resist, in turn sowing the seeds for World War II.

An example of the hazards of making use of existing racial or nationalist stereotypes or feelings can be found in a description, prior to World War I, by the noted scholar of crowd psychology, Gustav Le Bon, of his own attempts at shaping opinion in his community. A park in a Paris suburb was threatened with development. The people were not aware of this because the official name of the park, Villeneuve-l'Etang, was different from that by which the people knew it, St.-Cloud. After trying unsuccessfully to interest the press or the civic administration—which needed money from the sale—Le Bon resorted to the following persuasive technique. He found that the only serious buyer for the park was a German Jew, and he sent a note to a large newspaper announcing, "Sale of St. Cloud Park to the Germans." There was an immediate explosion of interest: masses of reporters descended on the community, and sensational articles appeared in the press. A political decision was quickly made during the outcry not to sell the park in the present or the future. Le Bon succeeded, in a good cause. However, he also added fuel to the potent force of nationalism and possibly to anti-Semitism. He does not say whether his note included reference to the buyer being Jewish, but the fact that he mentions this detail in his book suggests that he may also have done so in his note to the newspaper.[55] This was, after all, only 10 years after the uproar over the Dreyfuss Affair. The attitudes harnessed in his appeal, and thus reinforced by it, led shortly to total war, and a generation after that to genocide.

With hindsight, one can say that Le Bon's tactic was unethical because of the potent forces for evil that he encouraged (although at the time he did so without awareness, one can presume, of the full extent of this potential). However, acting as an early urban environmentalist saving a park, Le Bon at least was promoting a public good, thus providing a mitigating factor to his action.

Thirdly, while good arguments have been given for the use of emotional levers in persuasion, there is often resentment against this method for reasons mentioned above. These reasons become magnified when propagandist and propagandee strongly disagree about the morality of the end the propaganda is directed at achieving. We do not mind too much when our heartstrings are pulled for support of some downtrodden or starving group, but when disputing parties on, say, abortion, produce pictures and use tendentious language in support of their causes, they typically are led into increased hostility with no more light being thrown on the disputed question. If you see the other side as fundamentally wrong, the use of manipulative persuasive means will be seen as compounding the wrong. Furthermore, each side is concerned that the other side will win over a sizable part of the population through such means, without their own side getting an adequate hearing.

These observations support the idea of restraint in the use of emotional appeals, but not eliminating them altogether. Quite apart from Whately's reasons, there is Aristotle's point that appropriate style increases credibility; in other words, if the issue is morally powerful, it is right to speak with appropriate emotion. As Aristotle puts it:

> Appropriate style also makes the fact appear credible; for the mind of the hearer is imposed upon under the impression that the speaker is speaking the truth, because, in such circumstances. his feelings are the same, so that he thinks (even if it is not the case as the speaker puts it) that things are as he represents them; and the hearer always sympathises with one who speaks emotionally,

even though he really says nothing. This is why speakers often confound their hearers by mere noise.[56]

A fine example of a powerful communication having even greater force for its garbled syntax and literal near-unintelligibility is provided by Richard Lanham. He quotes the conductor Richter's impatient comment to the second flautist at Covent Garden: "Your damned nonsense can I stand twice or once, but some-times always, my God, never!"[57] The moral, amply supported by Lanham's other writings, is that we speak or write in a certain situation that may demand from us certain affective responses. If we ignore any semblance of passion in order to present some pure, distilled, objective truth, we may fall into a different kind of falsehood. Situational falsity might well coexist with efforts to preserve truth in our statements. Kierkegaard is a well-known exponent of this idea, illustrated by his story of the escaped lunatic who wants to persuade people he is sane by always saying something true. So he repeats saying "The world is round" over and over, but of course he is soon picked up again.[58]

All of this argues for the legitimacy of some appeals that will have the effect of by-passing the rational assessment of a communication; in other words, appeals that display a characteristic we have located in propaganda. It should be noted that we are thinking here of a sincere expression of emotion, not a stance cynically adopted to provide maximum impact. Whately makes a good practical point about simulated emotion. The person who becomes accustomed to engaging in histrionics even for justifiable reasons runs the risk of developing the habit of com-municating in ways that lack candour. The habit of disregarding right reason, truth, and fair argument in favour of emotional excess is not a habit easily unlearnt. He thinks this is debasing to moral character but also "ends up depriving the rhetori-cian of that air of simple truthfulness which has so winning a force and which is so impossible completely to feign."[59]

CONCLUSION: PROPAGANDA AND AUTONOMY

Propaganda, in the light of the definition we have adopted, involves manipula-tion of some kind. That is to say, it involves some form of misleading commu-nication, emotional pressure, appeals to the subconscious, and suchlike. In all such cases the autonomy of individuals is infringed, unless it is clear that these same individuals give approval to this activity. For example, as we have already seen, just as someone may prefer not to know the whole truth about his or her disease, so also someone may wish, in time of war, to be presented with atrocity stories in order to remove qualms and stimulate more enthusiasm among the troops, thus increasing the odds of winning. A Kantian defence of conscription refers to what a rational person would be deemed to accept. Autonomy in that way is not to be infringed, even though the demand that you lay down your life for the state seems the antithesis of autonomy. A similar argument can be made in defence of propaganda under very special circumstances, where preservation of the state is involved. A key assumption of this argument is that the individual rationally accepts both the need for preserving the state and, therefore, the obligation to come to its defence when under attack. However, if an individual feels that the state has too much power, that the war benefits the wealthy class and not the poor, and that all in all the state as so constituted is not worth defending, at least by this or that disadvantaged individual, then there is a real objection mountable on the basis of autonomy-violation.

The reverse side of this picture is the all-too-willing acceptance of propaganda under circumstances when it is unworthy to do so. Some people do not want to have the agony of decision-making. They would rather leave the problems of religion, life, and morality, to institutions such as the Church hierarchy or to some political saviour. So they give their assent to propaganda. This is one of Ellul's dominant themes: so many people want life to be simpler, and propaganda in its nature provides the illusion they want. Assuming this to be so, does the argument for condemning propaganda by reason of its autonomy-violation still have force? On the surface, the people targeted give their assent, and, as the saying goes, *volenti non fit injuria*—"to the consenting no wrong is done." However, it may be argued there is a wrong done against oneself in forfeiting an aspect of autonomy that should always be retained. If that is so, the propagandist becomes a co-conspirator in the joint effort to, in effect, partly enslave some willing people. Of course, in reply it can be argued that religious people sometimes surrender their autonomy to an abbot, and it would be presumptuous to regard this religious life as less moral than others. But there is, or ought to be, a difference in motivation. The religious calling places a life of prayer above all else and sets aside those things that, for such an existence, are a distraction. Such things include the continual openness to competing life choices and the constant study of challenging opinions from the irreligious. This approach is a reasoned one, and if one accepts the validity of a religious existence, it genuinely preserves the autonomy of what would otherwise be a loss of autonomy. In much the same way a husband and wife give up aspects of autonomy in order to give rise to a new expression of their autonomic choices. Without such a reasoned justification, the argument is sound that willingness to be propagandized does not automatically legitimize the propaganda. More will be said on autonomy in the context of arguments from John Stuart Mill in the next chapter.

NOTES

1   See for example Leviticus 20: 10-18, contrasted with 19:18 and with Matthew 5: 43-44 and
     7:1-5.

2   Plato, *The Republic*, I, 331c-332a; John Rawls, *A Theory of Justice* (Cambridge, MA, Harvard
     University Press), 48-50.

3   David Nyberg, *The Varnished Truth* (Chicago, IL: University of Chicago Press, 1993).

4   Sisella Bok, *Lying: Moral Choice in Public and Private Life* (New York: Pantheon Books, 1978).

5   St. Augustine of Hippo, "On Lying," *Treatises of Various Subjects*, vol. 16, ed. Roy J. Deferrari, Fathers of the Church (New York: Catholic University of America Press, 1952) 56.

6   Augustine, "Against Lying," *Treatises of Various Subjects*, vol. 16, ed. Roy J. Deferrari, Fathers of the Church (New York: Catholic University of America Press, 1952) 162.

7   St. Augustine, "On Lying" 57-58.

8   Augustine, "On Lying" 61 and 102.

9   Augustine, "Against Lying" 173.

10 St. Thomas Aquinas, *Summa Theologica*, trans. Fathers of the English Dominican Province (New York, Boston et al.: Benziger Brothers Inc., 1947) 2.2 ques. 110, arts. 2 and 3, 1664-1667.

11 Adapted from Immanuel Kant, *Fundamental Groundwork of the Metaphysic of Morals*, trans. H.J. Paton (New York: Harper and Row, Harper Torchbooks, 1964), 89-90.

12 Immanuel Kant, "On a Supposed Right to Lie from Altruistic Motives," *Critique of Practical Reason and Other Writings in Moral Philosophy*, ed. and trans. Lewis White Beck (Chicago, IL: University of Chicago Press, 1949).

13 Grotius, *On the Law of War and Peace*, trans F.W. Kelsey (New York: Bobbs-Merrill, 1925), bk 3, ch1, XI.

14 Grotius XII, XII.

15 Plato, *The Republic*, Book III, 389c and Book V, 459c.

16 See Kant, "On a Supposed Right to Lie from Altruistic Motives," excerpted in Bok 268-69. His foil was Benjamin Constant, but the ideas were similar to Grotius's.

17 Edward Dicey, "The Ethics of Political Lying," *Nineteenth Century* (June, 1889): 789-794. Direct quotes below are taken from this source.

18 *New York Times*, 25 February 1996.

19 Henry Sidgwick, *The Methods of Ethics*, 7th ed. (London: Macmillan, 1907); excerpted in Bok 273.

20 Bok 60.

21 Bok 24.

22 Bok 105.

23 Nyberg 25 and 5. The Steiner quotation is from George Steiner, *After Babel: Aspects of Language and Translation*, 3rd ed. (New York: Oxford University Press, 1998) 224. Curiously, Steiner invokes Socrates in defence of his view, claiming that Socrates' case in the *Lesser Hippias* is that "the man who utters falsehood intentionally is to be preferred to the one who lies inadvertently or involuntarily" (230). The dialogue is clearly a *reductio* of the view that doing wrong intentionally is better than doing it involuntarily and Steiner himself recognizes that the dialogue might have been "ironically *a contrario*," as he puts it (230). The dialogue puts clearly on the map the distinction between being skilled at doing something and using this skill for a good purpose. Steiner papers over this distinction with the word "preferred." Socrates clearly cannot accept that the man who utters falsehood is the better person and, thus, is to be preferred overall, even though he recognizes that such a man may be preferred for his skill.

24 Nyberg 59-60. Virginia Woolf, interestingly enough, was the niece of Sir James Fitzjames Stephen and thus biographically linked with the circle of thinkers mentioned earlier for whom the question of lying was a recurring preoccupation.

25 Albert R. Jonsen and Stephen Toulmin, *The Abuse of Casuistry: A History of Moral Reasoning* (Berkeley, CA: University of California Press, 1988) 205.

26 David Hume, *A Treatise of Human Nature*, ed. L.A. Selby-Bigge (1888; Oxford: Clarendon Press, 1960) 523.

27 Nyberg 151, quoting Samuel Oliner and Pearl Oliner, *The Altruistic Personality* (New York: Free Press, 1988) 107. A fictional treatment of this kind of problem of deception is included in Hilda van Stockum's *The Borrowed House* (Bathgate, ND: Bethlehem Books, 2000).

28 Nyberg 49, 50.

29 Nyberg 50.

30 See Arthur Koestler, *Darkness at Noon*, trans. Daphne Hardy (1941; New York: Signet Books, 1956) 117.

31 Gerth and Mills 77-128.

32 Gerth and Mills 125, 126.

33 Gerth and Mills 127, 128.

34 Albert Camus, *The Rebel* (Harmondsworth: Penguin, 1962); *Caligula and Three Other Plays* (New York: Knopf, 1958).

35 Michael Walzer, "Political Action and the Problem of Dirty Hands," *War and Moral Responsibility*, ed. Marshall Cohen, Thomas Nagel, and Thomas Scanlon (Princeton, NJ: Princeton University Press, 1974) 62-82. Hoederer is the exponent of the untrammeled ethic of responsibility in Jean-Paul Sartre's play, *Les Mains Sales (Dirty Hands)*, trans. *Crime Passionel* (London: Methuen, 1949).

36 Frank Knopfelmacher, "The Ethic of Responsibility," *Liberty and Politics*, ed. Owen Harries (New South Wales: Pergamon Press, 1976) 38-47.

37 *New York Times*, 11 March 1986: A25.

38 Knopfelmacher 43.

39 Plato, *The Republic* V, 414c ff; V, 459d ff; III, 389bc.

40 The President's Special Review Board (John Tower, Chairman), *The Tower Commission Report* (New York: Bantam Books, 1987) *passim*, and The National Security Archive (Scott Armstrong, Executive Director) *The Chronology* (New York: Warner Books, 1987) *passim*.

41 Clive Ponting, *The Right to Know: The Inside Story of the Belgrano Affair* (London and Sidney: Sphere Books, 1985) *passim*.

42 Commission of Inquiry Concerning Certain Activities of the Royal Canadian Mounted Police, Third Report, *Certain RCMP Activities and the Question of Governmental Knowledge* (Ottawa: Supply and Services Canada, August 1981) 7-8.

43 Halberstam 167-68.

44 FAIR, November 15, 2001. See <http://www.fair.org/articles/media-recount.html>.

45 Hans Classen, "Who Is in Charge of the Nation?" *The Time Is Never Ripe* (Ottawa: Centaur Press, 1972) 179, 180.

46 See the valuable table drawn up by William Brennan in *Dehumanizing the Vulnerable: When Word Games Take Lives* (Chicago, IL: Loyola University Press, 1995) 7.

47 Paul Grice, "Logic and Conversation," *Studies in the Way of Words* (Cambridge, MA: Harvard University Press, 1989) 22-40, 28.

48 Example taken from Trudy Govier, ed., *Selected Issues in Logic and Communication* (Belmont, CA: Wadsworth, 1988).

49 Fred Landis, "CIA Psychological Warfare Operations," *Science for the People* (January/February 1982).

50 Arthur Miller, *The Crucible*, ed. Gerald Weales (New York: Viking Press, 1971).

51 This comes from J.L. Austin, "Performative Utterances," in his *Philosophical Papers*, ed. J.O. Urmson and G.J. Warnock (Oxford: Clarendon Press, 1961). See also J.L. Austin, *How to Do Things with Words* (Oxford: Clarendon Press, 1962).

52 Jürgen Habermas, *Legitimation Crisis*, trans. Thomas McCarthy (Boston: Beacon Press, 1975). See, especially, the translator's very helpful introduction, xiii–xxiii. Direct quotes in this text are taken from this source.

53 Richard Whately, *Elements of Rhetoric*, 7th ed. rev. 1846. Direct quotes below are taken from this source.

54 The material in this subsection is taken from Richard Whately, *The Use and Abuse of Party Feeling in Matters of Religion*, lectures given at Oxford, 1822. I have occasionally paraphrased and added comments, but the phrasing is mostly in Whately's own language. I would like to thank the library at Trinity College, Dublin, for enabling me to discover and have access to this material.

55 Gustav Le Bon, *Les opinions et les croyances* (Paris: Flammarion, 1911) 231–32.

56 Aristotle, *Rhetoric* 1408a.

57 Richard Lanham, *Style: An Anti-Textbook* (New Haven, CN: Yale University Press, 1974) 1.

58 The relevant texts of Kierkegaard are *Concluding Unscientific Postscript*, trans. D. Swenson and W. Lowrie (Princeton, NJ: Princeton University Press, 1941); "Communication," *Journals and Papers*, ed. H.H. Hong and E.H. Hong, assisted by G. Malantschuk (Bloomington and London: Indiana University Press, 1967); and *The Point of View of My Work as an Author*, trans. W. Lowrie (1939; New York: Harper and Row, 1962).

59 Whately, *Elements of Rhetoric* 34. Cf. Aristotle, *Rhetoric* 1404b; and Richard Lanham, *Literacy and the Survival of Humour* (New Haven, CN: Yale University Press, 1983) 20.

FIVE

ADVERTISING AND PUBLIC RELATIONS ETHICS

Propaganda, in the English-speaking world, tends to be linked in people's minds primarily with ideology or political power. This is not so in the Spanish-speaking world, where the word for advertising is "propaganda." I discovered this in the early 1980s when I took out a classified advertisement in *Worldpaper* to ask for samples of propaganda. *Worldpaper* appears as a supplement to various newspapers around the globe and is published in Spanish and English. From South America only commercial advertisers responded. Despite the difference in meaning, there is a close similarity between ideological, political, and commercial forms of persuasion, at least so far as principles of persuasion are concerned. The same is true of related ethical issues. Together, advertising and its close relative, public relations, shape public consciousness. While the former is directly concerned with encouraging purchases, the latter is more diffuse, seeking to improve the public image of a corporation, to resist government control, encourage investment, head off consumer boycotts, and the like. In both cases questions of ethics in communication arise as important issues. Whether or not we apply the term "propaganda" to these cases, study of them is bound to contribute to our understanding of the ethics of propaganda.

ADVERTISING

The root of the word "advertise" is the Latin *advertere*, meaning to notice. Advertisements give notice of upcoming events or things for sale. Most constitute paid-for space or time, although they may be provided free of charge for some worthy charity or other cause. Advertising is usually commercial, but there can also be paid-for political or ideological advertising. Sometimes this goes by the name "advertorial," as when the space is used to publicize matter written in the form of a column or editorial. The expression "advocacy advertising" is also used in this connection. Government involvement in and legal controls over advertising will be addressed in Chapter 7, while the question of freedom of expression is the subject of Chapter 6. Here, our concern is with the ethics of advertising.

In evaluating advertising as a cultural phenomenon, it is wrong to treat it as a kind of monolith, as if everything one can say about advertising necessarily applies to all forms. It is true that advertising often gives information and is valuable for doing so, but some forms of advertising give precious little information, and even that little is wrong. Think of cigarette advertisements in which the company logo dominates a scene of pristine nature, with lakes, mountains, and healthy-looking individuals. The picture conveys the opposite impression to the dirty butts, stale breath, and poor health which are associated more accurately with the product. However, it is equally wrong to condemn all advertising, since it can perform a valuable service. The classified advertisement is a good example of a valuable and necessary form of communication: I have furniture for sale, and you are looking for a bargain; my classified ad brings us together for our mutual interest.

Beyond question, a significant part of advertising is valuable. However, many people do object to some advertising practices, which are seen as a threat to their autonomy, because it is designed not to inform but to persuade. As we noted in the case of cigarettes, it is not the reality of a product, but a consciously-fostered image that is often projected. The image is designed to respond to basic needs and aspirations, in line with fashionable trends in opinion and attitudes. Much research is done to determine what will motivate a target audience. Early this century, Walter Dill Scott's formulation of basic motivations included the maternal instinct, greed, emulation, the desire for health and good looks, the desire to be appreciated by others, etc. In the 1930s, advertisers began to use Freudian theory; by the 1950s, sexual imagery was being used in ads on a large scale.[1]

On the whole, advertising is a modern necessity. The modern world clearly benefits from economies of scale, and these are only possible through large-scale marketing. The question is how this marketing can be achieved. The answer until very recently was through the use of the mass media. Almost overnight, the situation has been revolutionized for some businesses by the introduction of the Internet, with its Websites giving buyers the opportunity to seek out sellers in a way literally unimaginable only a few years ago. Not every business has an equal chance to make use of this potent force for change, but already there have been clear winners, not surprisingly in the area of highly literate communities, such as the trade in secondhand books. There have also been losers, people with businesses at a Website with no callers. There is a premium to be paid for catchy, informative Website names, because people using the Internet use search engines, which pick all relevant sites featuring a key word. If you have the right name, you have an advantage in being more easily accessible to those trying to find you. It is too early to predict how the Internet will shape the future world, but it is clear that the potential is revolutionary, and that anything said about advertising today must be qualified by that recognition. Currently, the Internet is largely unregulated, but the major service providers have an enormous edge in influencing how people will use it. The fusion of the giant service provider America On Line (AOL) with the publishing and entertainment colossus Time-Warner is a signal as to how this future may develop: the AOL user is greeted with advertisements crowded onto the home page, at least for those starting up, and e-mail inducements to buy or sign up for some "free" service of the entertainment and publishing branch of the company.

The question is not whether advertising should exist, but what forms it should take. What ethics should govern advertising, and why? We will approach these questions as we did in the previous chapter, with one important caveat: an alleged overriding public interest justification for some form of otherwise immoral propaganda (deceptive atrocity propaganda in a war defensible on other grounds, for example) is less plausible here. The private, profit-maximization interest of an advertiser tends to dominate, and deception can be less easily justified.

Harms from Advertising

When an advertised product actually causes predictable harm, the advertiser may share some responsibility for such harm by virtue of success in increasing consumption of the product. Thus, one category of harms, and hence of ethical issues, relates to the product itself. A second category relates to the means used to sell a product. Such means may involve deliberate deception; exploitation of women; the presentation of a false social picture, demeaning to certain minorities; or the promotion of greed, envy, or a lifestyle not widely sustainable in the light of environmental concerns. The means may also be immediately offensive through noise, visual pollution of the landscape or cityscape, and the like.

A reasonably comprehensive catalogue of complaints against advertising includes the following:

1. First, and perhaps foremost, in terms of number of complaints received by different bodies set up to monitor advertising, is that advertising so often is misleading. Its benefits come from linking an interested seller to an interested buyer, by letting potential consumers become aware of what is on offer and for what price. Any misleading bit of information is likely to cause frustration, either from the inconvenience of seeking out a product only to find that the price is higher than indicated, or from discovering that the product is not what was expected (assembly being required, for example), or that the product does not perform as indicated. Such inconvenience is so great that in Canada laws exist against misrepresentation. These laws are regularly enforced, sometimes with steep fines.

2. Women have so often been demeaned in advertising that their exploitation is in a category of its own. Among the many offensive ways in which they have been portrayed, the following are some recurring themes from fashion, cosmetic, alcohol, cigarette, and laundry detergent advertisements: woman have unsatisfactory bodies, in need of weight-loss, skin-care products, hair conditioning, etc.; women exist primarily as sex objects for men; women need age retardants; women derive

their identity solely as home-providers; women are acceptable targets of sexual violence; and so on. Especially pernicious is the treatment of very young girls as sex objects. Fortunately, public hostility can be aroused against products associated with such advertising campaigns, making them a very risky business.[2]

3. Some advertising encourages greed. By depicting luxury items as requirements for a normal life and within the grasp of everyone with a credit card, advertisements have often tended to stimulate purchasing beyond what is wise, affordable, and socially responsible. The vice of prodigality has always been around, and advertisers have not invented it. However, there is no need to contribute to such a human failing by presenting imagery that encourages the idea that success or failure in life is tied to having or not having the material goods advertised.

4. Advertising sometimes encourages anti-social behaviour. Automobile television commercials are commonly irresponsible in this regard, featuring recklessness, such as cars speeding beyond safe limits. Tobacco advertising encourages a deadly, addictive, polluting, and disfiguring habit by suppressing all these features and presenting imagery suggestive of bonding, friendship, good times, sophistication, nature, and the like.

5. Advertising occasionally reinforces ethnic stereotypes. Sometimes this is done by omission—for example, by having a disproportionate number of models white-skinned in a racially diverse community. At other times ethnic stereotypes are exploited in an attempt at humour.

6. Another phenomenon worth special attention is the extent to which a gambling mentality is encouraged in modern advertising. Particularly offensive are misleading representations implying or suggesting that a person has already won some lottery, when in fact nothing of the sort has happened. They are asked to send in money for what turns out to be continued eligibility to win. In some cases they are told they are "guaranteed" to win, but the fine print says this means only that they will keep reentering a pool if they lose. The gambling mentality creates false hopes for many and gratification for only a few. In this regard the elderly are particularly susceptible, since they often see no other way in which their lives might be improved economically.

7. The targeting of children deserves special condemnation when they are used as a means of putting emotional pressure on parents to purchase objects. The booklet, "Ethics in Advertising," issued by the Pontifical Council for Social Communications in 1997 put it well: "Much advertising directed at children apparently tries to exploit their credulity and suggestibility, in the hope that they will put pressure on their parents to buy products of no real benefit to them. Advertising like this offends against the dignity and rights of both children and parents; it intrudes upon the parent–child relationship and seeks to manipulate it to its own ends."[3]

8. Advertising sometimes presents false imagery to create, through repetition, associations in our minds that are unrepresentative of reality and of which we are not fully conscious. This works to undermine our autonomy. In extreme form, subliminal advertising reaches us below the threshold of conscious awareness. The practice of "product placement," introduces brand-name products into a movie or television show in such a way that the viewer comes away with a greater awareness of the product. Mark Crispin Miller has described how Coca-Cola, after buying Columbia Pictures, gave a subtle, or perhaps not so subtle, boost to its product in the film *Murphy's Romance*:

> In Murphy's Romance, [Sally] Field's nice son goes looking for a job; and while "Coca-Cola" sheds its deep red warmth throughout Murphy's homey store, in a big supermarket where the kid is told abruptly that he isn't needed, two (blue) Pepsi signs loom coldly on the wall like a couple of swastikas.

A further unwelcome effect of this form of advertising is the impact it has on the creative process. As Miller writes:

> The rise of product placement has, however, damaged movie narrative not only through the shattering effect of individual plugs but also—more profoundly—though the partial transfer of creative authority out of the hands of filmmaking professionals and into the purely quantitative universe of the CEOs. All the scenes, shots, and lines mentioned above represent the usurpation by advertising of those authorial prerogatives once held by directors and screenwriters, art directors and set designers—and by studio heads, who generally cared about how their films were made, whereas the managers now in charge are thinking only of their annual reports.[4]

The Pontifical Council of Pope John Paul II, himself a playwright and philosopher, took note of the problem at a more general level:

> In the competition to attract ever larger audiences and deliver them to advertisers, communicators find themselves tempted—in fact pressured, subtly or not so subtly—to set aside high artistic and moral standards and lapse into superficiality, tawdriness and moral squalor.[5]

9. Some forms of advertisements put more emotional pressure on a targeted group than is warranted. Products that promote hygiene or safety are commendable, but often the objective can be reached by means other than use of the particular product advertised. It is especially abhorrent when the makers of formula milk suggest to inhabitants of developing countries that their children will be less healthy if they are breast-fed. The reverse is generally the case, not just because of the natural antibiotic content of the initial breast-feeding and of the

natural regulation of fat content in the milk as the baby grows, but also because of the unsanitary water supplies in so many developing countries.

10. General cultural attitudes are shaped, as well as followed, by advertising. Think of the amount of mental space taken up by the thousands of messages assaulting our minds every day. Earlier generations memorized poetry and songs, but today numerous commercial jingles populate our thinking, by sheer force of repetition; for example, the soft-drink company slogan, "Things go better with Coke," or "I'd like to buy the world a Coke" (which became an anthem of sorts in commercials showing choirs of children of many cultures singing to bring peace to the world through drinking the product).

The objection in the case of these and other jingles and slogans is that they take up permanent residence in one's mind in the place of more important and significant thoughts.

Some advertisements are in deplorable taste, such as those making fun of religion. Beethoven's "Ode to Joy" has been used to advertise milk, leading one to wonder what right advertisers have to tarnish such a venerable cultural legacy. Others encourage promiscuity, such as condom advertisements for those who "get lucky a lot." This carries an underlying message that those who don't get sex are unlucky, when in fact they may have many other exciting and wonderful things filling their lives. Many advertisements appeal to power and domination, whether men over women or women over men. Products are marketed on the basis that they will improve the power of the purchaser to attract and use another for sexual or status gratification. The socially valuable relationships of love and compassion are ignored in these appeals.

Efforts have been made to combat with some success the most pernicious forms of advertising. In Canada, legislation exists under the Competition Act to prohibit misleading advertising. In addition, a system of voluntary controls and guidelines has been set up under Advertising Standards Canada/Les Normes canadiennes de la publicité (formerly the Canadian Advertising Foundation/le Conseil des Normes de la Publicité), which drew up and enforces a Canadian Code of Advertising Standards and Gender Portrayal Guidelines. There is also a Broadcast Code for Advertising to Children, published by the Canadian Association of Broadcasters in cooperation with Advertising Standards Canada (ASC), for use in preclearance before an advertisement is aired. If an advertisement is found to be in violation of the code or guidelines, the various media and companies that participate in the control system must refuse to prepare or carry it in its objectionable form as a condition of their participation.

The code itself is periodically altered. In the most recent version, available in ASC's 1999 Ad Complaints Report, there are 14 clauses.[6] For many years, the most frequently complained-about code violations concerned Clause 1, concerning accuracy and clarity. Under this provision, advertisements must not "contain inaccurate or deceptive claims, statements, illustrations or representations, either direct or implied, with regard to price, availability, or performance of a product or service." The focus is on the general impression created in the recipient's mind, not the intention of the advertiser. Advertisements must also "not omit relevant information in a manner which, in the result, is deceptive." Details of any advertised offer must be "clearly and understandably stated." Any disclaimers and footnoted information "must not contradict more prominent aspects of the message and should be located and presented in such a manner as to be clearly visible and/or audible. All claims and representations should be supportable, and those which claim to be supported by test or survey data should have competent, state of the art, accepted research methodology." Lastly, still in Clause 1, "The entity that is the advertiser in an advocacy advertisement must be clearly identified as the advertiser in either or both the audio or video portion of the advocacy advertisement."

In 1999 for the first time a clause other than the first one generated more complaints than any other. This was the newly adopted Clause 14, "Unacceptable Depictions and Portrayals," which deems unacceptable advertisements that condone any form of personal discrimination, appear to "exploit, condone or incite violence" or "directly encourage, or exhibit indifference to, unlawful or reprehensible behaviour." Also unacceptable are advertisements which "demean, denigrate or disparage any identifiable person, group or persons, firm, organization, industrial or commercial activity, profession, product or service or attempt to bring it or them into public contempt or ridicule"; or those which "undermine human dignity, or appear to encourage or be indifferent to conduct or attitudes that offend the standards of public decency among a significant segment of the population."

Of the 1,075 complaints received by ASC in 1999, 365 involved Clause 14. Six complaints, including three petitions signed by 54 individuals, were lodged against a Quebec brewery, Brasserie Stroh, for a print advertisement identifying a woman as the new sex symbol for the advertiser's product in a campaign directed at men. Complainants said the advertisement was offensive and contemptuous towards women, and the ASC Council found it contravened the provision against "demeaning, denigrating and disparaging an identifiable group of persons," namely women. In another case there were six complaints against a manufacturer for a television commercial showing an individual participating in a religious sacrament. The complaint was that "the commercial disparaged a recognized religion and a dignitary of its faith." Council agreed that the result, although possibly unintentionally, was a trivialization of a sacrament fundamental to the adherents of the faith, thereby demeaning an identifiable group of persons. The manufacturer was not identified because the advertisement was either withdrawn or amended before the case was heard.

In the year 2000, the most recent for which figures were available on ASC's Website, the pattern continued. There were 563 complaints based on Clause 14, followed by 122 complaints concerning Clause 1.

Some of the other upheld complaints in 1999 revealed practices or depictions that are hard to read without a wry smile. One company advertised a service "in

24 hours," meaning three days of eight hours each, instead of one complete day. It was found to contravene Clause 1. Another was against Volkswagen Canada Inc.: "The commercial depicted a car chase in which police officers commandeered a Volkswagen vehicle and ordered its young driver to follow a criminal who fled the scene on a motorcycle. During the chase, the driver was pictured cutting off other drivers, driving under the forks of a forklift truck, and, at one point, driving at such speeds as to make the vehicle airborne." This was held in violation of Clause 10, Safety: "Advertisements must not without reason, justifiable on educational or social grounds, display a disregard for safety or depict situations that might encourage unsafe or dangerous practices, or acts." The same clause was invoked in a ruling against KIA Canada Inc. for a commercial that depicted, on national television, "two women drivers aggressively compet-ing with each other for the same parking spot." Council found that the use of a parking lot setting to depict the sports utility vehicle's off-road capabilities "displayed a disregard for safety and dramatized a situation that might encour-age others to perform unsafe or dangerous practices."

Whether depictions of reckless driving are likely to be imitated on the road is, of course, a contested question, and it can be argued that the code provisions are too severe, imagining harm to arise from depictions that do not in fact result in harm. The images are entertaining, or they would not be presented in the adver-tising. On the other hand, it is common experience that we take behavioural cues from observing those around us. For most people, the restraints against reckless driving prevail, but there is a small minority of "cowboy" drivers who do not feel such control. Such images give encouragement to those who might be tempted to this kind of behaviour, with potentially tragic consequences for others on the road. (The issue of free speech versus controls is dealt with in Chapter 6.) The threshold for judging unacceptable risk from a moral point of view is surely lower than the threshold required for imposing legal or other penalties. Of course, it would be easy to misuse this provision to enforce an unrealistic pic-ture of the world where everyone depicted is a model of good behaviour, but there is no doubt (to my mind, at least) that imitation plays a role in affecting behaviour, especially that of the young.

Other provisions of the code remind us of other potential harms from adver-tising. Disguised advertising techniques are prohibited, as are deceptive price claims. "Bait and switch" operations, in which real bargains are offered only in minute quantities, are also infringements. Guarantees are not allowed unless there is full explanation as to conditions and limits. It is a code violation to attack com-petitors unfairly. Testimonials must "reflect the genuine, reasonably current opin-ion of the individual(s), group or organization making such representations, and must be based upon adequate information about or experience with the product or service being advertised, and must not be otherwise deceptive." Spurious sci-entific claims are disallowed, and "any scientific, professional or authoritative claims or statements must be applicable to the Canadian context, unless otherwise clearly stated." Some of the code's ethical concerns deal with relations between advertisers. For instance, advertisers must not imitate the copy of another "in such a manner as to mislead the consumer," that is, to capitalize on another's advertising campaign or image. The remaining provisions are against preying on superstition and fears, exploiting the credulity of children, and advertising to minors products that are prohibited for sale to them.

These provisions show concern for the major ethical criticisms of advertising, and, provided the code is enforced, they ought to ensure a respectable practice of advertising. Unfortunately, because the code is enforced only on those companies voluntarily subscribing to the ASC, it does not affect all. There is also the problem that the enforcement appears to be reactive in nature, so that it is up to consumers to place complaints for the code to be effective. With a little over 1000 complaints for the whole of Canada in one year, it seems that public education in the use of this vehicle has still some distance to go. Much offensive material is imported from the US, particularly the cigarette advertisements and the product placements, so it is not clear how far the code's effectiveness can be extended. Anyone interested in lodging a complaint only has to contact the Website: <http://www.adstandards.com>.

The Dependency Effect

In the literature on advertising much has been written about the so-called "dependency effect" in advertising. Derived from the work of economist John Kenneth Galbraith[7] the expression draws attention to the propensity of some advertising to create wants, rather than to satisfy existing wants. Creating wants is not always bad, since new products may need to have their useful properties made known before people will want to buy them. The computer is a good example. Many asked, "who needs it?" when it first came out. Now, its benefits are recognized as enormous (although it also brings drawbacks!). For example, all kinds of material are available online, saving the scholar many hours of bibliographic searching. Thus, there is no reason to object to advertisers creating new wants. The legitimate objection captured by the expression "dependency effect," however, refers to the situation in which advertisers create wants such that the satisfaction of those wants leaves one no better off than before the wants were created. The net effect of the advertising is to get people to waste their money, buying things that give them no net value. Let us say that, before the advertising, the contentment level of the target audience was 10 units of whatever positive scale we choose. The advertising convinces the audience that they are rather miserable specimens of humanity without the particular soap, perfume, food, medicine, clothing, car, etc. They are made to feel worse as a result of the advertising, so for a while their contentment is down to level 8. They spend money and buy the product, but end up at level 9 because the product delivers less than it promises. That is one version of the "dependency effect," but there is a more insidious kind. In the case of cigarettes, addiction is created by the nicotine in tobacco. By creating and satisfying a want for the cigarette, a very long-lasting dependency can be created. As anyone who has smoked or knows someone who has smoked for a long period of time can testify, this dependency is fraught with cost, inconvenience, and health problems, which tend to outweigh the pleasure involved. There is a good case for asserting that the net effect from the advertising is negative for the targeted person who succumbs.

FALSE BELIEF AND REAL HAPPINESS

Given that we live in society and that advertising is a mass phenomenon, it can happen that advertising a spurious product gives rise to real wants. If enough people believe that having a particular gemstone or model of car is an indication of status, then, the nature of status being what it is, it becomes true that having it gives status.[8] Purchasing the object gives the status-seeker exactly what is desired. Although the world has always had its share of status-seekers, status-seeking is an unworthy enterprise, and anyone who can cash in and make a dollar out of this propensity is welcome to do so. Analogous arguments might be made about the deceptions practiced by P.T. Barnum. People want to be fooled, they get pleasure out of illusions, so why not cater to this long-standing desire? Barnum devised many gimmicks for separating a sucker from his money. Once, he hired someone to place four bricks one by one at busy New York intersections. The man carried a fifth brick and methodically exchanged each of the bricks after a rapid march. Every hour he walked into Barnum's Museum, and many people would pay to follow, hoping to solve the mystery of his odd movements.[9]

However, there is a difference between raking off a bit of someone's very disposable income for a bit of harmless foolery, on the one hand, and creating serious dependency on the other. Not everyone is immune to social disapproval of others, even when the disapproval is on spurious grounds. The environmental, ecological, and other damages resulting from excessive consumption of goods are a major concern, yet they are encouraged by the kind of advertising that links status with acquisition of the latest model this or that, leading to the junking of the old. The idea that only a diamond signifies the permanent commitment for a happy, lasting marriage can be a hardship to those who cannot manage the expense. At some point a line is crossed between innocent and fun-filled illusion-making and a contribution to serious social problems. To determine where that line is crossed would involve a case-by-case analysis, looking at effects of both production and consumption of the advertised product, along with the social repercussion of the attitudes and beliefs encouraged by the advertising messages.

It should also be reckoned into the moral equation that most of us would be unhappy to learn that our happiness is founded on an illusion. In such a case, there is a standing possibility of exposure to the truth and with it the destruction of such happiness. Perhaps something even more fundamental is at stake here; recall Socrates's dictum that it is better to be a dissatisfied human than a satisfied pig. As long as we have aspirations to knowledge and truth, we cannot be satisfied with the happiness derived from illusions, even when the illusions are held by others.

What we might do, though, as part of the search for truth, is to rank various forms of illusions from the dangerous to the relatively harmless and concentrate our energies on eradicating the dangerous kind.

PUBLIC RELATIONS ETHICS

In ancient Greece the orator directly confronted an audience, and persuasive skills were directed at winning it over, along lines described in Aristotle's *Rhetoric*. Today, that kind of direct confrontation is relatively rare. For the most part, large-scale communication is mediated through print, radio, television, and, more recently, the Internet. Communication through the Internet can be direct, but it is not necessarily reciprocally so. A Website can be visited by thousands who leave no indication of who they are and why they have visited, unless they choose to respond to requests for such identification. If the Internet has lessened the need for skilled public relations practitioners, this diminution was not picked up in the latest study conducted in 1999 for the US Commission on Public Relations Education and the US National Communication Association, which shows an increase in their numbers.

Public relations as a profession developed in the US in the twentieth century largely in response to the growth of the large-scale corporation and the mass media. News reports damaging to private railways or power utilities, with consequent demands for government intervention, created a need for both some kind of "damage control" and, more importantly, some means of heading them off before they happened. From the very beginning, public relations was a media-focused and media-conscious activity. Today it has become an accepted part of modern life. Partly because of this greater acceptance, but also perhaps because of increasing pressures from counterculture activists and other groups, public relations firms have reached "a size and scope undreamed of in the 1980s." The Commission on Public Relations Education refers to "the need for dialogue with groups of people who can and will influence [the] future [of] virtually every kind of institution." The need for skilled handlers when the mass media are involved is obvious. A public relations advisor will need to know what things will be treated as newsworthy by what vehicles of information dissemination and will need to be aware of deadlines in order to foster personal contact with key decision-makers, and so on. Yet, the Commission Report refers to "the veritable explosion of one-to-one communication and the technology to implement it,"[10] without any indication that this would diminish the need for public relations practitioners. Why? Perhaps one answer lies in the public relations disasters that can occur when e-mail messages or faxes reach the wrong destination. Institutions need to be reminded of the potential damage that can arise from a keyboard slip. Apart from that, effective one-on-one communication still requires knowledge of the principles of rhetoric; if key executives talk with individual members of the public, they need to be coached on the respects in which honest statements, meant to convey only the truth, might be misinterpreted by the message recipient. Furthermore, a hostile message receiver will look for any phrase that can be taken out of context to damage the institution, so a public relations consultant makes executives aware of the potential for damage in that respect.

At the core of the whole public relations endeavour is the problem of ethics. It arises the moment we contemplate the possibility that the best interests of a particular institution, public or private, commercial or noncommercial, may not coincide with the best interests of the public generally. The mass media provides a check on institutional wrongdoing. It is a great triumph for journalism when some illegal scam is exposed by intrepid reporters, and appropriate prosecutions and convictions result, leading to better, more honest institutional operations in the future. However, the institution, obviously, prefers that the matter be cleaned up from within, rather than have all the bad publicity. From the very beginning, then, there is a complicated question: "which interests should predominate—those of the institution or those of the public generally?" This question needs some refinement or contextualization. If we are speaking of philanthropic institutions, the public and institutional interests seem to mesh well, but for-profit institutions are not aiming at charity. They are looking, on the whole, for maximum profit for shareholders. Maybe the public interest is better served by reduced profits and lower-priced products, but that is not the customary orientation of the for-profit mentality; shareholders have grounds for complaint, if not civil action, against directors who turn such a company into a charitable enterprise. In one sense, then, the answer is fairly obvious: the public interest is opposed to the private institutional interest. But again, the situation is not so simple. It can be argued that it works out in the long run to have private, for-profit companies put their interests above the public interest, because, or so it is claimed, the profit incentive is a much more powerful goad to human enterprise than a concern for public welfare, and everybody benefits from this in the long run.

This is not the place to settle arguments about the relative virtues of socialism and capitalism. The experience of the last two centuries is that both systems have potential for abuses. The paradox for public relations is that in so many situations the most beneficial image an institution has is one of maximal concern for the public interest, and yet the greatest need for public relations advice comes when the interests of the institution and those of the public diverge. There is every good reason for practitioners to proclaim to the public that honesty, integrity, telling the truth, and credibility are essential components of good public relations. This is largely true, but what is unsaid is that if any naive, full, and unguarded disclosure of institutional policies and activities were made, there would be no need for their services. We are in the realm of *suppressio veri* and *suggestio falsi* again. Despite the contents of public relations codes of ethics, the truth undergoes some shaping and colouring at the hands of skilful PR practitioners.

To demonstrate this, let us contrast the activities to the public statements of Ivy Lee, sometimes regarded as the founder of public relations. Before doing so, we will examine some of the provisions of the Code of Professional Standards for the Practice of Public Relations, as adopted by the Public Relations Society of America in 1988, whose preamble includes a declaration of principles and a pledge that its members will act according to principles reflecting the value and dignity of the individual and of human rights, along with the freedoms of speech, assembly, and the press guaranteed in the US Bill of Rights. According to the code, members must conduct their professional life in accordance with the public interest, with honesty and integrity, dealing fairly and adhering to the truth in all cases, and avoiding the dissemination of information known to be false or misleading to the public and which might disrupt or corrupt the media or the government. Moreover, members must be willing to disclose the names of their clients and in whose interest they are acting.[11]

The Canadian Public Relations Society's (CPRS) Code of Professional Standards is less elaborate, but still provides that members "shall practice public relations according to the highest professional standards ... shall deal fairly and honestly with the communications media and the public ... shall practice the highest standards of honesty, accuracy, integrity and truth, and shall not knowingly disseminate false or misleading information."[12]

Critics within the profession have called attention to ways in which the obligations of public relations practitioners to their clients can be at odds with the proclaimed ethic concerns for the public good and for the highest standards of honesty and truth. Peter O'Malley, an Ottawa-based communications consultant and a member of CPRS for over 15 years, pointed out recently that, while transparency may often be helpful to a client, sometimes it is not. In many instances, he writes, the client's interest may lie in "seeing that a particular fact, or set of facts, never see the light of day." Or if they do it may lie in minimizing

> the impact, duration and even the clarity of any resulting reporting and public communications. This is called crisis avoidance and damage control. As we all know, it constitutes a large part of what we do for a living. It is also what many clients most value in our work.

O'Malley argues that where a client's culpability is low, the best strategy may lie along the path of "honesty, accuracy, integrity and truth," as happened when the makers of Tylenol, a pain-relieving pill, were victimized by someone who inserted poisons into bottles on drugstore shelves (this, by the way, led to the practice of applying safety seals to the lids of many such products). On the other hand, if culpability is high, as in the Bhopal disaster—a chemical leak from a factory in India that affected thousands—or the *Exxon Valdez* sinking—the oil tanker was run aground and broke up, causing severe environmental and ecological damage—"damage control almost always means being highly selective in what is said publicly, and very careful about when and where anything at all is said." O'Malley makes it clear that he is not defending lying, but the selective presentation of information and practice of secrecy to further the client's interest. This practice does not necessarily serve to "enlighten the public." In sum, he claims that, because we live with freedom of the press, it is important to have knowledgeable people defend an institution's interest by controlling what information gets passed on voluntarily to the media, and to "intervene in the reporting process in a manner that has a reasonable chance of influencing the reporting outcome in known ways."[13]

The philosophy expressed in O'Malley's thinking may have affected a change in the CPRS Code. The following provision from a previous code was dropped around 1993: "a) A member shall act primarily in the public interest in the practice of public relations and shall neither act nor induce others to act in a way which may affect unfavorably the practice of public relations, the community, or the Society...." However, the code available on the CPRS Website in January 2002 states that "Members shall conduct their professional lives in a manner that does not conflict with the public interest and the dignity of the individual, with respect for the rights of the public as contained in the Constitution of Canada and the Charter of Rights and Freedoms."[14]

It hardly needs stating that any attempt at secrecy must itself be kept secret or the policy of information restraint will backfire and give the institution an even worse public profile. In 1988, there were calls for resumption of international boycotting activity against Nestlé, in the light of accusations that the company once again was distributing free formula to clinics and hospitals in developing countries. When the PR firm Ogilvy and Mather gave advice to Nestlé to discourage media attention, the report containing the advice somehow was leaked to the press, with consequent negative publicity. The advice was to engage in the strategy of "pro-active neutralization" and to monitor grass roots activities.

> As always, the media have the potential to exacerbate the issue, create much greater awareness than desired, and continuously find negative in either neutral or positive news.
>
> In light of this, Ogilvy & Mather recommends that as a general rule Nestlé should be reactive regarding boycott materials and not initiate media communications. If the media ask questions or want a story, Nestlé representatives should judge and respond accordingly—not initiate. This avoids generating more awareness of the issue.

The same report also advised Nestlé to help "inoculate" against bad publicity by engaging in a positive "do good" public service campaign to give Carnation (a Nestlé subsidiary that markets infant formula) a good image. For this the report recommended "Carnation Care" (foster care for HIV-infected children and infants).[15]

A similar boomerang hit Ontario Hydro in 1990, following brownouts that occurred around Christmas 1988. Somehow the Energy Probe Research Foundation obtained a copy of a report prepared by Goldfarb Consultants and presented to Ontario Hydro officials earlier that year. In a newsletter, Norman Rubin, the foundation's director of nuclear research, detailed some of the advice in the report. The public was reluctant, it said, to go along with a $200 billion power expansion plan calling for, among other things, 14 Darlington-sized nuclear reactors. The report noted that it would be difficult to convince the public of the need for the expansion if there were few or no brownouts and blackouts. Three months later Hydro began to experience brownouts in parts of the province. "This year," wrote Rubin, "over a period of several months, Hydro denied repeatedly that this report existed, even though Hydro was required by law to divulge it at Ontario Energy Board hearings."[16]

Without commenting on the correctness or otherwise of Mr. Rubin's assessment of the legal requirements on Ontario Hydro regarding the report's contents, the incident does suggest one very important ethical restriction on a public relations strategy in which secrecy is vital. If the necessity for secrecy conflicts with legal requirements to divulge the secret matter, it is unethical to violate those legal requirements. Since it is unethical to sustain the strategy of secrecy under those circumstances, it sets the stage for a public relations disaster if such a strategy were adopted. Sound public relations advice, therefore, is against embarking on such a strategy.

Earlier, we mentioned Bok's criterion of publicity in connection with assessing the ethics of lying. The same test can be usefully applied, with some qualifications, to a public relations strategy. How would it look if the strategy became publicized? If the public resents being manipulated, it is likely that the strategy is wrong. However, we have seen Whately's argument, in the light of which not all deceptions are necessarily wrong; that kind of reasoning can apply here as well.

Ivy Lee and the Ethics of Public Relations

It is notable that one of the earliest, and most successful, practitioners of public relations, Ivy Lee (1877-1934), was outspoken about the importance of ethical behaviour in the profession. What he never ceased to emphasize in particular was the need to be upfront about the funding source of any campaign, for reasons that will be explored below. Lee is well-known in American PR circles. A University of Michigan study ranked him the most outstanding PR figure of the twentieth century.[17] Called "Poison Ivy" by labour sympathizers for his deceptive use of press releases on behalf of John D. Rockefeller's Colorado coal mine interests and other large corporations, he was a major force in developing the field of PR. He realized that companies could benefit greatly by taking public relations advice into account early in a planning process, rather than after the fact, when some disastrous policy mistake had been made.

Lee preached at times a rather austere PR morality, although the austerity was not always consistently maintained, except with respect to the feature mentioned above. However, some doubt if his practice was consistent with his teaching.[18] The purpose of PR, as Lee saw it, was to create or encourage a favourable image of a company in the public mind. Defined in this way, there is no necessary connection with any lack of ethics. Supposing that a company has been unjustly accused, it may be wise for the company to hire PR consultants to undo the damage to the extent possible. The consultants can help by pointing out the risks from engaging in a lawsuit as distinct, say, from taking out paid advertisements or using some other technique to neutralize the false story. On the other hand, it seems reasonable to suppose that, to the extent that damaging accusations are true, other things being equal, it will cost more to combat the message.[19] The less truth is on one's side, the more difficult it will be, generally speaking, to persuade a given public of the beliefs or attitudes one wishes to impart. The more difficult the task, the higher the fees one might expect to be levied for accomplishing the task.

In such circumstances, there is an obvious temptation to master and use whatever techniques of persuasion will accomplish a given job, always allowing for the fact that unethical techniques, if discovered, will tend to discredit the firm making use of them, as we have seen. If a firm has been thus tainted, potential clients will be dissuaded from hiring it, as the decision to do so will reflect badly. That is the reason why a firm should try to ensure it does not get caught in unethical practices. In addition, PR practitioners generally are concerned that the profession not be brought into disrepute.

What are some of the unethical practices that might tempt a PR firm? The Public Relations Society of America has made statistics available concerning cases brought before a Grievance Board or Panel between 1952 and 1985. Out of 165 cases, 75 involved matters of fairness in dealing with clients; 50 were listed under the rubric "intentional communication of false or misleading information"; 46 raised questions about whether professional life was conducted "in accordance with the public interest"; 37 disputed whether there was "adherence to truth, accuracy, standards of good taste"; 32 pertained to "engaging in practices that corrupt the channels of communication or processes of government"; 23 related to "intentional injury to professional reputation or practice of another member"; and 21 pertained to "using organizations purporting to serve one cause but actually serving an undisclosed special interest."[20]

Prominent in this list is one or another form of deception. One can infer, with reason, that if deception is attempted so often, it must get results and be profitable. Recall Aristotle and the importance of favourable ethos, what we might today call credibility. If US Widgets, Inc. is behind a whole series of articles favourable to its widgets, people who read the articles can discount in their minds what is said, on the ground of probable bias. On the other hand, if the source for the articles is misrepresented and accepted as a neutral evaluator, appropriate discounting will not take place. There is in this a deception, one that is favourable to the company.

It is, therefore, highly valuable for a company to find some public icon—a movie star, revered clergyman, famous scientist, or the like to endorse the product without any indication that they are paid to do so. In the 1920s John D. Rockefeller Jr., on the advice of Ivy Lee, provided $26 million towards the church of Harry Fosdick, a modernist preacher who proclaimed a message of tolerance and conciliation between fundamentalists and modernists. Conciliation and cooperation, as distinct from antagonism and competition, were ideas that conveniently suited the cartel-orientation of Lee and the oil interests. Fosdick was on the board of the

Rockefeller Foundation from 1916 to 1921. Lee, in the words of Marvin Olasky, "used all his PR skills to make Fosdick and his beliefs famous and influential." Perhaps Lee and Rockefeller simply liked Fosdick, but the obvious connection between his preaching and the corporate interests of Rockefeller suggests otherwise.[21]

A common method of diluting the immediate and obvious self-interest of a corporation in presenting a message is to form a separate group and fund it. Sometimes the title of the group is fairly revealing, at other times not. A "Sugar Institute" is fairly revealing of the interests represented. However, a "Smoker's Freedom Society" conceals to a significant extent that it may be supported by tobacco money. When a logging firm sponsors what purports to be an environmentally oriented group, there is positive deception if that funding source is not revealed.

The lobbying power of the tobacco interests is enormous, precisely because of their reach in the sense of controlling voices not likely to be identified with them. As an example of this power, consider a story that appeared in a Canadian newspaper in 1993 about the weakening of the Ontario government's resolve to curtail the sale of cigarettes by raising the legal age for tobacco sales to 19 and banning the sale of cigarettes in pharmacies and hospitals. A spokesperson for the cross-Canada chain, Shoppers Drug Mart, was quoted as saying that pharmacists would oppose the action and that a court challenge to the law would be a possibility: "It's not worth the battle, because if there is a constitutional challenge they won't win, and it's not one of the government's most important pieces of legislation." What the story did not reveal was that Shoppers Drug Mart, which had 678 stores across Canada that year, was part of the Imasco group of companies. Imasco, through its Imperial Tobacco cigarette brands, du Maurier, Matinée, and Player's, sold 66.2 per cent of manufactured cigarettes in Canada.[22] In another case, the British newspaper, *The Independent*, reported in 1996 that the well-known, outspoken British psychologist, Hans Eysenck, had received more than £800,000 in research monies through a secret US tobacco fund and the major cigarette companies. The story noted that Eysenck "has consistently decried the scientific consensus that smoking causes lung cancer." Eysenck said he had not profited personally from the funds, but the point is that people who heard his opinions should have been informed of the potential for conflict of interest so that they could make their own judgment about the credibility of the scientist.[23]

In the light of the important part played by credibility in influencing public opinion, it is not surprising that Ivy Lee, when he gave speeches or wrote articles on the ethics of public relations (which he often referred to by the name "publicity"), paid it close and repeated attention. He saw nothing wrong in sending press releases to newspapers, hoping to influence their editorial content, so long as the source of the releases was properly identified. Newspaper editors could make their own judgments about news value. To object to this practice, he said, was like objecting to a department store displaying many tempting goods. By contrast, he thought, "When public utilities buy newspapers and don't let the public know that they bought them, they are obviously making a wrong use of propaganda." If a newspaper is owned by a large business, its reports will favour those business interests. People have a right to know of such possible biases. Lee likewise condemned (rightly) the practice of some power companies of promoting in schools the benefits of private ownership of utilities as opposed to public ownership through governments. As he put it: "When power companies have school books written by professors in colleges and have these books put into schools without the knowledge of the people as to who is responsible for putting them there, that is a wrong use of propaganda."[24]

Lee recognized that "the truth" is often elusive, and that people's perceptions of the truth are coloured one way or another. However, people are entitled to have basic facts to make sound judgments. In that light they are entitled to know who is responsible for a certain expression of opinion or supposed fact. To this end Lee even endorsed the "inflexible rule" instituted by James Gordon Bennett of the *New York Herald* of allowing no anonymous interviews.[25] Such was the importance Lee attached to disclosure of a source's identity that he once wrote, categorically: "The evil of all propaganda consists in failure to disclose its source."[26] Taken literally, this has to be false. There are other evils connected with propaganda. Even if the source is known, there can be harmful lies or other disreputable communication. However, this likelihood is reduced when people know the source and can hold it to account if the lie is discovered. When the source is known, the public can be appropriately on guard.

In some of his high-minded writings, Lee showed considerable concern for the truth. The aim of PR, he wrote, is to get things done by "carrying out a truthful message to the public." At times he followed this principle. His advice to the copper industry, when it was threatened by a story that alcoholic liquids distilled in copper pots were poisonous, was that it should find out the truth and withdraw copper from such use if the story were true. He also condemned the practice of putting artificial pressure on the press, through advertising, to publish one-sided articles, or articles that the newspaper would "not print for its news value alone."[27]

Lee did oppose, as might be expected, disseminating false information, but his main concern was with the disastrous results of detection. He was not averse to the occasional *suppressio veri* with *suggestio falsi*. For instance, he posited a situation in which a tourist who speaks no Russian boards a Moscow train without a ticket; his advice is, "Whenever you get into a bad situation, make signs and smile." Obviously the tourist cannot fully articulate a literal falsehood, but can give the false impression that everything is all right. Lee's moral is more revealing: "It is only necessary for a man to tell his story in the best way he can, with such signs as he can manifest; to do it with a smile and with a pleasant attitude, and he can accomplish wonders."[28] Applied to the tourist, there is scarcely cause for concern, but, when we treat this as a model for the behaviour of huge corporations toward the public, we have, indeed, reason to be apprehensive. I can picture the complaint department of a retail organization smiling while disclaiming responsibility for a defective product.

Lee was aware of a certain unfairness occurring when one competitor can afford to spend large sums of money on public relations, while another is unable to do so. This situation results in advocacy for one side, without corresponding advocacy on the other. The truth no doubt suffers. His solution was to suggest that funds should be supplied by the other side of the controversy—obviously an inadequate reply when the "other side" lacks resources. In an article written for the mass-circulation magazine *Collier's* in 1925, Lee frankly admitted that he had no answer to the question of unfairness where there are unequal resources for PR available to contending parties.[29] One answer would be something like legal aid for public relations, but with current cutbacks to even basic legal aid, the outlook for such a scheme being adopted is not favourable.

Lee did not object to one-sided presentations of a case; as long as the source was upfront, he also approved explicitly a certain deviousness in persuasion. A case in point is that of Statler Hotels. Their regular advertisements in *Saturday Evening Post*, one of the widest-circulation magazines in the early part of the twentieth century, played up their wonderful service. The purpose of these advertisements, Lee revealed, was primarily to influence the staff themselves into giving better service. It was a clever bit of psychology, but somewhat manipulative. If the truth were told to workers, it would likely generate some, although probably not very serious, resentment at this trickery.[30]

One reason why Lee had few scruples about giving one-sided accounts of events was that he saw that even public officials were uncertain about what passes for truth. US President Calvin Coolidge had said, "Propaganda seeks to present a part of the facts, to distort their relations, and to force conclusions which could not be drawn from a complete and candid survey of all the facts." He also stated: "We don't want any propaganda." However, at the very time Coolidge made those remarks, his Secretary of the Treasury, Andrew Mellon, was carrying on what Lee judged to be an active propaganda campaign on behalf of the Mellon Plan, which involved reducing taxes on the rich. First presented to the House Ways and Means Committee in 1923, the plan was passed in 1926, following tremendous media support. Lee commented: "What he [Mellon] did was to give a selection of the facts," not a complete and candid survey of *all* the facts. Lee argued against Coolidge's lip-service condemnation of one-sided presentations, by asking rhetorically, "Can you kindly tell me of any situation in human history which has ever been presented to the people in the form of a candid survey of all the facts?"[31]

Lee's answer is an unsatisfactory response to Coolidge's complaint about propaganda, because he fails to deal with the entirety of what he reports as Coolidge's actual words. Coolidge spoke of conclusions that could not be drawn from a complete and candid survey of all the facts, not of those that are not, in fact, drawn from such a survey—the alternative being, of course, to draw the conclusion from a biased selection of the facts. Because Lee was in sympathy with the Mellon Plan, perhaps he thought that the conclusion in its favour could be drawn from such a complete and candid survey. We do not know what Lee's response would have been in a case where the conclusions could not have been supported from a survey of all the facts. One response to that hypothetical case, suggested by some of Lee's writings, involves simply hiding in a fog of relativity or scepticism. If nothing can be known for sure, then, it might be argued, you can never force any conclusions and, thus, never be guilty of propaganda in Coolidge's terms. However, this approach is not consistent with Lee's own characterization of propaganda as "something that insidiously plants wrong ideas in the mind and has an ulterior motive."[32] The reference to "wrong ideas" reflects a position other than complete scepticism. Lee seems to oppose outright deception, but not one-sidedness of presentation, where some worthy cause (in his mind) was at stake and where, in addition, there was an absence of any "all-sided" or objective account.

Public relations techniques, applied to promotion of goals that can be justified when all the pertinent facts are taken into account, is morally better than when they are applied to promote goals that cannot be so justified (other things being equal). This is true whether we are thinking subjectively, from the point of view of PR practitioners, or objectively, in relation to other people's evaluation of the goals. There remains a problem, however, when subjective and objective assessments are in conflict. What if the goals seem reasonable, to the PR practitioners, but not to the general public, when all the facts are in? In fact, the public is not usually given all the pertinent facts by PR practitioners, who are content to follow their own subjective valuation. At the heart of this problem is the one of grassroots democracy versus elitism. My tentative conclusion (although more discussion is reserved for Chapter 8) is that there are well-known dangers of biased judgment connected with the elitist perspective and that respect for democracy should discourage unfettered one-sidedness in presentations on policy matters.

Hill and Knowlton and the Gulf War: A Case Study[33]

An illustration of the clash between moral imperatives is provided by the Hill and Knowlton campaign, following the August 2, 1990, invasion of Kuwait by Iraq, to bring US opinion in favour of going to war against Iraq. One imperative was to get the job done, something the Reagan-Bush administration also supported. The other was to respect public relations ethics. The latter lost, according to Ivy Lee's major principle about being upfront regarding funding and information sources. The campaign was successful, and the US went to war in January 1991, ousting the Iraqis from Kuwait, but also causing huge damage to the whole Iraqi infrastructure, with consequent loss of life for many civilians. This success was linked directly to the violation of Lee's principle; in fact, the *Wall Street Journal* reported dissatisfaction within the public relations profession with the "discredit on our business" brought on by the company's tactics.[34] Prominent among the forces that helped sway opinion in favour of war was the incubator babies atrocity story: according to it, Iraqi invaders dumped 312 babies out of their incubators on to the cold floors of Kuwaiti hospitals and left them there to die, while they took the incubators to Iraq. The story seemed to reveal a deep-seated callousness and disregard for human life among the Iraqis. It received banner headlines in some newspapers when it was confirmed by Amnesty International. It was later discredited.[35]

The New York firm of Hill and Knowlton was responsible for presenting evidence to the public that this atrocity took place. With over $10 million from a group called "Citizens for a Free Kuwait" (CFK), the firm had ample means to publicize whatever version of truth or falsehood it chose. Most of the money, in fact, came from the Kuwaiti government. According to John MacArthur, "CFK reported to the Justice Department receipts of $17,861 from 78 individual US and Canadian contributors and $11,852,329 from the government of Kuwait."[36]

Not only was the identity of their client presented deceptively, but so was the identity of their most convincing witness to the atrocity, who appeared before a congressional human rights caucus. A Kuwaiti girl, identified to the public only as 15-year-old Nayirah, was discovered later to be the daughter of Shaikh Saud al-Nasser al-Sabah, the Kuwaiti Ambassador to the US. Had she been so identified at the time, her story might have been treated with more scepticism.[37] Congressman Thomas Lantos, co-chair of the congressional human rights caucus, admits that he was informed of Nayirah's identity, but the other co-chair, John Porter of Illinois, said he did not know her identity. Hill and Knowlton contradict him on this matter, and he does not sound very convincing in answer to questions put by Linden MacIntyre of the CBC's *the fifth estate* program. He makes an important admission, though, in saying that the rest of Congress and the public should have been informed:

> I think it [true identity of the girl] certainly should have been known at the time of the hearing. It would have had bearing on what she might have said. Yes, I think people—members of Congress certainly, and members of the public—were entitled to know the source of her testimony.[38]

Why was the story so effective? It supplied exactly the kind of attention-getting and emotion-arousing ingredients necessary to fuel the indignation of Americans against the enemy and thus provided the basis for widespread approval of the war. Atrocity stories abound in any war, as we have seen, but people have become accustomed to hearing about rapes, murders, and mutilations. This story was novel because the Iraqi invaders were pictured as brutes dumping innocent babies. The timing of the story—which hit the headlines first in October and even more resoundingly in mid-December 1990 (see below)—contributed to its effect. Coming that close to Christmas, when many people have in mind the newborn Christ and the massacre of the innocents by King Herod, gave it enormous resonance and impact. Furthermore, Christmas is a time for holidays, when people, preoccupied with various festivities, are not so likely to check on the accuracy of news reports. The momentum of the story was too great to stop without the most securely founded counter-evidence. Well-grounded rebuttals were difficult to obtain prior to the Christmas holidays, and by New Year's the story was fully rooted in people's consciousness.

What we do not know, and cannot expect to find out, is the precise connection between Hill and Knowlton and all the different forms in which the story appeared. This should not surprise us, since, as noted in Chapter 2, we still do not know, after more than 80 years, the full truth about the corpse utilization story of World War 1. It is worth contemplating some similarities between the stories. In both cases the story got an initial toehold in public consciousness through isolated reports without official acknowledgement. References in the press to theft of incubators began September 5, 1990, in the London *Daily Telegraph*, where the source was given as the exiled Kuwaiti housing minister, Yahya al-Sumait. Two days later newspaper reports of incubator atrocities, supplied by Reuters news agency and published in the *Los Angeles Times*, gave as sources women identified only by their first names. As MacArthur points out, it is a serious breach of journalistic practice to print only first names. If witnesses refuse to give their last names, their testimony should be treated warily.[39]

The first impact came with coverage by the news media on October 10, 1990, of Nayirah's testimony before the human rights caucus. Pictures of the tearful, distraught girl were widely published. On November 27, Dr. Ibrahim Bahbahani testified to the UN Security Council that he personally had buried 40 newborn babies who had been taken from their incubators. According to *Middle East Watch*, Dr. Bahbahani's testimony was arranged by Hill and Knowlton. It was discredited when it was discovered later that he was not a surgeon as he claimed, but an orthodontist; he admitted the bodies were buried without examination to determine their time and cause of death. In a March interview with ABC news, he said he buried around 30 and that he did not know whether or not the 120 babies buried by his group as a whole (according to his testimony) were taken from incubators at all.[40]

The crowning touch came on December 19, 1990, when Amnesty International was named as the source confirming the story of 312 incubator baby deaths. Apparently, the organization had been duped. In an April, 1991, news release, it admitted: "Once we were actually in Kuwait and had visited hospitals and cemeteries and spoken to doctors at work, we found that the story did not stand up."[41] Until this incident, Amnesty International's reliability was generally considered excellent. In the circumstances, it would have been hard to find a more credible source, and, understandably, the press treated their account as fact and exploited the story for all the publicity value they could get. The impact was such that it may well have made the difference to the number of votes in Congress, which narrowly voted in favour of the war; the Senate passed a resolution supporting the war effort on January 12 with only a five-vote margin. As MacArthur notes, "six pro-war senators (five Republicans and one Democrat) specifically cited the baby incubator allegation in their speeches supporting the resolution."[42] In fact, with the commencement of war in mid-January, US attention was completely diverted to the SCUD missile attacks and ground action. The question of the veracity of the atrocity story dropped out of sight from the mainstream press.

What is the truth about the alleged incubator baby atrocity? What was Hill and Knowlton's involvement, and how ethical or unethical was their role in all of this? Did they orchestrate the duping of Amnesty International, for example? In my analysis, both Hill and Knowlton and the Pentagon were heavily involved either in *suppressio veri* or lack of diligence toward finding and presenting the truth. A speech given on April 20, 1993, by Tom Eidson, then CEO of Hill and Knowlton, denied that the company engaged knowingly in any deception; coming after so many published reports on the actual funding of the PR campaign, the true identity of their star witness, and the numbers of babies who died, his account appears disingenuous at best. Eidson states, for example, that "Kroll Associates, the international investigative organization, issued a report that documented the atrocities and revealed official Iraqi documents ordering the removal of the incubators." He also referred to a Pentagon report in which, under the heading "Deaths Attributable to Iraqi Torture and Execution," there is the item "Premature babies removed from incubators ... 120."[43] But the Pentagon report itself says that the information was "obtained from hospital records and medical personnel"; earlier it gave the source as the Kuwait City medical records.[44] There is no indication that care was taken to evaluate the reliability of witnesses from whose testimony the figure of 120 incubator baby deaths was derived. Recall that Amnesty International also had received information from medical sources, but by their April 1991 report wrote: "Although some medical sources in Kuwait, including a Red Crescent doctor, were still claiming babies had died in this way, we found no hard evidence to support this. Credible opinion in hospitals discounts the allegations."[45]

Following the war, Kroll Associates was hired by the government of Kuwait to determine, among other things, the veracity of allegations concerning infant deaths caused by removal of incubators. It gives as its *most conservative estimate, based on corroborated eyewitness testimony ... that a minimum of seven babies died directly because of the looting of incubators and ventilators from pediatric wards at Al-Jahra and Al-Adan hospitals*" (emphasis in the original).[46] Nevertheless, there is an important credibility problem in the evidence. The date of the incident supposedly witnessed in 1990 by Nayirah al-Sabah when she visited Al-Adan Hospital is given only as "one day in late August." In other words, Kroll considered the reported incubator baby deaths at Al-Adan as among the seven for which, conservatively judged, solid evidence existed, although the report is unspecific as to the date. In response to a fax in which I sought more detail, Alice McGillion, Managing Director of Kroll Associates, replied in a letter July 8, 1993, that the nurses quoted in the report could say only that the incident occurred sometime during the week of August 26, 1990. I was puzzled that hospital records could not identify the date more precisely, since it is standard practice to maintain regularly updated charts on patients. In answer to my query, McGillion wrote on August 23, 1993, "As to your request for clarification of chart information, please remember that due to the emergency and resulting chaos of the situation, daily records on patient care and progress were not being kept with their usual care."[47] Now, one can make allowances for panic and the non-maintenance of charts at the time of the alleged incident, but, however sloppy the maintenance of charts might have been, they would at least be expected to note eventually the time when data ceased to be recorded by virtue of the disappearance of the baby.

If the evidence of incubator baby killing in the Al-Adan Hospital is solidly based, according to Kroll, how reliable are the cases where even Kroll is not willing to give its own "conservative" credence? Nayirah's testimony, widely televised, was: "I saw the Iraqi soldiers coming into the hospital with guns, and go into the room where 15 babies were in incubators. They took the babies out of the incubators, took the incubators, and left the babies on the cold floor to die."[48] Kroll says that Nayirah's experience "amounted to a glance or 'snapshot' impression that included chaotic commotion and the sight of one infant on the floor and the presumption that other infants, not seen, had also been removed from incubators."[49] They say she witnessed the scene for no more than seconds, hurrying out of the hospital in fear (given her identity) for her safety. It seems remarkable that between the nurses, Nayirah, and a friend who was with her, the date of this incident cannot be narrowed to within less than a week. What is certain is that disproof of the alleged sighting is made more difficult when the time frame is so extended.

Taking into consideration the deception involving the identity of their client and witnesses and their obstinacy in clinging to a number of baby deaths that subsequent reports proved to be false, it seems inescapable to conclude that Hill and Knowlton was not interested in the whole truth of the matter, but only in elements that would promote the interests of their real client and, therefore, of themselves.

Is this news? Should there be concern? Of course a business looks out for its own interests. So what? Suppose the following were true: The US, for defensible policy reasons, felt it necessary to go to war against Saddam Hussein. To do this, it required the support of the American people, a support that did not exist to the required extent. With the help of Hill and Knowlton, hired by Citizens for a Free Kuwait (which in turn was funded by the government of Kuwait), public opinion was altered sufficiently to implement the policy. Hill and Knowlton either invented or embellished the incubator babies story, or told its client what the Kuwaiti government needed to do to support it. Even if the details of the story were false, the Iraqis were certainly guilty of some well-documented atrocities. *Middle East Watch* does not mince its words: "Our own research on the occupation of Kuwait documented hundreds of gross abuses committed by Iraqi forces."[50] Why quibble about the details?

Supposing the truth of these statements, it is certainly arguable that deception may have been justified on the basis of the huge policy matters at stake. Many people felt that the US involvement in the Gulf War was vital to world peace. From that perspective, the usual "dirty-hands" arguments can be invoked to support the deception. There are few absolutists who would say that deception is never justified no matter how vital the stakes.

One answer to the "so what?" question is that democracy is a sham if those with government power feel it is acceptable to gain support for their policies through such deception. This answer does not settle the matter, for two reasons. First, not everyone wants genuine democracy. Second, a substantial number of people seem to accept deception, so long as it is for benign purposes. But, every so often, people glimpse the wrongdoing that lack of accountability encourages, and there is renewed demand for truthfulness and openness in government. Notable examples of this are Watergate and the Iran–Contra scandal. Recurring deceptions of the people have been used to impress on the public the need for more military expenditures. A problem with such deception is that it provokes a like response from the enemy. Perhaps the military gains from such a race, but not the general public. I.F. Stone noted the attempt to suppress information from a Coast and Geodetic Survey, which indicated that, contrary to the official position, underground nuclear explosions were detectable thousands of miles away.[51] The suppression was important for heading off calls for nuclear test bans and thus continuing the arms race. The *New York Times* revealed military deceptions on the cost and need for weapons in the 1980s.[52] Therefore, the argument against this kind of deception is that it can easily become rampant throughout the administration. If that happens, eventually cynicism and a sense of futility develop regarding the democratic process. This is good neither for the holders of power, nor for those subject to their decisions.

The argument as stated is consistent with deception being otherwise justified on a single-instance analysis, that is, not taking account of habit-forming repercussions. What if the actual decision, quite apart from the process used to enable it to be put into effect, is wrong? The outrage against the supposed 312 incubator baby deaths needs to be compared with the estimated 46,900 children under age five who died in Iraq between January and August 1991 as an indirect effect of US-led bombing, civilian uprisings, and a UN economic embargo.[53] Use of deception, we have seen, preempts the judgment of the people. It prevents such judgment from being made effective through choice of congressional representatives, by cutting it off from a grounding in proper fact, as distinct from grounding in selected information and misinformation disseminated by the power-holders.

Ivy Lee felt very strongly that it was wrong not to reveal to an audience the source of a PR message. This principle in the incubator babies case was violated with regard to the American people and to all but a few of the congressional caucus. The argument that concealment of Nayirah's identity was necessary to protect relatives in Kuwait sufficed to ward off critical scrutiny, but, considering the enormous stakes involved and the many lives lost during the war and as a consequence of it, the marginal increase in risk to such of her relatives who may have remained in occupied Kuwait hardly provides a convincing justification.

Although Lee was not as concerned as I am about one-sided presentations, I hope the evidence reviewed here will encourage the view that he ought sometimes to have been more concerned than he was. The one-sided account Hill and Knowlton gave of the incubator babies story contributes to burying the truth. According to their account, Hill and Knowlton were not at fault for the misleading information; they simply went with what they were told, taking the veracity of their sources for granted. On the contrary, since the story is shaky in its entirety, Hill and Knowlton did not serve the truth by pretending otherwise. The evasions and hyperbole, the "one-sided presentation" Lee referred to, continued to mask truths that the "other side" (in this case, MacArthur and *Middle East Watch*) painstakingly brought to public attention.[54]

CONCLUSION

It is sometimes argued that truth by itself is morally indifferent and that the value of a truth lies in its context, depending on the pragmatic implications of believing or acting upon it. What good does it do, it might be asked from this perspective, to chase after and expose deceptions that no longer have a role to play? The war is over, Kuwait was liberated, and exposure of deceptions will not undo any of the war's damage. Maybe those involved in the deception should be commended for helping to bring about such good as came of the war.

There are two answers to be given. One is pragmatic. If concern for the truth is not shown now, the message to decision-makers is that they have a free hand in pursuing deceptive means for accomplishing their goals in the future. Already we have seen reports that the figures of Serbian atrocities in Kosovo were greatly exaggerated. Without pursuing matters of truth, we open ourselves to accusations of disinterest in wrongdoing and share the responsibility that goes with willful blindness. If we are to have accountability, we need to know the truth about government-fostered deceptions, especially those that commit a nation to involvement in war, with all the resultant suffering and loss of life. So, the answer is that lack of concern for seemingly superannuated questions of truth has pragmatic consequences that cannot be ignored.

There is a second answer, very much in the spirit of St. Augustine. The question of whether pragmatic reasons are sound or not is itself a matter of truth or falsity. Without a strong precommitment to truth, the process of our reasoning is liable to corruption. The soundness or otherwise of the pragmatic considerations themselves must depend on their grounding in truth, and we cannot be confident that we have such truth if we turn our attention away from matters that, however uncomfortable to contemplate, are necessary for our enlightenment. Exposure of falsehood gives us a sense of protection against the arrival of an Orwellian world (or should one say the more complete arrival of an Orwellian world?), just as punishment for crimes helps to restore a sense of justice, even though we can expect that falsehood and crimes will both continue.

If a deception on the scale, and with the impact, of the incubator babies story is allowed to fade into remote history without a sense of apprehension about the ease with which people can thus be manipulated, the message given to future manipulators will surely be one of encouragement. It may be that controls against deceptive propaganda should be instituted. That question raises issues of free speech, to which we must now turn.

NOTES

1 Vance Packard, *The Hidden Persuaders* (New York: D. McKay, 1957).

2 See Jean Kilbourne's *Killing us Softly: The Image of Women in Advertising* (1979) and *Still Killing us Softly* (1987), Cambridge Documentary Films, a movie and video which make the points forcefully and with some humour.

3 Pontifical Council for Social Communications, *Ethics in Advertising* (Rome: Liberia Editrice Vaticano; and Ottawa: Canadian Conference of Catholic Bishops, 1997) 27-28.

4 An urban myth spawned by James M. Vicary, claimed that imperceptible (because they were shown for only one three-thousandth of a second) coaxings—"Hungry? Eat popcorn" and "Drink Coca-Cola"—during a showing of the film *Picnic* in Fort Lee, New Jersey, led to increased sales of those products. Mark Crispin Miller has reported that the "findings" were fabricated (*The Atlantic Monthly*, April 1990: 41-42), but the myth is still passed on as true, even by some students who are assigned the article as compulsory reading. Also Miller 43, 48.

5 Pontifical Council 20.

6 From the 1999 *Ad Complaints Report*, available at the Advertising Standards Canada Website: <http://www.adstandards.com>. All further quotations in this section are taken from this source.

7 John Kenneth Galbraith, *The Affluent Society*, 4th ed. (Boston: Houghton, 1984) Chapter 11.

8 For a more detailed discussion, see R.L. Arrington, "Advertising and Behavior Control," and Reese Miller, "Persuasion and the Dependence Effect," *Business Ethics in Canada*, 2nd ed., ed. Deborah C. Poff and Wilfrid J. Waluchow (Scarborough: Prentice-Hall, 1991).

9 P.T. Barnum, *Struggles and Triumphs or Recollections of P.T. Barnum written by himself* (London: Ward, Lock and Co., 1882).

10 See Commission on Public Relations Education, *Public Relations Education for the 21st Century*, October 1999. Online at <http://www.prsa.org/prssa4.html>.

11 Public Relations Society of America, *Code of Professional Standards for the Practice of Pubic Relations*. Downloaded 10 June 2000 from: <http://www.prsa.org/profstd.html>.

12 Canadian Public Relations Society, *Code of Professional Standards*, clauses 1-3. Downloaded 11 June 2000, from <http://www.cprs.ca>.

13 Peter O'Malley, "In Praise of Secrecy: The Ethical Foundations of Public Relations," available on the Website of the Canadian Public Relations Society, <http://www.cprs.ca>. Originally published in *Vox*, The Newsletter of the Ottawa Chapter of the Canadian Public Relations Society. I would like to thank Mr. O'Malley for permission to quote from this text (telephone conversation in Ottawa, 20 August 2001).

14 Canadian Public Relations Society, *Code of Professional Ethics*. A copy was kindly provided to me by CPRS. See the CPRS Website: <http://www.cprs.ca>.

15 "Corporate Cointelpro," *Harper's Magazine* (July 1989): 24.

16 Norman Rubin, Energy Probe *Newsletter* (1990).

17 D.L. Lewis, "The Outstanding PR Professionals," *PR Journal* (October 1970): 78.

18 Marvin Olasky, *Corporate PR* (Hillsdale, NJ: Lawrence Eerlbaum Associates, 1987) and "Ivy Lee: Minimizing Competition through PR," *PR Quarterly* (Fall 1987): 9-15.

19 The idea that truth is easier to prove than falsehood is found in Aristotle. John Thorp has an interesting discussion about this in "Aristotle's Rehabilitation of Rhetoric," *The Canadian Journal of Rhetorical Studies* (September 1993): 13-30, especially 16ff.

20   *PRSA Code of Professional Standards for the Practice of Public Relations: History of Enforcement* (New York: Public Relations Society of America, 1987).

21   See R.M. Miller, *Harry Emerson Fosdick: Preacher, Pastor, Prophet* (New York: Oxford University Press, 1985) especially 154 and 106; also Olasky, *Corporate PR* 48; Olasky, "Ivy Lee" 11; and H.R. Ryan, *Harry Emerson Fosdick: A Persuasive Preacher* (New York: Greenwood Press, 1989) 79, for more about payments for disseminating Fosdick's message.

22   Elizabeth Payne, "Proposed tobacco bill going up in smoke," *Ottawa Citizen*, 22 September 1993: A3; and Imasco Ltd., *Annual Report* 1992, 4.

23   *The Independent*, 31 October 1996.

24   Ivy Lee, "Problems of Propaganda," Ivy Lee Papers, Seeley G. Mudd Manuscript Library, Princeton University (23 February 1930): Box 3, Folder 2, 2.

25   Lee, "Editing Public Opinion," Ivy Lee Papers (n.d.). Box 2, Folder 1.

26   Lee, "Problems of Propaganda" 5.

27   Lee, "Constructive Publicity," Ivy Lee Papers (1922-23): Box 2, Folder 3, 1. See also, Ray Eldon Hiebert, *Courtier to the Crowd: The Story of Ivy Lee and the Development of Public Relations* (Ames, IA: Iowa State University Press, 1966) 170; and Lee, "Editing Public Opinion" 8-9.

28   Lee, "Editing Public Opinion" ch. III, 4.

29   Lee, "Editing Public Opinion" ch. I, 8. Also, Ivy Lee, "The Menace of Propaganda," typescript of an article produced from an interview with Samuel Crowther for *Collier's Weekly*. Approved by Lee 13 October 1925. Ivy Lee Papers (1925): Box 3, Folder 1, 21-22.

30   Lee, "Editing Public Opinion" ch. IV. 5.

31   Lee, "Problems of Propaganda" 1-2, 3-4.

32   Lee, "Constructive Publicity" 1.

33   This and the preceding sections incorporate material previously published in my "Public Relations Ethics: Ivy Lee, Hill and Knowlton, and the Gulf War" *International Journal of Moral and Social Studies* 8, 3 (Autumn 1993).

34   The *Wall Street Journal*, 12 January 1992.

35   See on this *Middle East Watch*, "Kuwait's 'Stolen' Incubators: The widespread repercussions of a murky incident," *Middle East Watch* 4, 1 (6 February 1992). Also John MacArthur, *Second Front: Censorship and Propaganda in the Gulf War* (New York: Hill and Wang, 1992); Randal Marlin, "A Matter of Credibility," *Content* (May/June 1991); and Linden MacIntyre, "To Sell a War," *the fifth estate*, CBC Television, (7 January 1992). As a result of seeing my *Content* article, *fifth estate* researchers contacted me early in December 1991, to see what ideas I might have to offer. I suggested that they find out the identity of "Nayirah," the Kuwaiti girl who was such an effective witness for the incubator babies story. It seemed to me that, with her excellent English, she was no ordinary Kuwaiti girl but had made a perfect "credible witness" for the American audience and that her connections would probably be revealing. Such turned out to be the case, as "To Sell a War" demonstrated so well.

36   MacArthur 50.

37   Nayirah's age generally has been given as 15 and appears that way in every press account I have seen. Hill and Knowlton, in answer to a written query from me, gave the age as 14 at the time of her testimony (letter from Thomas Ross, Senior Vice-President, 10 June 1993), and I suppose they would have access to knowledgeable sources. However, her age does have a small role to play: her credibility was important at the time of her testimony, and being 15 carries greater

weight than 14. On the other hand, in 1993 her supposedly impressionistic rendering of events and unreliable memory at the time of her testimony was the issue, and this would fit slightly better with a 14-year-old.

38 See McIntyre, "To Sell A War."

39 MacArthur 54.

40 See *Middle East Watch* 5. Also United Nations Security Council, *Provisional Verbatim Record* (27 November 1990): S/PV. 2959, 37; there Dr. Bahbahani is identified as "Witness #3." The *Middle East Watch* report also discredits the testimony of other key witnesses. In particular, Dr. Abdel-Rahman al-Sumait is identified as Amnesty International's anonymous source for the information which led AI to publicized the figure of 312 incubator baby deaths, a figure he denies providing, although he vouches for claiming to bury 72 babies at Al-Rigga cemetery around 16 August 1990. See *Middle East Watch* 7. Curiously, Kroll Associates (see below in the main text) state that they "unsuccessfully attempted" to locate Dr. Abdul Rahman Sumaid (*sic*—spellings of the name differ), whom they describe as "a Red Crescent doctor who is reported to have stated that he participated in the burial of 72 babies at Al-Rigga Cemetery." Kroll Associates Inc., "Investigation into allegations regarding deaths of neonatal patients at Al-Adan Hospital, Al-Jahra Hospital, and Al-Sabah Maternity Hospital during the Iraqi occupation of Kuwait, and the status of handicapped care at the social welfare institutes," (April 1992).

41 Amnesty International News Release, Canadian Section (English speaking), (Ottawa,), 18 April 1991: 37.

42 MacArthur 70.

43 Tom Eidson, speech (no title) on Hill and Knowlton's work on behalf of Citizens for a Free Kuwait, Church of the Incarnation, "Ethics in Media" luncheon, 20 April 1993. I would like to thank Hill and Knowlton for sending me this document.

44 Secretary of the Army, *Report on Iraqi War Crimes (Desert Shield/Desert Storm)*, unclassified version, 8 January 1992; submitted to UN Security Council, 19 March 1993, as document S/25441. Relevant pages are 14, 41, and 51.

45 Amnesty International 9-10.

46 Kroll Associates 6 (emphasis in the original).

47 Personal correspondence, Alice McGillion, 8 July 1993 and 23 August 1993.

48 *Middle East Watch* 5.

49 Kroll Associates 3.

50 *Middle East Watch* 2.

51 I.F. Stone, *I.F. Stone's Weekly*, dir. Jerry Bruck, Boston, 1973.

52 Tim Weiner, "Military accused of lies over arms," *New York Times*, 28 June 1993.

53 These estimates are taken from a study by an international team of researchers, led by Dr. Alberto Ascherio of the Harvard School of Public Health. Originally published in the *New England Journal of Medicine*, it is quoted here from "Gulf War caused huge jump in infant mortality, study finds," *Ottawa Citizen*, 24 September 1992.

54 There are others who deserve recognition, such as Alexander Cockburn, *The Nation*, 4 February, 8 April, and 13 May 1991. See also his "Human Rights and Wrongs," *London Review of Books*, 9 May 1991: 12. Cockburn's early scepticism about the number of incubators in prewar Kuwait was justified in the light of the Kroll report, which placed the number as between 235 and 260 (see Kroll Report 15).

SIX
FREEDOM OF EXPRESSION
Some Classical Arguments

Our discussion so far has focused on the ethics of communication. Unethical behaviour, when recognized as such, elicits disapproval from others in society. This is not always verbally expressed, since few people wish to appear self-righteous, but disapproval can be detected easily in the usual non-verbal forms of communication, such as facial expressions. Discussion about ethics can encourage or discourage any questionable activity, since ethics is not merely "academic," but concerns how we live our lives. Given social disapproval, controls follow a consensus that a certain activity is morally undesirable. Whistling at women, socially tolerated in North America in the 1950s, is now unacceptable, because of a change in attitude that now sees it as harassment. Sometimes a change in attitude is sufficient by itself to restrain unethical and anti-social behaviour, sometimes legal or quasi-legal controls are needed, and sometimes the important attitude change only comes about after the adoption of legal or quasi-legal controls.

There is an important two-way influence between law and public opinion. Law that flies in the face of deeply entrenched public opinion will be unenforceable, or enforceable at unacceptable cost. But law that touches an area where age-old prejudices show signs of being discarded can speed up the process dramatically. Sexual harassment is a case in point. The introduction of human rights legislation and the commissions to enforce it has given legal teeth to attitudes in support of women and minority groups. They have the right to work unmolested, verbally or otherwise, in jobs hitherto closed to them, but for which they are well-suited. While not universally successful, the overall profound change in access has been accelerated by legislative means, and along with this change has come a reinforcement, for the most part, of the attitudes which led to adoption of the legislation.[1] Over a century ago, Sir James Fitzjames Stephen, architect of the criminal code that became the foundation for Canadian criminal law, noted how attitudes toward duelling were greatly altered when inflicting death on another in a duel was ruled to be murder.[2]

The need for legal controls on incitement has long been recognized. "Spreading false news" was an offence under Edward I of England and remains so in the Criminal Code of Canada, although without force and effect since it was judged unconstitutional by the Supreme Court in 1992. The Criminal Code provisions against hate propaganda have survived the constitutional scrutiny of the courts, and the continued existence of the civil law of defamation in most jurisdictions provides a disincentive to malicious communications. In various times and to various degrees, a wide variety of communications has been subject to legal controls. At one time, it was a crime of sedition in England to "excite disaffection against the person of her Majesty, her heirs or successors, or the government and constitution of the United Kingdom, as by law established, or either House of Parliament, or the administration of justice...."[3] This involved something as innocent, by today's standards, as selling a copy of Tom Paine's *Rights of Man*. Obscenity and pornography, libel, violation of copyright, fraudulent misrepresentation, incitement to lawbreaking, treason, contempt of court, divulging of state secrets, breach of trust, broadcasting without a licence, etc.—all are subject to criminal or civil legal sanctions, and the list is by no means complete. Virtually every attempt to restrict freedom of expression has a plausible-sounding reason, stated in some general terms, for imposing the restriction. However, it is hard to think of any form of restriction of free expression that has not at some time been abused. Even that great defender of liberty, Voltaire, to whom Tallentyre attributed the attitude, "I disapprove of what you say, but I will defend to the death your right to say it,"[4] was quite merciless in his prosecution of the publisher Grasset, who printed uncomplimentary things about him.

Our concern here is with what might be called the jurisprudence of propaganda controls. The scope includes hate propaganda, incitement to war, and controls over the media, advertising, and public relations. Although we include pornography insofar as that can be construed as hate propaganda, discussion of controls over erotica, as such, are beyond the scope of this book. The inclusion of the words "as such" is necessary, because it is clear that dissemination of erotic and scatological materials is often bound up with attempts at persuasion. Our focus is on the "ought" question: are some forms of controls justified in the areas concerned and, if so, what kind? Pertinent to these questions is the underlying and persistent value of free expression. It is important, therefore, to review the classical arguments in favour of such freedom by thinkers such as Milton, Locke, Voltaire, Rousseau, Mill, Meiklejohn, and Chafee, to name only a few. These defenders of free speech (treating this here as meaning free expression) had outspoken critics; for instance, the first five all had inconsistencies in their theories, or actions, or the two taken together. As we review the arguments of John Milton and John Stuart Mill, we will find free-speech defenders invoking the following values: truth, self-fulfilment and self-development, autonomy, democracy, balance between stability and change in society, social interaction and community, avoidance of the slippery slope to tyranny, and, more recently, self-legitimation or self-respect.

JOHN MILTON

John Milton (1608-74) argues passionately against the power of the state to suppress a publication through the requirement of a licence, which it can withhold or revoke. This power, exercised largely through the Court of Star Chamber until 1641, was re-enacted by Parliament in 1643 in an Act "to regulate printing: that no book, pamphlet, or paper shall be henceforth printed, unless the same be first approved and licensed by such, or at least one of such as shall be thereto appointed." Having attracted threats of censorship as a result of his publishing, without a licence, what some preachers called a "wicked" pamphlet on divorce, Milton wrote his famous *Areopagitica* in opposition to the whole process of government licensing. Echoes of his arguments can be heard in virtually any contemporary debate on free speech versus censorship.

According to his book, Milton opposed censorship generally, but he is especially critical of licensing because it involved what later came to be termed, in the US, "prior restraint." The special harm attaching to prior restraint is that the government can keep materials from reaching the public, so there can be no accountability, no judgment by the people that the power to suppress was wrongly exercised. Some of Milton's phrases apply to both prepublication and post-publication censorship: "as good almost kill a man as kill a good book ... he who destroys a good book, kills reason itself, kills the image of God, as it were, in the eye."[5] Perhaps his main argument is the argument from truth, that by prohibiting publication, the learning process is stifled. If a book is in error, free discussion will reveal the errors. As Milton writes so eloquently:

> And though all the winds of doctrine were let loose to play upon the earth, so Truth be in the field, we do injuriously by licensing and prohibiting to misdoubt her strength. Let her and Falsehood grapple; who ever knew Truth put to the worse in a free and open encounter? Her confuting is the best and surest suppressing. (JM 50)

Licensing, he says, in a frequently adopted mercantile metaphor, "hinders and retards the importation of our richest merchandise, truth" (JM 41).

Milton brings other powerful arguments to bear:

1. Our abilities will be blunted if we are constantly protected from error. We should actively engage in the process of filtering truth from error and should not rely on someone else to do it for us.
2. Censorship will not succeed—scandalous, seditious, and libellous works will still circulate. Nor will evil cease. Evil forms of activity can be learned without books.
3. Censorship requires censors, who will have to read the materials. If the material is corrupting, what will happen to the censors themselves?
4. Censorship of publications puts us on a slippery slope: if books are regu-

lated, why not also dance and music? Why not all recreations and pastimes, what we eat, drink, and wear? Even our talk might come to be regulated (JM 23–24).

5. If state control prevents us from contact with all things that might incline us to do evil, what role will there be for individual virtue? (JM 25–26). If God has so ordained things that evil and good both exist in the world, why should we act differently? God has given people a trial on earth. By what right should anyone take away this trial?

6. If a person believes some doctrine only by virtue of the bidding of a pastor or legislative authority, then, even if the belief is true, there is heresy of a kind, because freedom of conscience is thereby negated (JM 37).

7. The only kind of people who would want to take on the job of censor are suspect, likely being: "either ignorant, imperious, and remiss, or basely pecuniary" (JM 28). The censor will likely be the inferior of the scholar, who wants to be published.

8. What guarantee of truth will there be to a teacher, when all texts are under the control of the patriarchal licenser? The office charged with censorship will likely accept for publication only what fits in with the preconceptions of the general public. (Milton was keenly aware of the degrading task involved in editing a complicated and laboriously worked text, only for the purpose of satisfying some blinkered and uninspired censor's mind.)

In spite of all the rousing things Milton has to say in defence of free expression, he does not believe that "anything goes" and quite definitely endorses the censorship of two classes of persons: Roman Catholics and atheists. The passage in which he says this deserves to be quoted in full, since it will otherwise be difficult to believe he actually said it:

> I mean not tolerated popery and open superstition, which as it extirpates all religions and civil supremacies, so itself should be extirpated, provided first that all charitable and compassionate means be used to win and regain the weak and the misled: that also which is impious or evil absolutely, either against faith or manners [=morals], no law can possibly permit that intends not to unlaw itself. (JM 52)

These exceptions to his general principles will seem most odd to a contemporary audience, but it should be borne in mind that Milton feared that if Catholics regained power, freedom for people like himself to express themselves openly would disappear. The increased tolerance of today may stem from diminished fear of the consequence of a religious group gaining power in our western democracies. Consciousness of the degree of unfreedom allowed under the Taliban government in Afghanistan can heighten our awareness of the problem. The Victorian writer John Morley spoke insightfully about tolerance in the early twentieth century, in his book *On Compromise*:

We constantly hear the age lauded for its tolerance, for its candour, for its openness of mind, for the readiness with which a hearing is given to ideas that forty years ago would have excluded persons suspected of holding them. Before, however, we congratulate ourselves too warmly on this, let us be quite sure that we are not mistaking for tolerance what is really nothing more creditable than indifference. These two attitudes of mind, which are so vitally unlike in their real quality, are so hard to distinguish in their outer seeming.[6]

Milton's thinking parallels writers of the 1950s who felt that censorship of Communist literature was justified because, if the Communists came into power, they would readily impose censorship themselves. "No freedom for the foes of freedom," is one form of expression for the thinking involved. As for atheism, such was the intertwining of religion and morals in Milton's day that an attack on God was seen as an attack on morality as well. Once again, the modern reader is so used to the idea that morality can exist despite disbelief in God's existence that Milton's view seems both inconsistent and unacceptable. A modern equivalent of what Milton was contemplating—that is, something that allegedly undermines the morality of our fellow citizens—is the case of mind-altering drugs. Fear of such an outcome, whether or not well-founded, has helped to fuel opposition to marijuana use today.

John Locke (1632-1704) explicitly shares Milton's opinion that atheists and those who subject themselves to a religion tied to a foreign state, such that their civil allegiance to the crown might conflict with their religious obligations, should not be tolerated by the civil magistrate. Nor, for Locke, should those be tolerated who profess to have special privilege or power, derived from religion, over the civil authority, or who "will not own and teach the duty of tolerating all men in matters of mere religion"[7]; "mere" presumably referring to religions not tied to political power. Missing from Locke's account, as Fitzjames Stephen argues in a critique, is the principle that "free inquiry is the great, and indeed almost the only possible guarantee for the truth of any doctrines whatever. Persecution destroys this guarantee, and is therefore unfavourable to any intelligent and real belief in the truth of any creed whatever."[8] Fitzjames Stephen is clearly indebted to John Stuart Mill for this insight, though he criticizes Mill as well.

JOHN STUART MILL

Mill's *On Liberty* deserves a preeminent place among texts devoted to defence of a liberal theory of free expression. The influence of this essay in the English-speaking world has been enormous. His arguments, or variations on them, still form part of the arsenal that civil libertarians use to defend such freedom today. They are interesting philosophically, because they are not merely polemical broadsides aimed indirectly at promoting a particular cause, with free speech invoked for that ulterior purpose. On the contrary, they are linked to the project of providing a coherent view of human social and political existence. For that very reason, Mill can be turned against himself, by adapting one or other of his basic contentions to support a different outcome than the one he envisages. His arguments in favour of free speech warrant close study, as do also the exceptions he allowed to his basic principle of maximizing such freedom.

Underlying Principles

Mill's book begins with an epigraph from a treatise on government written by the noted German scholar, sage, and politician, Wilhelm von Humboldt, whom he clearly admires. Humboldt's central doctrine is that "the end of man … is the highest and most harmonious development of his powers to a complete and consistent whole" and that from "freedom and variety of situations" comes the desired object: "the individuality of power and development."[9] This supports Mill's anti-paternalistic stance. The idea that the state should act as a kind of nanny to grown persons, by legislating to protect them from making bad decisions affecting themselves, was abhorrent to him. He says:

> [T]he only purpose for which power can be rightfully exercised over any member of a civilised community, against his will, is to prevent harm to others…. His own good, either physical or moral, is not a sufficient warrant. The only part of the conduct of anyone for which he is amenable to society is that which concerns others. In the part which merely concerns himself, his independence is, of right, absolute. Over himself, over his own body and mind, the individual is sovereign. (JSM 13)

In other words, the state has no business forcing people to refrain from unhealthy eating or drinking habits, or preventing them from skydiving or mountain-climbing, so long as others are not endangered thereby. There are immediate free speech implications to be drawn from this premise. If an adult wants to hear someone else's dangerous, corrupting thoughts and theories, he or she should be permitted to do so. On the face of things, this seems to mean that incitement to treason, encouragement to use of drugs, tobacco advertising, counselling of suicide, pimping, and so on, should be permitted. The philosophy seems to say that people are free to go to hell anyway they choose, so long as they don't harm others. In fact, Mill does not draw such an unequivocal conclusion. He provides exceptions to the principle of free speech, but, even before that, he provides exceptions to his basic anti-paternalistic principle. The exceptions are threefold:

> It is, perhaps, hardly necessary to say that this doctrine is meant to apply only to human beings in the maturity of their faculties. We are not speaking of children or of young persons below the age which the law may fix as that of manhood or womanhood. Those who are still in a state to require being

taken care of by others must be protected against their own actions as well as against external injury. For the same reason we may leave out of consideration those backward states of society in which the race itself may be considered in its nonage ... (JSM 13-14)

In other words, paternalism is acceptable where children are concerned, but also, more generally, where people are not in possession of mature faculties. This presumably includes those who are insane and unable to look adequately after their own interests in a predatory environment. His third exception is part and parcel of the British colonial mentality of his time, and at the very least has to be rephrased to get a sympathetic hearing today. The idea that a whole people could be so backward as to vitiate a right of free speech is of course repugnant to modern ears attuned to signs of racism.

Crucial to Mill's defence of his anti-paternalist stance is his distinction between what is in the sphere of an individual's interest and what is in society's interest. He thinks that there is, indeed, a sphere of action which is directly in an individual's interest and in which society has "if any, only an indirect interest: comprehending all that portion of a person's life or conduct which affects only himself or, if it also affects others, only with their free, voluntary, and undeceived consent and participation" (JSM 15-16). He recognizes that what affects oneself can also indirectly affect others and that problems for his theory can arise from this fact. A second major difficulty comes from disagreement about whether the fallout from a person's activity, when it does affect others, can be construed as harm or not. Perhaps someone doesn't like the message carried on a placard in a political demonstration. Perhaps a message supporting a right to abortion gives distress to some, while a message seeking to criminalize it upsets others.[10] At what point does this distress become harm justifying suppression?

Two other questions arise from Mill's essay on liberty: can his exceptions be meshed consistently with his philosophy? And is his proclaimed utilitarianism consistent with either the underlying principle of non-paternalism or with the exceptions he makes? Before looking at these questions, we need to examine Mill's arguments in favour of free speech and the reasons he gives for requiring exceptions.

Free Speech Arguments

Mill brings a battery of considerations and arguments to bear on his free speech principle, which is concisely stated in a footnote to his Chapter Two. The principle is that "there ought to exist the fullest liberty of professing and discussing, as a matter of ethical conviction, any doctrine, however immoral it may be considered."

SELF-DEVELOPMENT AND SOCIAL BENEFIT

The tendency to conformity is strong, and people with original, but challenging, ideas are likely to be silenced if there is no recognition of the value of nonconformity. George Bernard Shaw was later to put this idea very succinctly when he said, "The reasonable man adapts himself to the world: the unreasonable one persists in trying to adapt the world to himself. Therefore all progress depends on the unreasonable man."[11] Mill acknowledges that there is a need to protect a minority not only against tyranny by the state, but also against the formidable social tyranny that is more difficult to escape, penetrating as it does "much more deeply into the details of life, and enslaving the soul itself." From this comes Mill's call for resistance to this social tendency:

> Protection, therefore, against the tyranny of the magistrate is not enough; there needs protection also against the tyranny of the prevailing opinion and feeling, against the tendency of society to impose, by other means than civil penalties, its own ideas and practices as rules of conduct on those who dissent from them; to fetter the development and, if possible, prevent the formation of any individuality not in harmony with its ways, and compel all characters to fashion themselves upon the model of its own. (JSM 7)

Thus, the twofold benefit from free expression is both to individual self-development and to the society that profits from the new ideas.

INFALLIBILITY AND LEGITIMACY

A quite different thread in Mill's argument concerns legitimacy. The strength of an idea cannot be measured without giving it a fair hearing. Truth is not to be determined by political power, but by examining its claims in the light of relevant evidence. The power to silence expression of non-conforming views is illegitimate: "If all mankind minus one were of one opinion, mankind would be no more justified in silencing that one person than he, if he had the power, would be justified in silencing mankind," because there is an implicit assumption of infallibility when one engages in such suppression. "To refuse a hearing to an opinion because they are sure that it is false is to assume that their certainty is the same as absolute certainty. All silencing of discussion is an assumption of infallibility" (JSM 21-22). If we allow that we are not infallible, then we must recognize the possibility that the view we want to suppress is true, and, if so, we do wrong to suppress it. Therefore, the preservation of truth is one reason for allowing maximal liberty in expression.

In fact, Mill concedes that some people bent on censorship do not necessarily claim infallibility; instead, they claim certainty strong enough to warrant action. As he phrases the objection, in reference to power-holders: "To prohibit what they think pernicious is not claiming exemption from error, but fulfilling the duty incumbent on them, although fallible, of acting on their conscientious conviction" (JSM 23). Government leaders constantly have to make tough decisions, affecting the lives of others, without having absolute certainty. To Mill's credit, he puts the objection to his own position quite forcefully: "There is no such thing as absolute certainty, but there is assurance sufficient for the purposes of human life. We may, and must, assume our opinion to be true for the guidance of our own conduct; and it is assuming no more when we forbid bad men to pervert society by the propagation of opinions which we regard as false and pernicious" (JSM 24). Mill's answer to this objection is impressive. He ties it to an old adage in law, that one should hear the other side to a dispute: "Complete liberty of contradicting and disproving our opinion is the very condition which justifies us in assuming its truth for purposes of action; and on no other terms can a being with human faculties have any rational assurance of being right" (JSM 24). This is a centrally important observation, not just for individual expressions of isolated doctrine, but for a whole philosophy of democratic government. Mill's argument has staying power, but an immediate reply can be made along the following lines: If the problem is that government leaders need to legitimize their judgments by hearing the other side, why can they not satisfy the requirement by hearing the views they desire to suppress expressed behind closed doors? If the leaders give these views full consideration, and win the argument in debate with the person whose ideas are to be suppressed, then the legitimacy problem has been solved for some, at least. Mill is aware of this type of argument and notes the practice of the Roman Catholic Church of allowing members of the hierarchy to read books forbidden to most of the faithful for the purpose of being better able to refute them.

In reply, Mill notes that, without dissemination, a doctrine will not get a full and effective hearing. Yet, such a hearing is necessary, so that other highly intelligent people may be convinced and become involved in its defence. Without dissemination, these other potential defenders will be kept out of action. Mill's defence of his infallibility argument thus mutates into a legitimacy question, but as such it carries weight. Secondly, he argues that it is all very well for a select group of officials to satisfy themselves that the dissenting doctrines are without merit, but does that justify them in preventing others from hearing those doctrines and deciding for themselves? No! This is Mill's point in using the word "infallibility." As he says, "it is not the feeling sure of a doctrine (be it what it may) which I call an assumption of infallibility. It is the undertaking to decide that question for others, without allowing them to hear what can be said on the contrary side" (JSM 29). Mill bolsters his arguments against the assumption of infallibility by reflecting on historical cases—those of Socrates, Jesus, and Christianity under Emperor Marcus Aurelius—where, from a later perspective, the persecutors of a new doctrine were wrong. As Mill notes, any of the arguments that might be used to suppress atheism could have been used, suitably modified, to support Aurelius's action against Christianity.

Mill also takes note of the value of continual self-correction. Progress comes from recognition of the corrigibility of what we believe, and the development of a habit of openness to correction will improve the process of learning. We need people who listen to what others have to say, not people who put blinkers around cherished ideas for fear of losing them. Stifling unpopular opinion discourages development of this beneficial character trait of openness.

PARTIAL TRUTH

As a second general line of argument, Mill observes that even if the doctrine, taken as a whole, is in error, a vigorous defence of it may lead us to discover new truths or to recover aspects of older truths that have been forgotten. By not allowing its expression, we cut ourselves off from access to some aspects of truth that may be enlightening. We need to encourage bold thinkers, who are not afraid to follow reason where it may take them, instead of aborting an inquiry when it threatens to end in some heretical conclusion. The harm of suppression is not only done to the suppressed thinkers. "The greatest harm," Mill claims, "is to those who are not heretics, and whose whole mental development is cramped and their reason cowed by the fear of heresy" (JSM 41). No great thinker can subordinate the pursuit of truth to predetermined conclusions, he claims. "Truth gains more even by the errors of one who, with due study and preparation, thinks for himself than by the true opinions of those who only hold them because they do not suffer themselves to think" (JSM 41).[12] Not silencing expression of a doctrine permits us to benefit from such part-truths as may be contained in the doctrine we wish to suppress. When there are conflicting doctrines, it is unlikely that one is wholly true and the other wholly false. More likely they share some part of the truth between them (JSM 56). The real problem comes from taking an incomplete set of truths for a complete set. Opposition helps those with open minds to realize what is missing from their own set. This can be so even though the challenged view may start with the greater amount of truth.

VITALITY OF BELIEF AND COMPREHENSION OF THE DOCTRINE

Quite apart from the possible truth of all or part of a heretical doctrine, Mill recognizes the great benefit provided by challenges to received opinion, namely, the stimulus to holding those views with vitality. Without any challenges, a view may become simply "dead dogma." The result of avoiding all critical reflection about a doctrine one subscribes to is that one becomes unable to defend the view against the most superficial objections. Apart from that, the holding even of true opinion through prejudice is unworthy of a rational being and does not constitute knowledge (JSM 43). We do not fully understand the justification for our believing in our own doctrines if we do not understand what arguments are brought against them. How can we say that some contrary view is wrong, when we don't even know what that view is? To experience a proper challenge to received opinion, it is not enough, Mill thinks, to get a secondhand statement of heretical opinions. It is important to hear from people who actually believe these statements and who can present their case in the strongest form.

Added to the question of vitality is the matter of comprehension. Mill argues that absence of challenge does not lead only to diminishing intellectual enthusiasm for a set of beliefs. It also results in atrophy of understanding: the beliefs become more and more imperfectly understood. Eventually only the "shell or husk" of an idea is retained, while the "finer essence" is lost (JSM 48). In fact, this was the state for most of Mill's contemporaries regarding their belief in Christianity.

This situation was very different from that of the early Christians, who had to struggle to defend and spread their beliefs.

Finally, Mill notes how easy it is for upholders of the received view to denounce challengers as being immoral people and to demand that they be less strident in their expression. This polemical debating weapon introduces unfairness into the debate, since the challenger cannot so easily attack the character of a defender of the status quo. If anything deserves protection, Mill argues, it is the view that challenges orthodoxy. Better still is a moral judgment by the community to disapprove of attacks on character and to encourage disputants to stick to the matters under debate.

Mill's Exceptions and the Matter of Consistency

If we try to apply Mill's theory to some of the specific issues concerning us today, we find some problems. Take, for example, the question of whether it is legitimate to suppress tobacco advertising. It is clear that Mill had in mind the propagation of doctrines, whether scientific, religious, or political. Modern advertising does not express doctrine, although it may hint at certain unstated claims. The same is true with regard to hate propaganda, some of which can be a matter of doctrine. However, most use insulting epithets or a deliberately falsified version of history. Mill's argument depends to some extent on the merit of hearing a passionate defender of some heterodox opinion. He has not envisaged for us, other than in passing,[13] the cynical disseminator of falsehoods who knows them to be false. Can we be confident that what is thus disseminated will still contain some partial truth?

When Mill considers specific free speech problems in his own time, he takes into account cases where the model is not that of a doctrinal dissenter, but of someone much more practically oriented, or whose expressions have immediate practical consequences. We need to examine the matter of consistency between the exceptions and his stated principles.

CHILDREN

Mill specifically excepted children from the ambit of his remarks. Some general readers take this to mean "children should be seen and not heard"; in other words, it is all right to silence them. Certainly, there are circumstances in which children are rightly silenced by parents or guardians, although it would be ludicrous to claim that they should not be allowed to express their thoughts about God, morality, music, what's wrong with school, parents, etc. This is not Mill's point. He is concerned with what law and morality have to say about curtailing expression, and the argument that adults should not have to be protected from corruption by communications from others clearly is not applicable to children. Children do not have the experience and knowledge to evaluate critically what they are told. Parents have the right and the duty to protect their children from evil influences. Once we understand curtailment of free speech in this way, Mill's exception becomes acceptable. That children should be protected in some respects against the free expression of others is uncontroversial today, although there are disagreements concerning specific matters, such as whether a parent or the state should prevail on the matter of exposing young children to sex education, the teaching of evolution in schools, etc.

INFIRM ADULTS AND PEOPLE "IN THEIR NONAGE"
Mill also made exceptions for adults suffering from some relevant kind of infirmity, affecting, for example, their reasoning or judgmental powers (although he does not spell this out). Once again, we must object to Mill, if we think this means measures such as gagging or sedating mental patients. However, if we think of the predations of unscrupulous marketers, who exploit the deteriorating judgment of elderly persons, the picture changes (for an explanation of what I have in mind, see Chapter 5, page 178).

INCITEMENT
Mill makes an exception to his principle in the case of incitement, where the damage is immediate. Since his philosophy is based on the advantages of hearing different sides to a disputed doctrine, the benefits only arise under circumstances where time permits formation of a balanced judgment. However, he recognizes that there are situations in which provocative remarks can trigger off harmful actions, and he makes an exception for such cases. He illustrates his point by a story about corn-dealers who support tariffs, thus raising the price of grain for the British people:

> An opinion that corn-dealers are starvers of the poor, or that private property is robbery, ought to be unmolested when simply circulated through the press, but may justly incur punishment when delivered orally to an excited mob assembled before the house of a corn-dealer, or when handed about among the same mob in the form of a placard. Acts of whatever kind, which without justifiable cause do harm to others may be, and in the more important cases absolutely require to be, controlled by the unfavourable sentiments, and, when needful, by the active interference of mankind. (JSM 67-68)

This is an important restriction on his principle, and it immediately raises questions of the following sort: just how immediate must the threat be to the life of the corn-dealer? Does it matter if the effect of the incitement is felt right away or instead results a few days later in death by stealth? Does it make any difference whether what is said is true or false? In American jurisprudence, Justice Oliver Wendell Holmes Jr. introduced the "clear and present danger" test for deciding whether or not a speech act was seditious (and therefore punishable by law). It can be argued that false accusations over time, in a situation where the communicatees are not able to find out the truth, can lead to systematic harms against a person or group. Why should the time lapse make this situation different from the case of the corn-dealer, where Mill allows an exception to his principle? Another important question is whether deliberately deceptive propaganda should be treated differently from honest expression of opinion.

COMMERCIAL SPEECH

Mill thinks that commercial speech is on a very different footing from the expression of beliefs concerning doctrines in science, religion, or politics. He says, "Whoever undertakes to sell any description of goods to the public, does what affects the interests of other persons, and of society in general; and thus his conduct, in principle, comes within the jurisdiction of society" (JSM 117). At first one may question the distinction. Someone who gives a political speech also affects people. The words of Karl Marx, Jesus, and Socrates, for example, affected many people. However, consider a situation in which a person is selling poison. If the poison is not properly labelled, people's lives are put at risk right away. The effect of such mislabelling is much less under anyone's control than the case of political speech. Mill favours free trade, but he feels that controls to enhance safety are permissible, so long as they are restricted to what is necessary to reduce involuntary harms from the sales. If the poison has some legitimate use, the legitimate users should not be barred access to it simply because others might want to use it for murder. Thus, the state can properly require labelling of the poison. The buyer "cannot wish not to know that the thing he possesses has poisonous qualities," Mill writes (JSM 117). Where articles are regularly used for criminal purposes, the state legitimately may require the seller to register the name and address of the buyer, quantities sold, etc. Mill's suggestion has been acted on in many jurisdictions, including Canada, with regard to firearms.

Mill recognizes the duty of public authority to prevent accidents, and he defends this duty in the case where a man is about to cross an unsafe bridge, not knowing of its hazardous condition. If there is no time to warn him, the police have the right to physically prevent him from crossing, without any real infringement on his liberty. If there is time to explain all the dangers, and a person decides to enter upon risky activity anyway, Mill thinks he should not be prevented from taking the risk, because only that person knows his motives well enough to judge whether the risk is worth taking or not. We are speaking, of course, of adult persons who are not in some condition rendering their judgment unfit (see above). Few people will quarrel with Mill's judgment that it would be right to stop the person who does not know of the risk, but his language is so broad that it opens the door to potential abuses of authority. Any authority can reason that no one desires the harms from smoking or alcohol abuse; therefore, it is no infringement of liberty to prevent either of these activities. Once we link freedom to what people would choose if they were fully informed, instead of first informing them and seeing what they do choose, we are on the road to endorsing Rousseau's notion of "forcing people to be free." Freedom on Rousseau's account implies a distinction between a person's higher self and his or her lower self, and a totalitarian state could pass all kinds of restrictive legislation in the name of such a higher self. For the libertarian, there is a need to protect the individual against such possible legal restrictions. Perhaps it is worth repeating that Mill himself was not advocating Rousseau's approach.

Mill supports the right of mature individuals to purchase drugs such as opium, even though it had become a social problem in some areas of British rule during his lifetime. He is at odds on this point with his critic, Fitzjames Stephen, who deplores the imposition of free trade in such drugs on China, correctly predicting the animosity against British rule which the callous implementation of this policy engendered.[14] Mill, in fact, makes some statements that can be marshalled against his free trade position regarding drugs. He specifically defends the legal non-recognition of contracts by which a person might sell himself or herself into slavery because "by selling himself for a slave, he abdicates his liberty.... The principle of freedom cannot require that he should be free not to be free" (JSM 125). Why not import some of this theory into the treatment of highly addictive drugs? The addict also loses freedom regarding the future craving for the addictive substance. This should have some implication for advertising of such addictive substances.

In fact, Mill considers very carefully the question of counselling people to do things that society judges is wrong and comes up with opposing views. He neither favours permitting the advertising of harmful products nor prohibiting such advertising. He takes the example of pimping, presenting the dilemma in the following way. On the one hand, giving advice and inducements to others is a social act and affects others. On the other hand, if people must be allowed to engage in what concerns themselves only, to act as seems best, why should they not also be free to seek out the advice of others? "*Whatever it is permitted to do, it must be permitted to advise to do*" (JSM 120, italics added).

Having said that, though, Mill makes an exception for commercially motivated advice. The question, he says, is "doubtful only when the instigator derives a personal benefit from his advice, when he makes it his occupation, for subsistence for pecuniary gain, to promote what society and the State consider to be an evil." Since Mill believes that consensual prostitution should not be outlawed, the italicized principle quoted above should lead him to accept the advertising of such services. But he is in two minds about whether people should be allowed to induce others to engage in such activity. He considers an argument for denying such freedom: the state or the public "cannot be acting wrongly in endeavouring to exclude the influence of solicitations which are not disinterested, of instigators who cannot possibly be impartial—who have a direct personal interest on one side, and that side the one which the State believes to be wrong, and who confessedly promote it for personal objects only" (JSM 121). There is nothing lost, according to this argument, by having people make up their minds free from inducements by others. Even if some people will continue to engage in the socially disapproved behaviour, others will be dissuaded by the element of secrecy involved, and a good effect will have been achieved.

Mill admits that there is a moral anomaly here, according to which the principle activity—fornication or gambling—would be legal, but the accessory behaviour of the pimp or gambling-house keeper would be punishable offences. He does not resolve this anomaly either way. He puts the case on the "exact boundary line" between the principle classifying inducement as a social act needing control and the principle of freedom for individuals to seek out whatever advice they wish.

The basis for Mill's backtracking from the full application of the liberty principle is tied to the argument from truth. As long as extraneous motives, such as profit, enter into discourse, one cannot expect that communications will have the truth as a primary object, any more than "product placements" built into the scripts of movies are likely to enhance their artistic merit. For some people, all commercial speech should be excluded from constitutional protection, but, while such a view is attractive when some forms of advertising are contemplated, it has the drawback of allowing the prohibition of the use of all but some designated language in all advertising. This in turn means acceptance of a form of linguistic tyranny. Whether the Quebec government's restrictions on the use of the English language in advertising are justifiable or not is a debated matter, but the idea that the minority should have no rights whatever in such matters of expression does not seem right to many people on both sides of the linguistic divide.

Assuming the considerations Mill adduces to be evenly balanced, further arguments ought to be able to tip the scales in one direction or another. As earlier mentioned, the freedom-threatening nature of addictive drugs ought to weigh on the side of permitting government restraints on advertising them. The fact that tobacco advertisements are so often targeted at youth (under 18-year-olds) is another factor. Moreover, there is the consideration that much tobacco advertising, as we have seen, is misleading.

Mill's Critics

Mill has been criticized by libertarians, some of whom believe that he is too much of an instrumentalist in defending free speech on the basis of the goods that flow from it. They feel that free speech should be seen as constitutive of a good life and of democratic society. It is not that some good will come of it, rather, that part of what it means to have a democratic society is that free speech is protected.

Mill has also been criticized by socialists (and others) on the grounds that the harms resulting from his hands-off approach to communications are greater than those that would follow from more restraint, particularly in the area of, for example, the potential for violence resulting from racist speech. Conservatives are more likely to think of the need for controls on pornography or seditious behaviour, but they, too, reject what they see as Mill's hands-off approach to interfering with free speech.

JAMES FITZJAMES STEPHEN

Fitzjames Stephen (1829–94, and so-named to distinguish him from his eminent father, Sir James Stephen) provides a book-length critique of Mill's essay in his *Liberty, Equality, Fraternity*. Although Fitzjames Stepen once stood as a candidate for the Liberal Party, his thinking was generally conservative, and he resisted the progressive side of Mill's thinking. From 1869, he lived in India for over two years, where, as a legal member of the Law Commission, he was charged among other things with providing codified bodies of law. He was fully attuned to questions of morality and law, having to adapt the thinking of a Christian-based society to something that would result in a workable system of law for Hindus, Muslims, and others. What bothers Fitzjames Stephen about Mill's principles is not the end result, since he more or less agrees with the extent of freedom allowed as it pertained to India. Rather, he rejects the universalist language in which Mill expresses himself. Fitzjames Stephen thinks that freedoms that are suitable in one social and political environment may not be suitable to another. He also feels that certain key distinctions in Mill needed clarification.

One such distinction is that between actions affecting ourselves alone and those that also affect others. Self-protection can be construed broadly or narrowly, Fitzjames Stephen writes. Revolutions are a clear case in which actions taken by one group of people, to satisfy their own interests, have an impact on everyone else as well. Human conduct is guided by innumerable influences that become embedded in our outlooks. We accept these influences without thinking much about them. To the extent that we are aware of the hostile prejudices of other people, we may understandably feel afraid. In Fitzjames Stepen's words:

> The life of the great mass of men, to a great extent the life of all men, is like a water-course guided this way or that by a system of dams, sluices, weirs and embankments. The volume and quality of the different streams differ, and so do the plans of the works by which their flow is regulated, but it is by these works—that is to say, by their various customs and institutions—that men's lives are regulated. Now these customs are not only in their very nature constraints, but they are restraints imposed by the will of an exceedingly small numerical minority and contentedly accepted by a majority to which they have become so natural that they do not recognize them as restraints.[15]

The upshot of this argument is that there is always an impact that the conduct of some people has on others, even if it is only by force of example. This has important applications to modern questions of hate propaganda and pornography containing a component of violence. To many, the thought that some men take pleasure from depictions of sadistic sexual assaults on women is frightening. That the state should freely allow such materials to circulate will knock away one of the "weirs and embankments" by which the mass of people take their cues for behaviour. It is not irrational to fear that such materials, if allowed to circulate, will have a deleterious effect on men's attitudes towards them.[16]

Fitzjames Stephen also takes issue with the exceptions Mill allows for children and a nation "in its nonage," that is to say, in an undeveloped state (or, in the language used in his time, a "backward" nation). Mill reasons that such people, lacking education, are not in a position to benefit from free discussion. But

Fitzjames Stephen counters that not only children, but also many adults in supposedly advanced societies are often not improved by discussion. In fact, he says, there is never a time when discussion will necessarily lead or not lead to improvement. Therefore, compulsion is never justified or always justified, depending on how you construe things.

Fitzjames Stephen, himself, has a low opinion of the capacity for the masses to be improved by discussion: "If we look at the conduct of bodies of men as expressed in their laws and institutions, we shall find that, though compulsion and persuasion go hand in hand, from the most immature and the roughest" societies "up to the most civilized, the lion's share of the results obtained is due to compulsion...."

> Parliamentary government is simply a mild and disguised form of compulsion. We agree to try strength by counting heads instead of breaking heads, but the principle is exactly the same. It is not the wisest side which wins but the one which for the time being shows its superior strength ... The minority gives way not because it is convinced that it is wrong, but because it is convinced that it is a minority.[17]

Fitzjames Stephen's criticism comes from the standpoint of what is sometimes called managerial liberalism, the Benthamite attitude that looks at overall social good rather than individual rights. Mill, on the other hand, is concerned with the need for individual self-development. On Mill's view, even if people choose the wrong solution to a problem, they are better for having developed the critical capacities within themselves to discuss and deal with the problem. As an answer to Mill, then, Fitzjames Stephen's critical observations are incomplete.

Fitzjames Stephen does pay attention to individual development in some contexts. He approves of coercion in the form of taxes to subsidize libraries, art centres, orchestras, and cultural activity generally, thinking this is the right thing to do even if, after discussion, it is not what the population at large would agree to. So, while he is enthusiastic about self-development when it arises as an end-product of social planning, he is far less concerned with this self-development when it pertains to grassroots discussion in the process of arriving at political decisions. From today's standpoint, his critique seems elitist—not surprisingly, given his family background.

Finally, Fitzjames Stephen makes the very telling point that libel law, the existence in some form or other of which is generally supported, conflicts with the amount of freedom Mill's theory allows. Because Mill is thinking of doctrinal matters, not defamation, some qualifications need to be made if libel law is to be accommodated to his theory. For example the "clear and present danger" test can hardly be appropriate in determining what is libellous. Character assassination is harmful to a person whether it happens immediately or after some delay. People need to be protected against unjust and irresponsible slanders whether or not these are certain to result in measurable harm.

OTHER CRITICS

In 1957 a replay of the Mill-Fitzjames Stephen debate was sparked in Britain by the publication of the Report of the Committee on Homosexual Offences and Prostitution, otherwise known as the Wolfenden Report.[18] The committee's liberal recommendations brought a reaction from Lord Devlin, who published his British Academy Lecture, "The Enforcement of Morals" first in 1959 and then as part of a book, *The Enforcement of Morals* in 1968.[19] Recalling Fitzjames Stephen's work, H.L.A. Hart thoroughly critiqued Devlin's position, in *Law, Liberty and Morality* two years later.[20] The debate centred on the question as to whether society had a right to legislate on matters of morality, which appeared to many to be a matter of private choice rather than a public concern, homosexual acts between consenting adults being a prime case in point. The question of free speech also entered the debate with the case, discussed by Hart, of *Shaw v. Director of Public Prosecutions* (1961), which involved a procurer who wanted to publicize, with a Ladies Directory, the various offerings available to potential clients. Some nude photographs were included. Having consulted police, who apparently could find no definite grounds on which the publication would be illegal, he went ahead, only to be prosecuted and convicted on three charges, one of which was the centuries-old common law offence of "conspiracy to corrupt public morals." The conviction was upheld on appeal, and he was sent to jail. The vagueness of this last charge opened up a large area of potential convictions for crimes not known as such to the doer. As Hart commented: "As a result of Shaw's case, virtually any cooperative conduct is criminal if a jury consider it ex post facto to have been immoral."[21] Shaw's case falls squarely within the realm envisaged and unresolved by Mill, in which two strong principles collide; although the *ex post facto* issue, a form of retrospective legislation in effect, should work for Mill in Shaw's favour.

Shortly thereafter, two Australian philosophers, H.J. McCloskey and D.H. Monro, also clashed, the former as a critic and the latter as a defender of Mill. McCloskey argued that certain beliefs, such as those concerning racial inferiority, are not only false, but dangerously wrong and deserve severe censure. Mill, he thinks, places too high a valuation on possible true belief as against the evils that may result from preparing a receptive environment for it, namely, one that tolerates all kinds of dangerous falsehoods. Our willingness to accept the limitations of freedom of expression in the case of libel and defamation rests in part on our belief that we can reach a high degree of probability in these areas about which views are true. McCloskey does not mind claiming infallibility about the judgment that sadistic torturing by parents of unwanted children is a grave evil. From the absurdity of supposing this is not wrong, he argues that our supposed fallibility is insufficient to disentitle society from legislating against forms of expression that encourage such outrageous acts. This may seem a cumbersome way of saying that such legislation is justified, but, of course, there are other arguments to consider than that of fallibility. For example, there are practical concerns as to whether legislation is enforceable, whether it will do more good than harm, and whether more effective alternative routes to the goal might exist.

Mill's argument that suppression denies the population some truth does not apply with such force when it is a matter of denying the expression only in a particular time and place. McCloskey is sympathetic to such a possibility:

> [I]f it were to be found that the publishing of the true figures concerning Negro crime rates in the USA in respect of murder and rape, incited mob violence, and opposition to poverty relief measures, it would be reasonable for enlightened legislators to consider temporarily restricting the publication of these figures.[22]

Monro agrees with McCloskey that in some areas—such as the fact that arsenic is poisonous—it is important to know the truth, not just the reasons on which it is based, and so restraints on mischievous false assertions in that regard might well be justified. However, he says, this situation hardly applies to politics, morality, and religion. Censorship harms its own cause in the long run by generating the suspicion that the view suppressed cannot be shown to be false, if it has been censored. Nor are the people in government charged with making censorship decisions likely to be those whose opinions one would readily trust. This point is clearly illustrated by a recent case in Ottawa. A person submitted a roll of film for developing. The roll contained a few pictures of his three-year-old son in a state of nudity. The pictures were handed over by a clerk to police on the grounds that they fell foul of the child pornography law. Charges were dropped, but the person involved had legal expenses and had to undergo with his wife and son some counselling from the local Children's Aid Society.[23]

Suppression of crime statistics, Monro argues, "would lead people to suspect the truth (indeed to suspect rather more than the truth) and so would defeat its own purpose."[24] By making exceptions to the free speech principle the atmosphere of free discussion is destroyed, in the long run causing more harm than good. Of course, Monro assumes that the facts of suppression are discovered. It can be argued that, if censorship operated in the form of behind-the-scenes pressures, no such information would become public, and so there would be no change in the atmosphere of public discussion. Such an argument assumes the existence of the kind of controls and philosophy associated with a closed society, with all the dangers associated with such a society. I prefer the notion of an open society that lies behind Monro's assumption.

MODERN COMMUNICATIONS MEDIA: A FREE AND OPEN ENCOUNTER?

It is often observed that, with the modern mass media of communication, the "free and open encounter" envisaged by both Milton and Mill hardly obtains. Some people wield enormous power over the content of the media. Others lack such power. Whether one gets a hearing or not depends on the editorial judgment of those to whom one submits an article or letter. The media have their own particular interests in increasing circulation and attracting advertisers, so that the truth may sometimes take a back seat to the question "Will it sell?" Complex arguments stand less of a chance of being published in a letter to the local newspaper, because editors rightly surmise that a majority of readers will not have the time to read carefully and prefer the gist of an argument to its full explication. The problem of unequal space, attention, and emphasis was succinctly put by Charles Rembar in an article for *The Atlantic Monthly*: "If you and I are opponents, and I speak through a bullhorn while you speak through a kazoo, you have no freedom of speech."[25] The question that should be asked is: who has more money to spend?

A second point to note regarding the premises of Mill's thinking is that he was thinking of arguments and the need to develop the ability to expose and defend oneself against superficially plausible, but faulty, reasoning. However, today the messages thrown at us are often surreptitious and appeal to the subconscious. It is not clear that exposure to this form of communication strengthens people's characters.

The appropriateness of the Milton–Mill "open encounter" concept was called in question by a special committee set up in Canada in the 1960s to examine the feasibility and philosophical justification for legislating against hate propaganda. The committee of seven members included the distinguished jurist, Maxwell Cohen, Dean of the McGill University faculty of Law, as chair, and two rising stars, Pierre-Elliot Trudeau, later prime minister of Canada, and Mark R. MacGuigan, a future minister of justice. In their report, published in 1966, the committee states that it does not share Milton's faith in the simple truth. When emotion displaces reason, people can be swept away by emotion, allowing their rationality to be flooded by emotion.

> The successes of modern advertising, the triumphs of impudent propaganda such as Hitler's, have qualified sharply our belief in the rationality of man. We know that under strain and pressure in times of irritation and frustration, the individual is swayed and even swept away by hysterical, emotional appeals. We act irresponsibly if we ignore the way in which emotion can drive reason from the field.
>
> Radio, television, motion pictures, the pervasiveness of print are new elements in the twentieth century which the classic supporters of free speech never had to reckon with. Their arguments from the seventeenth century to the nineteenth century assumed scattered isolated readers or a small literate audience within the range of a man's natural voice. They had not to consider

the impact of speech associated with colour, music and spectacle on the feelings of great multitudes of people.

In the committee's view, the great confidence that defenders of free speech had in
Mill's time that truth would prevail has been undermined by experience since then:

> We know that, as well as individual interests, there are social interests to be
> protected, and these are not always protected by unrestricted individual free-
> dom. The triumphs of Fascism in Italy, and National Socialism in Germany
> through audaciously false propaganda have shown us how fragile tolerant
> liberal societies can be in certain circumstances. They have also shown us the
> large element of irrationality in human nature which makes people vulner-
> able to propaganda in times of stress and strain. Both experience and the
> changing circumstances of the age require us to look with great care at abuses
> of freedom of expression.[26]

This report led to the adoption of the hate propaganda legislation currently
contained in sections 318 and 319 of the Criminal Code of Canada. It contains
numerous defences, along with the provision that the consent of the attorney general is required before proceedings under some of its provisions can take place.
There are considerable safeguards for free speech in this legislation, but some civil
libertarians feel there are not enough. In any case, the legislation has been subjected to scrutiny by the Supreme Court of Canada and has been accepted as constitutional.

We will examine the hate propaganda law in Chapter 7. For the moment, our
concern is with the Milton-Mill notion of the "free and open encounter."
Sometimes, as with Milton himself, there appears a mercantile metaphor. Justice
Holmes referred to "free trade in ideas ... the power of the thought to get itself
accepted in the competition of the market"[27]; it is important not to be blinkered
by this metaphor. If taken literally, it suggests that a sufficiently wealthy buyer
could take over the market, but free speech theory could hardly want to guarantee the possibility of such a monopoly.

Talk about monopolization of the media needs to be updated to include reference to the Internet, which has come to play a central part in the life of almost
everyone who can afford a computer and an access provider. In theory, the
Internet provides the ability to escape the domination of the few owners of the
major media networks, by linking individuals with other individuals, each with
their own particular sources of information. Informal networking of individuals in theory provides more immediate access to news and opinion than the
major networks can provide. In practice, there are numerous roadblocks in the
way of developing an anarchy of cyberspace. These will be discussed later in
Chapter 8. For now, it is enough to say that talk about media monopoly is not
yet outdated. Alternatives to corporate dominance over the media exist, but

they suffer from the lack of inducements and support available from the dominant corporate players.

ADDITIONAL FREE SPEECH ARGUMENTS

Mill's case for free speech rests on the argument that it promotes the truth, self-fulfilment and self-development, autonomy, and progress. His arguments are mostly instrumentalist: free speech is a means to something good. But the idea that free speech is tied to free thinking is also present. He values free thinking, and so his argument includes the idea that free speech is valuable for more than just what it will lead to. It is, therefore, as some have said, constitutive of autonomy and a good life, not just a means to that end. This gives the preservation of free speech added weight when competing policy considerations are adduced. Mill posits a fifth, non-instrumentalist argument, namely, the argument from validation discussed earlier. One does not have the authority to put forward claims if the opposing side has not been granted a hearing.

Other writers have introduced new arguments or given greater attention and development to ideas implicit in Mill, and to these we now turn. The arguments are: democracy, a good balance between stability and change in society, social interaction and community, opposition to tyranny and to the slippery slope leading to it, and legitimization of lifestyles. Each of these arguments deserves some attention.

Democracy

The argument from democracy is possibly the most powerful argument for an uncompromising protection of freedom of expression. Eric Barendt calls it "probably the most attractive and certainly the most fashionable free speech theory in modern Western democracies."[28] Its most notable proponent has been, in the US at least, Alexander Meiklejohn. According to this argument, the concept of democracy is that of self-government by the people. For such a system to work, it is necessary that the electorate be enlightened and informed. In order to be appropriately knowledgeable, there must be no constraints on the free flow of information and ideas. Democracy will not work, will not be true to its essential ideal, if a group of people in power are able to manipulate the electorate by withholding some information and stifling criticisms by charges of sedition, violation of state secrecy requirements, or threats of libel, etc. The argument is particularly significant where considerations of prior restraint are the issue, because use of this mechanism prevents the people from knowing even what it is they are not permitted to know.

The desire to manipulate opinion can stem from the highest motive of seeking to bring about an important, good objective for society. However, choosing manipulation negates, in its means, the democratic ideal. As Meiklejohn writes:

> [T]he point which we are making is that the externalized measuring of the play of forces which serves the purposes of business or of science is wholly unsuited to our dealing with problems of moral or political freedom.... We are experts in the knowledge and manipulation of measurable forces, whether physical or psychological. We invent and run machines of ever new and amazing power and intricacy. And we are tempted by that achievement to see if we can manipulate men with the same skill and ingenuity. But the manipulation of men is the destruction of self-government.[29]

A classic defence of free speech on the basis of democracy was made by Justice Brandeis of the US Supreme Court, in *Whitney v. California*:

> Those who won our independence believed ... that public discussion is a political duty; and that this should be a fundamental principle of the American government. They recognized the risks to which all human institutions are subject. But they knew that order cannot be secured merely through fear of punishment for its infraction; that it is hazardous to discourage thought, hope and imagination; that fear breeds repression; that repression breeds hate; that hate menaces stable government; that the path of safety lies in the opportunity to discuss freely supposed grievances and proposed remedies; and that the fitting remedy for evil counsels is good ones. Believing in the power of reason as applied through public discussion, they eschewed silence coerced by law—the argument of force in its worst form. Recognizing the occasional tyrannies of governing majorities, they amended the Constitution so that free speech and assembly should be guaranteed.[30]

In Canada, Justice Rand spelled out in *Boucher v. The King* how alterations in the view of public authority over the course of the last few centuries have modified the concept of seditious libel:

> Up to the end of the eighteenth century it was, in essence, a contempt in words of political authority or the actions of authority. If we conceive of the governors of society as superior beings, exercizing a divine mandate, by whom laws, institutions and administrations are given to men to be obeyed, who are, in short, beyond criticism, reflection or censure upon them or what they do implies either an equality with them or an accountability by them, both equally offensive.... But constitutional conceptions of a different order making rapid progress in the nineteenth century have necessitated a modification of the legal view of public criticism; and the administrators of what we call

democratic government have come to be looked upon as servants, bound to carry out their duties accountably to the public.[31]

All of these remarks are powerful statements in favour of protecting criticisms directed against state authority and of the freest possible discussion of public affairs. Worries are raised, however, when we contemplate, in the context of this argument, the ability of a few wealthy individuals to control the mass media of communication. Legislation against such monopoly control arguably enhances the value of democracy invoked here. The case of *United States v. Associated Press* elicited remarkably trenchant comments from the judiciary on just this matter. The case involved the attempt to freeze out the Chicago *Sun* from membership in the Associated Press, thus giving the *Sun's* competition, the Chicago *Tribune*, an enormous advantage. Hearing the case in New York, Justice Learned Hand stated that the newspaper industry serves one of the most

> vital of general interests: the dissemination of news from as many different sources, and with as many different facets and colours as possible. That interest is closely akin to, if indeed it is not the same as, the interest protected by the First Amendment; it presupposes that right conclusions are more likely to be gathered out of a multitude of tongues, than through any kind of authoritative selection.[32]

When the case reached the US Supreme Court, Justice Hugo Black issued another memorable pronouncement:

> The First Amendment ... rests on the assumption that the widest possible dissemination of information from diverse and antagonistic sources is essential to the welfare of the public, that a free press is a condition of free society.... Freedom of the press from governmental interference under the First Amendment does not sanction repression of that freedom by private interests.[33]

A Good Balance Between Stability and Change

The argument that freedom of expression helps to provide for a good balance between stability and change is a corollary to the argument from democracy. It pays special attention to the way such freedom can act as a kind of "safety valve" to let off steam when people might otherwise be bent on revolution or other destructive social action. Thomas I. Emerson outlines this argument in his article "Toward a General Theory of the First Amendment," as follows:

> The principle of open discussion is a method of achieving a more adaptable and at the same time more stable community, of maintaining the precarious balance between healthy cleavage and necessary consensus. This may not

always have been true, and may not be true of many existing societies. But where men have learned how to function within the law, an open society will be the stronger and more cohesive one.

Attitudes and ideas are likely, on this reasoning, to become stereotyped and institutions to lose their vitality when opposing voices are suppressed. "Opposition serves a vital social function in offsetting or ameliorating this normal process of bureaucratic decay."[34]

Social Interaction and Community

Unlike the two previous arguments, which are suited to considerations of relations between the individual and the state, this argument looks at relations between individuals within the state. According to this argument, developed by Richard Moon, the value of freedom of expression lies with social interaction. He writes:

> By communicating an individual forms relationships and associations with others—family, friends, co-workers, church congregation, countrymen. By entering into discussion with others an individual participates in the development of knowledge and in the direction of the community.
> The value attached to freedom of expression, then, is based on the recognition that the good of the individual is bound up with the community. Expression is the way we interact with others and so participate in social goods such as friendship and self-government. And through expression individuals develop their human capacities.[35]

This argument is not advanced by Moon as a way of forcing others to speak against their will—specifically a newspaper to publish an advertisement—but it can be argued that, for instance, in refusing to print a classified advertisement for a gay publication, the Vancouver *Sun* was choking off lines of communication. If communication between individuals is such an important activity, the controllers of dominant media should not have the right arbitrarily to deny access to anyone.[36]

Moon conceives his argument as giving a broad scope for freedom of expression. It protects "various forms of symbolic communication such as dance, music, painting and sculpture." He also recognizes that the value of social interaction and community is not the only value, and he takes self-development and autonomy into account when he considers the question of pornography. There is, he says,

> the certainty that pornography does not advance the values that underlie the freedom—the development of an individual's capacity for intelligent thought and emotional experience and for establishing relationships with others. Indeed, pornography, by portraying human beings as objects for sensual

gratification, may actually inhibit the capacity of the consumer to experience complex emotions and relate to other individuals.[37]

Here, of course, the definition of pornography comes into question. Moon proposes that the legislature concern itself only with the most offensive pornography, that which depicts the use of violence against other human beings and has no other purpose than sexual stimulation.

The Slippery Slope to Tyranny

Any restrictions to freedom of expression will always open the door to possible others, because analogical reasoning can mount arguments showing why this or that class of objects is closely similar to those for which exceptions have been made.

Precisely because the case for free speech is complex and rests on different considerations, it becomes impossible to draw a sharp line between what restrictions should be permitted and what not. We are right to recognize that with each new restraint there comes the possibility of new analogies in the light of which further restraints become permitted. From fear of the slippery slope some thinkers have thought, at different times in history, that freedom of expression should be absolute and that there should be no government interference with free speech whatsoever.

But this position is untenable. Even if one distinguishes between "regulation" of speech and "interference" with speech, so as to support, for example, rules of order in debate or the regulation of airwaves, there are generally agreed-on needs for restraint such as cases of libel, public mischief, fraud, copyright, military secrets in time of war, professional confidentiality, government confidentiality, fair trials, names of juvenile offenders, etc. Most people also draw the line to prohibit the most offensive kinds of obscenity or hate propaganda. Being on the slippery slope, we do not have to assume that any additional restraint will send us inexorably down the perilous slide. The answer to the slippery slope argument must be that each new case for restraint must be looked at carefully in the light of the whole battery of philosophical arguments.

Justice Learned Hand's decision in *United States v. Associated Press*, referred to earlier, is a model for dealing with slippery slope reasoning. He argued for prohibiting Associated Press from having a monopoly arrangement with one newspaper in Chicago. He recognized that one could extend the anti-monopoly reasoning to an unacceptable extent and considered the problem of finding limits to the protection of competition:

> Does [the principle] apply to the engagement of a single reporter by a single editor? ... The answer to such questions need not embarrass us: their pertinency presupposes that whatever is true in small matters, must be true in large; and

the greater part of the law is founded upon a denial of exactly that; for in law differences in quantity again and again become decisive differences in quality.... [I]t is enough that in the case at bar AP is a vast, intricately reticulated, organization, the largest of its kind, gathering news from all over the world, the chief single source of news for the American press, universally agreed to be of prime consequence. Wherever may be the vanishing point of public concern with any particular source of information, that point is far beyond this service.[38]

Legitimation of Lifestyles

A society that disapproves of a certain lifestyle may decide that a limited level of tolerance is better than an attempt to eradicate the activity entirely. The rule, written or unwritten, may be that the activity will be tolerated if it is not carried out too openly. Under these circumstances, as the old saying has it, hypocrisy will be the tribute that vice pays to virtue. The flip-side of this thinking is that restrictions on freedom to express oneself in this area are likely to reinforce public attitudes against the activity in question. It follows that those who have hitherto been denied openness—unfairly, in the view of practitioners—will want to ensure that it is granted, precisely in order to remove the stigma that comes from having expression of their lifestyle prohibited.

Joseph Raz presents arguments in favour of free speech that "turn on the fundamental need for public validation of one's way of life, and on the need for public recognition as a way of transmitting, preserving, and developing ways of life." He makes the point (surely a valid one) that, in a genuinely pluralistic society, there will be a need to grant recognition to a range of different conflicting world outlooks. Freedom to express those outlooks will be essential to the sense of self-worth of individual members of different religious, moral, or ethnic groups. This freedom he treats as "a foundational part of the political and civic culture of pluralistic democracies."[39] In other words, it is not only a means to an end, although harmony is likely to be promoted by it, but it is also constitutive of what a pluralistic liberal democracy means.

CONCLUSION

How do these general philosophical considerations of free speech principles apply in setting proper limits to legislation or informal restraints against propaganda? It makes sense for us now to turn our attention to existing legislation and to evaluate it in the light of the arguments above. We may also speculate about what new forms of control might reasonably be instituted.

NOTES

1   This analysis is the reflection of one who has followed for three decades or so day-to-day manifestations of opinion in newspapers, radio, and the university workplace. It is certainly open to challenge should anyone have a well-designed empirical study that gives contrary evidence. I am fairly confident that human rights legislation will have produced a counter-productive backlash in certain strata or pockets of society, at least for a time. My remarks have to do with overall tendencies.

2   "The rule that a deliberate intent to fight with deadly weapons is malicious, and that as a consequence, death inflicted in a duel is murder, is remarkable as an instance in which the law has had a great influence in bringing about change in the moral sentiment of the country, and the rather, because convictions for murder, by duelling, were almost unknown. Had it been once conceded that to kill in a duel is not murder, duels would have been sanctioned by practice much longer." James Fitzjames Stephen, *A General View of the Criminal Law of England* (London and Cambridge: Macmillan, 1863) 120.

3   James Fitzjames Stephen, *A Digest of the Criminal Law of England* (London: Macmillan, 1877) 56.

4   S.G. Tallentyre, (pseudonym for Beatrice Hall), *The Friends of Voltaire* (New York: U.P. Putnam's Sons, 1907) 199.

5   John Milton, *Areopagitica and Of Education*, ed. George H. Sabine (Northbrook, IL.: AHM Publishing, 1951) 6. References to this work come from this edition and will be indicated by JM and page number in brackets in the text.

6   John Morley, *On Compromise* (London: Macmillan, 1923) 104.

7   John Locke, *A Letter Concerning Toleration*, ed. John Horton and Susan Mendus (London and New York: Routledge, 1991) 46.

8   James Fitzjames Stephen, "Locke on Toleration," *Horae Sabbaticae*, Essay 10 (London: Macmillan, 1892) 171.

9   John Stuart Mill, *On Liberty*, ed. Currin V. Shields (1859; Indianapolis: Bobbs-Merrill, 1956) 69. References to this work come from this edition and will be indicated by JSM and page number in brackets in the text.

10 The example is not merely hypothetical. The *Globe and Mail* reported that Ontario Supreme Court Justice Janet Scott issued an injunction against anti-abortion demonstrators, ruling among other things that the word "killing" in signs they carried was "defamatory." See "Anti-Abortionists Ordered Not To Picket Near MD's Office," *Globe and Mail*, 14 July 1987. I wrote a critical letter to the same newspaper, "Free expression limited on abortion," *Globe and Mail*, 12 August 1987. Also, in November-December 1981, the Toronto Transit Commission cancelled an advertisement by the Toronto Right to Life Association, following public pressure, although it met the standards of the Advertising Standards Council.

11 George Bernard Shaw, *Man and Superman*, 1905.

12 Compare on this point, Kierkegaard: "When truth conquers with the help of 10,000 yelling men—even supposing that that which is victorious is a truth: with the form and manner of the victory a far greater untruth is victorious." See Robert Bretall, ed., *A Kierkegaard Anthology* (New York: The Modern Library, 1946) 431.

13 Mill seemed to be including the liar in his argument, where he talks about the inadvisability of the law suppressing a controversialist simply for misrepresenting an opponent's position.

14 Fitzjames Stephen wrote in a letter to Lord Lytton, Viceroy of India, the following: "I have not often felt smaller, or less well satisfied with myself, than I did when Sir Rutherford Alcock expounded at the Council room of Calcutta the views taken by the Chinese of the opium traffic and of the treaty by which they are obliged to tolerate it. Most of the Council treated their remonstrances and appeals to justice and common morality as a sort of joke and as wretched cant. I did not agree with them at all and I suspect that some day or other, we shall see cause to regret bitterly the line we have taken and are taking with them." See, Fitzjames Stepen MSS., Cambridge University Library, Add. 7349/14/1. I wish to thank A.E.B. Owen, Keeper of Manuscripts, for assistance in interpreting the handwriting and verifying the reference.

15 James Fitzjames Stephen, *Liberty, Equality, Fraternity* (1874; Cambridge: Cambridge University Press, 1967) 63-64.

16 For more on this topic see my "Censoring Pornography," *Women and Public Policy: Reprints from Policy Options*, ed. Doris Anderson (Kingston: The Institute for Research on Public Policy, 1987) 64-69.

17 Fitzjames Stephen 69-70.

18 Committee on Homosexual Offences and Prostitution, *The Wolfenden Report* (New York: Lancer Books, 1964). See also, *Report*, CMD 247, 1957.

19 Patrick Devlin, *The Enforcement of Morals* (Oxford: Oxford University Press, 1968).

20 H.L.A. Hart, *Law, Liberty and Morality* (Oxford: Oxford University Press,1963).

21 Hart 12. The case is *Shaw v. Director of Public Prosecutions* (1961) 2 A.E.R. 446. (1962) A.C.

22 Fitzjames Stepen was a believer in codification of the criminal law as well as in the legal enforcement of morality, including the prohibition of homosexual acts. Therefore, he would have been sympathetic to Hart's Benthamite objection concerning the uncertainty brought about by the general crime of "conspiracy to corrupt morals," but he would have had no difficulty in seeing Shaw's book as in violation of criminal law on other counts. See Fitzjames Stephen, *A Digest of the Criminal Code* Article 172.

22 H.J. McCloskey, "Liberty of Expression: Its Grounds and Limits (I)," *Freedom of Expression*, ed. Fred R. Berger (Belmont, CA: Wadsworth, 1980) 42-57.

23 Margaret Wente wrote two columns for the *Globe and Mail* on the subject in April and May 2000.

24 D.H. Monro, "Liberty of Expression: Its Grounds and Limits (II)", Berger 58-70.

25 Charles Rembar, "For Sale: Freedon of Speech," *The Atlantic Monthly* 247, 3 (March 1981): 25-32, 31.

26 Special Committee on Hate Propaganda in Canada, *Report* (Ottawa: Queen's Printer, 1966) 8, 9.

27 *Abrams v. United States* (1919): 250 U.S. 616.

28 Eric Barendt, *Freedom of Speech* (Oxford: Oxford University Press, 1987) 19.

29 Alexander Meiklejohn, *Free Speech and Its Relation to Self-Government* (New York: Harper and Bros., 1948) 8.

30 *Whitney v. California*, 1927: 274 U.S. 347, at 375-76.

31 *Boucher v. The King*, 1 Dominion Law Reports (1951): 657.

32 Justice Learned Hand, *United States v. Associated Press* (1943): 52 F. Supp. 362, DCSD, NY.

33 *Associated Press* v. US 326, US Reports 1, 17-20 (1945).

34 Thomas I. Emerson, "Toward a General Theory of the First Amendment," *The Yale Law Journal* 72 (1963): 877, 884.

35 Richard Moon, "The Scope of Freedom of Expression," *Osgoode Hall Law Journal* 23,2 (1985): 331, 348.

36 The reference is to *The Gay Alliance Toward Equality v. The Vancouver Sun* (1979) 2 SCR 435, decided in favour of the Vancouver *Sun*, Chief Justice Bora Laskin dissenting.

37 Moon 353, 355.

38 Hand.

39 Joseph Raz, "Free Expression and Personal Identification," *Free Expression: Essays in Law and Philosophy*, ed. W.J. Waluchow (Oxford: Clarendon Press, 1994) 28.

SEVEN
THE QUESTION OF CONTROLS

In the light of arguments reviewed in the previous chapter, any attempts to justify limits to freedom of expression and to implement controls of any kind will have a heavy burden of proof to discharge. This is especially true in jurisdictions such as Canada and the US, where freedom of expression is a constitutionally protected right. Nevertheless, some forms of legal and quasi-legal controls have already been tested in the courts of those countries and have survived the test, although not always in a way that gives confidence in their permanent survival.

Should government exert control through legislation over the media and advertising? Is it better to leave matters of press responsibility and advertising and public relations ethics to the relevant responsible elements in those professions, or would this be like putting the fox in charge of the henhouse? Since attempts at self-policing have existed for some decades, we will look at what they have accomplished, focusing on three things: advertising, and the standards developed in that business; press councils, notably the Ontario Press Council; and government information, with suggested guidelines for its provision. One aspect of government information is directly linked to both of the previous concerns: a large volume of advertising may be thought to curry favour with the media whose pockets are thus lined with lucrative contracts.

CONTROLS ON HATE PROPAGANDA

The need for some kind of control over hate propaganda was mentioned in Chapter 6 in connection with the Report of the Special Committee on Hate Propaganda in Canada (also known as the Cohen Committee). Internationally, there is also a consensus for such a need, and agreements to institute and enforce such controls have been implemented. But international agreements tend to combine calls for prohibition against, say, racist speech, with ringing affirmations of the right to freedom of expression. This leaves the judiciary much to do in the way of interpretation. The UN International Covenant on Civil and Political Rights is one such agreement. Under Article 20 it prohibits propaganda for war and advocacy of national, racial, or religious hatred that might lead to violence or discrimination. Balancing this is Article 19, which guarantees the right of individuals to freedom of expression and the right to hold opinions without interference, as long as these rights do not infringe on the rights of, and respect for, others or with national security or public order. The UN also passed the International Convention on the Elimination of All Forms of Racial Discrimination, which condemns propaganda and organizations based on racist or discriminatory theories and which vows to adopt measures to counter incitement to, or acts of, such discrimination.

The European Convention on Human Rights in its Article 10 also provides for a balancing of free speech rights—both freedom to hold opinions and ideas and to receive and impart information without interference by governments—against other rights, such as national security, public safety, prevention of crime, protection of health, protection of reputation, and maintaining the authority and impartiality of the judiciary.[1]

The Canadian Constitution since 1982 has incorporated a Charter of Rights and Freedoms, which builds in restrictions on the extent to which rights, such as freedom of expression, might otherwise undermine perfectly good and sensible law. The main restriction of this kind is section 1 of the Charter, which "guarantees the rights and freedoms set out in it subject only to such reasonable limits prescribed by law as can be demonstrably justified in a free and democratic society."[2] It incorporates many of the exceptions that judges in the US have found necessary to recognize, despite the uncompromising wording of some of the US Constitutional Amendments.

Hate Propaganda and the Supreme Court of Canada

We will briefly examine two cases that have been at the centre of constitutional debate about hate propaganda in Canada. The first involves Ernst Zundel, who published materials denying the Holocaust, the massive and systematic killings of Jews in areas under Nazi domination during World War II. The statute under which he was initially convicted—the "spreading false news" statute, s.181, of the Criminal Code of Canada—was considered by the Supreme Court of Canada to be too broadly drawn, and it was struck down. When a statute is too broad, it threatens more speech than the kind targeted by the legislation.

A few points of interest pertaining to the Zundel case are worth mentioning. The "spreading false news" provision did not require the consent of the attorney general to launch a prosecution. In striking down that statute, the Supreme Court weakened the power to stifle hate propaganda, because an offended individual cannot launch a criminal action merely by going to a crown attorney. For exactly this reason, it removed at the same time a possible source of intimidation against free speech. Secondly, the "spreading false news" statute, unlike the hate propaganda provisions, is specifically linked to speech that is false and, furthermore, speech that the speaker *knows* to be false. In other words, this statute criminalizes lying speech that causes harm. It shares this feature with s.300 of the Criminal Code, which states that "Every one who publishes a defamatory libel that he knows is false is guilty of an indictable offence and liable to imprisonment for a term not exceeding five years." To the extent that we rely on Mill for the philosophical underpinnings of free speech protections, we have reason to question whether they support the protection of lying speech. Recall that Mill was concerned to defend the professing and discussing "as a matter of ethical conviction" of any doctrine "however immoral it may be considered." Someone who lies is not defending what the lie purports to say "as a matter of ethical conviction." The liar may want to defend the use of the lie as an instrument to accomplish something good, but that is very different from defending what the lie purports to say. From the standpoint of Mill's most basic defence of free speech—the argument for giving truth the best possible chance of a hearing—lying speech hardly warrants any protection at all.

Zundel was acquitted eventually, because the law under which he was convicted was found to be overbroad. By contrast, an Alberta high school teacher was found guilty of violating provisions of the hate propaganda legislation in the Criminal Code of Canada. James Keegstra was charged in 1984 under what is now s.319(2) of the Criminal Code for teaching and requiring his students to repeat in class and on exams that "Jewish people seek to destroy Christianity and are responsible for depressions, anarchy, chaos, wars, and revolution. According to Mr. Keegstra, Jews 'created the Holocaust to gain sympathy' and, in contrast to the open and honest Christians, were said to be deceptive, secretive, and inherently evil."[3] He was convicted; the conviction was reversed on appeal, but he was reconvicted upon retrial after the Supreme Court of Canada upheld the constitutionality of the law in 1990.

The Supreme Court had to decide whether the section of the Criminal Code under which Keegstra was charged was an infringement of freedom of expression as guaranteed by the Charter, and if so, whether the infringement could be justified by s.1. Secondly, it had to decide whether the presumption of innocence, also guaranteed by the Charter, had been infringed by virtue of putting the burden of proof in a truth defence on Keegstra, to support the truth of what he allegedly said, instead of requiring the Crown to prove its falsity beyond a reasonable doubt. In the end, although it ruled that the law did infringe both rights, the infringements could be justified by s.1 of the Charter.

In his judgment on the case, Chief Justice Brian Dickson reviewed some of the US constitutional history of freedom of expression. He noted that the 1952 ruling in *Beauharnais v. Illinois*,[4] wherein the US Supreme Court upheld a statute against group defamation, had been subsequently weakened, but not overturned. Interestingly, in the light of the Zundel case, he noted that the effect of some subsequent decisions had been to "protect public invective as long as the speaker has not knowingly lied and there exists no clear and present danger of violence or insurrection." However, doubts about the tenability of the *Beauharnais* ruling were raised in 1978 by the decision that a municipal ordinance prohibiting public demonstrations inciting "violence, hatred, abuse or hostility toward a person or group of persons by reason of reference to religious, racial, ethnic, national or regional affiliation," was unconstitutional.[5] The ruling gave members of the American Nazi Party the right to march in the Jewish suburb of Skokie, Illinois, where many Holocaust survivors resided. Despite the ruling, in the end no march was held.

Dickson favoured the *Beauharnais* ruling, noting that a growing body of academic writing supported the idea that the First Amendment can be squared with restrictions on racist and sexist speech. American constitutional history shows that the courts are not always content-blind when evaluating the extent to which different forms of expression merit protection.[6] Dickson concluded that, despite the uncompromising wording of the First Amendment—"Congress shall make no law ... abridging the freedom of speech, or of the press..."—it is far from clear that a law such as the Canadian hate propaganda legislation would necessarily be found unconstitutional in that country. He also mentioned the pernicious effects on society of hate propaganda, drawing on material from the Cohen Committee, including the quotation from Justice Jackson of the US Supreme Court in *Beauharnais* about how hate propaganda's "sinister abuses of our freedom of expression ... can tear apart a society, brutalize its dominant elements, and persecute even to extermination, its minorities."[7]

Dickson regarded hate propaganda as low in the order of expression representing the core values of the Charter of Rights, saying, "I am of the opinion that expression intended to promote the hatred of identifiable groups is of limited importance when measured against free expression values." In giving his reason for this opinion, he eschewed relativism regarding truth. His position is that we do have greater and less certainty about different things, and this is not a purely subjective matter. We can be fairly sure that some things are erroneous, and erroneous things are going to be less helpful for discovering truth. He depicted hate propaganda as detrimental to truth and unlikely to lead to a better world.

Dickson argued that the word "hatred" must be defined according to the context in which it is found. In his view, the word "connotes emotion of an intense and extreme nature that is clearly associated with vilification and detestation." He also identified it with specific characteristics as follows:

> Hatred is predicated on destruction, and hatred against identifiable groups therefore thrives on insensitivity, bigotry and destruction of both the target group and of the values of our society. Hatred in this sense is a most extreme emotion that belies reason; an emotion that, if exercised against members of an identifiable group, implies that those individuals are to be despised, scorned, denied respect and made subject to ill-treatment on the basis of group affiliation.[8]

Whether or not one agrees with this contextual interpretation of hatred as a rendition of ordinary English usage, the result of this legal, authoritative analysis is to narrow the scope of the term for purposes of the law. As if to anticipate that not everyone will automatically think of hatred in the way he describes, Dickson indicated that future juries should be directed by judges in such a way as to "include express mention of the need to avoid finding that the accused intended to promote hatred merely because the expression is distasteful." That warning will help, he thought, to avoid limiting freedom of expression more than is necessary.

Dickson wrote the judgment of the Supreme Court of Canada. This means that the scope of "hatred" for purposes of the law is what *he* said the scope is. To whatever extent ordinary English may be vague about the scope of "hatred," that vagueness is removed by the decision of the Court.

Some qualifications should be made here. First, hate propaganda is not defined in terms that require falsity in the statements. One very effective way of fomenting hatred is by uttering a selection of truths to create an unbalanced view of another individual or group. Secondly, according to Mill, truth is not a matter only of correspondence between what a person believes and reality; it can be a matter of the vitality with which a belief is held, and that vitality can be stimulated by lively opposition. Dickson recognized this point in a later caveat, saying, "It can also be argued that it is partly through a clash with extreme and erroneous views that truth and the democratic vision remain vigorous and alive," but that did not cause him to alter his opinion. Thirdly, there is the idea that there will be some truth somewhere in what motivates the hate propagandists. By allowing them to express themselves we will have a better chance to discover whatever truth may be behind the nonsense they often propound. Dickson did not say that because hate propagandists have very little chance that "their vision of society will lead to a better world," their speech should be criminalized, but that in the overall balancing process this feature should count to some extent in the decision to give constitutional acceptance of such criminalization. That is why it is important to see all the nuances of the argument from truth.

In my view, hate propaganda has the potential for setting off a destructively vicious spiral of racially or ethnically motivated attacks by one group on another. As such, it warrants the seriousness of criminal sanction, but only as a last resort. The chilling effect can be greatly reduced if people are instructed to see the law as one of rare application. It is a matter of educating attorneys general as to how the law should be applied.

Wayne Sumner, in his article "Hate Propaganda and the Charter of Rights," gives reasons for turning away from a civil libertarian view of the anti-hate law to one at least not hostile to it. First, such law seems to have a chilling effect on the actual targets of the legislation, the hate-mongers themselves. Another is a disposition among otherwise perfectly ordinary Canadians to be receptive to messages of hatred and intolerance, such as those spread by Zundel and Keegstra. Further, the targets for Canadian hatred have multiplied: not only Jews but francophones, native peoples, blacks, Asians, and Muslims have been subjected to racially or ethnically motivated attacks. He concedes that the empirical evidence to support the law is not strong, but neither in his view is there much support for the civil libertarian position that the law has been ineffective and counterproductive. In light of the safeguards built into it, he feels that "there is no convincing case against the statute in its present form," but that we should hold our views on the matter with "considerable modesty and circumspection," given the many uncertainties involved.[9]

ADVERTISING

The Case Against Government Controls

The case against government controls on advertising was usefully articulated in an article, "Advertising and Ethics," by Phillip Nelson, a professor of economics at the State University of New York.[10] He argued against government sanctions for controlling advertising, because he felt that government control would be wasteful, ineffective, and unnecessary in the light of possible alternatives. The arguments are far from compelling, but they are worth critiquing inasmuch as they articulate ideas that have some plausibility.

1. Government regulation has had a bad track record, in particular a record of counter-productivity. For example, by controlling rents at a fixed level, accommodation prices are kept lower and the stimulus to build new housing is lessened, thus making low-cost accommodation more difficult to obtain. This may be so, but that is only one area of government regulation. There are many others that show no obvious counter-productivity; for example, motor vehicle licensing. The abandonment of a government system of water supply testing has emerged as a contributing factor in the outbreak in Walkerton, Ontario of a deadly e.coli infection. So the argument against government regulation of advertising, on the basis that government regulation in general is bad, is not very strong.

2. Advertising generates social well-being. That is true of some advertising, perhaps even of most advertising. However, it doesn't address the question of how to deal with advertising that misleads, insults, demeans, or is otherwise reprehensible.

3. There is a distinction between advertising of experience qualities and advertising of search qualities (qualities that can be determined prior to purchase, such as cost, size, shape, etc.). Nelson points out that if there is any deception in the description of the search qualities, people will not buy the product. In the case of experience qualities, the customer might be fooled once, but will not be in line for repeat purchases. Therefore, false advertising will not pay for any company that wants to stay in business for long. Since self-interest will dictate truthfulness in the advertising of experience qualities, legislation should not be needed. If people are rational and act in their own interest, there ought not to be any false or misleading advertising. This argument has some merit, but, like the legendary bumblebee that ought not to be able to fly in the light of aerodynamic principles, this kind of deceptive advertising of experience qualities nevertheless occurs and with

some frequency, as can be seen from convictions obtained in Canada under the Competition Act.

4. Some forms of deception are harmless, because they trick people into doing what they ought to do in their own interest anyway. Strangely, he views this kind of deception as a case of providing information, because it leads people to act in the way they would act if they were fully informed.

5. If advertising were deceptive, people would not believe it; thus, in the long run, deception would not be in the interest of advertisers. That is true, but the observation does not support the case against regulation. So long as the majority of advertisers are truthful, there will be a tendency to believe advertisements. However, if this tendency exists, it can be exploited by a few unscrupulous advertisers for their own benefit.

6. Because it is not possible to prevent all fraud, Nelson suggests putting up with existing abuses, rather than trying to regulate them out of existence. There are costs to all forms of legal enforcement, and there are diminishing returns the closer one moves toward reducing crime to zero. That point is sound, but limited in scope. From the valid point that one cannot prevent all fraud, we cannot infer that it would be inadvisable to try to prevent some fraud.

7. Perhaps Nelson's least impressive argument is one in defence of advertising products that are of no real intrinsic benefit to the customer, on the grounds that "if I don't make/sell it, someone else will." The form of that argument is identical to the rationalization of any protection racket operator, contract killing organization, or suchlike. Even if it is true that someone else will do it anyway, that does not serve as a justification for my doing it.

Burton Leiser gives a few illustrations, not intended to be a complete list, of the kinds of deceptions to be found in advertising.[11] Among those he lists are the following:

1. offering for sale at a "reduced" price what was never offered for sale at the supposedly "regular" price;
2. offering "free" sets of encyclopedias, but asking for a small monthly service charge for a 10-year research service;
3. advertising "free" books or records to join a club, when they are not free, but are consideration in a binding contract to purchase a certain number of books or records;
4. small type to obscure limitations on, for example, insurance coverage; and
5. misleading language, as when a health insurance policy advertises that it "will pay your hospital bills," but not all hospital bills and maybe not all of the bills themselves.[12]

Leiser makes a strong case for government intervention where products are advertised in ways that mask health or safety risks to consumers, though he would prefer advertisers to behave in ways that would make such intervention unnecessary.

Canada's Competition Act

Canadian legislation spells out some particular kinds of prohibited deceptions in the Competition Act. The following are excerpts and paraphrases from some of the provisions, not meant to be a complete statement of the law, outlined in Industry Canada's Misleading Advertising Bulletin, of October-December 1995:

> *Section 52(1)(a)*: All representations, in any form whatever, that are false or misleading in a material respect are prohibited.
>
> *Section 52(1)(b)*: Any representation in the form of a statement, warranty or guarantee of the performance, efficacy or length of a product, not based on an adequate and proper test, is prohibited.
>
> *Section 52(1)(c)*: Any representation that purports to be a warranty or guarantee of a product, or a promise to replace, maintain, or repair an article, or any part of an article are prohibited where their form is materially misleading or where there is no reasonable prospect that the warranty, guarantee, or promise will be carried out.
>
> *Section 52(1)(d)*: Any materially misleading representation as to the price at which a product is ordinarily sold is prohibited.
>
> *Section 54*: Where two or more prices are clearly shown on a product, its container, or wrapper, the product must be supplied at the lower price; in other words, the product must be offered for sale at the lowest price depicted.
>
> *Section 57*: Advertising a product at a bargain price when the advertiser does not have reasonable quantities of the product available for sale is prohibited.
>
> *Section 59*: This prohibits any contest that does not disclose the number and approximate value of prizes or important information relating to the chances of winning in the contest, that does not select participants or distribute prizes on the basis of skill or on a random basis, or in which the distribution of prizes in [sic] unduly delayed.

Standards of veracity are quite stringent. Dominion Stores, carrying on business under the generic name Best for Less, displayed in-store signs, which compared its price to a "why pay up to" price, followed by a list of savings. Dominion was convicted and fined when it was established that items were available from competitors at lower prices than the "why pay up to" prices.[13] When Simpsons Ltd. conducted a one-day "mini casino" promotion in October 1985, it was charged and found guilty under sections 52 and 59 for not disclosing adequately the chances open to "players." Advertisements said, "you could save 10%, 15%,

20% or 25% on practically everything in the store." It did not disclose that 90 per cent of the cards contained the 10 per cent symbol under all four tabs, while the remaining cards contained all four percentage symbols.[14]

Section 57 is recognizable as what is more commonly known as legislation against "bait and switch" operations. The deal involves advertising a popular item at ridiculously low prices to bring people into the store. When they arrive, the advertised item is out of stock, but a substitute is offered that is not a bargain.

The arrival of the Internet, to be discussed more generally in the last chapter, has caused concern about the ability to enforce provisions of the Competition Act. In Industry Canada's April-June 1996 issue of the *Misleading Advertising Bulletin* some of the implications of the new technology for marketing were discussed by Rachel Larabie-LeSieur, Deputy-Director of Investigation and Research (Marketing Practices).[15] What is new about the Internet is that its interactivity provides for instant transactions following advertising of a product. This is a great convenience, but it also tends to facilitate fraud. "Ease of entry and low initial cost means that the Internet is fertile ground for scam artists," she said. "Victims will be precluded from the safeguards that time and distance have traditionally afforded." Illegitimate marketers could present misleading representations as online entertainment, especially where children are concerned. Larabie-LeSieur did not see this kind of fraud to be different in content or subject matter from what has already been experienced in other media; however, the Internet tends to be resistant to regulation, nationally and internationally. How do you enforce national laws in a borderless medium? What steps can be taken, for instance, when a buyer resides in Canada, the seller is located in Colombia, the good is shipped from Japan, and the financial transaction is cleared through a bank in Switzerland? Where does the offence occur? Which country's laws and standards should prevail? How will conflicts between different legal regimes be resolved?

Among the solutions Larabie-LeSieur contemplated were increased use of computer technologies to combat illegal activities with a focus on the intermediaries, the service providers. But "under which circumstances, if at all, should online service providers be held liable for advertisers' deceptive practices?" One of the attractions of the Internet is that communications are not subject to the usual filters and controls of the established mass media, as with telephone communications. There are many who would like to keep things this way, and to handle problems of misleading advertising (or hate propaganda, or libel, etc.) by self-policing. Here the service providers already have taken the initiative in some cases. Larabie-LeSieur acknowledged that the Internet "may indeed be suitable to some form of self-policing since consumers can and do provide quick feedback service to advertisers and service providers," but she thought that under the influx of millions of new users in the years to come, "it seems unrealistic to rely overly on the culture of the Internet to ensure effective deterrence against fraudulent practices." Her proposed solution was to seek efficient cooperation among enforcement agencies on a global scale.[16] Legitimate businesses have an obvious stake in combatting fraud on the Internet, since people who have been victimized in scams will have less to spend on legitimate business. In any case, enforcement of the Competition Act relies to some extent on complaints from the public.[17]

In the present political climate, government intervention on a larger scale to protect consumers seems unlikely. But interesting explorations of other possibilities were undertaken in the 1970s by a study team headed by Michael J. Trebilcock, a law and economics professor at the University of Toronto. The team's "Study on Consumer Misleading and Unfair Trade Practices" set out to decide whether there was a case to be made for imposing restrictions based on persuasive, as distinct from simply informative, content.[18] In other words, should there be restrictions beyond what is simply false or misleading? In particular, should there be a disclosure requirement to force advertisers to tell truths they would rather not state?

Beyond literal inaccuracies, such as falsely advertising a reduction in price, it is not possible in many cases to assess an image appeal in terms of truth and falsity. The study notes, "[T]he principal attacks against image advertising are directed against its tendency to distract consumers from other, arguably more important, issues concerning the product at hand and against those claims which exploit the susceptibilities of the audience to which they are directed."[19] The problem is measured by the effects produced in the mind of the consumer, not the abstract characteristics of the claim itself. Insufficient information can as readily mislead a person to make unwanted purchases as false information. So, at first sight, it seems as though a broader "information ethic" could gain a foothold and provide a basis for legislation.

However, the study questions whether the aim of advertising is to inform; it more often is meant to persuade, and detailed, technical information may interfere with this. Advertising is a form of advocacy, so one does not expect it to give the whole picture. Here the study expresses reluctance to pursue a more global truth requirement: "To condemn resort to persuasion and polemics in advertising, while tolerating similar tactics in the classroom, in the pulpit and on the hustings, smacks of discrimination.... It seems there is a point beyond which positive legal requirements cannot go."[20]

The study advocates a restricted role for government advertising controls, enforcing truth only on matters of factual claims, and not on esoteric general impressions received by the potential consumer.

Advertising Standards Canada/Les Normes canadiennes de la publicité

The current body known as Advertising Standards Canada (ASC) in English and Les Normes canadiennes de la publicité in French existed for many years as the Canadian Advertising Foundation (CAF). The latter in turn was preceded by the Canadian Advertising Advisory Board (CAAB), founded in 1957 and "dedicated to the improvement of the industry's image through the harnessing of the powers of advertising in the public interest."[21] The CAAB first became involved in self-regulation in 1963, sponsoring the first Canadian Code of Advertising Standards. At the time of the name change from CAF to ASC, in May 1997, the President and CEO, Linda Nagel, commented that the new name better described the role of the organization as the advertising industry's self-regulatory body.[22] This seems to indicate more of an acceptance of the self-policing job than in earlier years. In 1980 Keith McKerracher, President of the Institute of Canadian Advertising, told the Kent Commission:

> ...[T]he Advertising Standards Council was not really set up to regulate advertising. It was set up to provide an industry body to which the public could complain about advertising rather than to complain to a government agency and the reason may well have been that we were afraid in our industry that complaints against advertising to governments might invoke more government regulations, and if we could head off complaints by creating our own complaints bureau, if you like, we might be able to provide a foil between the consumer and the advertiser to get those complaints diminished. It is only lately that Advertising Standards Council has got into this sort of regulatory business and that was, again, to head off what was regarded within the industry as almost certain government regulation if it didn't.[23]

Government has already involved itself in the business of controlling misleading advertising, but there are many other concerns, such as taste, sex-role stereotyping, ethnic stereotyping, and other matters, which have been the source of complaints against the industry. It is not surprising, then, that the self-policing role has become more active than in the past. Perhaps the organization hopes that, if effective self-regulation can be shown to exist in these areas, the Competition Act might be trimmed by the Canadian judiciary on the ground that at least some provisions of the existing law are no longer needed. However, before that can happen voluntary membership in ASC would have to include virtually all advertisers. The membership list is currently very long. The main sanction of ASC, as with the CAF before it, is the exclusion of non-complying advertisers from membership in the organization. This is true of print media, but there are also arrangements with the Canadian Association of Broadcasters whereby English-language material is sent to ASC for pre-clearance. Since the Broadcast Code for Advertising to Children is endorsed by the CRTC, which has the power to withhold a broadcaster's licence, there are real teeth to ASC's functions. This means that the distinction between "voluntary self-regulation" and "government control" has become blurred.

Continued membership serves as an indication of a clean bill of moral health for the advertiser. Ultimately, the sanction of membership exclusion is only as powerful as the desire of advertisers to be seen to be operating in line with current moral standards. But any individual advertiser, who may or may not care to be a member of ASC, will likely have to deal with other members who are. For example, if someone wants to advertise in a newspaper, the chances are that the paper is a member of ASC and will be guided by the Canadian Code of Advertising

Standards. So, to the extent that the newspaper is to be an outlet for the advertising, the "voluntary" control is every bit as effective as any punitive, government-enacted control might be. In fact, the civil libertarian might well have reason to be concerned whether self-censorship might not go too far, since decisions are often made by a committee behind closed doors.

The effectiveness of this self-regulatory body will no doubt be affected by the extent of public participation in the complaints process. Although the Canadian Advertising Foundation did not publicize its decisions, that policy has changed with the change of name. This will give more clout to the decisions made against an advertiser. The ASC provides a focal point for publicity, and that is a service in itself, especially in such matters as the appearance of conflict of interest when a major corporation or government heavily advertises in a medium. On August 19, 1996, the *Ottawa Sun* appeared with a four-page wraparound supplement that appeared under the *Sun* logo, but which was, in fact, an advertising feature written by Bell Canada; the ASC ruled that the Code had been violated. Four days earlier, in a *Globe and Mail* article, Marina Strauss discussed an upcoming special edition of the *Financial Post*, in which Bell Canada was to be the sole display advertiser. "The Post edition," she wrote, "raises thorny questions about the potential of advertisers to erode journalistic integrity—and independence—if the very existence of the editorial product becomes so dependent on one company."[24] (This issue relates more to the ethics of the newspapers themselves than to the advertising self-regulators, and so will not be pursued.) One other aspect of the Bell Canada advertising blitz may be worthy of note. In both cases the advertising appeared the same day as the CRTC began its hearings to determine the future of the $7-billion local phone market and the form in which competition should be allowed.[25] The recent purchase by Bell Canada Enterprises (BCE) of both the *Globe and Mail* and CTV raises the question whether a column as critical of Bell as Marina Strauss's is likely to appear in that paper in future. Having already shown its desire to exert its influence through the media, how much easier will it be when BCE owns such a large and influential section of it?[26]

A number of useful initiatives have been taken by ASC in relation to consumer complaints. Sex-role Stereotyping Guidelines were produced in 1981 and updated twice to become in 1993 what are now called the Gender Portrayal Guidelines. These encourage such things as the equal representation of women and men in roles of authority "both for the characters within the actual advertising scenario and when representing the advertiser through announcers, voice-overs, experts, and on-camera authorities"; equal portrayal of women and men as single decision-makers for all purchases "including big-ticket items"; and the showing of women and men in "the full spectrum of diversity and as equally competent in a wide range of activities both inside and outside the home." Advertisers are told to avoid "inappropriate use or exploitation of sexuality of both women and men." More specifically, they are told that they must not portray boys and girls under 16 as displaying adult sexual characteristics, nor should adult women be portrayed as "girls or with childlike characteristics while maintaining adult sexual characteristics." Women and men should be portrayed as equals, and stereotypes such as male dominant/female submissive should not be reinforced. The guidelines also prohibit use of a woman's sexuality to sell a product with no relation to sexuality, exploitation of nudity, "irrelevant segmentation of body parts," sexual harassment, objectification, "commodization," violence, and threats of domination. Finally, advertising "should avoid language that misrepresents, offends or excludes women or men." As an example, they recommend use of "firefighter" instead of "fireman" and "synthetic" instead of "man-made."[27]

The ASC currently operates in conjunction with independent National and Regional Community Response Councils, consisting of industry and public representatives who adjudicate complaints based on alleged Code violations. There are also advisory panels on gender portrayal in Toronto and Montreal, operating at the national level in English and French respectively. Over 1000 complaints were handled in 1999, and the number is expected to grow with the increased use of the Internet for advertising and as more publicity is given to the work of the ASC.[28] However, the ASC 's limitation for regulating advertising is the same as that which gives it its strength and purpose; namely, it is not a punitive body. Instead, it seeks only to make sure that offensive advertising does not reappear. For those who are concerned simply with the end product—that is, more acceptable advertising— it makes little difference how this result is achieved; the less fear, trouble, and "chilling" of legitimate expression, the better.

The ASC can expect to be a continuing focal point for hotly disputed questions pitting opponents of "political correctness" in advertising against progressive forces seeking to promote equality of race, ethnicity, and gender in the media.

Tobacco Advertising and the Supreme Court of Canada

Mill's observation, that advertising is not disinterested, has a role to play in downgrading the importance of protecting it for the sake of truth. However, some advertising, such as advocacy advertising, mixes the commercial with the political. And, since one can pay to express oneself on any matter, paid advertisements can also be purely political or ideological. There is clearly no basis for lessening the importance of free expression merely because a person pays to express it. On the contrary, it shows that the person believes in the ideas sufficiently to pay out of his or her pocket to disseminate them!

Even when we deal purely with the commercial realm, there are core values at stake. One is self-expression and self-fulfilment: a person really believes in the product he or she is marketing and that the good life really and truly is bound up with marketing it. There is also the self-fulfilment of potential recipients of the message to take into account. The right to express oneself in one's mother tongue, particularly in one of Canada's official languages, is a right to be jealously guarded in the commercial no less than in political or religious discourse.

This is the philosophical context in which the Supreme Court of Canada decided the question as to whether a total tobacco advertising ban, in the form of certain sections of the 1988 Tobacco Products Control Act, was an unjustifiable infringement of the Charter guarantee of freedom of expression or not. The Court's answer, in *RJR-MacDonald Inc. v. Attorney General of Canada* and *Imperial Tobacco Ltd. v. Attorney General of Canada et al.*, was handed down September 21, 1995.[29] The Court ruled that the statute in question restricted more expression than was demonstrably necessary to reduce the social harm of smoking. It conceded the important point that some prohibition of tobacco advertising was consistent with the Charter, even though conclusive scientific evidence connecting advertising with increased consumption was lacking.

The reasoning in *RJR-MacDonald* shows that a majority of the Supreme Court at the time viewed the arguments in favour of a total prohibition against tobacco advertising to be insufficient to justify viewing it as a reasonable limitation under the guarantee of free expression in the Charter. What seems to have tipped the scales in the delicate balance between the right to free expression and the pressing social interest of life and health was the appearance of a cavalier attitude on the part of the government on the matter of minimal impairment. The Court was worried perhaps about the kind of precedent that would be set if the government's suppression of evidence were overlooked.

Certain facts about tobacco advertising can be adduced, and were adduced, to demonstrate that the kind of expression that is tobacco advertising is not worthy of much protection, since it advocates the use of an addictive substance that both kills people in large numbers and causes numerous health problems to the user and to others subjected to environmental pollution caused by smoking. The existence of injurious health effects related to smoking was not disputed by the tobacco companies.

Much tobacco advertising is misleading imagery, whose motivation, quite naturally, is to persuade the recipient to buy the tobacco product and smoke it. It is not intended to enlighten the recipient about its hazards or environmental drawbacks. Why bother, then, to protect this damaging kind of expression? Does freedom of this kind of expression actually weigh more heavily than the lives and health of young people (who must be targeted if new smokers are to be generated)?

Justice Beverley McLachlin, writing for the majority, agreed that the objective of saving lives and health was of sufficient importance to warrant an infringement of freedom of expression, but she questioned whether the Act minimally impaired that freedom, and also whether the Act's rational connection with the objective sought had been sufficiently demonstrated. There was "no indication" that purely informational or brand preference advertising would have the effect of increasing consumption of tobacco. She would have accepted a partial ban, however, on lifestyle advertising only, advertising aimed at children and adolescents, and labelling requirements only. These would have been a reasonable impairment, as distinct from an unreasonable total ban.

The failure of the government to provide evidence that a less intrusive ban would not have been equally effective seemed to her noteworthy as well. Because the government did not present as evidence the results of a study it was known to have had made on alternatives to the total ban, the Court had to infer that these results did not justify the government's position. The government had a duty, in her view, to show that the infringement on freedom of expression did not exceed what is reasonable and "demonstrably justified in a free and democratic society." In her opinion it failed to do this.

However, McLachlin's argument strikes me as missing, or giving inadequate attention to, important considerations relating to the question of minimal impairment regarding restrictions on tobacco advertising. These include:

1. The enormous financial power of the tobacco interests to affect public consciousness—a power they have shown themselves willing and able to use to circumvent even the supposedly "total" ban when it was in place, prior to having sections struck down. For instance, the advertising of companies sponsoring sports or cultural events links their name or logo to that event.

2. The persistent directing of advertising at young people. Since the Supreme Court decision advertisements linking cigarettes with guitars have been published in newspapers, such as university newspapers and free cultural papers such as *Ottawa X-Press*, which are known to appeal to young audiences.

3. The history of deceptive advertising by the tobacco industry.

4. The difficulty of separating informational advertising from "lifestyle" or equivalently persuasive advertising. The repetition of information, carried on long enough, has psychological effects beyond the information itself. Furthermore, even typographical design can convey exotic or trendy associations, leading to a more favourable attitude towards the product.

All in all, it seems to me, we ought to consider the expression of tobacco advertising as of a low order of protection-worthiness.[30] It entices people, especially young people, to take up an addictive, health abusive, and life-shortening habit, whose environmental affects may harm those around them. Anything short of a total ban opens up loopholes exploitable by a determined party, which the industry has shown itself to be. New legislation, less broad than the 1988 statute, has succeeded in reducing the visibility of tobacco advertising to a great extent. The exception is that of sponsorships, where look-alike logos make their appearance at sporting and other events. However, once again the tobacco companies are seeking to have such legislation overturned; their new case will be heard by the Supreme Court in fall 2002.

GOVERNMENT CONTROLS ON THE MEDIA

When freedom of expression is coupled with media controlled in the interests of profit-oriented private enterprise, the public need for detailed knowledge helpful for meaningful political involvement is not likely to be satisfied, for the simple reason that doing so is not profitable. Two government commissions in Canada and a private commission in the US have investigated the role of the government in controlling the media and whether, indeed, there is a need for such control.

The Commission on Freedom of the Press (Hutchins Commission, 1947)

The Commission on Freedom of the Press, headed by Robert M. Hutchins, chancellor of the University of Chicago, was set up in 1943 with a grant of $200,000 from Time, Inc. and $15,000 from Encyclopedia Britannica, Inc. After hearing testimony from 58 people connected with the press, as well as many other interviews, it produced a report, *A Free and Responsible Press*, in 1947. It also sponsored and published six other works, including W.E. Hocking's *Freedom of the Press: A Framework of Principle* and Zechariah Chafee Jr.'s *Government and Mass Communications*.

The philosophy of the Hutchins Commission (as it came to be known) can be summarized as follows. The press in the modern age has an important democratic role to play. This role can no longer be overlooked by *laissez-faire* attitudes. Technology has meant increasing concentration of media. This in turn opens the door to possible abuses of power. Hitherto, the role of the state has been to ensure freedom of expression to the provider of information and ideas. The right to receive these has been protected at the same time. However, under modern circumstances, the same confidence in simultaneously protecting both rights can no longer be presumed, because the media may not find it economically in their interest. Therefore, some means should be found to ensure that they act responsibly. Since government action, however, may destroy the very freedom it seeks to protect, it should only be used as a last resort. The power of persuasion, and the use of education, should be the first means of improving the press. The press "must now take on the community's press objectives as its own objectives."[31]

Before Isaiah Berlin published his influential *Two Concepts of Liberty* in 1958 the Commission advanced the doctrine that "As with all freedom, press freedom means freedom from and also freedom for." In addition to the social service obligation, the major media also should act as a common carrier of ideas, open "to all who have something worth saying to the public, since the essential object for which a free press is valued is that ideas deserving a public hearing shall have a public hearing." In the view of the Commission, "The important thing is that the press accept the public standard and try for it. The legal right will stand if the moral right is realized or tolerably approximated. There is a point beyond which failure to realize the moral right will entail encroachment by the state upon the existing legal right."

The Commission felt that the government had a supplementary role to play in disseminating information useful to the public, but which commercial vehicles would find unprofitable:

> Government may and should enter the field of press comment and news supply, not as displacing private enterprise, but as a supplementary source. In so doing, it may present standards for private emulation. While in our experience a democratic government is one in which government itself is one of the main objects of public discussion and can therefore never be allowed to control or to regulate the debate, it is not inconceivable that a government by the people should also be a powerful instrument for the people, in respect to educational and other noncommercial possibilities of the developing press.

One obvious way in which a government could help would be by subsidizing the cost of gathering news in foreign locations, since the payoff in terms of reader interest in foreign affairs is not usually present in large enough numbers to make the cost of a permanent foreign correspondent in many locations worthwhile. However, Zechariah Chafee drew attention to a number of risks attached to affirmative government activities. He pointed out three ways in which well-intended subsidies could have a harmful effect on freedom of the press.

First, there was the risk of accidental discouragement. The general tendency of any widespread government action was to produce unexpected results. In order to strengthen a Portuguese alliance, England reduced tariffs on Portuguese wines, resulting in increased consumption of port. Unintentionally, the "result was to afflict two centuries of Englishmen with gout." The good intentions in developing highways hurt railroads. More specifically, the Mail Classification Act of 1879 established low second-class rates for the benefit of newspapers and magazines, but to the detriment of books. The Copyright Act of 1891 protected British authors, but with the result that "contemporary English writers are almost inaccessible at any price, except for an occasional best-seller."[32] Secondly, there was the possibility of deliberate government discouragement. For example, when a government is in charge of licensing, officials may become "reluctant to benefit an ungrateful recipient." A precedent for fearing such a result is the case of eighteenth-century British prime ministers who "did not grant literary pensions to vigorous critics of their administration." Any new form of regulation or subsidy brings with it an opportunity for discriminatory use "in accordance with an official's judgment of meritoriousness" (GMC 477). Thirdly, there was a growing habit of government concern with communications. Chafee alludes to the slippery slope, with each new government initiative providing arguments for further intrusions and for controls on forms of expression. Favours bestowed by government on media could result in control. He did not specifically mention advertising, but his remark was certainly applicable to the Canadian scene.

The Commission explicitly rejected what it saw as the Canadian model for government involvement in the information business, as voiced by John Grierson, former general manager of the Canadian Wartime Information Board (WIB), who acted as a foreign advisor to the Commission. As summarized by Chafee, this model involved a very active role for government in disseminating information. It did more than pass on information sought by the media, it also did in-depth research the press were unwilling or unable to do for themselves and produced reference papers prior to events of interest.

Interestingly, this remark, made in 1947, would have to be thoroughly revamped today. A Royal Commission in the early 1960s recommended putting a brake on government information in Canada, specifically to reduce or eliminate propaganda.[33] Subsequent policy papers moved in the direction of providing more information, and the Access to Information Act was passed in the 1980s. Meanwhile under the Reagan administration, large budgetary increases were given to support US propaganda around the world, and foundations were encouraged to promote propaganda at home. The control of media by government became especially tight for war correspondents in Grenada, the 1991 Persian Gulf war, the 2001 war on terrorism in Afghanistan, and other areas of combat.

The Commission drew special attention to the fact that the Canadian government was the largest advertiser in newspapers and that here was "a powerful means of directly influencing newspapers to co-operate" (GMC 740). Nothing has changed in this regard. On the other hand, the existence of a government network for distributing its documentary films in public theatres no longer exists, although such films are available in public libraries and are sometimes shown on television. The Commission report also revealed some clever manipulation by the WIB. Recognizing that its own output would be distrusted, WIB arranged to get a noted American columnist to publish material. Chafee commented, "Only the exigencies of war against the deadliest of enemies could, I believe, justify the full extent of the Canadian government's participation in the distribution of news and ideas" (GMC 744-45). Not surprisingly, Chafee's thinking did not encompass the possibility that Canadian nationalist aspirations might need some protection from the perpetual threat of submergence in a sea of US media outputs.

Grierson wholly supported government information initiatives to prepare for public acceptance of government policies. It could reasonably be described as government propaganda. Grierson himself was discredited later for his involvement in the Gouzenko affair,[34] but the problem for democracies in combatting propaganda from private and extra-territorial sources still remains. His views are expressed in the following passage, reproduced by Chafee:

> We claim certain rights in carrying out a plan of government or national management which has been in general agreed to by Parliament. We try to make that national plan successful. We claim the right to give information that is news, and also information that is pre-news, in order to prepare people for a situation so that they are not caught. We also claim the right to create civic

interest and therefore to promote healthy discussion. We also claim the right to motivate actions... We would be very foolish if we confused that large educational duty with the party in power.... If we feel that we are secure on general consent, then we go ahead. (GMC 746).

Chafee's reaction to this was surprisingly similar to that which followed a Canadian information initiative with the founding of Information Canada in the 1970s: "You are putting a professional group of a very special kind between the government and the media. You are refusing direct access to the government more and more. The government's statements of policy are all gone over before they are issued. They are interpreted by this specialized group before they hit the media proper" (GMC 748).

Evidently, such an arrangement could undermine the power of the media to criticize government effectively. The Commission rejected such a proposal, because it was concerned to see the media improve through self-regulation rather than from government-imposed sanctions or manipulative actions. But the nub of the "residuary legatee" theory is that, failing such self-regulation, some government action was necessary, and the Canadian experience was sufficiently unappealing to the media as to encourage self-regulating steps on their part.

The Royal Commission on Newspapers (Kent Commission, 1981)

Unlike the Hutchins Commission, the 1981 Royal Commission on Newspapers (hereafter referred to as the Kent Commission, after its chairman, Thomas Kent) was not afraid to recommend immediate government action to deal with concentration in the media. There were numerous allegations of abuse of power by the owners of newspaper chains, and an especially glaring case of self-censorship by the *Toronto Star* at the very time the Kent Commission held hearings in Toronto. There was public support for the institution of a "CBC in print," the newspaper equivalent of the public broadcaster, but the Commission declined to make such a recommendation, reasoning that the newspaper industry could soon be in decline and that the effect of starting a competing government newspaper might be to put some out of business. There could also be a constitutional problem: radio and television are federal licensing responsibilities, but how would the initiative in print be regarded constitutionally? Further, there would always be the suspicion that politics was influencing the newspaper even when it was not. The Commission felt that, faced with the constant threat of criticism concerning motivations against a history of newspapers with identifiable political points of view and readers' expectancy of such, such a government-sponsored newspaper would be bland.[35]

The Kent Commission's primary recommendation—at least the one that excited the most violent reaction from Thomson Newspapers, one of the two biggest chains at the time—was a limitation placed on existing chains to prevent expansion and a suggestion that the existing Thomson empire be dismantled.

The Commission proposed the enactment of a Canada Newspaper Act, which would stipulate that "a company owning or controlling a daily newspaper which is printed in two or more distinct locations in separate provinces of Canada shall not, either directly or through associated companies, own or control any other daily newspaper in Canada."[36] Thomson would have to divest itself of either the *Globe and Mail* or its 40-odd other newspapers, constituting a third of the Canadian total of daily newspapers. Such legislation today would force Izzy Asper to decide between owning the *National Post* or his extensive Southam chain of newspapers across Canada. The recommendation was made, not on the basis of proven decline of newspapers under chain ownership, but primarily because the Kent Commission felt that such ownership put too much power into the hands of a very few people and was, therefore, undemocratic.

The Commission did not concede that there had been no decline in the quality of newspapers under chain ownership, although its own commissioned research failed to establish any such decline. Numerous anecdotes in testimony covered in over 7,000 pages of transcripts give useful material to anyone who wants to make such a case, however. For example, Frank Withers, New Brunswick Chairman of the Media Club of Canada, testified that the Irving brothers' industrial empire combined with control over the media led to soft-pedaling negative stories about the former in his province. "Never does it seem to occur to the man on the street that never in the Irving press has there been an editorial attacking or criticizing any face of an industrial combination which owns or controls a huge proportion of the New Brunswick economy, and also the principal means of telling the people what to think about it." Julian Walker, editor of the *St. Croix Courier* testified that he had made critical remarks about the Irving press in a *Maclean's* article and the "*St. John News* truck, which carried all copies of *Maclean's* magazine and every other magazine that week to Charlotte County, our home area, caught fire." The delivery truck was owned by Irving. Reporters in the Irving press, he said, were kept busy in the "rubber chicken circuit" and did not have time to do in-depth reporting on an Irving company. "An editor at the *Evening Times-Globe* is simply not going to direct a reporter, for example, to dig into why the province recently granted a major tax concession to the Irvings for oil pipeline and oil storage facilities.[37]

RECOMMENDATIONS

The Kent Commission proposed a Canada Newspaper Act, whose features we will now discuss.[38]

1. Significant further concentration of the ownership and control of daily newspapers and of the common ownership of these newspapers and other media would be prohibited.

The Commission suggested that the same person, company, or associates, should not be allowed to acquire more than five daily newspapers, that the combined circulation owned not exceed 5 per cent of total daily newspaper circulation in Canada, and that the point of publication be not less than 500 kilometres distance from any other paper under the same ownership. Some flexibility in the rules might be obtained through the Press Rights Panel (described below under point 5). As for cross-media ownership, between radio, television, and print media, the Commission proposed that the proprietor not own a television, radio, or cable system if 50 per cent or more of the population within good reception lived in the circulation area of the newspaper. Again, doubtful cases would be decided by the Press Rights Panel. Southam, the Commission said explicitly, would have to sell its 30 per cent interest in Selkirk Communications, a major television and radio company, which had 11 radio stations and two television stations in BC and Alberta and large interests in three other BC television stations; Southam had six daily papers in the two provinces. In New Brunswick the Irving interests would have to divest themselves of either of their two-in-one papers in Saint John or their similar Moncton papers. Other cases were also mentioned.

2. The very worst cases of concentration of media then existing would be corrected.

The recommendations applied only to conglomerates and chains, where there was reason to feel that editorial integrity might be compromised by other interests. The Commission supported the freedom of the proprietor to do what he liked with his products *"provided that newspaper is his principal property"* (italics in original).[39] The justification for legal controls was squarely based on the social responsibility theory of the press. The Commission felt that where proprietors had other media interests, or stores or oil wells or pulp mills or suchlike, their power should not be accepted unconditionally. The Commission pointed to the Canadian Daily Newspaper Publishers Association's own declaration:

> The newspaper must hold itself free of any obligation save that of fidelity to the public good.... Conflicts of interest, and the appearance of conflicts of interest, must be *avoided*. Outside interests that could affect, or appear to effect, the newspaper's freedom to report the news impartially should be *avoided*. (Italics added.)[40]

The reader can smile on reading this. In 1995, at a safe distance from any political pressures to enact any of the Kent Commission proposals, the Canadian Daily Newspaper Association changed its Statement of Principles on precisely this point, so that it now reads:

> The newspaper's *primary* obligation is fidelity to the public good. It should pay the costs of gathering the news. Conflicts of interest, real or apparent, should be *declared*. The newspaper should guard its independence from government, commercial and other interests seeking to subvert content for their own purposes. (Italics added)[41]

3. An incentive to widen the ownership of newspapers and to establish new newspapers and magazines would be offered.

The Act would provide a special inducement, through tax haven provisions, for the purchase of shares in companies that acquired newspapers in consequence of the Act.

4. The Act would raise the status and enhance the freedom of journalists by protecting their rights, in cases where owners had major interests outside the newspaper; this would also provide an opportunity for the voice of the community, whose citizens have a particular stake in the quality of the local newspaper, to be heard.

This would protect editors of newspapers belonging to a chain or conglomerate, by requiring that the editor-in-chief be appointed under a written contract, the nature to be spelled out in statute, for a period of not less than three years and not more than seven. The editor would decide news, and his judgment could not be overruled, although he would be advised by a committee of four "in-house" members and three representative people from the community. This committee would publish an annual report, and comments would be published in the newspaper.

5. The Act would establish, in conjunction with the Canadian Human Rights Commission, a Press Rights Panel which would monitor the implementation and effectiveness of the legislation.

The Press Rights Panel, which was to operate within the Human Rights Commission, would have many functions, including the monitoring of the press. It would provide guidance to advisory committees and would review and provide flexibility in cases of proposed acquisitions. It would have power to get information from newspapers on matters pertinent to its work. It would, rather importantly, have up-to-date information on all business interests with which the ultimate proprietor was in any way associated. It would also observe the performance of newspapers in Canada and publish an annual review of that performance.

6. A tax credit and surtax to encourage newspapers to devote more of their resources to the provision of information would be provided.

The idea is quite simple and seems worthy of adoption. The only two objections to it are a general objection to a Newspaper Act, on the grounds that, once in place, such an Act might facilitate Orders in Council, with the government acquiring a weapon against disliked media and, secondly, an encouragement to wasteful expenses to get the tax benefit and avoid paying the surtax.

7. Matching grants to help improve the news services within Canada and for Canadians about the world would be provided.

The Commission felt that Canadians should be better informed about general national and international news. A financial incentive would encourage more such coverage. For instance, if the Canadian Press were to increase expenditure by $100,000, then the Treasury would pay a grant of $50,000 to the news service the following year.

CRITICISM OF THE KENT COMMISSION REPORT

There were many criticisms, some of them expressed in terms of outrage, by the media at these proposals. H. Perrin Beatty, a Progressive-Conservative MP (later president and CEO of the CBC) focused on the discretionary power that would lie in the hands of the Press Rights Panel. "What is so dangerous about this board of the Government's friends is that it has the power to determine whether a newspaper can stay in business. It is this panel that decides whether the law will apply and, of course, if it doesn't feel the law goes far enough, it has the right to recommend changes to the Government." He was concerned that self-censorship would take place "if newspapers had to worry about keeping the favour of a panel of the government's friends."[42]

The recommendations went virtually nowhere, since the Trudeau government was in the thick of its battle to amend the Constitution and bring in the Charter of Rights and Freedoms. It could ill afford to alienate the media any more. Despite this other preoccupation, a much-reduced set of proposals was presented by Jim Fleming, Minister of Communications, in May 1982, at a time when, he noted, 77 per cent of the national newspaper circulation was controlled by chains compared to 58 per cent in 1970. His proposed Canadian Newspaper Act would not allow any one owner to acquire more than 20 per cent of the average Canadian circulation of daily newspapers. (Two owners already in excess would be allowed to keep their existing holdings, but not acquire more.) There would be a Canadian Advisory Council on Newspapers, reporting biennially and promoting public debate. "Canadians must have some objective place to air their grievances against newspaper stories short of a costly setting," Fleming said.[43]

The cabinet approved the bill, but the legislation was not introduced in Parliament. Two cabinet decisions were announced instead. One directed the Canadian Radio and Television Commission (CRTC) to prohibit newspapers from holding a controlling interest in broadcast media in the same area. This had the effect of delaying the licence renewal of one of the Irving radio stations in New Brunswick, although in 1985 the federal cabinet, under the new Progressive Conservative government, abandoned its effort to prevent newspaper owners from keeping broadcast outlets. The other cabinet directive was for an equal cost-sharing program to establish new out-of-province or foreign news bureaus, to a maximum of $50,000. The total amount granted would not exceed $1 million. I am not aware of the offer having been taken up by any news organization.

The overall effect of the Kent Commission should not be measured simply in terms of proposed legislation that went nowhere. It clearly had the effect of encouraging self-regulation in the media, and it brought to light many of the potentials for abuse in the media. It is surely no coincidence that shortly after the Report appeared, every daily newspaper in Ontario became a member of the Ontario Press Council. Yet, the concentration of ownership has increased, curiously for a while in the direction of ownership by one individual, Conrad Black (until he sold his Canadian papers in 2000-01), who has been more "hands-on" than the previously preeminent press baron in Canada, Kenneth Thomson. Black has thrown some obstacles at those who would criticize his power over the media. For example, the papers have been opened more than ever before to input from the public in terms of letters to the editor and columns (in the *Ottawa Citizen* at least). Two full pages of letters are published on most days in that newspaper. The complaint that surfaced in the US Commission on Freedom of the Press—that newspapers were denying the public the common carrier function of allowing exchange of ideas—could not be pressed against Black, unless a systematic bias (in choice of letters) against some particular viewpoint could be found. The possibility for abuse of power is still there in other respects, such as control over the timing and prominence of the viewpoints expressed in letters and the usual question of ignoring worthwhile news items or printing biased accounts that are in accord with Black's, or his editors', dominant ideology. This kind of analysis needs constant updating and involves some tedium. The new magnate to watch, with his close ties to the Liberal party, is Izzy Asper and his family, whose extensive CanWest Global holdings include the Southam chain. Already controversy has been created with his new requirement that the chain carry a centrally written editorial from time to time. The *Globe and Mail* reported on September 1, 2001, that Michael Goldbloom, publisher of Montreal's daily newspaper the *Gazette*, was quitting, citing a difference in perspective between himself and the new CanWest Global Communications owners. The *Globe* said sources at the *Gazette* confirmed that "senior editors at the paper were told in August to run a strongly-worded, pro-Israel editorial on a Saturday op-ed page." Aside from political power, there are also the commercial ends of the paper which arguably may clash with the social responsibility criterion. Here again, careful analysis over time is needed to produce any substantial critical impact.[44]

THE MEDIA CONTROLS ITSELF

The UK Press Complaints Commission

As with self-regulation in advertising, the move to self-regulation in the press has been stimulated by the threat of government legislation and by periodic surges in public opinion supporting government intervention. In Britain, the Royal Commission on the Press recommended in 1977 that the Press Council draw up a code of behaviour on which to base its adjudications. Concerns about invasion of privacy by the press triggered the appointment in 1989 of a departmental committee, which two years later recommended setting up a Press Complaints Commission to take the place of the existing Press Council. This independent commission was to adjudicate a code of practice agreed to by publishers and editors. The new commission was given 18 months to demonstrate "that non-statutory self-regulation can be made to work effectively."[45] It has continued in existence for over a decade now, producing monthly reports listing every complaint.

The Press Complaints Commission's Code of Practice has numerous clauses dealing with the gathering of information; for example, it condemns misrepresentation in a general way, but allows subterfuge "only in the public interest and only when material cannot be obtained by any other means" (PCC Clause 11). It also exposed some of the falsifications used to impress readers, such as interviews presented as in person when they were conducted on the telephone. Accuracy, opportunity for reply, privacy, identification of victims, and intrusion into grief and shock are among the concerns covered. Propaganda-related matters include conflicts of interest, suppression of news, avoidance of hate propaganda, ethnic stereotyping, and the like. Clause 13 states: "Discrimination: (i) The Press must avoid prejudicial or pejorative reference to a person's race, colour, religion, sex or sexual orientation or to any physical or mental illness or disability; (ii) It must avoid publishing details of a person's race, colour, religion, sexual orientation, physical or mental illness or disability unless these are directly relevant to the story."

On matters of accuracy and libel, the Commission has shown itself willing and able to stem biased reporting and editing. For example, a letter writer complained that the *Daily Mirror* edited her letter about AIDS, substituting the word "plague" for "illness." The Commission supported the complainant's view that the substitution "carried the implication that she regarded AIDS as a form of divine retribution for moral corruption. The editor should not have printed this alteration without [her] consent."[46] Letters are supposed to be edited for style and space reasons, but it is not unusual to find unflattering references to the newspaper or one of its staff removed or toned down. In this case it seems that an ideological perspective was being advanced and imputed to the writer. It is a very old form of propaganda to impute to others ideas one wants to advance in public. The complaints system performs an important restraint on this kind of activity and is welcome for that reason. To be effective, though, there must be publicity. In 1993-94 the Commission set out on a promotional tour in municipal libraries of major UK cities, and publishers offered nearly £230,000 of advertising space.

The Commission, in the words of its first chairman, Lord McGregor of Durris, "does not wield and will not seek enforceable sanctions." Its aim is to "assist the industry to observe the code that it has framed." It handles complaints, gives advice on the code and on journalistic ethics, indicates shortcomings in the code, and seeks to gain credibility for the self-regulatory process. It sees itself as having the duty "to promote generally established freedoms, including freedom of expression and the public's right to know, and the defence of the press against improper pressure from government or elsewhere."[47] In 1993 the body appointing members to the Commission was restructured to provide a clear majority of members independent of the industry. It also undertook to ratify the code and changes to it in future, so that the PCC would share responsibility for the code as well as for its implementation.[48]

The most recent version of the code, ratified by the Commission on December 1, 1999, includes some fairly extensive and noteworthy changes. On the matter of privacy, the new code prohibits the use of long-lens cameras to take pictures of people in private places without their consent. It requires a newspaper or periodical to report fairly and accurately the outcome of an action for defamation to which it has been a party. On harassment, "persistent pursuit" has been added to a list of prohibited activities. A new Clause 8 prohibits the obtaining or publishing of material obtained "by using clandestine devices or by intercepting private telephone conversations."[49] In a recent annual report, the new chairman, Lord Wakeham, explained that the reason why the PCC does not monitor the press more proactively and does not have sanctions in the form of fines is that the industry would not cooperate under such circumstances. The PCC would be turned into a "Press Control Commission," which would undermine self-regulation "because publications would, rightly, cease to be so co-operative with the PCC. They would see us as the first rung on a legal ladder, not as the alternative dispute resolution mechanism that we are."[50] It hardly differs then from what an American writer perceived the earlier British Press Council to be: "It endeavours to protect citizens from abuse by the press, while protecting the press against far worse censors than itself."[51]

In summary, the PCC fulfills a useful, but limited role. Just how effective it is likely to be in the future will depend on the energy with which the public makes use of the existing code in the complaints process and continues to consider government-sponsored regulation, since this threat is obviously a powerful motivating force for the self-regulatory system.

The Ontario Press Council

In Canada the threat of government intervention in the media stimulated on at least two occasions activity of a self-regulatory nature. The Ontario and Alberta press councils were formed in 1972, shortly after the Special Senate Committee on Mass Media presented its scathing evaluation of the press in Canada, together with its recommendation for a National Press Council; there was an upsurge in membership of these councils following the 1981 Kent Commission Report. I will focus on the workings of the Ontario Press Council, with which I am most familiar. (This does not imply that the Ontario Press Council is superior in any way to other Canadian press councils. Indeed, a recent writer in the *Canadian Journal of Communication* says that the Quebec Press Council is "considered to be the most dynamic press council in North America, and perhaps anywhere."[52])

The Ontario Press Council (OPC) was founded in 1972 with Davidson Dunton at the helm. Since its foundation it has heard, at the 1998 count, 2,966 complaints.[53] Like many other such councils, it has several different functions. It is intended to speak out against government interference with the press, while at the same time correcting the worst abuses in the press that might fuel public demand for government control. It acts as an adjudicative body, deciding to uphold or dismiss complaints and giving reasons for its decision. There are no sanctions other than the requirement that, as a condition of membership in the council, newspapers publish decisions involving complaints against themselves. That is not an insignificant requirement; it provides a moral victory to complainants who see themselves vindicated, as well as having a deterrent effect on the future behaviour of newspapers. Where the British PCC appears to be more concerned about privacy, the OPC deals primarily with issues of stereotyping, hate propaganda, and the like. This may be due to greater intrusivenes on the part of the British Press, particularly regarding royalty (of 13 cases reported in the February 7, 2001 MediaGuardian as "landmarks" or "notorious," 10 dealt with privacy issues); it could also be a reflection on the fact that Canada has human rights commissions and hate propaganda legislation. One cannot safely conclude, though, that self-regulation is necessarily triggered by the existence or threat of more restrictive legal controls. The popular morality which supports one will support the other, and the same cause may affect both.

The purpose of the OPC is set out in a preamble, adopted in a 1989 revision. Acknowledging that it exists because "newspapers recognize that a democratic society has a legitimate and fundamental interest in the quality of the information it receives," it goes on to list the various unfair conducts for which papers can be called to account by the public: "invading privacy without justification, condemning people by innuendo or hearsay, ignoring commonly-accepted ethical standards, reporting conjecture as fact, distorting accounts of events, or failing to acknowledge error." While claiming independence from the newspapers who founded it, the OPC "vigorously defends the independence of the press and full freedom of public expression ..." and "speaks out for the public on ...freedom of public expression and access to government information."[54] Its objectives, as stated in its constitution, are:

(a) to defend the freedom of the press on behalf of public and press alike;

(b) to serve as a medium of understanding between the public and the press;

(c) to encourage the highest ethical and professional standards of journalism;

(d) to consider specific, unsatisfied complaints from the public about the conduct of the press in gathering and publishing news, opinion and advertising; to consider complaints from members of the press about the conduct of individuals and organizations toward the press; and to report publicly on action taken;

(e) to review and report on attempts to restrict access to information of public interest.

(f) to make representations to governments and other bodies on issues related to the purposes of the Ontario Press Council; and

(g) to publish periodic reports recording the work of the Ontario Press Council.[55]

A policy statement issued in 1997 emphasized that the OPC "does not deal with complaints based only on the differences of opinion between complainant and newspaper," but that "newspapers have a responsibility to provide a forum for expression of counter opinions"; it affirmed its determination "to continue to consider complaints involving opinion if complainants contend that they are based on erroneous information or are erroneous in themselves or that the language used was unnecessarily hurtful."[56] In early 1985 the OPC announced it would not deal with complaints about rejection of letters to the editor "unless the Council considered that the issue involved warranted an exception to the general rule."[57]

In early years a complainant had to undertake, as a condition of being heard, to waive his or her rights to legal redress. The 1982 annual report states, in the procedure section of its constitution: "Every complainant shall sign a waiver agreeing not to take legal action on any complaint heard by the Council on which the Council makes a finding." Davidson Dunton told a student interviewer at the time that the OPC rarely insists on complainants signing, but the requirement was an important check. "If, say, you get a case starting before the Council and, at the same time, they're (the complainants) starting a libel case, then one party can be using the proceedings before the Council to get material for their legal case."[58] The case of John and Judi McLeod of the *Brampton Daily Times* suggests that other forms of legal redress than that related to libel might also be barred to complainants. They were fired following their investigative-style coverage of city council meetings. They wanted to take their case to the OPC, but were unwilling to sign the waiver and so dropped it. This led to a charge in 1984 by the spokesperson for the Centre for Investigative Journalism that some Canadian journalists were being "victimized' by press councils.[59] In the updated version, the rule is that "under some circumstances" the OPC "may ask a complainant to sign a waiver agreeing not to take legal action...[etc]."[60]

According to most recent figures there are currently two English-language daily newspapers which are not members of the OPC—the *Belleville Intelligencer* and the *National Post*. The OPC's revenue comes from member newspapers. In 1998 it was $180,593, down from $186,292 in 1997. Considering that revenue was $109,195 in 1982, it seems not to have kept up with inflation over the years.[61]

The current OPC has shown itself to be reactive rather than adventurously pro-active in exploring issues of journalistic ethics.[62] Early sceptical comments about the OPC and what it might accomplish seem no less appropriate today than they were some 20 years ago. With Izzy Asper replacing Conrad Black as the dominant force in Canadian media, will there be any change? This remains to be seen.

The Role of Canadian Press Councils

When the OPC was first set up in 1972, the Canadian correspondent for the *New York Times*, Jay Walz, commented "until a nationwide council is created, there is no chance to consider the implications of the trend towards concentration and monopoly that the Davey committee found to be advancing so ominously in Canada."[63] That seems in retrospect to be a prescient remark, underscoring the limited role played by press councils in Canada.

In 1972 the *Globe and Mail*, not a member of the OPC at the time, editorialized that "Press councils have no punitive power to control recalcitrant members who continue to go their merry way—as the British council experience has demonstrated. Publishers go on buying scandal-case confessions while the council worries itself over such problems as the use of the word 'Mister' in second reference to persons in the news."[64] The root of the problem is that the councils, as mentioned earlier, are financed by the industry itself, which is interested foremost in staving off government interference and gaining public confidence. A limited usefulness cannot be denied, to judge by the experience of the OPC, but the nature of the limits depends largely on the public mood and the enthusiasm of publishers themselves for the highest standards of journalism, which may or may not coincide with perceived financial interests.

In his chairman's remarks in the 1990 annual report of the OPC, former Supreme Court of Canada Justice Willard Z. Estey remarked that voluntary bodies "bring about a moderation of the exercise of the right of freedom of expression by the press through group influence and peer pressure and by regular reminders of the use of common sense by the reporter or commentator." These voluntary restraints, he wrote, "have proven to be more successful than heavy-handed direct intervention by the state into the relationship between the writer and the reader." Critical to the success of self-regulation is that it not operate "in a manner which will curtail or suppress legitimate dissemination of fact and comment." Regulatory intrusion into everyday life, he wrote, is evident everywhere in our daily life and virtually the only "pruning mechanism" against the growing tentacles of government, outside of the political process, is the "free and independent press":

> Without a dedicated investigative press, service by all levels of democratic organs of government to the community is diminished.... Access-to-information legislation accelerates this modern vital role of the journalist. Competition amongst the press excites the exercise of the right of access. This competition ensures a better-informed public. That same pressure, however, elevates the importance of the organization and exercise of self-restraint by the voluntary institution, the press council.[65]

GOVERNMENT INFORMATION

The American progressive and independent journalist, I.F. Stone, made the point that too many establishment journalists have been co-opted by government, so that carefully contrived deceptions are passed on uncritically to the public. Politicians in power attempt to hide wrongdoing and rationalize coverups in the name of the national interest as perceived by the party in power. The news correspondent is brought into the government official's confidence so that he or she begins to feel like a statesman, rather than a critical newsperson.[66] However, those in government who are responsible for disseminating information are often frustrated with the media, which are often interested in the sensational rather than in what people need to know for the better working of society. A major attempt to show off an important function paid for by taxpayers' money may be scuttled because of other media needs.[67]

In modern democracies, governments work to ensure measures they deem necessary will be received favourably by the people. They are concerned that their actions not be misinterpreted, that the reasons for various measures be understood. However, since governments are formed from political parties, there is always some two-sidedness to any campaign of government information. On the one hand, there is the aim of informing; on the other, there is the temptation to spend public money to promote a favourable image of the political party in power. This latter use of public funds gives an enormous advantage to the party in power. Public money may also be spent with a view to giving a favourable image to a government department, thus enhancing budgets and the prestige of officials in that department. The film "Red Nightmare" was made in the 1950s by the US Department of Defense with Warner Brothers. It promoted fear of communism, along with glorification of the role of the military; in the last scene of the film, armed forces personnel join hands in a display of brotherhood and nationalism. The message of the film encouraged public support for large defense expenditures.

Governments may also suppress information they do not wish the public to hear or they may practice disinformation. A conspicuous example of the latter was the campaign by the Reagan administration against Mu'ammer al Qaddafi in the summer of 1986. The *Wall Street Journal* proclaimed that a military attack against him was in the works. Two months later, the *Washington Post* published a memo from National Security Advisor John Poindexter indicating that the story had been leaked to the press as part of a disinformation campaign against Qaddafi. In Britain a disinformation campaign by the Thatcher government to support the sinking of the *Belgrano* at the time of the Falklands/Malvinas war was exposed by Clive Ponting in his book *The Right to Know*.[68]

Canada has devoted an unusual amount of attention and several major studies to the problem of disseminating information to the public. Periodically Canadian newspapers snort with indignation about the avalanche of government advertising that swells their own pages. They also profit from it, and sustained pressure to do away with such "advocacy advertising" has not yet happened. The Conservatives will berate the Liberals for the practice and then do the same themselves when in power.

The Canadian government has wrestled several times with philosophical questions relating to provision of information. During World War II, the Bureau of Public Information—later renamed the Wartime Information Board (WIB)—worked to shape public attitudes to the war. Its general manager, John Grierson, believed in participatory democracy, and during his tenure, the WIB issued pamphlets explaining how Canadians could have influence on the political system. These pointed out that only a few men controlled the press and radio, apart from the public system; they also enthusiastically supported labour activities and accomplishments.

When a general election was called in June 1945, the Liberal Party chose a WIB slogan for its campaign: "Building a New Social Order for Canada." The Liberals won handily, benefiting from the WIB propaganda. In the long run, Grierson's ideas were too left-wing to be acceptable to the Liberal establishment, and his credibility was further weakened by his involvement in the Gouzenko Inquiry.[69]

Government-sponsored studies of its own provision of information have varied in purpose, intent, and conclusions. In the early 1960s, restraint was the general message. At the end of the decade, when participatory democracy was in full flower, the aim was to empower the less fortunate by giving them more information directly and subsidizing their ability to make themselves heard. Information Canada in the early 1970s was touted as a more democratic, because more efficient, information provider, but the media saw it as an institution that would consolidate information and make government propaganda easier. They may have been right on this, but their motives were also open to suspicion, since any direct contact between government and people has a diminishing effect on the media's importance.

The Glassco Report

An important examination of government information policy was carried out by the Royal Commission on Government Organization, headed by J. Grant Glassco. Volume III of its 1962 report dealt with information services. It noted that the development of special machinery of government information had been gradual, starting with the Editorial and Information Division of the Department of Mines. In 1910 the Department of Agriculture, having issued farmers' bulletins since 1887, created a Publications Branch. In 1920 the new Department of National Health established a Publicity and Statistics Division to enlighten the public on maternal and child welfare and the dangers of various diseases and how to treat them. World War II had a "catalytic effect" on information services. The machinery was set up to engage in propaganda. It was dismantled after the war, but "the wartime experience left a lasting impression on political leaders and administrators and during the next few years most departments and agencies which had not already established information services did so."[70]

The report listed four main categories of tasks:

1. services to the public, such as the census, weather-forecasting, research information, etc;
2. enlisting public support; for example, urging people to file income taxes early, using postal codes, recruiting for national defence, etc.;
3. responding to a public right to be informed. "Knowledge of government activities is a public right, and indeed a necessity; but the growing size and diversity of government make the satisfaction of this need more and more difficult. The machinery and processes of government are therefore taking increasingly into account the public demand to be informed" (GR 67).

The report noted that business people suffered when the government dragged its heels on classifying goods for import duty;

4. publicizing of government activities. Here is where the provision of government information entered the area of controversy. The report noted that proper limits of such activity become "debatable." Obviously, if a museum is established, people should be told so they can see it. But when governments go beyond the obviously acceptable minimum and publicize their activities on the basis of general newsworthiness they enter an area which "is not always easy to draw" between "releasing news and 'telling a Department's story.'" The publicity may enter a realm of political controversy. "There is no fixed line between exposition and argument, between publicity and propaganda" (GR 69).

The report then drew three conclusions. First, general government publicity should be "strictly factual and as far as possible objective." The task of information services is "to inform rather than to persuade." The "ultimate decision as to what is news and how it should be presented must be left to the media." Secondly, there should be "restraint and balance in volume." Even when "information is objective in character, sheer volume can transform it into propaganda." Finally, an important distinction should be drawn between "material which genuinely informs and that which is calculated only to impress; the latter has no place in the information activities of government." It is tempting, the report noted, to issue news stories, pictures or films depicting weapons, laboratories, and engineering works as marvels of the age—begging the question of their function and worth (GR 70).

The report further noted that the role of the public relations person for private industry is on a different footing from that in government, in that maximal favourable exposure for the company is a legitimate goal. But the commissioners denied that similar approaches are permissible in government. "Keeping the mass media supplied with a flood of so-called news releases is not a function of a department." Taxpayers' money "should not be spent to impress people with the quality of performance" (GR 70-71).

The commission felt that the Department of National Defence had gone overboard. During a two-week period in November and December 1961 there were 68 press releases, including 10 "major stories," 7 news-feature releases, more than 2,500 photographic plates distributed and more than 100 radio, TV, and film assignments completed. More than 700 radio tapes and 500 TV tapes were produced and distributed (GR 71-72).

The report did not state that it was essential for government departments to speak with one voice, but was concerned about duplication of effort from a cost standpoint. It recommended that government advertising accounts be awarded on the basis of tender in the manner of other government contracts. The reason was that "vast differences in value" were often received from different advertising agencies (GR 95).

The Glassco Report's philosophy and recommendations are no less pertinent today, with the burgeoning of government advocacy advertising to be described shortly.

The Task Force on Information

With the election of a Liberal government under the leadership of Pierre-Elliot Trudeau in the late 1960s an energetic change in attitude towards government information came to Ottawa. Like Trudeau, Gérard Pelletier, who became Secretary of State, was influenced by London School of Economics Professor Harold Laski[71] and sought ways of making democracy more meaningful. In his book, *La crise d'octobre* (*The October Crisis*) Pelletier expressed his concern very succinctly. The ordinary citizen, "while being assailed twenty-four hours a day by the written press, radio, and television, often has no other means of expression than the placard at the end of a stick, as in 1850."[72] In line with this philosophy, the federal government provided a wide array of subsidies for alternate media, with programs such as Opportunities for Youth and Local Initiatives. The interest in media was further strengthened by the hearings of the Special Senate Committee on Mass Media in 1969 under Senator Keith Davey, who had proposed the idea for such an investigation in November 1968.

In 1969 the Task Force on Government Information produced its report, *To Know and To Be Known*,[73] with recommendations that led to the establishment of Information Canada. The report included results of a national public opinion survey, which found:

> Canadians are generally ill-informed on the responsibilities of their provincial and Federal governments; and a majority of the public want more information than they are now receiving. (TK 50)

Evidently, the government needed to find some better way of getting information out to the public. The task force confronted the accusation that government advertising was tantamount to propaganda:

> Exposure to federal advertising and use of available information sources do not seem to influence attitudes that might favour the Federal Government. Those who remember seeing federal advertisements are not predisposed to be more favourable toward the government; nor does their exposure apparently make them more favourable. (TK 50)

This interpretation of the data showed that additional government information was not successful as propaganda; therefore, the government could not reasonably be judged to be motivated by propaganda considerations in seeking extended information channels.

The report began its recommendations urging that "[t]he right of Canadians to full, objective, and timely information and the obligation of the State to provide such information about its programs and policies be publicly declared and stand as the foundation for the development of new government policies in this field." Its fifth recommendation sought "[s]teps … to reach sections of the Canadian public that are at present outside the mainstream of the government information flow." Among the suggestions was inviting the cooperation of provincial and municipal governments, private agencies, and voluntary organizations to establish and finance Citizens Advisory Bureaux and neighbourhood councils. It sought also an "enhanced role of the information function" and the strengthening of relations with media and with particular publics nationally and regionally. It called for "[a] central resource and services organization, to be known as Information Canada" to be established in an existing ministry. Information Canada "should ensure that the two official languages are used as equal instruments of creativity and communication." It was to be given the function of public advocate in matters of access to federal information and timeliness of replies to citizen's queries, with adequate staff to fulfill this function. Other recommendations included the setting up of an audiovisual unit in Information Canada to "advise government, departments and agencies on policy and to conduct approved operations of limited scope in this field." Also included among the proposals was that "[a] daily, analytical press digest on significant developments and views within and outside Canada (when they involve this country) be produced for officials and, on request, for other interested persons and organizations" (TK 61). Once again there was concern about the securing of advertising contracts, with a recommendation that an independent board, knowledgeable about media and advertising but free of conflicts of interest, get the best value for money when choosing advertising agencies for government assignments.

D.F. Wall Report

Information Canada came into being shortly after the task force report was issued, and hopes were created about its ability to provide, free of charge, answers to complex questions about government and the law. From the beginning the media tended to treat it with distrust, some seeing it as a propaganda tool. Certainly, if one were interested in having the government engage in propaganda, the centralizing of information would be the first step. No effective propaganda of that kind can be carried out when different branches of government say contradictory things. In any case, for whatever reason, Information Canada did not last long. A report, *The Provision of Government Information*, was prepared by D.F. Wall for the Privy Council and circulated in April 1974. It provides a very interesting analysis of what went wrong, while defending a philosophy of government information favouring openness in dealings with the public. Since this was also the task force's philosophy, it is interesting to look at Wall's analysis of its failings.

Wall identified four main policy objectives:

1. to keep secrecy to a minimum;
2. to detect and expose existing problems in the provision of information services;
3. to deal with concerns that special interest groups were getting better access to information than others, even backbench MPs;
4. to deal with concerns that government had become too anonymous and faceless.

The basic flaw in existing information practice was that the Canadian government would "release only that information which was considered advantageous or harmless, and automatically ... withhold the rest."[74] The operative principle, he wrote, seemed to be "When in doubt—classify it!" He quoted the Minister, Don Jamieson favourably:

> Somewhere, way back, we started from the assumption that everything was secret and that only the minimum possible information should be released. Surely a far better and more democratic approach would be to proceed on the assumption that everything is open, and only to withhold information from the general public when this is clearly necessary on the grounds of public interest or for security reasons. (WR)

One obstacle to the free disclosure of information was the Public Service Employment Act, s. 23, which required civil servants to take an oath: "I ... solemnly and sincerely swear ... that I will not, without due authority in that behalf, disclose or make known any matter that comes to my knowledge by reason of [my employment in the civil service]." Thus, Wall wrote, the civil servant had often nothing to gain and everything to lose by giving out information of a sensitive nature. Interestingly, evidence that the oath might still be an obstacle to giving out information was provided as recently as a Senate committee hearing in late 1999. Dr. Shiv Chopra, a science researcher at Health Canada, said that he was told by higher officials in government that, in testifying to the Senate Committee on Agriculture about Bovine Growth Hormone, he and others "might be in conflict of two oaths: one, our existing oath to the public service and the oath that we would take before the Senate Committee on Agriculture. We were told that the only person who can give evidence is the minister or his delegate, and so we will have to be careful."[75]

Wall interviewed 100 public servants and 60 non-governmental people; almost without exception they felt the government did not do an adequate job of explaining not only policies and programs to the public, but also their rationale and how programs fitted with policy. Part of the reason was the very human factor of inter-ministerial rivalry. There was "a propensity of some Ministers and their offices to seek maximum publicity for themselves and their programs, often to the exclusion of other programs" (WR). Lack of appropriate co-ordination often resulted in provincial governments getting most of the publicity for projects initiated and largely funded by the federal government. Information papers handed out on an occasional or on a one-shot basis were not as useful as a constant stream. Some said there was too much bureaucratese in the language used. Another complaint was that government information was not adequately targeted to its appropriate audiences. Hans Classen, an information officer whom I interviewed in 1979 (he died within a few years), confirmed the existence of much wastage—warehouses of undistributed pamphlets, for example. For that reason he recommended using the media to get things out, despite the unpredictable nature of news demands on any given day. Even when the material is distributed, there is no guarantee it will be read. The media, on the other hand, edit and publish material on the basis of what people will read.

With regard to special interest groups having privileged access, Wall's response was to recommend more regular access to officials at the middle and senior levels. Over time, he felt this would "reduce the growing suspicion and scepticism between government and Parliament, and government and the media, and would help to establish clearer and more acceptable ground rules as to attribution, adversary partisan use of information, withholding publication in the public interest, publication of 'leaks,' etc." (WR). He felt that civil service "anonymity" had been carried too far, even though, understandably, civil servants did not want to become centres of public controversy in which they would be unable to defend themselves.

As to giving more of a human face to government information, Wall suggested that admission of wrong would sometimes improve a government's credibility rather than the reverse. Nothing is as informative or persuasive, he wrote, than the combination of "clarity, objectivity, simplicity, and pertinence." These qualities were "often found lacking in governmental statements, press releases, speeches and pamphlets, inserts and so on, sometimes to the extent that credibility was seriously strained, and the objective lost" (WR).

INFORMATION CANADA: WHAT WENT WRONG?
Since there are indications that in the fall of 2001 the Canadian government is again looking at the idea of consolidating information, the objections Wall found against Information Canada are worth reviewing. They were:

1. that the present terms of reference were unclear;
2. that its relationships with departments and agencies were so little developed that it was not given much substantive information to disseminate;
3. that, as a result, the initiatives it did take were often annoying to departments and unsatisfactory to its public clientele;
4. that in any event it could not possibly direct, control, operate, or even fully coordinate substantive information programs in defiance of statutory departmental and ministerial responsibilities and "dollar control";

5. that its officials did not have sufficient knowledge of the nature and substance of government operations; and

6. that, for many of these reasons, it was not attracting staff of the necessary quality to make it credible and effective within its existing terms of reference.

Even those positively disposed towards Information Canada did not feel it had
become adequately coordinated with other departments.

Wall's study went beyond Information Canada to look at the overall functioning
of government information. He found in his discussions that a recurring strand
of concern was that information officers were ineffective for several reasons: first,
they did not have enough access to or participation in the processes of policy formation, so they didn't fully understand what they were supposed to convey.
Second, they tended to be used for cosmetic purposes, apologists for ill-con-
ceived or poorly explained initiatives. Third, many were failed journalists who didn't
command respect. Finally, the development of an information community within
the public service had the effect of isolating this community rather than integrating
its members into the broader functions of public service and the government as
a whole. Emphasis was more on career patterns in terms of more pay, etc., than
on the essential function of informing the public.

One other constant problem in government is the existence of leaks, which
can undermine a government's policy. Why do people engage in the practice?
Junior people may be frustrated that their ideas are not getting through to the top
echelons, or they may shift their loyalties in the direction of causes such as Quebec
independence, minority rights, etc. Some may be sympathetic to the political opposition. The oath of office, mentioned earlier as a source of a penchant for secrecy,
for some people lacked credibility because of the absence of clear sanctions for violation and so lacked restraining influence. More often than one would suspect,
leaks were by persons with no axe to grind, pranksters out to shake people up in
the higher ranks. Finally, in some cases there was the desire to leak something judi-
ciously at an appropriate time to bring favourable public reaction to a minister,
who would then be favourably disposed to the leaker.

The problem with leaks in Wall's view is that they have negative and damaging aspects: they arouse interest in the fact of the leak rather than the substance;
they almost invariably lead to distortion; they can engender inequality, market instability, and an atmosphere of "doubt, suspicion, and loss of confidence"; they are
wasteful, since clarification will be needed and there will be efforts to track the
leak; they tend to upset an orderly approach to government priorities; overall, they
are at best an inefficient way of informing the public.

Sydney Freifeld added further observations about possible motives for leaks, such
as currying favour with the news media. Leaking a hot item will benefit a reporter,
who may repay the favour by writing up an item of dubious newsworthiness, but
beneficial to the leaker. Freifeld made an interesting suggestion relating to journalistic ethics in dealing with leaks from anonymous sources. Wherever possible
the circumstances of the leak should be made clear, so that the reader can make

some inference as to whose axe is being ground and, thus, can approach the news item with appropriate scepticism. Obviously, the recipient of the leak cannot betray a source, but short of that, it is often possible to convey much relevant information about the circumstances. Freifeld contends first, that the editor be told of the source in confidence and, secondly, that the public be told as much about the circumstances of the leak as is relevant to making an informed assessment and yet does not violate the code of source confidentiality. This will not always be easy, since it is often a temptation to give the reader the impression that intrepid investigatory reporting was behind the story, rather than that it was handed on a platter. No one said the ethical is always easy to carry out.[76]

Wall concludes that information officers ought to be more involved in the decision-making process. Too often they have been viewed as "the PR boys who are always boozing it up at the Press Club when you need them" (WR). Information should be viewed as an integral function of government in general. He writes that experience has surely made it clear that information unjustifiably withheld almost inevitably finds its way out, and usually in circumstances which provide not one but several targets for critics, some of them impossible to miss. Not just the government, but the whole process, suffers as a result.

In the light of the Somalia affair[77] years later, and the protracted attempts at covering up which have come to light, the final warning seems prescient.

Government Advertising as Propaganda

If we hark back to the Glassco Report and look at government information in Canada in the decades since the 1960s we can see no diminution of government advertising, and we have reason to recall the admonition that sheer quantity can turn government information into propaganda. Bursts of advertisements accompany every new federal-provincial rivalry, and spending limits are sidestepped with subliminal messages paid for by the taxpayer. For instance, in the May 1980 referendum on Quebec independence, the federal side was to vote "non" and the separate side "oui." One advertisement for not mixing drinking with driving, sponsored by a federal department, read "NON" in big letters; the overt intent was to indicate not drinking alcohol before driving, but the covert intent was which vote should be cast. The PQ government responded with an employment billboard with large letters featuring the acronym of the Office de la Securité d'Emploi—OSE. The word "ose" in French means "dare." In other words, the billboard suggested that people dare to vote for Quebec sovereignty. One argument in justification for the federal blitz was that, since the province had control over the teaching system and the CEGEPs (schools straddling high school and post-secondary education), the Quebec government had an unfair advantage. Certainly it made use of this advantage at the time of the introduction of the 1981 Constitutional Amendment (later to become the 1982 Amendment), when it circulated to history departments in all the schools and in public places such as liquor outlets an emotional 21-page booklet with the heading "Minute Ottawa!" The booklet contained a tendentious presentation and interpretation of the constitutional amendments.[78]

With the referendum over, the advertising competition did not stop. The Quebec government, in anticipation of constitutional changes, placed a two-page advertisement in August 1980 in *Le Devoir* setting out its own position, the federal position, and the position of other provinces on a number of constitutional and policy issues. The federal government produced a large amount of advertising of its own, prompting an indignant column by W.A. Wilson in the *Ottawa Journal*, "Ads tread fearful line between information and propaganda." Wilson's comments are worth recording:

> The real problem with propaganda, as opposed to information, is that it is intended to condition the public mind by evading the questions and need for answers which are inherent in the information process. That is why media manipulation, a form of propaganda, is so popular during election campaigns— the purpose is not to spread information but to condition the popular mind....[79]

The federal government's National Unity Office also came up with television advertising showing trees, canoes, and Canada geese in flight, thus promoting a "feel-good" attitude towards the nation. This brought an expression of disgust from *Ottawa Citizen* columnist Charles Lynch: "B-R-A-A-A-C-K says it all." The geese received so much exposure that an editorial page cartoon still made reference to them in the same paper seven years later; one flying goose says to another, "A Free-Trade TV commercial? ... No way!...I can still feel the buckshot we took on those National Unity ads."[80]

Perhaps the 1980 referendum gave the federal government a taste for massive advertising. About three-quarters of a page in the *Ottawa Citizen* on September 4, 1980, was taken up with an advertisement by Employment and Immigration Canada showing a group of young people; its headline was, "Help wanted before September 29. Canada's employment plans won't work without you."[81] This conveys the impression that the government was doing something about unemployment, in this case through community development projects. Typically, an advertisement in one paper such as the *Ottawa Citizen* is indicative of an advertisement circulating in other newspapers as well. I asked for and obtained from the department a list of newspapers and insertion dates for one such advertisement. For Ontario alone, 43 daily newspapers from the *Barrie Examiner* to the *Woodstock Sentinel Review* were listed, all within the same week. Of course all the major papers, the *Toronto Star*, the *Globe and Mail*, and so on were included. The advertisement was listed as having a space size of 1500 lines and was in black-and-white. Two other lists were involved, one of weekly English newspapers, the other of French-language weeklies outside Quebec. Only two insertions were allotted to the weekly newspapers in either language. Thus, the total reach of the advertisement is huge and at considerable cost to the taxpayer.[82]

A full-page advertisement of a scene showing farmland at the foot of the Rocky Mountains was headed "Canada —We have a lot to offer each other," and went on to say that the Government of Canada spends $160 million annually to support Agriculture Canada research, and other favourable items. Across Canada an expensive campaign was carried out to promote the ill-fated new national energy policy. Full-page advertisements proclaimed "Completed energy security for Canada is this close." And a picture of a greatly enlarged digital finger and thumb about an inch apart was portrayed.[83]

There was another incident in the same year, 1982, in which the distinction between government advertising and reported news was blurred. A full-page advertisement from Supply and Services Canada was placed in the *Moncton Times*, in a 10-page section devoted entirely to a new federal building at Shediac, in which the department was the major occupant. The advertisement proclaimed "In Shediac 442 new jobs serving Canadians." Pictures of Supply and Services Minister Jean-Jacques Blais and Oceans and Fisheries Minister Romeo LeBlanc were placed on page one with the headline "LeBlanc, Blais to officiate at opening of Shediac offices." A story on page three detailed the history and organization of the Department of Supply and Services. On another page were profiles of Blais and Paul Cosgrove, Minister of Public Works, and a further story on page nine dealt with how Supply and Services is "in contact with all aspects of life in Canada."[84]

Not surprisingly, in areas where federal and provincial interests were at cross-purposes, the provinces retaliated. A federally sponsored advertisement in the *Montreal Gazette* in February 1983 brought a full-page response from the Saskatchewan Department of Agriculture opposing the federal changes to the Crow rate. Where the federal advertisement said "The Crow goes without a flap," the Saskatchewan advertisement, published in the *Globe and Mail* two months later, produced such a flap, telling readers to write to Pierre Trudeau and other federal ministers to oppose the measures.[85]

Verbal and pictorial duelling between Ottawa and Quebec reached mammoth advertising proportions in 1999 over health care and other areas of shared financial responsibilities. A full page in *Le Devoir*, proclaiming Ottawa's unpaid bills to Quebec was faced by a half-page advertisement by the Canadian government showing that Quebec, with 24 per cent of the population was going to receive a 34 per cent increase in transfer payments in the 1999 budget. Josh Freed devoted a column describing the "avalanche of ads" in the Montreal Gazette.[86]

The problem with this jousting is that it is paid for by the taxpayer and enriches the media, introducing conflict between the two sets of interests. Under the circumstances a fierce attack by the media upon this practice appears, humanly speaking, unlikely. Pressures to stop it would then have to come from the general public. A solution might be to strike a committee, reflecting both viewpoints, to examine and clarify the opposing positions and communicate the results to the public.

In January 1984 the Liberal government hit on the idea of flying student newspaper editors to Toronto where they were told by Employment and Immigration Minister John Roberts about "cafeteria programs" available for jobless youth.

He announced that the job creation budget would be increased to $1.2 billion for 1984. He also asked for suggestions and criticisms about existing programs. As a way of gaining favourable publicity for the program, this meeting backfired. A story in the *Globe and Mail* focused on the cost of flying the students in and accommodating them in a good hotel, although it did mention that they had been given a tour of employment centres. A student from Simon Fraser estimated that his expenses cost $1,000. All of this came after a report in the *Ottawa Citizen* that the Trudeau cabinet was "Putting the finishing touches on an $11-million, election-year advertising blitz to sell federal government programs." The story quoted Conservative MP Perrin Beatty as saying the campaign appeared to be an attempt "to polish their own image in preparation for an election." However, Roberts, identified as chairman of a 12-member Cabinet communications committee, was said to have insisted that the advertising would not be "advocacy" in nature. "He says it will be informational, aimed at informing citizens what programs are available, based on surveys pointing to information gaps with the public."[87]

There is nothing new in the practice of flying appropriate opinion leaders to a location where they are likely to be impressed. Aside from the British in World War I, and other cases mentioned earlier, there is the US Pentagon propaganda machine that defused opposition to missile sites by choosing community leaders and flying them to a place where they received red carpet treatment, briefings, and displays.[88]

Despite denunciations of federal advertising overkill, the Progressive Conservatives did much the same thing when in power. Thus, an eight-page newsprint brochure in English and French, "Objective: Canada's economic recovery," was distributed, proclaiming highlights of the 1991 budget with charts and graphs putting a favourable slant on the budget. Liberal finance critic Herbert Gray was quoted, saying, "This ad and its brochure are nothing more than Conservative propaganda, and they should be paid for by the Conservative Party—not the hard-hit taxpayer."[89] A half-page advertisement in the *Kingston Whig-Standard* in 1985 with the name of Employment and Immigration Canada Minister Flora MacDonald at the bottom proclaimed "help a student step into the working world, and we'll foot the bill." In this case there was cooperation with the provincial government, since the name of the Ontario Minister for Youth, Phil Gillies, also appeared at the bottom with the Ontario logo.[90]

One of the most insidious aspects of government advertising is the attempt to use it to buy coverage in the news columns of a paper. A Canadian Press story in 1986 detailed such an offer:

> Newspapers across the country are being offered a lucrative advertising deal if they agree to publish a number of Government articles provided by the federal Energy Department.
>
> The department has agreed to buy a full page of advertising if the newspapers agree to print six of 30 articles it provides on transportation technology.
>
> Earl Matthews, the department's marketing manager, says he sees nothing wrong with putting conditions on the advertising purchase.

"Basically it's to get the message out," Mr. Mathews said in a telephone interview from Ottawa, and not an attempt to control editorial content in the newspapers.

"We're saying here's 30 articles, print six. You pick what you want to print," he said. "You can take our copy and rewrite it if you wish… as long as the facts are straight."

As the *Globe and Mail* editorialized two days later, "The facts, of course, are those selected by Energy Canada, as may be imagined from a recent title: Federal Energy Minister Shows Alternative Fuel Leadership." The editorial made the following useful ethical analysis of the situation: "The department is using public money to feed its political message to readers disguised as something it is not—an article according to the newspaper's usual editorial standards of what is important and what is balanced. The Government seeks to rent not just advertising space, but the newspaper itself. The intrusion should be fought by all who value an independent press." Two days after the editorial the chairman of the Canadian Daily Newspaper Publishers Association was reported as denying that member newspapers would accept such a deal: "Daily newspaper publishers throughout the country would not accept a contingency advertising order which requires them to publish material in their news columns as a condition of acceptance." Energy Minister Pat Carney was also reported as suggesting in the Commons that there was no such advertising deal and that such a practice would be deplorable. But one of her aides said the minister was not denying the existence of the deal, only denying an allegation that the government-written stories were propaganda. In a further editorial the *Globe and Mail* reiterated, "Instead of paying for the privilege of having its words run, or leaving it to editors to make a judgement on the quality of articles submitted, the department is bribing the newspapers to shape their standards to conform with the Government's—and to give up a measure of their freedom."[91]

There is no indication that government advertising tantamount to propaganda is diminishing in recent years. The Ontario government under Premier Mike Harris has engaged in extensive newspaper and direct-mail advertising, such as in its battle with striking teachers. As one news report put it, some of the advertisements "tell the truth but not necessarily the whole truth about what's happening to the province's healthcare system." Ontario's advertising met with a response from the federal government in an advertisement in the *National Post* proclaiming, "$11.5 billion more is a real shot in the arm for our healthcare system."[92]

As recently as March 11, 2002, the Ontario government paid a share of the costs of a six-page supplement to the *Globe and Mail*, with no mention made of this fact. According to government sources, the copy was provided by the government in consultation with advertisers. The supplement was titled "Ontario's Electricity," followed in smaller type by "Lighting the way to a brighter future" and "A special supplement on Ontario's new electricity market." At the top of each page, with the exception of page M4, in the space which journalists designate the "flag" or the "folio" there appeared in unusually large bold capital letters "The Globe and Mail, Monday, March 11, 2002." Among the sub-headings was "Customer protection paramount." Energy Probe has found some questionable statements and omissions in the supplement pointing to disguised advertising in favour of the government's policies, contrary to the Advertising Code and to principles of journalistic ethics.[93] One may well ask what has happened to the earlier fierce independence of the *Globe and Mail?* An obvious candidate for the answer is the takeover of the newspaper by Bell Canada Enterprises. Let the CRTC take note on the next occasion that the CTV network, also owned by Bell, appears before it.

NOTES

1   Ian Brownlie, ed., *Basic Documents in International Law*, 2nd ed. (Oxford: Clarendon Press, 1972) 170, 194, 195, 210-11.

2   Canada, *The Charter of Rights and Freedoms: A Guide for Canadians* (Ottawa: Minister of Supply and Services Canada, 1982) 33.

3   Supreme Court of Canada, *R. v. Keegstra*, [1990] 3 S.C.R., 714. Subsequent quotations in the text are taken from this source, hereinafter referred to as *Keegstra*.

4   *Beauharnais v. Illinois*, 343 US 250.

5   *Collin v. Smith*, 578 F.2d 1197 (7th cir. 1978) *certiori* denied 439 US 916 (1978). The quoted passage is from page 1199.

6   He refers among other things to obscenity rulings in commercial speech cases such as *Posadas de Puerto Rico Associates v. Tourism Co. of Puerto Rico*, 478 U.S. 328 (1926), and T. Alexander Aleinikoff, "Constitutional Law in the Age of Balancing," *Yale Law Journal* 943, 96 (1987): 966-68.

7   *Keegstra*, 748. Dickson's direct reference is to the *Report of the Special Committee on Hate Propaganda in Canada* (Ottawa: Queen's Printer 1966) 59; indirectly to *Beauharnais* 304.

8   *Keegstra* 777.

9   Wayne Sumner, "Hate Propaganda and Charter Rights," *Free Expression*, ed. W.J. Waluchow (Oxford: Clarendon Press, 1994) 172.

10 Phillip Nelson, "Advertising and Ethics," *Ethics, Free Enterprise, and Public Policy*, ed. Richard T. de George and Joseph A. Pichler (New York: Oxford University Press, 1978) 187-98.

11 Burton Leiser, "The Ethics of Advertising," de George and Pichler. The examples below are taken from pages 173-86 of this text.

12 Leiser 182.

13 Canada, Department of Consumer and Corporate Affairs, *Misleading Advertising Bulletin 4*, July/September 1986: 10.

14 Canada, Department of Consumer and Corporate Affairs, *Misleading Advertising Bulletin 2*, January-March 1989: 3.

15 Rachel Larabie-Lesieur, notes prepared with the assistance of Roy Jackson, *Misleading Advertising Bulletin 2-1996* (Ottawa: Industry Canada, Competition Bureau, 1996). See 5, 6.

16 Larabie-Lesieur 7.

17 The toll-free number, 1-800-348-5358, was still in service September 2001. A Website has replaced the *Misleading Advertising Bulletin*. It is viewable through Industry Canada's site,

<http://strategis.ic.gc.ca>, or more particularly <http://strategis.ic.gc.ca/SSG/ct01250e.html>, from which the legislation, news releases, and other information can be downloaded.

18   Michael Trebilcock et al., *Study on Consumer Misleading and Unfair Trade Practices: Proposed policy directions for the reform of the regulation of unfair trade practices in Canada* (Ottawa: Information Canada, for the Department of Consumer and Corporate Affairs, 1976). Quotations below are taken from this study.

19   Trebilcock et al.

20   Trebilcock et al.

21   From a brochure, "Canadian Advertising Foundation: Advertising Self-Regulation Activities," provided by the CAF around 1995.

22   Linda Nagel, in Advertising Standards Canada, *Communiqué* 1,1 (September 1997): 3.

23   Keith McKerracher, President, Institute of Canadian Advertising, in testimony to the Royal Commission on Newspapers (n.p.) Transcript 6129.

24   Marina Straus, "When one sponsor 'buys' a newspaper," *Globe and Mail*, 15 August 1996: B9, discussing the *Financial Post*, 19 August 1996. See also *Ottawa Sun*, 19 August 1996.

25   Scott Feschuk, "Battle over local phone service begins," *Globe and Mail*, 20 August 96.

26   Part of the answer to this question may have come with the publication of the February, 2002 *Report on Business Magazine* carried in *The Globe and Mail*. See my "Disguised Corporate Advertising in the Media?," *Straight Goods*, 4 February 2002, <http://www.straightgoods.ca/ViewMediaFile.cfm?REF=147>.

27   ASC, *Gender Portrayal Guidelines* <http://www.canad.com/en/Standards/Gender.html>.

28   The 1997 *Ad Complaints Report*, Advertising Standards Canada (Toronto) is online at <http://www.canad.com/en/Standards/Complaints_Report/1997ReportE.pdf>. To make a complaint, all a person has to do is to access ASC's Website at <http://www.adstandards.com> and follow the links.

29   *RJR-MacDonald Inc. v. Canada (Attorney General)* [1995] 3 S.C.R., 199. Further quoted passages referring to this decision and found in the text come from this source.

30   This section and the previous chapter have incorporated and adapted portions of a study I did for Health and Welfare Canada: "Freedom of Expression, Bill C-51, and the Canadian Charter of Rights and Freedoms," March 1989. I am grateful to Health and Welfare Canada for their support of that project.

31   Commission on Freedom of the Press, *A Free and Responsible Press* (Chicago, IL: University of Chicago Press, 1947) 126. Quotation appears in italics in the original. Quotations below from 128, 129.

32   Zechariah Chafee Jr., *Government and Mass Communications: A Report from the Commission on Freedom of the Press*, Vol II (Chicago, IL: University of Chicago Press, 1947) 475. Further references to this work are taken from this edition and will be indicated by GMC and page number bracketed in the text below. Vol. II begins with page 471.

33   J. Grant Glassco, *Royal Commission on Government Organization* (Ottawa: Queen's Printer, 1962).

34   Igor Sergeievich Gouzenko defected from the Soviet Embassy in Ottawa in September 1945 with documents proving to Canadian authorities that there was a Soviet spy ring in Canada.

35   Canada, Royal Commission on Newspapers, *Report* (Ottawa: Supply and Services Canada, 1981) 231. Hereafter known as the Kent Report.

36   Kent Report 243.

37 Kent Report transcripts 4135, 4262, 4264.

38 Kent Report 237-38.

39 Kent Report 246 (italics in the original).

40 CDNA, 1977. A copy is reprinted in the Kent Report.

41 CDNA, "Statement of Principles," no date appears on the one-page statement itself. At the bottom, the statement appears: "Adopted by the Canadian Daily Newspaper Association in 1977, revised in 1995." A news release announcing the change was issued by the CDNA 4 October 1995. It announces the addition of two new clauses, "Community Responsibility" and "Respect," but is silent about the change in wording from "avoided" to "declared." The Association, now re-named the Canadian Newspaper Association, has its Statement of Principles online at <http://www.cna-acj.ca/about/sp.asp>.

42 Perrin Beatty, "Freedom of Press at Stake," *Globe and Mail*, 4 February 1982.

43 Jim Fleming, public announcement 25 May 1982 in connection with a draft Bill which met with Cabinet approval but did not reach Parliament.

44 I have tried to engage in the kind of analysis described on several occasions. One concerned a misleading headline, "No harm from secondhand smoke," in the *Ottawa Citizen* (8 March 1998), concerning the effects of passive smoke. The second involved what I have argued was a sensationalist attack on the newly appointed CEO of the Ottawa Hospital, David Levine. See my *The David Levine Affair*. Another involved a critique of tobacco advertisements that had appeared in many newspapers, including the *Ottawa Citizen*. Though submitted to many newspapers, my critique was printed only in *The Gazette*, Montreal, 3 March 1997.

45 UK, Press Complaints Commission (PCC), *Report* #1, (London: January-June 1991) 2. The Code of Practice which appears on page 6 has been updated, and clause numberings given in brackets are to the code as accessed online 13 February 2002 at <http://www.pcc.org.uk/cop/cop.asp>.

46 PCC, *Report* #1 24, 23.

47 PCC, *Report* #1, 4.

48 PCC, *Report* #17 (London: March-April 1993), 5.

49 From the PCC 's Website, <http://www.pcc.org.uk>.

50 From the PCC 1998 *Annual Report*, taken from the Website <http://www.pcc.org.uk/annual/98/chairrep.htm>.

51 Patrick Brogan, *Spiked: The Short Life and Death of the National News Council* (New York: Priority Press, 1985) 105.

52 David Pritchard, "The Role of Press Councils in a System of Media Accountability: The Case of Quebec," *Canadian Journal of Communication*, downloaded July 2000 from <www.cjc-online.ca/Backissues/16.1/pritch.html>.

53 Doris Anderson, "Forward," 26th *Annual Report*, Ontario Press Council (1998) 5; also available on <http://www.ontpress.com/1_about/1_about.html>.

54 Preamble to the constitution, taken from the Ontario Press Council Website <http://www.ontpress.com/about/council_constitution.asp> 14 February 2002; used with permission. It appears also in the annual reports. The current preamble has not changed since 1989.

55 OPC Constitution, rev. 1998, available online (see note 37).

56 OPC, Policy Statement, 24th Annual Report 1996 (Toronto, 1997) 18.

57 OPC, "How to Complain," 24th Report 35.

58 Quoted in Giuliano O. Tolusso's, "The Ontario Press Council: Challenges of a Second Decade," honours research project, School of Journalism, Carleton University, (1983) 9. At the time Davidson Dunton was a senior fellow of the Institute of Canadian Studies at Carleton.

59 Sherri Barron, "Journalists to investigate actions of press councils," *Ottawa Citizen*, 27 February 1984: 4.

60 OPC, 26th Annual Report (1998) 75 .

61 Figures are taken from OPC 26th Annual Report (1998) 60; OPC 10th Annual Report (1982) 52.

62 See, for example, complaints detailed in OPC News releases on 29 October 1998, 17 January 1998, 4 November 1996, 20 March 1998; and in OPC 's Annual Reports for 1992, 30–32, and 1993, 26–29.

63 Jay Walz, "A Press Council Set Up in Ontario," *New York Times*, 20 August 1972: 23.

64 *Globe and Mail*, 25 April 1972.

65 Willard Z. Estey, "The Chairman's Foreword," Ontario Press Council, 18th Annual *Report* (1990) 2, 3.

66 Stone, *I.F. Stone's Weekly*.

67 Hans Classen, a long-time information officer with the Canadian Department of Energy, Mines and Resources, told of elaborate preparations made for a media event, following the return to Halifax of a scientific research vessel that wintered in the Arctic. The publicity was scheduled around the return of the ship into Halifax harbour. Unfortunately, the event clashed with the start of the six-day war between Egypt and Israel, and the event was pushed off the pages of the media! (Personal interview, tape-recorded in Ottawa, 1979.)

68 *Wall Street Journal*, 25 August 1996; *Washington Post*, 2 October 1996; Ponting.

69 Comments about the WIB are taken from a very interesting manuscript by William R. Young, "Mobilizing English Canada for War: The Bureau of Public Information, the Wartime Information Board, and a View of the Nation During the Second War" (n.p., n.d.)

70 Canada, Royal Commission on Government Organization, *Report*, Vol 3 (Ottawa: The Queen's Printer, 1962) 62. Following references are from this source and will appear as GR and page number bracketed in the text.

71 A fact he revealed to me in a taped interview in Bordeaux in 1979–80, when he was Canadian Ambassador to France.

72 Gérard Pelletier, *La crise d'octobre* (Montréal: Éditions du Jour, 1971) 43. The more lengthy passage is as follows: "Dans cette perspective, il est urgent que l'Etat mette concrètement à la disposition de certains groupes défavorisés les moyens techniques de faire entendre leur cause et d'exposer leurs idées. C'est chose faite dans un certain nombre de secteurs. Mais, comme le soulignait un homme politique anglais, le citoyen ordinaire, qui vit dans un monde où la technologie des communications est extraordinairement développée, se retrouve malgré tout seul dans la rue, comme il y a cent ans, le jour où il veut dire aux autres des choses qui sont importantes pour lui. Alors qu'il est assailli vingt-quatre heures par jour par la presse écrite, la radio et la télévision, il n'a souvent pas d'autre moyen d'expression que la pancarte au bout d'un baton, comme en 1850." (Footnote omitted).

73 Canada, Task Force on Government Information, *To Know and to Be Known*, Vol. 2 (Ottawa: The Queen's Printer, August 29, 1969). Further references are from this source and will be indicated in the text by TK and page number in the text below.

74   D.F. Wall, "The Provision of Government Information" (Ottawa, mimeographed paper, 1974). Further references are from this source and will be indicated in the text by WR.

75   Canada, Senate Committee on Privileges, Standing Rules and Orders, *Proceedings 4: Evidence* (Ottawa: 7 December 1999) 6. Downloaded from <www.parl.gc.ca/36/2/paribus/commbus/senate/com-e/RULE-E/04EV-E.HTM>.

    In the event, Dr. Copra testified he was persuaded that Senate rules protected his submission and that he spoke freely before the Committee on Agriculture.

76   Sydney Freifeld's remarks were delivered in an annual guest lecture given in my "Truth and Propaganda" course at Carleton University in the 1980s.

77   The Somalia affair relates to, among other things, the torture and murder of a Somali teenager by Canadian airborne soldiers in 1993. An inquiry in 1994-95 widely publicized the existence of a culture of racism and brutality among the soldiers. See Canada, Report of the Somalia Commission of Inquiry (Ottawa: Public Works and Government Services Canada, 1997; available online at <http://www.dnd.ca/somalia/somaliae.htm>.

78   *Ottawa Citizen*, "Pamphlets from PQ cause fuss," 15 October 1981.

79   W.A. Wilson, *Ottawa Journal*, 20 August 1980.

80   Charles Lynch, *Ottawa Citizen*, 10 October 1980; *Ottawa Citizen*, 8 January 1987.

81   *Ottawa Citizen*, 4 September 1980.

82   Department of Employment and Immigration Canada, personal communication from David McConnell, Advertising Services, Public Affairs Division, n.d.

83   For an example, see *Globe and Mail*, 16 November 1981; 2 September 1982.

84   *Moncton Times*, 8 July 1982.

85   *Montreal Gazette*, 21 February 1983; *Globe and Mail*, 21 April 1983.

86   93. *Le Devoir*, 28 February 1999; *Montreal Gazette*, 27 February 1999.

87   *Globe and Mail*, "Bewildered journalism students wonder why they were sent for," 28 January 1984; *Ottawa Citizen*, 10 January 1984.

88   J. William Fulbright, *The Pentagon Propaganda Machine* (New York: Random House-Vintage, 1971) 7-9.

89   Herbert Gray, *Globe and Mail*, 19 March 1991.

90   *Kingston Whig-Standard*, 23 March 1985.

91   Canadian Press, *Globe and Mail*, 19 May 1986; editorial, *Globe and Mail*, 21 May 1986; Tom Crowther, "Daily papers would reject government ad deal, publisher says," *Ottawa Citizen*, 23 May 1986; editorial, *Globe and Mail*, 27 May 1986.

92   *Ottawa Citizen*, "Ontario health ads tell selective truths," 25 January 1995; *National Post*, 27 February 1999.

93   The present writer has joined with Tom Adams of Energy Probe in registering a formal complaint with Advertising Standards Canada. A letter to the editor, for publication, and to the publisher of the *Globe* was also sent. The text of both documents can be seen on the Website <www.energyprobe.org>.

EIGHT

PROPAGANDA, DEMOCRACY, AND THE INTERNET

THE PROMISE OF THE INTERNET

To many, the arrival of the Internet has been a gift, an answer to the problem of media concentration and corporate dominance. It is no longer necessary to rely on the newspaper or television for vital information or interpretations not available in the daily press. The world's best newspapers, including *Le Monde Diplomatique* and *The Irish Times*, are online. A wealth of government documents can be downloaded from a decent Internet-equipped computer costing under $2,000; many organizations, pressure groups, propagandists, bureaucratic documents, and even such esoteric entities as a flat-earth society can be found at the click of a button on any good search engine, such as google.com. When I read, in the *Globe and Mail* on July 12, 2000 about the International Panel of Eminent Personalities and their report on genocide in Rwanda, I was able to download the whole report of 24 chapters the same day. Robert Fisk's thoughtful, courageous, and historically sensitive reporting from the Middle East is accessible daily on *The Independent's* Webpage <http://news,independent.co.ul/world/middle_east/>. Critics of Fisk can be found at <http://honestreporting.com>. A gateway to a large and important worldwide selection of media has been assembled by an Ottawa news junkie, Pierre Bourque, and is accessible through search engines by typing in "Bourque Newswatch," or going directly to <http://www.bourque.org/>. A more academically oriented selection can be found at Arts and Letters Daily found at <http://www.aldaily.com>.

The power of the Internet to affect political and economic decision-making was made manifest in Seattle in 1999. A high-level World Trade Organization meeting was effectively shut down by a mass of highly co-ordinated protesters. In the "old days" (meaning a few years ago) a social critic who wanted to have some influence was handicapped by delays in accessing court judgments, government reports, or other documents. The time delay meant that the critic was at a disadvantage compared to those whose jobs were bound up with the media. To a large extent that is no longer true. Government press releases in Ontario appear not only in the media but, at the same time, are posted on the government Web pages, with links to actual documentation.

The field is wide open for independent journalists to set up their own Web pages. Indeed, Boyce Richardson, a retired journalist and filmmaker in Ottawa has done just that; "Boyce's Paper"—found by typing that name into the search engine—provides regular insightful commentaries on the media, books, politics, sports, and whatever else captures his attention. What is special about this publication, updated every few days, is that it gives an unapologetic socialist viewpoint unobtainable, at least on any regular basis, in any Canadian mainstream publication that I know. However, without an advertising budget, how many know of its existence? Long ago Albert Camus dreamed of a critical journalism that would outline the biases of the writers, owners, news sources, and so on, and would give the reader the benefit of the journalist's experienced judgment as to the likelihood of their veracity. This form of meta-journalism would draw attention to contradictory accounts, rather than suppressing them, thus putting the reader on guard against credulity. He was optimistic about the technical possibility of such journalism, without going into further detail.[1] Today various Websites can be found that approximate the function described by Camus, FAIR being one such (<http://www.fair.org>). All that is lacking, for many people, is awareness of where such sites are to be found. Can we expect a new era of democratic involvement? Or is this new technology likely to follow in the footsteps of the telephone, radio, and television, touted in similar ways, but falling far short of the promises made by some on their behalf?

Anyone familiar with the marvels of the Worldwide Web can hardly fail to see that we have entered a new era in communications on a scale perhaps comparable to the invention of the Gutenberg press. However, it is impossible to predict with confidence how this new technology will be developed. What seems limitless at first runs up against the fact of human boredom. Already news accounts have reported that, after a spurt of across-the-field experimentation, people tend to settle on a few Websites which they visit with regularity, until they step out of the virtual world to the real one, with its full human interaction. The Web is full of outdated, because not maintained, sites. After the initial discovery of cyberspace's potential, some more sober assessment is in order. Jacques Ellul, long before the arrival of the Web, made some comments on information technology that seem likely also to apply with poignancy to the Internet. He said:

> The technical possibilities of a wide variety of benefits [of a computerized society] are there, but it is illusory to suppose that the benefits will necessarily come about. The computer and other information devices enter an existing social order.... Inevitably, information systems will become concentrated and centralized.... The ordinary citizen will be given access to information, but how will he know where to look for what he wants, which data bank to tap? Social privilege will flow even more than now to the big administrators, intellectuals, and pressure groups or unions, whoever has the resources to get per-

tinent information.... Secrecy will also be favored, inasmuch as there will eventually develop two levels of information. The first will be what goes into the data banks. The second, and more important, will be the information not provided by the banks but known to those who fed the data into the computer, who decided what to put in and what to leave out. This will be one of the gravest threats to our future freedom.[2]

This prediction, made in 1980, about the difficulty of getting new technology to support grassroots democracy against established commercial interests, seems to be verified by contemporary developments. According to Donald Gutstein, a communications professor at Simon Fraser University, the development of the Internet is repeating what happened with previous communications technologies. As long as the technology is in its infancy, it is promoted as a public good, and public money is demanded and obtained for its development. Then, when the big cost hurdles are overcome, pressure is put on the government to allow private corporations to use the new technologies for commercial purposes. CA*net, the Internet in Canada, was funded through universities and the National Research Council. An industry-dominated organization was formed—the Canadian Network for the Advancement of Research, Industry, and Education (CANARIE)—and financed by the Mulroney and Chrétien governments to "upgrade CA*net and turn it over to the private sector—Bell Canada as it turned out." However, some of the companies involved in this organization, Bell included, stood to benefit from the demise of CA*net, since they planned to set up private Internet access companies. "CANARIE made no provision in its programs for public information access. Nonprofit and community projects were specifically excluded from support unless they had private sector partners."[3]

Currently the Internet has plenty of space for independent voices. These appear either on commercial Websites or on sites hosted by nonprofit organizations such as National Capital Freenet (www.ncf.ca) in Canada's capital. Freenet has provided e-mail and specific interest discussion groups since the early 1990s and now hosts a large number of sites. It survives on donations. What is worrying, however, is the idea that the BCE or other Internet-involved conglomerates might use their enormous technical, financial, and political capital to undermine the potential of the Web to become an effective counterculture voice. BCE controls, as we have seen, the major outlets of the *Globe and Mail* and CTV. Will it also end up dominating the Internet? One way this could happen is through the "synergy" of the different media outlets it controls. One media outlet discusses what is going on in a sister-publication, carefully directing the reader to a relevant paper, program, or Website. These in turn repay the favour by citing material from the first. Something comparable has already happened in the new newspaper-television synergy, less than a month after the CRTC declined to impose segregation of business from editorial interests in the cases of both BCE and CanWest Global. For example, the *Ottawa Citizen* carried a banner headline "Global newscast aims to be different," over a full page of copy highlighting the new newscast season of

CanWest Global Communications. There was not even the pretence of impartiality between Global Television and its competitor CTV.[4]

Those with money can arrange to have their own Websites posted higher in the lists delivered by the different search engines. Furthermore, one of the central features of the Web are linkages, which can be arranged in such a way as to direct the Web-surfer onto the pages which the company or organization desires, rather than those which the surfer wants. For example, in researching the *Ottawa Citizen's* archive early in September 2001, I find that when I clicked to go back to what I thought would be the *Citizen's* home page I was linked to CanWest Global's page instead. The use of pop-ups is another way of constraining the user. Pioneered mainly by the porn industry, it provides an endless linking of one porn site to another; each time a porn site is closed, another pops open in its place, providing a high level of meaningless "hits" for the porn trade. The only way to break the chain in some cases is to shut down the computer.

UNCERTAINTIES AND NEGATIVE FEATURES

Currently, the Internet is treated in the media as a big question mark. I have been speaking of the Worldwide Web, but in fact we need to bear in mind four different things, which together are referred to by the word "Internet." First is electronic mail—e-mail—by which written messages are conveyed through computer hookups to any part of the globe, virtually instantaneously. This seems likely to continue to grow. Bulletin boards are places where ideas are floated, questions asked, debates pursued, etc. To some extent the success of these will depend on the willingness of discussants to show restraint and tolerance, as well as patience. Some of these have diminished in interest as people became tired of "flamewars" (insulting exchanges) and the like. It is a democratic form of communication, since everyone gets to contribute in those sites that have no filters, but it also shows the limitations of unfiltered democracy. Those with the largest egos dominate the space with endless arguments directed against some equal and opposite obtuse and unyielding mind. Third are the circular mailing lists by which whole groups contact each other directly. This is a powerful mobilizing force. Last are the Websites already mentioned and the search engines, which provide ready access to a huge range of information.

One obstacle to the maximization of the potential for information access through the Web is cost. Who will pay? People buy computers to access the Web, but are not rushing to buy from many of the businesses set up there. In 2000-01 the money did not come in fast enough to meet expectations, and a huge loss of confidence in the high-tech industry resulted. Nortel, the electronics giant, saw its stock drop from $122.75 to less than $9 in a year. Some businesses have done well on the Net. Secondhand booksellers have profited from this service, which links buyers with books so much more efficiently than before. Judging from the proliferation of pornography sites, that particular business appears to profit as well. One theory is that the Internet will challenge the huge corporate structure by allowing small-scale entrepreneurs to interact with clients and with each other, avoiding major overhead costs and intermediaries. But there is still the problem of how to inform the public about one's Website, and how to keep them checking in. It is difficult to predict developments with any certainty. If access is through the telephone line, will the practice of not charging for time on local calls continue? If access is through an Internet service provider, will the rates stay the same once large numbers of people rely on this service for their livelihood? How will the cable companies benefit from high-speed connections, and how will lines—both cable and telephone—be shared between different companies?

Although the Internet's future is uncertain, our chief concern here is with its impact on all the questions that have been raised so far in this book. Will successful propaganda be made easier or more difficult (through the possibility of counter-propaganda) by the Internet? Does the existence of the Internet mean that arguments against monopolization of the mass media no longer have the same force? Or does the fact that "convergence"—the joining together of dominant interests in the entertainment and news industry, such as the merger of America Online with Time-Warner or the sale of Conrad Black's Canadian newspapers to Izzy Asper's CanWest Global—mean that any independent counterculture is doomed to continuous marginalization? Looking at the flip-side of democracy and human rights, should Canada's hate propaganda legislation be used to cut off access to racist Websites?

Much careful thinking has already gone into such questions. Interestingly, such thinking is itself largely accessible on the Internet, discoverable by simply typing in the words "democracy," "propaganda," and "Internet" on a search engine. Not surprisingly, there is a wide variety of opinion on the matter, but even the most pessimistic hold out some positive hope for the use of the Internet in democracy-friendly ways. What needs sorting out are the different conceptions of democracy and their relation to the marketplaces. For some, the market epitomizes democracy, and the less government involvement of any kind, the better. Others take the view that an unregulated marketplace begins to resemble corporate boardroom democracy, where one share equals one vote rather than one person. In other words, in the final analysis, marketplace democracy means dollar democracy, which is nothing but plutocracy. There are various conceptions of the ideal marketplace, and some people who accept the marketplace as embodying democracy reject monopolistic practices as contrary to the ideal, which involves free buyers choosing products offered by free sellers. In a monopoly situation one side or the other loses the ability to choose among comparable offerings by others. Hence, there is a large measure of agreement, not just among the political left, that at least some government interference with the marketplace is warranted, although special interests work fiercely to ensure that their own particular form of monopoly power is outside the range of government restraining powers. Aside from this minimalist conception of the role of government, there are stronger versions of democracy, according to which a commitment to democracy means a commitment to a form that will work, that is to say, one in which there is meaningful participation by the ordinary citizenry in the running of a country. This in turn requires meaningful education and access to information, not giving a free hand to the media to slant the news in favour of the business interests of the controlling group.

These issues have been discussed in connection with the ill-fated Kent Commission proposals, but we need now to consider their ramifications in connection with the Internet. Two different sets of questions arise. One deals with the need to recast the earlier issues of media monopoly, since the Internet theoretically provides individuals and groups with the ability to communicate with others on a large scale while not requiring large resources. (The cost of a computer which can enable one to reach millions of people is thousands of times less than a printing press, paper, ink, and delivery service to do the same thing.) The second relates to free speech issues and the possible regulation of the Internet itself. The Internet is sometimes viewed as unregulable, since so many pathways exist between communicator and communicatee that a practical way of intervening becomes difficult and, some believe, impossible. Who will the courts judge responsible for a hate-communication? The sender may operate through another's account and not be identifiable. An Internet service provider who knowingly permits hate messages regularly might be convicted, but the capability of examining every message does not exist, so the defence of lack of knowledge looms large. If certain key words are monitored by computer, the exclusion of such messages will likely expunge much innocent expression.[5] This takes us back to the question of the value of the Internet as a whole, in particular its value as an untrammelled form of communication between individuals and groups within the same neighbourhood, city or nation, or all over the globe.

I believe that the potential for the transformation of society does exist with this medium. What is not clear is whether the transformation will necessarily be for the better. First, let us explore the good features of the Internet. Unlike ham radio, for which similar hopes were held, no special skills are needed to "surf the Net." A good computer linkup is all that is needed to be within seconds of access to information of hitherto unimaginable breadth and depth. Instead of relying on one's own government information sources, it is possible to be in direct contact with the government information of any country and, more importantly, with individuals in that country. An unparalleled array of information sources have been opened up to the world. The important question remains: how reliable are they? One individual will not have the ability to sift through all the information sources. Of course, like-minded individuals can form groups. Nongovernmental organizations with similar aims can pool their information sources. Each organization can perform its own search and filtering service, passing the results on to others. Indeed, the operation is as simple as posting their results on a Website, where anyone interested can find it. That is already happening. Specific for-profit alternate media sources also exist on the Net. Some sites, including that of the not-for-profit *Z-Magazine*, are offshoots of existing paper publications, which presumably hope to attract donations or subscriptions through the Website operation. Other alternate media sites have been started with the aim of eventually becoming financially self-sustaining.

What is needed is enough time to allow a general audience to find trustworthy "filters" of news and information, so as to properly assess the mainstream media's accounts of what is going on in the world. We can anticipate difficulties: it should not be difficult for the corporate culture, should it see its interests threatened, to put forward its own representatives in the guise of disinterested seekers of truth in the media or even of counterculture activists. It could become difficult to distinguish between the genuine article and a cleverly constructed fake. We have seen similar happenings with the formation of company-friendly environmental groups. The difficulties are not limited to biases from the right, and the genuine truth-seeker should guard against turning a blind eye to distortions and deceptions merely because they appear to advance his or her own agenda, whether from leftist or rightist perspectives.

STRATEGIES FOR DEMOCRATIZING THE NET

Gathering information is costly, but much can be done to democratize information if people develop a strong sense of the public interest. Recall the dictum that the "public interest" is not necessarily what the public is interested in, hence the ease with which the public is distracted from the task of political involvement. Every so often things happen which cause the public to sit up and take notice—the e.coli tragedy in Walkerton, Ontario, has already been mentioned—and this is where gains can be made in terms of people recognizing the need for attending to alternate sources of news and opinion. From my own experience in a local community organization, which was very active in the 1970s, I can testify that the real empowerment to the community association came from professional planners and architects who were frustrated by the way in which city planning was directed by the needs of developers, rather than by overall concern for the community. By bringing their expertise and knowledge to the public, they were able to advise the association on how to be effective at getting certain changes, in particular a comprehensive traffic plan, accepted. As we were advised on one occasion, it would be possible to win over the politicians by a combination of public pressure and supportive bureaucrats or politicians. But one can never win when politicians and bureaucrats are united against one. Therefore, the task had to be one of convincing one or other second member of the triad to accept what the community association members felt was necessary for the survival of their community.[6] The volunteer members of the community association were professionals giving of their time freely for work they saw as contributing to community betterment. Not every professional takes complete satisfaction in his or her work. Sometimes the need to make one's living conflicts with one's best judgment. Working outside these traditional constraints clearly gave some volunteers great satisfaction. The same hope may also exist regarding journalists or public servants, that they will find some way, consistent with their primary professional obligations, of assisting what could well become a whole new generation of information disseminators on the Internet.

Increasing democratization of the Internet can happen in various different ways. First, the government could give more support to existing freenets. The National Capital Freenet in Ottawa, for example, has done much to further public discussion. It has many limitations, some of which can be overcome with additional financing. However, government and institutional support is waning, and government tax policy so far has not favoured treating donations to the freenets as tax deductible. There seems no good reason that institutions like the Fraser Institute, which clearly favours a right-wing political philosophy, should have their donations tax-deductible, while the freenet, which exists to facilitate communication of all kinds (barring libel, etc.) does not have this benefit. I expect that this situation will change. A third problem is that access to e-mail facilities is now provided free by private companies, thus removing one of the incentives for joining a freenet.

A second way in which the Internet could become increasingly democratic is through the active initiatives of non-governmental organizations, or the for-profit kind of operation which Straight Goods—an Ottawa-based, left-of-centre, online news magazine—embodies. If the latter is to succeed, there must be people willing to do first-class investigative reporting for relatively small financial reward. There is so far no sign of enough money on its way to support alternative media, even when the usual distribution cost overheads are removed through utilization of the Internet.

In the early days of political activism in the 1960s, and in many volunteer organizations today, one often heard—and still hears—the remark that the same small knot of people show up for all the different causes and try to do all the organizing and other work involved, because not enough other people were interested. A similar challenge faces any task of making the Internet more democratic. It is necessary to attract numbers. Some may find that, as a result of a worthwhile bit of information from some non-governmental organization on an issue which affects them most directly, they come to value reports passed on or recommended by that organization in future. That means the possibility of a steady growth of audiences for alternative news and opinion suppliers on the Internet.

Public Journalism

The project of democratizing news media is not new, and has been promoted by Arthur Charity, among others, in *Doing Public Journalism*.[7] This reform movement was started by journalists disillusioned with the gap between the news and opinion they saw as properly needed for serving the public interest in towns, states, and the nation and what was allowed to surface in their own newspapers or other media outlets. The objective of such public journalism is to make it easier for ordinary citizens to make intelligent decisions about public affairs and to get these decisions carried out. Among the tasks faced by public journalists—and here Charity credits Daniel Yankelovich for pioneering thought in this area—are those of raising the consciousness of the public concerning important issues, then allowing for public debate in which the consequences of different possible choices are clearly spelled out, with the ethical implications of each choice highlighted. The aim is to bridge the expert-public gap, promoting two-way communication; special efforts would be made to keep discussion on the level of civility. Finally, journalists can be helpful in prodding the political level to adopt measures approved by citizens.

Charity also draws upon Jay Rosen's work. Rosen, director of the Project on Public Life and the Press, argues that journalists are not simply detached observers, but have a role to play in making public life work by taking citizens' concerns more seriously.[8] This does not mean "dumbing down" a newspaper—the practice of eliminating or reducing in-depth research by which a journalist is able to understand and explain some complex issues. Such complex articles are difficult to read because the matters they deal with are difficult. The art of a good investigative reporter lies in signalling in the introduction why it is important to come to grips with the serious matter that follows. The reader can then decide whether he or she has the patience to tackle the matter. It is extremely important, for a good democracy, that such materials be made available. Although only a minority may read the articles, these will be an influential minority compared with the average reader. On the other hand, the "dumbing down" philosophy favours producing what great numbers of people, often in a hurry, will actually read. This is often gossip, entertainment, and sensationalized or quirky news of no real consequence. G.K. Chesterton, who made many trenchant comments about the press nearly 100 years ago, commented once that the "silly season" of the summer months is actually a time when newspapers "begin to discuss the things which are really important to human society." He had in mind the discussion of institutions taken for granted but having a huge impact on society, such as that of marriage.[9] His point, as I see it, is that conventional journalism often passes over serious issues, perhaps because they lack novelty, in favour of issues that have the power to attract attention but have no lasting importance. Good journalism will seek out the issues that need airing and discussing, even though the public may show little enthusiasm for the matter at the start.

The Internet, far from competing with public journalism, is in a position to contribute to it, for very different reasons. First, the Internet is able to provide information and gossip easily and faster than newspapers. In other words, the scope of the Internet is so very large that it contains within it a "dumbing down" beyond what newspapers can provide. Radio and television are also fast in delivering news, but people have to be listening at the right time, and most people do not have time to do this for more than a few hours a day. The Internet is accessed when the user is ready, and keeps the information until the user is ready for it. On this score the existing mass media are not able to compete, which may be one reason why they have decided to join with the Internet rather than fight it. Most major newspapers have their own Website. In any case, the parallel supply of "dumb-down" materials on the Internet should allow for some additional uncertainty about pursuing this form of journalism in the major media. Will people pay for it on paper when they can access it free online? Susanne Craig, a media columnist for the *Globe and Mail*, gave examples of cases where Internet sites scooped the established press: "For instance, reporters from the relatively unknown TheSmokingGun.com were first to reveal that the Who Wants to Marry a Multimillionaire? groom, Rick Rockwell, was once the subject of a restraining order. That discovery made world head-lines." So far, she observes, newspapers and at least one newsmagazine have rushed to get their scoops on their Websites as quickly as possible. It is good for a news-paper to be known as the one with a great many scoops, but she wonders about the wisdom of posting "less sexy exclusives," since people might decide not to buy the morning newspaper when so many of the important matters are freely acces-sible on the relevant Website.[10] As a result, newspapers might want to give a higher proportion of space to public journalism; people will have a good reason to subscribe when they know there is a high degree of likelihood of seeing some important and durable think-piece brought to their attention each day. Such items, unlike the gossip materials, which can be picked up and posted by others, are not so easily pirated. Even when the same material is on the Internet, the need to down-load the serious material provides at least some incentive to pay to get it in the format where it first appeared.

A second, and less tentative reason why the Internet is likely to contribute to public journalism is the comparatively low cost of disseminating ideas on this medium. There are people willing to do the research necessary to produce in-depth articles, and there are people strongly interested in finding and reading those results. As mentioned earlier, journalists and civil servants can contribute to the public journalism project by taking a little extra time to post materials. Journalists who have their materials spiked by their mainstream media editors can now find an outlet in one of the alternative news Websites. That may provide an additional incentive for their employers to publish more of such material, so as not to lose readers to these alternative sites. If a journalist fears the wrath of an employer, he or she can always contribute material under a pseudonym or anonymously.

A third way in which the Internet can contribute, and already does contribute, to public journalism is through making it easier to get information relevant to at least some aspects of reporting and to share this information among other journalists themselves. I.F. Stone made his living by analyzing government documents, pick-ing them up from department offices when they were printed. Today one does not have to live in Washington, as did Stone, to access such documents in a timely way.

All of these are positive features of the Internet, so far as the goals of public jour-nalism are concerned. Not all writers about the Internet are so sanguine about its prospects, and it is important to take note of the drawbacks of this form of com-munication for democracy. The first, and obvious, point is that not everyone has access to it. Since we are talking about giving a voice to those who currently lack power in the system, that voice extension misses a section in society that may well need it most. Even those who log on do not necessarily have equal access. There is an enormous difference in speed and nature of access between, for instance, an "iMac" and the older Mac Classic, where pictures did not come through and texts accessed through Lynx came through only extremely slowly. Some will have the right kind of software to access videos, complicated documents, and suchlike. The fortunate will be able to download, edit, and forward texts much faster and more efficiently than others. The question is not necessarily what views will be posted, but which will prevail in the context of technological inequlaity.

What Others Have Said

THE INTERNET ENHANCES DEMOCRACY

There are many ways in which the Internet can contribute to democracy. One, as already seen, is by providing opportunities for discussion and dissemination of information outside the range accepted in the mainstream media. Another is by facilitating contact between voters, their representatives, and the media. One organization which exists to promote interaction between the public and their elected representatives in the US is Capitol Advantage, founded 14 years ago and employing 55 people early in 2000. Robert Hansan, its founder, reminds us that "the Internet makes it easier and less intimidating to become politically active," since "you can do it from the comfort of your home, on your own time."[11] The site provided easy access to all candidates running in the 2000 election; the link to the Ralph Nader Website for instance, rewarded me with policy statements, pictures, and a video showing him giving a speech. The quality of reproduction was suitable for use in campaigning. It appears that such access should provide a powerful tool for information dissemination; however, Nader received considerably less than the 5 per cent of support he had been hoping for at the polls that November.

Capitol Advantage also provides a search engine to locate media reporters and editors, but only to senders with US addresses. It advertises that "More than 500 associations, portals, media organizations, and corporations use CapWiz [one of the pages in this site], including some of the Internet's most highly-trafficked sites." This sounds as though it will, indeed, enhance democracy, but it is not difficult to imagine how money and the existing power structure can still have a dominant effect. Those with money can use all the traditional means of persuasion at their disposal to persuade ordinary citizens to send a certain message to their elected representatives. The problem with the Internet is information overload, which means that no single individual will have time to sort through all the conflicting information. Most people have to rely on others to do some of the sifting for them, and that is where existing money and power can continue to have influence.

SCEPTICAL ATTITUDES TO THE INTERNET

Some of those who have done a lot of thinking about the Internet often show, at best, a qualified optimism for the future of this medium as regards democracy. One such person is Robert W. McChesney, professor in the School of Journalism and Mass Communication at the University of Wisconsin-Madison.[12] In 1996,

McChesney correctly forecast the trend of convergence in media, at a time when the mergers of Disney with Capital Cities/ABC and Time Warner with Turner Broadcasting were just under way, and that between AOL and Time-Warner was still to come. In Canada the sale of the bulk of Conrad Black's newspapers to Izzy Asper's CanWest Global Communication continues the trend of linking content providers with electronic media.[13] (Those familiar with Black's previous activities should have no reason to doubt his word that he may well return. Presumably, if newspaper stocks become undervalued, he will be back in the market.)

McChesney noted two opposite tendencies with these developments, so far as the future of democracy is concerned. On the one hand, there are arguments that domination of the media by increasingly concentrated commercial interests is bad for democracy. On the other hand, as McChesney puts it, "newly developed computer and digital communication technologies can undermine the ability to control communication in a traditionally hierarchical manner," and the Internet in particular "permits inexpensive, global, interactive, and mass computer communication, as well as access to a previously unimaginable range of information." Whether this new technology will eclipse the development of the printing press, as one of his sources claims, is a matter that remains to be seen. But the impressiveness of the Internet leaves no doubt that the point is at least debatable. McChesney's pessimism comes from his assessment of the 1995 Communications Act in the US: "perhaps one of the most corrupt pieces of legislation in US history ... effectively written by and for business." What should have been a profound, soul-searching debate about the implications of this act did not take place. The news media simply covered the issue as a business story, not a public policy story, he writes, with the result that an "informed and mobilized citizenry ready to do battle for alternative policies" never had a chance to form.

McChesney believes that control of the new information super-highway should be determined by the kind of debate that in the 1920s led the Aird Commission in Canada to establish public control over the airwaves and a nonprofit public broadcaster. With the 1996 US Telecommunications Act, which permitted dominant firms to get larger through mergers and acquisitions,[14] private corporations have been determining the future of the Internet. Reformers would like to generate a "viable nonprofit and noncommercial sector in the information highway," but to get taken seriously they need to concede that they are fighting a battle for the margins and not of regaining public control over information exchanges. As Gutstein put it in the Canadian context, we have seen the enclosing of the information commons.

Ralph Nader has used the direction taken by the corporate media as an issue in his campaign for the presidency, stating:

> It's the corporate media ... it's exactly another reason why the power is so concentrated and the voice of the people is not expressed. You have one company owning 800 radio stations, and before 1996 it was illegal to own more than 12, after the Telecommunications Act. Six major media conglomerates now control most of the circulation of magazines, newspapers, and the audi-

ence of radio and TV…. The electronic media now is into trivialization, sensationalism. You know, they are looking for the nonfiction soap operas like O.J. Simpson and Elián and Lewinsky. And that crowds out enormous journalism because of the time it takes, the space it takes.[15]

On the opposite, more optimistic, side of the ledger is the fact that the Internet is distinct from the situation with previous communications technologies in that by its nature it is not amenable to centralized control. McChesney has no doubt that a citizen-based, nonprofit sector of cyberspace will survive and even thrive, but for him the issue is whether the Internet will be able to radically transform our societies for the better. Will we achieve the ideal speech situation described by Habermas (discussed in Chapter 4)? McChesney looks at the history of capitalism and how it developed public relations in answer to democratic threats to its interests. Analogous developments might emerge to hobble the use of the Internet for radical democracy. Alex Carey has studied and nicely documented this public relations response in his book *Taking the Risk Out of Democracy.*[16] However, the Internet, as well as facilitating global commerce, has also made it easier for capitalism to run around any gains that workers may have achieved in their own country. The future prospects are bright for the very rich, but not for those opposed to environmental recklessness, instability, or a deteriorating public sector.[17]

What McChesney wrote about the US in 1996 can easily be applied to the current Chrétien government of Canada or the Harris government of Ontario: "There is nothing short of a wholesale assault on the very notion of democracy, as the concept of people gathering, debating, and devising policy has been supremely truncated."[18] Backbenchers such as Richard Patten (Liberal) in Ontario have been outspoken against the diminished role of the ordinary Member of the Provincial Parliament (MPP), and similar feelings have been expressed in the federal arena. On the evening of December 16, 1997, Mike Harris's Tories "proceeded with a motion that grouped together five separate Bills from different ministries"; by doing this, Patten says, "they shut down debate on five separate, important pieces of legislation. As an Opposition MPP, I questioned why I was even in the legislature."[19] For McChesney it is not just a question of a crisis in national sovereignty, but of "sovereignty writ large," since nations are "required either to toe the global capitalist line or to face economic purgatory." Interestingly, McChesney links the powerlessness of democratic procedure with "antirationalist, fundamentalist, nationalist movements that blame democracy for capitalism's flaws and threaten to reduce humanity to untold barbarism."

With negative features of the Internet acknowledged, McChesney returns to a very qualified reason for some optimism. There are generally acknowledged positive features, such as the ability to reach like-minded others for discussion, thus creating a sense of empowerment. This has its negative side. Months before the 9/11 tragedy, *Wired News* carried a story about how the FBI feared Osama bin Laden was using steganography—the practice of concealing one message inside another—to communicate with his terrorist allies and evade law enforcement.[20] Pro-democracy forces can communicate with people in other countries. As mentioned already several times, it is almost impossible to censor the Internet, which was designed so that messages reach a destination through no particular route. It is virtually instantaneous, allowing for concerted action over virtually the whole world, in fact.

McChesney concludes that the Internet may be indeed a boon for democracy, but that certain qualifications are needed. First is the problem of universal access and computer literacy. Without that, of course, the people who are worst off get the least access to communications, guaranteeing that their situation in life will not improve, perhaps even worsen. Secondly, he wisely observes that people come to the Internet bulletin boards already conditioned by other forces in society, and there is no reason for believing that they will not perpetuate those attitudes in the new media. Rather than politicizing people, it may help to commercialize them more.[21]

Thirdly, McChesney worries that many people will not be up to discussing the details of important political issues as these become more complicated. Here is a role for the academic, to go online and explain matters to the public, even though "such behaviour runs directly counter to the priorities, attitudes, and trajectory of academic life." Good public journalism also has a role to fill in making the Internet live up to its potential for democratizing society. However, professional journalists have had to work for organizations that have become oriented to "infotainment." Who will support financially the work of a committed investigative journalist? Certainly not the market. It comes down, once again, to the need for a public policy to support such work and to paying for it. A danger McChesney sees is that illusory benefits of the Internet will successfully persuade a population to accept the industry line that antimonopoly controls over the media are not needed.

McChesney does not take a defeatist line, but rather proposes a Herculean task for structuring communications in the future. He agrees with William Greider[22] in believing that the reform of communication must be part and parcel of a movement to reform the global political economy. Universities will have to provide the research for this purpose. Unfortunately, as McChesney recognizes, universities have suffered cutbacks, putting pressure on academics to seek funding from the corporate sector. So, at the time when university autonomy is most needed, it is also under severe threats to its mission. The academics in the communications disciplines must resist the temptation to cultivate ties with the business communications sector. They will need to do this, he thinks, in order to maintain a university tradition of commitment to independent inquiry, in furtherance of democratic values.

In a more recent interview, McChesney reiterated his view that "unless there is explicit social policy to develop cyberspace as a noncommercial, nonprofit entity, it is going to be taken over by the most powerful elements in our society." The Internet, he says, is becoming a hierarchical commercial entity, even though it is still a useful tool for social activists. He still is optimistic in the light of successful movements in Sweden, New Zealand, Australia, India, Brazil, etc. to gain popular support for the idea of taking control of the media away from corporations and advertisers and making it instead " central to the project of building a democratic society."[23]

MORE SPECULATION

Any attempt to say something new and worthwhile about the Internet may well become obsolete in the time lag between the writing and publishing of this book. With that caveat, it seems to me worth risking some speculation about the scope of impediments to democratization of the Internet. Assuming that a public segment of the Internet will continue, just how potent is the threat of its increasing marginalization? Here are some ideas that occur to me as at least possibilities for ruining the Internet as a tool for democracy, although I cannot predict the likelihood of their happening.

1. As more and more people enter the Internet through a commercial provider, there are many ways in which their access to relevant progressive sources of information could be discouraged, curtailed, or even cut off. Assuming that the Internet Service Provider (ISP) has control over speed, it could gradually discourage Websites not able to upgrade and of which it does not approve.

2. With the new commercial orientation of the Internet, many distractions appear. For example, I used a search engine to look up "Democracy Watch." Immediately I was bombarded with advertisements for all different kinds of watches, including wrist-watches. This has its funny side, but such a plethora of alternate sites and objects distract attention from the goal of increasing political involvement. Given the forest of information available, the key to sustained investigation will be adequate linkages. If the linkages are plentiful to commercial sites, but scarce to political sites, or to sites of only a particular political colouring, the result will be an impoverished political debate. The Center for Media and Democracy (CMD) provides many linkages useful for the study of public relations, but I found it deficient when it came to the tobacco industry. Mentioned and linked were tobacco industry sites and those of their apologists, but no link was made to the Non-Smokers' Rights Association of Canada (NSRA), which has been so very active and effective at combating the pro-tobacco propaganda. This omission is explained easily by the fact that the main concern of CMD is to observe PR in operation. And, since it views PR negatively, it might not wish to include an organization whose PR it might value. However, for those who wish to combat the PR of the tobacco industry, the NSRA is a valuable source of information and would have been usefully included in a list of linkages. The CMD list has a section headed "Activism," and NSRA might have been placed there.[24]

3. The element of distraction needs further comment. It is a simple matter for someone other than the user to track Website visits by any user of the Internet and thus create a user profile. This is especially easy when an Internet surfer wittingly or unwittingly allows "cookies" to be inserted into his or her computer. Ordinarily

the surfer is informed before they are inserted and has the opportunity to reject them. But not everyone understands the significance of this choice. "Cookies" relay information about Internet usage effected through the computer to whoever plants the cookies. So, someone who is crazy, say, about horses is alerted to every new horse-related happening commercial interests care to exploit and is distracted from other searches. A mission to pursue political matters could easily be derailed. Whatever a person's obsession, it can be determinable over time if the person is a frequent user of the Internet and if the "cookies" are not removed from the computer—something the average user may not know how to do. There are often inducements for free access to certain sites, or other benefits, so long as a subscriber allows "cookies" to be placed in his or her machine. In that way the movement to distraction toward the commercial is made easier.

4. One of the key aspects of political use of the Internet is e-mail. People can get organized with others through e-mail, either directly or through a list reachable automatically through a listserv. But what is to stop hundreds of people e-mailing a person at one time, thus burying relevant messages and consuming time? Such "mail bombs" can overwhelm an individual's account and even crash a server. Already I, like many others, receive half a dozen unsolicited e-mails—or "spam"— a day. If they are artfully presented—for example, in a form which suggests they are responding to a request—it may take several minutes of reading to realize what they are. If the user responds with a request to be removed from the sender's list, this verifies that the email account is active, and more messages may be sent. What is manageable in small numbers rapidly becomes unmanageable, in the sense of screening out the worthwhile messages. Software exists to screen out "spamming," or the sending on a huge scale of unsolicited mail, but, so far, it is a matter of software countering other software, and breaches in the devices designed to protect against spamming are possible. Democratic use of the Internet seems to me vulnerable on this score.

5. It is also possible for members of the established power structure—or any wealthy individual with an axe to grind—to pay agents to contribute to public discussions in order to shape the agenda on various bulletin boards. If a discussion site is monitored and certain views are censored, the discussion site loses some credibility. On the other hand, if it is unmonitored, anyone can enter the discussion. Blake Harris, in a 1999 article in Infobahn ("The Magazine of Internet Culture"), quotes an anonymous post, which expresses the problem:

> Internet is a fascinating lab for the study of idea dissemination. A number of times I have watched how an idea briefly mentioned in one post will suddenly get a great deal of play a few weeks later. Even more interesting is how the idea might suddenly appear in posts in another group. My study of this is informal and intuitive, but I have a sense that somebody who carefully studied the communication dynamics (and coincidences in the cases where causal

effects are hard to find) could exert a great deal of control over what was discussed and how. Since Internet originated ideas have a small, but growing influence over the "mass consciousness" of the nation, this capacity could be exceedingly useful to tacticians and strategists who want to have some voice in the "national agenda."[25]

There are many examples of how widely misinformation posted on the Internet can travel and, in so doing, gain legitimacy. One such notice claimed that a study had shown that George W. Bush has the lowest IQ of any US president in the past 50 years. This "study" was proven to be a hoax, but not before Garry Trudeau had accepted it and made it the subject of a Doonesbury cartoon on September 1, 2001.[26] In another instance, Pierre Salinger, former Kennedy press secretary, claimed to have documents proving that TWA Flight 800—a Boeing 747-131 that crashed off Long Island July 17, 1996, killing 230 passengers and crew—had been hit by a stray US navy missile. This claim was widely circulated on the Internet, although he was contradicted by the Chicago-based Emergency Response and Research Institute, which, in an equally widely circulating post, maintained that Salinger's information had come via the Internet from Parveez Syad, an alleged Iranian/extremist Muslim propagandist, who operated from a base in Birmingham, England, at the time. Whether or not ERRI was right about Sallinger, the episode reveals a potential for misinformation from the Internet.[27]

6. In earlier discussions of freedom of the press and Zachariah Chafee's *Government and Mass Communications* (see Chapter 7), we observed that legislation to promote freedom in communications can have unintended consequences. Not discussed then was another of Chafee's ideas: to require by law that the ownership and business links of a major newspaper be very clearly stated in the newspaper itself, either annually or more often when changes are frequent. However, as he points out, this requirement could work against progressive causes, since people might be reluctant to make donations to a progressive publication if they thought that doing so could expose them to investigation by a McCarthyite committee, should one ever come into being again.[28]

A similar reluctance to support radical causes might develop from the awareness that the FBI or other investigators can track Websites visited by an individual. Unlike secret meetings, the Web is easily monitored. Not long ago a high Canadian naval officer was court-martialled, because he was caught visiting pornographic sites from his office computer.[29] Since, as we have seen above, it is possible from an outside source to identify which Websites users visit, so policing agencies could compile lists of alleged subversives—those who visit anarchist or Communist Websites. Thus, the freedom of the Internet will last only as long as people feel free of such Big Brother scrutiny, since no one will want to expose themselves to becoming the subject of a loyalty inquisition, along the lines of the McCarthy Cold War hunts.

7. From a world perspective, the problems of information imbalance may well be exacerbated in some respects. Most powerful search engines are heavily weighted toward things American, which is not surprising or unjust given that US funding was behind the development of the Internet. What we see with the convergence of media is the bringing together mainly of US media and entertainment, so that what is readily accessible on the Internet, and reflected in the search engines, can hardly be expected to differ from customary US concerns. That could change, of course, if more people in the US come to take an interest in other parts of the globe and if other countries develop rival search engines with the same capabilities.

Having said this, it is necessary to underscore the point that, despite the obstacles on the path to a more balanced flow of information worldwide, the Internet has provided a remarkable opportunity for by-passing the normal media filters. As an example, my sister who lives in Kenya and is a citizen of that country was able to send me an interesting and fairly lengthy report on the fallout from the explosion at the American Embassy in Nairobi. She knew some of the victims, being originally American herself, and the impact was presented more significantly than in the usual media accounts.

The reception given the McBride Report by the Western media was so overwhelmingly negative that it is hard to imagine a similar kind of response with the Internet in existence today. Sean McBride's *Many Voices, One World* was a UNESCO publication, whose subtitle indicates its purpose: "Towards a new more just and more efficient world information and communication order."[30] Its conclusions were roundly derided by the press at the time of its publication in 1980. The word about media bias is certainly getting out,[31] and today more people are willing to challenge the one-sided preoccupation with free speech issues that governed the report's reception in the industrialized countries of the West. Granted that reaction focused on serious concerns that free speech would be threatened by the recommendation of government interference with the media, still the problem of adequate reporting of third-world issues and the swamping of the world with Western perspectives are problems that should be addressed seriously, not dismissed out of hand as they were then. Western media reports on the UN-sponsored World Conference on Racism in Durban, South Africa, in September 2001, rightly called attention to its anti-Israeli and anti-American bias and properly denounced the overt anti-Semitism of some of the participants, but they also tended to ignore or avoid serious treatment of other issues raised there, such as the high price of patent medications for victims of AIDS. Some left-oriented Website publications helped to restore balance, in a way not possible in the early 1980s. When protests took place in Quebec City in April 2001 against the meetings of the Free Trade Areas of the Americas, a wide variety of reports appeared on the Internet, supplementing the accounts in the established media.[32]

8. The human factor must not be forgotten. The ability to summon up a lot of in-depth material is not the equivalent of reading it carefully and digesting it. Staring at a screen is less pleasurable than holding a book or newspaper in one's hand, with the possibility of getting up and moving about. A reaction against this mode of information access may be setting in, as people ask themselves why they are spending so much time indoors watching a screen, perhaps developing health problems with eyes glued to the imagery and text for such extended periods. Another point to consider is that while contact is possible with people worldwide, it is also mediated contact. That does not matter so much when we contact people we already know, but those we meet only through the Internet seem less likely to inspire the same confidence and trust than those we meet in person. We do not have access to the facial cues and body language that accompany expression of ideas.

Participation even in local political discussion groups dissipates as the computer with its Internet access ceases to be a toy and becomes an accepted tool of everyday life, demanding time and energy perhaps spent more productively elsewhere. Although the Internet makes useful information easily available to activists, they may feel pressured to disseminate and act upon the new information, leading some who engage in this type of work to regret the amount of time consumed. This phenomenon is not new, but it becomes more threatening when involvement is increased.

Interesting information about the kind of people who get information from the Internet was provided by the Annenberg Public Policy Center, as reported in a column by Jeffrey Simpson for the *Globe and Mail*. Surveying 48,000 people during the first six months of 2000, this study found that those using the Internet for political information tended to be men who earn a median income of $57,500. Only 20 per cent of those interviewed said they got their news online, 45 per cent having Internet access but not using it for news, the other 35 per cent not having any access to the Internet at all.[33] This profile does not encourage the thought that the Internet is rapidly radicalizing the population.

Since part of the problem with democratizing the Internet comes from the ways in which PR techniques can be adapted to this new medium, part of the solution will consist in the general population becoming familiar with different techniques of propaganda and persuasion. For this reason it is appropriate to turn our attention to procedures for recognizing and analyzing such techniques, which are, of course, applicable to the whole range of media and not just the Internet. Some have existed for centuries or millenia, but the arrival of the Internet has introduced a wider scope of application. Some techniques, such as digital enhancement, are new, but the related ethical concerns and principles involved share common ground with, for instance, a Renaissance portrait artist's falsification of a subject's attributes.

PROPAGANDA ANALYSIS

Various suggestions for systematic propaganda analysis have been made elsewhere, and these can be usefully applied to the analysis of materials on the Internet. The following are pertinent questions to ask.

What is the Source?

This is the most important question. Who is the real author of a given message? Unless we know who the source is, we cannot make an adequate appraisal of the likelihood of authority against possible bias. Getting to the original source of an idea can be difficult, but also telling. Someone expresses a startling idea or notable fact, which we discover had been printed in the morning's newspaper. How did the article come to appear in the paper? Was it from a press release? Who provided the press release? Was it from government or industry? Was it from an industry "think-tank"? How open is the newspaper to covering "think-tank" materials from institutions of a different political persuasion? Even events may have been subject to control for their public relations impact. What influences may have been behind the timing of a given event? If there is a story about a group protest, we want to know whether this is a genuine expression of concern by informed citizens, or whether this is a group artificially created by commercial interests to fight grassroots opposition. Sometimes a group protesting clearcutting of a forest does not consist of environmental activists but is a "fair environmental practices" group, covertly sponsored by the industry, which seeks nice-sounding, but ineffective, constraints to clearcutting.

What Is the Message?

When we look for propaganda, we have the obvious job of asking what messages are being propagated. Not all messages are straightforward, but contain subtexts, not stated but insinuated in the main message. Remember the point made in Chapter 3 that a barrage of facts, truthful in themselves, may nevertheless create a false impression. By noting the source, the less obvious message can be seen. The fact that a doctor has left Canada to work in the US can be presented to suggest either that Canada's health system is no good and should be privatized, or to indicate that Canada's health system should be better supported with public money. Or it could have no significance at all: the doctor has decided that he or she has put up with one blizzard too many. So in asking the question "What is the message?," we need to differentiate between direct message and the subtext—what is presupposed in, and reinforced by, the message and implication (conclusions the message recipient reaches on the basis of earlier conditioning).

Who Stands to Gain?

The old Latin watchword, "Cui bono" (literally: "to whom the good"), should always be part of any propaganda analysis. It can be the clue to identifying the source when that is unknown. If the source is known, it may help to uncover hidden alliances between source and beneficiary of a message. The Internet has made it much easier to verify the ownership structure of the various media and the related business interests that might benefit from slanting of the news. It allows for speedy determination of the names of those involved in a conglomerate, along with their other connections.

Techniques Used to Impart the Message

Propaganda analysis seeks to spell out the methods used to impart a message. The wide array of analytical tools involved include rhetorical analysis, suggestions we have encountered from the Institute for Propaganda Analysis (see Chapter 3), and many similar proposals. There is the phenomenon of orchestration, whereby a planned assault on many different media at the same time conveys to the receiver the idea of unquestionable truth. Is repetition part of what helps to get the message accepted? Is the recipient bombarded with more information than he or she can deal with in a critical state of mind? Is the message presented in a way that "piggybacks" on some favoured cause or personality popular at the moment? Is the piggybacking legitimate, or is it artificial in the sense of twisting facts to give a false appearance of connected interests? If the message is communicated through a news story, ask whether the news is genuinely important or whether its value is doubtful. If the latter, it is legitimate to look for possible extraneous reasons for appearance of the message. Was it free copy for the editor, supplied by industry or government? Is there significant advertising in the media outlet to suggest favouring the message-supplier? Are there connections between the media ownership and the interests supported by the message? It is not stretching the word "technique" to see it applied to the practice of providing lavish tourist accommodation to a freelance writer in order to encourage a favourable write-up of some travel destination. It is up to the analyst to spot any significant possible influences affecting the dissemination of a message in such a way as to warrant regarding it as propaganda in some sense.

Contexts and Truth-Reliability

It is important to pay attention to the many different ways in which contexts affect a given message. A one-sided presentation may be only a legitimate response to a heavily-biased presentation in the opposite direction, presented earlier. Questions to bear in mind are: what opportunity has there been for challenges to a message or its premise to be heard? Is the context one of government control or monopoly ownership? Speaking of the Internet, an obvious case of imbalance is one where a message is presented on thousands of different Websites, all controlled by an individual or a small group, whereas only several sites exist to provide a contrary opinion or contrary data. Following Habermas, one needs to assess any message in the light of the existence or nonexistence of an adequate opportunity for rebuttal of the main arguments or sources of information at the base of the arguments. Few people will know adequately the details of most social and political questions of moment, but they can at least find other people who have more knowledge, and they can question those people as to whether a sufficiently representative range of facts and opinion have been presented to the public for debate. We can think of "truth-reliability quotient" as related to the reliability of claims measured by their openness to critique. When facts or events are suppressed, it may well be because they are true but threatening to some established interests. Where there is the possibility of rebuttal, the doctrines propagated gain reliability if they are not rebutted despite the existence of an opportunity to do so. Of course, something could be true despite the suppression of contrary opinion. However, the reliability is affected by the suppression, and very strong reasons would be needed to justify suppression.

Contexts cover a large territory, so the existence of counter-propaganda, if any, should be part of any appraisal of the context of any propaganda. What are the background presuppositions of a given target and propagandist? What is the recent history? In dealing with armed conflict especially, what are the reasons given by each side as to why peaceful negotiation is no longer possible, if it ever was? What is the track record, in terms of truth or deception, of the spokespersons for both sides? Or of the administrations which appointed them? Are there dominant myths affecting cases on either or both sides? Can these myths be deconstructed, meaning taken apart and exposed as not worthy of continued dominance?

Fairness in Propaganda Assessment

It is all too easy to judge material to be propaganda when no such intent is involved, particularly if we disagree strongly with the message communicated. We should ask: what is the most charitable construction to be placed on the message and the motives of the message giver? This does not mean we have to whitewash something we strongly suspect to be deliberate propaganda. It does mean, however, that the language used should be appropriately circumspect and qualified, so that a fair assessment is given of different likelihoods: whether the message-giver knows the truth and is engaging in deception, or whether he or she is confused or ignorant and sincere. As Whately remarked, propaganda analysis easily can backfire if carried out sloppily for the purpose of engaging in counter-propaganda of one's own.[34]

Propaganda Technique and the Future of World Peace

Propaganda analysis can contribute to world peace by exposing those techniques that lead to armed conflict by creating misapprehension of reality. Under certain circumstances the understanding of the mechanisms of persuasion can help individuals to fight currents of opinion they see as likely to lead to unnecessary violence and injustice. Making use of propaganda techniques involves losing the high ground in any area of controversy. In campaigning against mind-manipulation, it is more effective if the same charge cannot be made against one's own activities. Recognizing that propaganda techniques may at times be necessary, a level of openness and sophisticated understanding should be encouraged so that not only will use of such techniques not be necessary, but they also will likely be counterproductive.

In that spirit, the following activities and objectives may further the aims of a more democratic and informed society, one that will be better in process as well as in results. Rather than a world in which commercial powers concerned mainly about profit maximization dominate the political and social agenda, I posit one in which living conditions and the environment, education and health are given the priority one hopes an intelligent and caring majority desires and deserves.

1. Encourage the dissemination of knowledge about the activities of various lobbyists, both those officially registered and the unofficial providers of news releases, hospitality offerings, and other forms of inducements. Sometimes letter writers to newspapers have connections not mentioned when they should be. There is work still to be done to expose connections between groups that front for some commercial interest and groups that exist under a deceptive name. This is where the Internet can be most helpful. Just as the Ethics Commissioner in Canada has a resource base for finding out about official lobbyists, so also there might be an unofficial clearing-house run by some philanthropically established group to provide information about vested interests connected with any journalist, columnist, or letter-writer. Failing such a centralized body, individual interest groups can form to fulfill some of that function.

2. The informed section of the population should share expertise with voluntary groups to make the actions of the latter more effective. It helps to know what strategies are doomed to failure and which ones have some possibility of success. When Lord Durham wrote his report on Lower Canada,[35] he noted the power which French-Canadians obtained by virtue of their family structure. With large families, only a few children could remain on the farm. The rest would have to work for someone else or join one or other of the professions. Many became labourers of course, but others joined the clergy or became surgeons, lawyers, or notaries in numbers exceeding the demand. As a result, so-called class differences were contained within a single family. Most families had a knowledgeable sibling or cousin, who informed them about political issues, told them for whom to vote and why,

and specified which issues were worth fighting for, and how hard to fight. The people trusted their sources of information this way. The large family is, generally speaking, a thing of the past, in Canada at least, but community associations and interest groups have filled the role of bringing together people with disparate economic and educational backgrounds. Perhaps something of the same kind of information exchange may develop, and possibly this could occur on the Internet— if trust can be developed there.

CONCLUSION

The Internet provides a new focal point for some very old concerns about democracy. It would be foolish to pretend that empowering all protest groups will necessarily solve the world's problems. Protesters can get things wrong too. Democracy has the potential for all the faults that Plato saw: the ordinary seamen can still take over the ship from the captain and navigator.

Today, however, satellites have simplified navigation, and the Internet has made possible acquisition of specialized knowledge, so that the ordinary citizen is often in a position to second-guess the supposed experts. My definition of democracy entails a political situation in which the problems of the worst-off in society are put prominently on the agenda, as distinct from the problems facing wealthy investors seeking to maximize profits. The interests of the privileged classes often are not presented as such, but are couched in language that makes them appear to be the interests of the general population. The Internet gives an opportunity for altering those informational structures to some extent. Whether the result in the long run is for the better will depend on many things, including a willingness to sift through evidence, to listen to many different voices, and to show generosity of spirit to those with whom we disagree. The history of propaganda shows how easy it is to manufacture enemies through misinformation and distortion. Use of propaganda may be justified in extreme cases, but we should have learned by now how counterproductive propaganda can be.

The best goal for propaganda analysis is to develop such an understanding of the phenomenon that it will no longer be profitable for people to engage in it. In that way a citizenry can concentrate on trying to find the right way to accommodate the many different interests among its population, rather than on how to herd people efficiently along a road the only clear merit of which is that it has short-term benefits for a privileged few. The challenge is not only to journalists to provide the new, more critical, presentation of news, but for audiences to read, listen, and respond to them. This will require much more effort than the comfortably-ensconced television viewer is accustomed to, but democracy worthy of the name demands nothing less. Complacency leads to servitude; hard-won freedoms are easily eroded through inattention.

NOTES

1   Albert Camus, "Le Journalisme Critique," *Combat* (8 September 1944) in *Oeuvres complètes d'Albert Camus* Vol. 5 (Paris: Gallimard et Club de l'Honnête Homme, 1983) 68–69.

2   Randal Marlin, trans. and ed., "Jacques Ellul's Lectures on Forecasting and Planning," *Futures Research Quarterly* (Winter 1985): 32

3   Donald Gutstein, *e.con: How the Internet Undermines Democracy* (Toronto: Stoddart Publishing, 1999) 2. For a richly rewarding exploration of the different forms and implications of control, or lack thereof, in Internet development, see also Lawrence Lessig, *Code and Other Laws of Cyberspace* (New York: Basic Books, 1999).

4   *Ottawa Citizen*, 3 September 2001: 4.

5   I would like to thank Diane Dubrule for drawing my attention to this point.

6   These remarks are drawn from my experience with the Glebe Community Association as president in 1972, traffic committee chairman in 1973, and executive member for several additional years. Some of these experiences have been recounted in more detail in Susan Hendler, ed., *Planning Ethics* (New Brunswick, NJ: Rutgers University Press, 1995).

7   Arthur Charity, *Doing Public Journalism* (New York and London: The Guilford Press, 1995), 1-2.

8   See for example Jay Rosen, *Getting the Connections Right: Public Journalism and the Troubles in the Press* (Washington: Century Foundation Press, Brookings Institute, 1996). Available online at
<http://www.tcf.org/Publications/Media/Getting_the_Connections_Right/Preface.html>.

9   G.K. Chesterton, *The Collected Works*, Vol. 27, ed. Lawrence J. Clipper (San Francisco: Ignatius Press, 1987) 543.

10 Susanne Craig, "Media," "Internet turns up heat on newspapers," *Globe and Mail*, 10 March 2000.

11 Paul Tolme, "Capitol Advantage grows along with Internet democracy," *CANOE news*, 22 February 2000. Online at <http://www.canoe.ca/TechNews0002/22_democracy.html>.

12 Robert W. McChesney, "The Internet and US Communication Policy-Making in Historical and Critical Perspective," an interview with David Peterson, *The Journal of Communication* 46,1 (Winter 1996). Online at <http://www.ascusc.org/jcmc/vol1/issue4/mcchesney.html>. Quotations in the following text are taken from this site.

13 April Lindgren, "CanWest seals mega-merger," *Ottawa Citizen*, 31 July 2000.

14 Edward Herman and Robert McChesney, interview, *Z Magazine*, October 1997. Online at <http://www.lol.shareworld.com/zmag/articles/petersonoct97.htm>.

15 Ralph Nader, interview, *The Bay Guardian*, 26 May 2000. Reproduced on the Ralph Nader for President Website <http://www.votenader.com/issues/MASS-MEDIA.html>. Nader is referring in this quote to the media circus surrounding the trial of football star O.J. Simpson for the murder of his wife and her friend; the return of young Elián Gonzales to his father in Cuba after his mother drowned attempting an illegal entry into Florida, where her relatives tried to keep him; and the sexual affair between Washington intern Monica Lewinsky and US president Bill Clinton.

16 Carey.

17   See for example William Greider, *Who Will Tell the People?* (New York: Simon and Schuster, Touchstone, 1992) Chapter 17; or Greider, *One World, Ready or Not* (New York: Simon and Schuster, 1997) *passim.*

18   McChesney, "The Internet...," section "Salvaging Political Culture" (note 12 above).

19   Richard Patten, "Democracy in Ontario: Fade to Black," *Ottawa Life* (March 2000): 23.

20   See <http://www.wired.com/news/politics/0,1283,41658,00.html>.

21   Here I can bring some of my own experience to bear. Having started the "Propaganda and Media" bulletin board on the National Capital Freenet in its early days, I have seen it grow to a participation of about 60 or more, who visited the site over 500 times a week. Participation has dropped to about 35 recently, partly because participants do not restrain themselves sufficiently in one-on-one debates that bore others. With free e-mail available on the more advanced commercial servers such as Netscape, people have drifted away. More recently, the National Capital Freenet has increased its speed and capacity, including Web capabilities. It remains to be seen whether its proportion of regular Internet users can be recaptured. It may also be, though, that with the new commercial emphasis entering the arena, potential Internet surfers will be distracted from the political and towards the commercial.

22   Greider, *Who Will Tell the People?*

23   McChesney and Peterson (note 12).

24   When I typed in "NSRA" to various search engines, I came up with the Tennessee National Street Rod Association, the National Shoe Retailers Association, and the Norfolk Squash Rackets Association. Someone looking for the Non-Smokers Rights Association might well give up, although in some search engines it was not far down the list of entries. When I typed in "Non Smokers Rights" (without adding "Association"), I got a New York City group called CLASH who are actually a group opposed to controls on tobacco; there was no mention of the Canadian Non Smokers Rights Association.

25   Quoted in Blake Harris, "The Geopolitics and Cyberspace," *Infobahn* ("The Magazine of Internet Culture" <http://www.interlog.com/~blake/geopolitics.html>) 9.

26   *Ottawa Citizen,* "Bush 'IQ' study bogus," 7 September 2001: A15.

27   For the record the US National Transportation Safety Board concluded in a final report in August 2000, that "the probable cause of the accident was an explosion of the center wing fuel tank, resulting from ignition of the flammable fuel/air mixture in the tank. The source of ignition energy for the explosion could not be determined with certainty, but, of the sources evaluated by the investigation, the most likely was a short circuit outside of the CWT (center wing fuel tank) that allowed excessive voltage to enter it through electrical wiring associated with the fuel quantity indication system." See the NTSB Website, specifically <http://www.ntsb.gov/Publictn/2000/aar003.htm>. But Boeing's lawyers had earlier maintained that until the source of ignition energy is determined, ignition sources external to the aircraft—of any type—could not be ruled out. For Boeing's and other contrarian viewpoints see <http://seattletimes.nwsource.com/news/business/html98/twa_19991209.html> and <http://abcnews.go.com/sections/us/DailyNews/TWA800Missile000716html>.

28   Chafee 494.

29   "Commander guilty of surfing porn," cnews, 16 August 2001 <http://www.canoe.ca/CNEWSLaw0108/16_navy-cp.html>.

30   Sean MacBride, *Many Voices, One World: towards a new more just and more efficient world infor-mation and communication order* (Paris: International Commission for the Study of Communication Problems, 1980).

31   John Seigenthaler, of NBC, told a meeting of the Radio-Television News Directors Association in Minneapolis, September 2000, that "It's no secret that all news media suffer from a loss of credibility" and added that the public often considers the credibility of journal-ists to be on par with auto dealers and politicians. Online at <http://www.rtndf.org/news/2000/senrec.html>.

32   My own such account was published in <http://www.straightgoods.com> and has also been archived in <http://www.ncf.ca/civil-liberties/specialreports/quebecreport.html>.

33   Jeffrey Simpson, "So who's using the Internet? Political junkies," *Globe and Mail*, 9 August 2000.

34   See Chapter 4, p. 168 for Whately's analysis.

35   Gerald M. Craig, ed., *Lord Durham's Report* (Toronto: McClelland and Stewart: 1963) 29-30.

SELECTED BIBLIOGRAPHY

Books, Articles, Reports, Unpublished Documents

Adams, Ephraim Douglass. *Great Britain and the American Civil War.* Vol. II. Gloucester, MA.: Peter Smith, 1957.

Aleinikoff, T. Alexander. "Constitutional Law in the Age of Balancing." *Yale Law Journal* 943,96 (1987): 966-68.

Allen, Barry. "A Note on the Definition of 'Propaganda.'" *The Canadian Journal of Rhetorical Studies* 3 (September, 1993).

Anderson, Doris. "Forward." Ontario Press Council 26th *Annual Report* (1998). <http://www.ontpress.com/1_about/1_about.html>.

Aquinas, St. Thomas. *Summa Theologica.* Trans. Fathers of the English Dominican Province. New York, Boston et al.: Benziger Brothers Inc., 1947.

Aristotle. "Rhetoric." *The Basic Works of Aristotle.* Ed. Richard McKeon. Trans. W. Rhys Roberts. New York: Random House, 1941.

Arrington, R.L. "Advertising and Behavior Control." *Business Ethics in Canada.* 2nd ed. Ed. Deborah C. Poff and Wilfrid J. Waluchow. Scarborough: Prentice-Hall, 1991.

Austin, J.L. *How to Do Things with Words.* Oxford: Clarendon Press, 1962.

——. *Philosophical Papers.* Ed. J.O. Urmson and G.J. Warnock. Oxford: Clarendon Press, 1961.

Barendt, Eric. *Freedom of Speech.* Oxford: Oxford University Press, 1987.

Barnum, P.T. *Struggles and Triumphs or Recollections of P.T. Barnum written by himself.* London: Ward, Lock and Co., 1882.

Baron, Samuel *Plekhanov.* Stanford, CA: Stanford University Press, 1963.

Berger, Fred R., ed. *Freedom of Expression.* Belmont, CA.: Wadsworth, 1980.

Bernays, Edward. *Crystallizing Public Opinion.* New York: Boni and Liveright, 1923.

Black, Conrad. *A Life in Progress.* Toronto: Key Porter Books, 1993.

Bok, Sisella. *Lying: Moral Choice in Public and Private Life.* New York: Pantheon Books, 1978.

Bolinger, Dwight. "Truth is a Linguistic Question." *Language* 49,3 (1973).

Bracken, Brendan. *Parliamentary Debates.* Fifth Series. Vol. 401.

Brennan, William. *Dehumanizing the Vulnerable: When Word Games Take Lives.* Chicago, IL: Loyola University Press, 1995.

Bretall, Robert, ed. *A Kierkegaard Anthology.* New York: The Modern Library, 1946.

Brogan, Patrick. *Spiked: The Short Life and Death of the National News Council.* New York: Priority Press, 1985.

Brownlie, Ian, ed. *Basic Documents in International Law.* 2nd ed. Oxford: Clarendon Press, 1972.

Bryce, James. "Report of the Committee on Alleged German Outrages, as Presided over by The Right Hon. Viscount Bryce, O.M." London: HMSO, 1915.

Buchan, John (Lord Tweedsmuir). *Augustus.* London: Hodder and Stoughton, 1937.

Buddicom, Jacintha. "The Young Eric." *The World of George Orwell.* Ed. Miriam Gross. London: Weidenfeld and Nicolson, 1971.

Buitenhuis, Peter. *The Great War of Words.* Vancouver: University of British Columbia Press, 1987.

Butterfield, Steve. *Amway: The Cult of Free Enterprise.* Montreal and Buffalo: Black Rose Books, 1986.

Camus, Albert. *Algerian Reports, Resistance, Rebellion and Death.* Trans. Justin O'Brien. New York: Modern Library, 1963.

——. *Caligula and Three Other Plays.* New York: Knopf, 1958.

——. *Oeuvres complètes d'Albert Camus.* Vol. 5. Paris: Gallimard et Club de l'Honnête Homme, 1983.

——. *The Rebel.* Harmondsworth: Penguin, 1962.

Canada. *The Charter of Rights and Freedoms: A Guide for Canadians.* Ottawa: Minister of Supply and Services Canada, 1982.

——. Commission of Inquiry Concerning Certain Activities of the Royal Canadian Mounted Police. Third Report. *Certain RCMP Activities and the Question of Governmental Knowledge.* Ottawa: Supply and Services Canada, August 1981.

——. Department of Consumer and Corporate Affairs. *Misleading Advertising Bulletin.* 1986. 1989. 1996. <http://strategis.ic.gc.ca> and <http://strategis.ic.gc.ca/SSG/ct01250e.html>.

——. House of Commons Special Committee on Participation of Visible Minorities in Canadian Society. *Equality Now!* Ottawa: Supply and Services Canada, 1984.

——. Law Reform Commission of Canada. *Hate Propaganda,* Working Paper #50. Ottawa: Supply and Services Canada, 1986.

——. Royal Commission on Government Organization. *Report.* Vol 3. Ottawa: The Queen's Printer, 1962.

——. Royal Commission on Newspapers. *Report.* Ottawa: Supply and Services Canada, 1981).

——. Senate Committee on Privileges, Standing Rules and Orders. *Proceedings 4: Evidence.* Ottawa: 7 December 1999. <http://www.parl.gc.ca/36/2/paribus/commbus/senate/com-e/RULE-E/04EV-E.HTM>.

——. Somalia Commission of Inquiry. Report. Ottawa: Public Works and Government Services Canada, 1997. <http://www.dnd.ca/somalia/somaliae.htm>.

——. Special Committee on Hate Propaganda in Canada. *Report.* Ottawa: Queen's Printer, 1966.

——. Standing Committee on Health and Welfare. *Minutes of Proceedings and Evidence.* 2 November 1967.

——. Standing Committee on Social Affairs, Science and Technology. *Minutes of the Proceedings on the Subcommittee on Veterans Affairs.* 7th Proceedings. 6 November 1992.

——. Task Force on Government Information. *To Know and To Be Known.* Vol. 2. Ottawa: The Queen's Printer, 1969.

Canetti, Elias. *Crowds and Power.* Harmondsworth: Penguin Books, 1960.

Carey, Alex. *Taking the Risk Out of Democracy: Corporate Propaganda versus Freedom and Liberty.* Champaign, IL: University of Illinois Press, 1997.

Chafee, Zechariah Jr. *Government and Mass Communications: A Report from the Commission on Freedom of the Press.* Vol II. Chicago, IL: University of Chicago Press, 1947.

Charity, Arthur. *Doing Public Journalism.* New York and London: The Guilford Press, 1995.

Chesterton, G.K. *The Collected Works.* Vol. 27. Ed. Lawrence J. Clipper. San Francisco: Ignatius Press, 1987.

Chomsky, Noam. *Chronicles of Dissent.* Vancouver: New Star Books, 1992.

Cicero, Marcus Tullius, *De Oratore.* I, LIV. Trans. H. Rackham and E.W. Sutton. Cambridge, MA: Harvard University Press, 1988.

Cicero, Quintus (?). "Handbook of Electioneering," *Cicero XXVIII*. Trans. W. Glynn Williams, M. Cary, and Mary Henderson. Cambridge, MA.: Harvard University Press, The Loeb Classical Library, 1972.

Classen, Hans. *The Time Is Never Ripe*. Ottawa: Centaur Press, 1972.

Cobban, A.B. *The Medieval Universities: Their Development and Organization*. London: Methuen 1975.

Cohen, Elliot D., ed. *Philosophical Issues in Journalism*. New York and Oxford: Oxford University Press, 1992

Cole, J.A. *Lord Haw-Haw*. London: Faber and Faber, 1964.

Commission on Public Relations Education. *Public Relations Education for the 21st Century*. October 1999. <http://www.prsa.org/prssa4.html>.

Craig, Gerald M. ed. *Lord Durham's Report*. Toronto: McClelland and Stewart: 1963.

Crick, Bernard. *George Orwell: A Life*. Harmondsworth: Penguin, 1980.

Crossman, Richard. "The Creed of a Modern Propagandist." *A Psychological Warfare Casebook*. Ed. William Daugherty. Baltimore, MD: Johns Hopkins Press, 1958.

Daugherty, William E. *A Psychological Warfare Casebook*. Baltimore, MD: Johns Hopkins, 1958.

Department of Publicity in Enemy Countries. "Analysis of German Propaganda, May 1-16, 1940" (27 May 1940). C 6592/18/18, 1. Sir Campbell Stuart papers, Imperial War Museum, London.

Department of Publicity in Enemy Countries. Document C 6592/18/18. Sir Campbell Stuart papers, Imperial War Museum.

Devlin, Patrick. *The Enforcement of Morals*. Oxford: Oxford University Press, 1968.

Dicey, Edward. "The Ethics of Political Lying." *Nineteenth Century* (June, 1889): 789-794.

Domenach, Jean-Marie. "Leninist Propaganda." *Public Opinion Quarterly* (Summer 1951): 265-73.

Doob, Leonard. *Public Opinion and Propaganda*. 2nd ed. Hamden, CT.: Archon 240.

Ellul, Jacques. *FLN Propaganda in France During the Algerian War*. Trans. Randal Marlin. Ottawa: By Books, 1982.

——. *Histoire des Institutions*. Paris: Presses Universitaires de France, 1961.

——. *Histoire de la propagande*. Paris: Presses Universitaires de France, 1967.

——. *The Political Illusion*. 1967. New York: Random House, Vintage Books, 1972). Trans. of *L'Illusion politique*. Paris: Robert Laffont, 1965.

——. *Propaganda: The Formation of Men's Attitudes*. Trans. Konrad Kellen. New York: Random House, Vintage Books, 1973.

——. "Propagande." *Larousse, La Grande Encyclopédie*, 1975.

——. *The Technological Society*. New York: Random House, Vintage Books, 1964.

Elwood, Carter. "Lenin and *Pravda*, 1912-1914." *Slavic Review* 31 (June 1972).

Emerson, Thomas I. "Toward a General Theory of the First Amendment." *The Yale Law Journal* 72 (1963.

Fanon, Frantz. *The Wretched of the Earth*. New York: Grove Press, 1963.

Fox, Robin Lane. *Pagans and Christians*. London: Penguin, 1988.

Freifeld, Sidney. "Nazi Press Agentry and the American Press." *Public Opinion Quarterly* (Summer 1942): 221-235.

——. "The War of Nerves in the News." *Contemporary Jewish Record* (February 1942): 2-31.

Fulbright, J. William. *The Pentagon Propaganda Machine*. New York: Random House-Vintage, 1971.

Gagnon, Georgette, and Dan Rath. *Not Without Cause*. Toronto: HarperCollins, HarperPerrenial Edition, 1992.

Galbraith, John Kenneth. *The Affluent Society*. 4th ed. Boston: Houghton, 1984.

George, Richard T. de, and Joseph A. Pichler, eds. *Ethics, Free Enterprise, and Public Policy.* New York: Oxford University Press, 1978.

Glassco, J. Grant. *Royal Commission on Government Organization.* Ottawa: Queen's Printer, 1962.

Goodis, Jerry, *Have I Ever Lied to You Before?* National Film Board of Canada, 1976.

Govier, Trudy, ed. *Selected Issues in Logic and Communication.* Belmont, CA: Wadsworth, 1988.

Greider, William. *One World, Ready or Not.* New York: Simon and Schuster, 1997.

——. *Who Will Tell the People?* New York: Simon and Schuster, Touchstone, 1992.

Grice, Paul. "Presupposition and Conversational Implicature." *Radical Pragmatics.* Ed. Peter Cole. New York: Academic Press, 1981.

——. *Studies in the Way of Words.* Cambridge, MA: Harvard University Press, 1989.

Grotius. *On the Law of War and Peace.* Trans F.W. Kelsey. New York: Bobbs-Merrill, 1925.

Gutstein, Donald. *e.con: How the Internet Undermines Democracy.* Toronto: Stoddart Publishing, 1999.

Habermas, Jürgen. *Legitimation Crisis.* Trans. Thomas McCarthy. Boston: Beacon Press, 1975.

Halberstam, David. *The Powers That Be.* New York: Alfred Knopf, 1979.

Hardy, Forsyth. *Grierson on Documentary.* 1946. New York: Praeger, 1971.

Harris, Blake. "The Geopolitics and Cyberspace." *Infobahn,* "The Magazine of Internet Culture." <http://www.interlog.com/~blake/geopolitics.html>.

Harris, John. *Dunkirk: The Storms of War.* Newton Abbot: David, 1980.

Harrison, S. "Augustus, the Poets and the Monuments." Corpus Christi Classical Seminar. Oxford. 18 November 1987.

Hart, H.L.A. *Law, Liberty and Morality.* Oxford: Oxford University Press,1963.

Heiber, Helmut. *Goebbels.* New York: Hawthorn Books, 1972.

Hendrick, Burton J. "Propaganda of the Confederacy." *A Psychological Warfare Casebook.* Ed. William E. Daugherty. Baltimore, MD: Johns Hopkins, 1958.

Hengel, M. *Crucifixion.* London: SCM Press; Philadelphia, PA: Fortress Press, 1977.

Herman, Edward, and Robert McChesney. Interview. *Z Magazine.* October 1997. <http://www.lol.shareworld.com/zmag/articles/petersonoct97.htm>

Hiebert, Ray Eldon. *Courtier to the Crowd: The Story of Ivy Lee and the Development of Public Relations.* Ames, IA: Iowa State University Press, 1966.

Hiley, Nicholas. "'Kitchener wants you' and 'Daddy, what did YOU do in the Great War?': The Myth of British Recruiting Posters." *Imperial War Museum Review* 11 (1997): 40-58.

History of the Communist Party of the Soviet Union (Bolsheviks). Moscow: International Publishers, Inc., 1939. Online at <http://gate.cruzio.com/~marx2mao/Other/HCPSU39ii.html#c5s1>.

Hitler, Adolf. *Mein Kampf.* Trans. Alvin Johnson and John Chamberlain. New York: Reynal and Hitchcock, 1939.

——. *Mein Kampf.* Trans. Ralph Manheim. Boston: Houghton Miflin, 1943, 1971.

Holtman, Robert B. *Napoleonic Propaganda.* Baton Rouge, LA.: Louisiana State University Press, 1950.

Huff, Darrell. *How to Lie with Statistics.* New York: Norton, 1954

Hunt, Lynn. "Engraving the Republic: Prints and Propaganda in the French Revolution." *History Today* (30 October 1980): 11-17.

Imperial War Museum, *British Propaganda during the War 1914-1918* (n.d)

Jonsen, Albert R. and Stephen Toulmin. *The Abuse of Casuistry: A History of Moral Reasoning.* Berkeley, CA: University of California Press, 1988.

Kant, Immanuel. *Critique of Practical Reason and Other Writings in Moral Philosophy.* Ed. and trans. Lewis White Beck. Chicago, IL: University of Chicago Press, 1949.

Kenez, Peter. *The Birth of the Propaganda State: Soviet Methods of Mass Mobilization 1917-1929.* New York: Cambridge University Press, 1985.

Keshen, Jeffrey A. *Propaganda and Censorship During Canada's Great War.* Edmonton: University of Alberta Press, 1996.

Kierkegaard, S. "Communication." *Journals and Papers.* Ed. H.H. Hong and E.H. Hong, assisted by G. Malantschuk. Bloomington and London: Indiana University Press, 1967.

——. *Concluding Unscientific Postscript.* Trans. D. Swenson and W. Lowrie. Princeton, NJ: Princeton University Press, 1941.

——. *The Point of View of My Work as an Author.* Trans. W. Lowrie. 1939. New York: Harper and Row, 1962.

Kilbourne, Jean. *Killing us Softly: The Image of Women in Advertising.* Cambridge Documentary Films, 1979.

——. *Still Killing us Softly.* Cambridge Documentary Films, 1987.

Klein, Naomi. *No Logo.* Toronto: Alfred A. Knopf, 2000.

Klemperer, Victor. *I Will Bear Witness, 1933-1941.* New York: Modern Library, 1999.

Knightley, Philip. *The First Casualty.* London: André Deutsch, 1975.

Knopfelmacher, Frank. "The Ethic of Responsibility." *Liberty and Politics.* Ed. Owen Harries. New South Wales: Pergamon Press, 1976. 38-47.

Koestler, Arthur. *Darkness at Noon.* Trans. Daphne Hardy. 1941. New York: Signet Books, 1956.

Landis, Fred. "CIA Psychological Warfare Operations." *Science for the People* (January/February 1982).

Lanham, Richard. *Literacy and the Survival of Humour.* New Haven, CN: Yale University Press, 1983.

——. *Style: An Anti-Textbook.* New Haven, CN: Yale University Press, 1974.

Lasswell, Harold. *Propaganda Technique in the World War.* London: Kegan Paul, Trench and Tubner 1927; New York: Alfred Knopf, 1927.

Le Bon, Gustav. *Les opinions et les croyances.* Paris: Flammarion, 1911.

Lee, Alfred McClung, and Elizabeth Briant Lee, eds. *The Fine Art of Propaganda: A Study of Father Coughlin's Speeches.* New York: Harcourt Brace and Company, 1939.

Lee, Ivy. Ivy Lee Papers. Seeley G. Mudd Manuscript Library. Princeton University.

Leiser, Burton. "The Ethics of Advertising." de George and Pichler.

Leith, James A. *Media and Revolution.* Toronto: Hunter Rose Company for CBC Publications, 1968.

Lenin, V.I. *Que faire?* Pékin: Éditions du Peuple, 1972.

Lessig, Lawrence. *Code and Other Laws of Cyberspace.* New York: Basic Books, 1999.

Levick, Barbara. "Propaganda and the Imperial Coinage." *Antichthon* 16 (1982): 104-16.

Lewis, D.L. "The Outstanding PR Professionals." *PR Journal* (October 1970).

Locke, John. *A Letter Concerning Toleration.* Ed. John Horton and Susan Mendus. London and New York: Routledge, 1991.

Lutz, William. *Doublespeak.* New York: HarperPerennial, 1990.

MacArthur, John. *Second Front: Censorship and Propaganda in the Gulf War.* New York: Hill and Wang, 1992.

MacIntyre, Linden. "To Sell a War." *the 5th estate.* CBC Television. 7 January 1992.

Mackenzie, A.J. *Propaganda Boom.* London: John Gifford, 1938.

MacLean, Eleanor. *Between the Lines: How to detect bias and propaganda in the news and everyday life.* Montreal: Black Rose Books, 1981.

Manvell, Roger, and Heinrich Fraenkel. *Doctor Goebbels: His Life and Death.* New York: Simon and Schuster, 1960.

Marketing Law Reporting Service. Vol. 3. Cobourg, ON: Business Law Reporting Ltd, 1984.

Marlin, Randal. "Censoring Pornography." *Women and Public Policy: Reprints from Policy Options*. Ed. Doris Anderson. Kingston: The Institute for Research on Public Policy, 1987.

——. *The David Levine Affair*. Halifax: Fernwood, 1998.

——. "Disguised Corporate Advertising in the Media?" *Straight Goods*, 4 February 2002, <http://www.straightgoods.ca/ViewMedia File.cfm?REF=147>.

——. "Freedom of Expression, Bill C-51, and the Canadian Charter of Rights and Freedoms" Health and Welfare Canada. March 1989.

——. "A Matter of Credibility." *Content* (May/June 1991).

——. "Propaganda and the Ethics of Persuasion." *International Journal of Moral and Social Studies* 4,1 (Spring 1989).

——. "Public Relations Ethics: Ivy Lee, Hill and Knowlton, and the Gulf War," *International Journal of Moral and Social Studies* 8, 3 (Autumn 1993).

Marlin, Randal, trans. and ed. "Jacques Ellul's Lectures on Forecasting and Planning." *Futures Research Quarterly* (Winter 1985).

Masterman, C.F.G. "Work Conducted for the Government at Wellington House." Third Report. Foreign Office News Department 49/3 (41) 01. 3.

MacBride, Sean. *Many Voices, One World: towards a new more just and more efficient world information and communication order*. Paris: International Commission for the Study of Communication Problems, 1980.

McChesney, Robert W. "The Internet and US Communication Policy-Making in Historical and Critical Perspective." *The Journal of Communication* 46,1 (Winter 1996). <http://www.ascusc.org/jcmc/vol1/issue4/mcchesney.html>.

McCloskey, H.J. "Liberty of Expression: Its Grounds and Limits (I)." Berger.

McHardy, A.K. "Religious Ritual and Political Persuasion: The Case of England in the Hundred Years War." *International Journal of Moral and Social Studies* 3,1: 95-110.

McKenzie, Vernon. *Through Turbulent Years*. London: Geoffrey Bles, 1938.

Meiklejohn, Alexander. *Free Speech and Its Relation to Self-Government*. New York: Harper and Bros., 1948.

Messinger, Gary S. *British Propaganda and the State in the First World War*. Manchester and New York: Manchester University Press, 1992.

Meyvaert, P. "Medieval Forgers and Modern Scholars: Tests of Ingenuity." *Bibliologia* 3. Ed. P. Ganz. Turnhout: Brepols, 1983.

Mill, John Stuart. *On Liberty*. Ed. Currin V. Shields. 1859. Indianapolis: Bobbs-Merrill, 1956.

Millar, F. "State and Subject: The Impact of Monarchy." *Caesar Augustus: Seven Aspects*. Ed. F. Millar and E Segal. Oxford: The Clarendon Press, 1985.

Miller, Arthur. *The Crucible*. Ed. Gerald Weales. New York: Viking Press, 1971.

Miller, R.M. *Harry Emerson Fosdick: Preacher, Pastor, Prophet*. New York: Oxford University Press, 1985.

Miller, Reese. "Persuasion and the Dependence Effect." *Business Ethics in Canada*. 2nd ed. Ed. Deborah C. Poff and Wilfrid J. Waluchow. Scarborough: Prentice-Hall, 1991.

Milton, John. *Areopagitica and Of Education*. Ed. George H. Sabine. Northbrook, IL.: AHM Publishing, 1951.

Monro, D.H. "Liberty of Expression: Its Grounds and Limits (II). Berger. 58-70.

Moon, Richard. "The Scope of Freedom of Expression." *Osgoode Hall Law Journal* 23,2 (1985.

Moore, Robert J. "Reflections of Canadians on the Law and the Legal System: Legal Research Institute Survey of Respondents in Montreal, Toronto and Winnipeg." *Law in a Cynical Society? Opinion and Law in the 1980s*. Ed. Dale Gibson and Janet Baldwin. Calgary and Vancouver: Carswell Legal Publications Western Division, 1985.

Morley, John. *On Compromise*. London: Macmillan, 1923.

Murphy, James A., and Richard A. Katula, et al. *A Synoptic History of Classical Rhetoric*. Davis, CA.: Hermagoras Press.

Nagel, Linda. *Communiqué* 1,1 (September 1997): 3.

Nelson, Phillip. "Advertising and Ethics." de George and Pichler.

Nobécourt, R.G. *Les secrets de la propagande en France occupée*. Paris: Fayard, 1962.

Nyberg, David. *The Varnished Truth*. Chicago, IL: University of Chicago Press, 1993.

Olasky, Marvin. *Corporate PR*. Hillsdale, NJ: Lawrence Eerlbaum Associates, 1987.

——. "Ivy Lee: Minimizing Competition through PR." *PR Quarterly* (Fall 1987): 9–15.

Oliner, Samuel, and Pearl Oliner. *The Altruistic Personality*. New York: Free Press, 1988.

O'Malley, Peter. "In Praise of Secrecy: The Ethical Foundations of Public Relations." CPRS <http://www.cprs.ca>

Ontario Press Council. <http://www.ont-press.com/about/council_constitution.asp>.

——. Annual *Reports*. 1982. 1990. 1992. 1993. 1997. 1998.

Orwell, George. *Collected Essays*. London: Mercury Books, 1961.

——. "A Farthing Newspaper." *G.K.'s Weekly* (29 December 1928).

——. *Homage to Catalonia*. 1938. Harmondsworth: Penguin Books, 1962.

——. *Nineteen Eighty-Four*. Harmondsworth: Penguin, 1949.

Orwell, Sonia, and Ian Angus, eds. *The Collected Essays, Journalism and Letters of George Orwell*. Vol. 1 and 2. Harmondsworth: Penguin Books, 1970.

Packard, Vance. *The Hidden Persuaders*. New York: D. McKay, 1957.

Paine, Robert. "'Presence' and 'Reality', and a Smallwood Speech." *Propaganda and the Ethics of Rhetoric. The Canadian Journal of Rhetorical Studies* 3 (1993): 57–73.

Paulos, John Allen. *A Mathematician Reads the Newspaper*. New York: Basic Books, 1995.

Pelletier, Gérard. *La crise d'octobre*. Montréal: Éitions du Jour, 1971.

Plato. *The Collected Dialogues of Plato*. Ed. Edith Hamilton and Huntington Cairns. Trans. W.D. Woodhead. New York: Pantheon Books, 1961.

Plekhanov, Georghi. *Selected Philosophical Works*. Vol. 1. Moscow: Progress Publishers, 1974.

Ponsonby, Arthur. *Falsehood in Wartime*. London: George Allen and Unwin, 1928.

Pontifical Council for Social Communications. *Ethics in Advertising*. Rome: Liberia Editrice Vaticano. Ottawa: Canadian Conference of Catholic Bishops, 1997.

Ponting, Clive. *The Right to Know: The Inside Story of the Belgrano Affair*. London and Sidney: Sphere Books, 1985.

Pritchard, David. "The Role of Press Councils in a System of Media Accountability: The Case of Quebec," *Canadian Journal of Communication* (July 2000). <http//www.cjc.online.ca/Backissues/16.1/pritch.html>.

Public Relations Society of America. *Code of Professional Standards for the Practice of Pubic Relations*. 10 June 2000. <http://www.prsa.org/profstd.html>.

Public Relations Society of America. *PRSA Code of Professional Standards for the Practice of Public Relations: History of Enforcement*. New York: Public Relations Society of America, 1987.

Quine, W.V.O. "Reference and Modality." *From a Logical Point of View*. Cambridge, MA: Harvard University Press, 1961.

Quintilian. *Institutio Oratoria*. Book XI. Trans. H.E. Butler. Cambridge, MA: Harvard University Press, 1979.

Rapoport, Anatol, ed. *Clausewitz on War*. Harmondsworth: Penguin Books, 1968.

Rawls, John. *A Theory of Justice*. Cambridge, MA, Harvard University Press, 1971.

Raz, Joseph. "Free Expression and Personal Identification." *Free Expression: Essays in Law and Philosophy*. Ed. W.J. Waluchow. Oxford: Clarendon Press, 1994.

Reimann, Viktor. *Goebbels*. Garden City, NY: Doubleday, 1976.

Rosen, Jay. *Getting the Connections Right: Public Journalism and the Troubles in the Press*. Washington: Century Foundation Press, Brookings Institute, 1996. <http://www.tcf.org/Publications/Media/Getting_the_Connections_Right/Preface.html>.

Rousseau, Jean-Jacques. "The Social Contract or Principles of Political Right." *Social Contract*. Intro. Sir Ernest Barker. Trans. Gerard Hopkins. Oxford: Oxford University Press, 1947.

Rubinstein, Shimon. *German Atrocity or British Propaganda, The Seventieth Anniversary of a Scandal: German Corpse Utilization Establishments in the First World War*. Jerusalem: Academon, 1987.

Ruchames, Louis, ed. *Racial Thought in America*. Vol. I of *From the Puritan to Abraham Lincoln*. Amherst: University of Massachusetts Press, 1969.

Rudinow, Joel. "Manipulation" *Ethics* 88 (1978): 338-47.

Russell, Bertrand. *Education and the Social Order*. 1932. London: George Allen and Unwin, 1967.

Ryan, H.R. *Harry Emerson Fosdick: A Persuasive Preacher*. New York: Greenwood Press, 1989.

Sanders, M.L., and Philip Taylor. M. *British Propaganda During the First World War, 1914-18*. London and Basingstoke: Macmillan, 1982.

Santillana, Giorgio de. *The Crime of Galileo*. Chicago, IL: University of Chicago Press, 1955.

Sartre, Jean Paul. "A Plea for Intellectuals." *Between Existentialism and Marxism*. New York: Morrow Quill Paperbacks, 1979.

Schauer, Frederick. *Free Speech: A Philosophical Enquiry*. Cambridge: Cambridge University Press, 1982.

Sidgwick, Henry. *The Methods of Ethics*. 7th ed. London: Macmillan, 1907.

Simpson, Colin. *Lusitania*. Harmondsworth: Penguin Books, 1972.

Sinclair, Upton. *The Brass Check*. Passadena, CA.: n.p, 1920.

Sington, Derrick, and Arthur Weidenfeld. *The Goebbels Experiment*. New Haven: Yale University Press, 1943.

Smith, Bruce L. "Propaganda." *Encyclopedia Britannica Macropedia*. Chicago: Encyclopedia Britannica, Inc., 1985.

Spenser, Edmund. *A View of the State of Ireland*. Ed. Andrew Hadfield and Willy Maley. Oxford: Blackwell Publishers, 1997. St. Augustine of Hippo. *Treatises of Various Subjects*. Vol. 16. Ed. Roy J. Deferrari. New York: Catholic University of America Press, 1952.

Steiner, Claude, and Charles Rappelye. "Interview with Jacques Ellul." *Propaganda Review* (Summer 1988).

Steiner, George. *After Babel: Aspects of Language and Translation*. 3rd ed. New York: Oxford University Press, 1998.

Stephen, James Fitzjames. *A General View of the Criminal Law of England*. London and Cambridge: Macmillan, 1863.

Stephen, James Fitzjames. *A Digest of the Criminal Law of England* (London: Macmillan, 1877) 56.

——. *Horae Sabbaticae*.London: Macmillan, 1892.

——. *Liberty, Equality, Fraternity*. 1874. Cambridge: Cambridge University Press, 1967.

Stevenson, Charles. *Ethics and Language*. Yale University Press, 1944.

Stockum, Hilda van. *The Borrowed House*. Bathgate, ND: Bethlehem Books, 2000.

Stone, I.F. *I.F. Stone's Weekly*. Dir. Jerry Bruck. Boston, 1973.

Strickland, Lloyd, and Tzvetanka Dobreva-Marinova. "Bekhterev's Conception of Mental Phenomena, Activity, and Persuasibility." International Society of Political Psychology, Annual Scientific Meeting, 1995.

Sumner, Wayne. "Hate Propaganda and Charter Rights." *Free Expression*. Ed. W.J. Waluchow. Oxford: Clarendon Press, 1994.

Tallentyre, S.G. *The Friends of Voltaire*. New York: U.P. Putnam's Sons, 1907.

Taylor, Edmond. *The Strategy of Terror*. Rev. ed. Boston: Houghton Miflin, 1942.

Taylor, Richard. *Film Propaganda: Soviet Russia and Nazi Germany*. London: Croom Helm, 1979.

Thomson, Oliver. *Easily Led: A History of Propaganda*. Phoenix Mill, England: Sutton 1999.

Thorp, John. "Aristotle's Rehabilitation of Rhetoric." *The Canadian Journal of Rhetorical Studies* (September 1993): 13-30.

Thucydides, *The Peloponnesian War*. Trans. Rex Warner. Harmondsworth: Penguin Books, 1954.

Tolme, Paul. "Capitol Advantage grows along with Internet democracy." *CANOE news*, 22 February 2000. <http://www.canoe.ca/TechNews0002/22_democracy.html>

Tolusso, Giuliano O. "The Ontario Press Council: Challenges of a Second Decade." School of Journalism, Carleton University, 1983.

Trebilcock, Michael, et al. *Study on Consumer Misleading and Unfair Trade Practices: Proposed policy directions for the reform of the regulation of unfair trade practices in Canada*. Ottawa: Information Canada, for the Department of Consumer and Corporate Affairs, 1976.

Tudiver, Neil. *Universities for Sale*. Toronto: James Lorimer, 1999.

UK. Committee on Homosexual Offences and Prostitution. *The Wolfenden Report*. New York: Lancer Books, 1964.

——. Defence Committee of Inquiry. *Minutes of Evidence taken before the Defence Committee*. 21 July 1982.

United Nations Security Council. *Provisional Verbatim Record* (27 November 1990): s/PV. 2959, 37.

US. Commission on Freedom of the Press. *A Free and Responsible Press*. Chicago, IL: University of Chicago Press, 1947.

US. Secretary of the Army. *Report on Iraqi War Crimes (Desert Shield/Desert Storm)*. Unclassified version, 8 January 8 1992. UN Security Council, 19 March 1993: s/25441.

US. Senate. *Covert Action in Chile, 1963-1973*. Staff Report of the Select Committee to Study Governmental Operations with Respect to Intelligence Activities. Washington, DC: US Government Printing Office, 1975.

Virgil. *The Aeneid of Virgil*. Trans. C. Day Lewis. London: The Hogarth Press, 1961.

Wall, D.F. "The Provision of Government Information." Ottawa: n.p., 1974.

Walzer, Michael. "Political Action and the Problem of Dirty Hands." *War and Moral Responsibility*. Ed. Marshall Cohen, Thomas Nagel, and Thomas Scanlon. Princeton, NJ: Princeton University Press, 1974.

Weber, Max. *From Max Weber: Essays in Sociology*. Trans. and ed. H.H. Gerth and C. Wright Mills. New York: Oxford University Press, 1946, 1958.

Weeks, Albert L. *The First Bolshevik*. New York: New York University Press, 1968.

Wells, Colin. *The Roman Empire*. London: Fontana Books, 1984.

Whately, Richard. *Elements of Rhetoric*. 7th ed. rev. 1846.

——. *The Use and Abuse of Party Feeling in Matters of Religion*. 1822.

Wheeler, Michael. *Lies, Damn Lies and Statistics*. New York: Dell, 1976.

Wilde, Oscar. *A Woman of No Importance*. Ed. Ian Small. London: A&E Black, 1993.

Young, William R. "Mobilizing English Canada for War: The Bureau of Public Information, the Wartime Information Board, and a View of the Nation During the Second War." (n.p., n.d.)

Newspapers and Newsmagazines

Boston Globe

Extra (FAIR)

Globe and Mail

Harper's Magazine

The Independent

Kingston Whig-Standard

Le Devoir

Manchester Guardian Weekly

Moncton Times

Montreal Gazette

National Post

New York Times

Ottawa Citizen

Ottawa Journal

Times (London)

Wall Street Journal

Selected Websites

Arts and Letters Daily.
    <http://www.aldaily.com>.

ASC (Advertising Standards Canada).
    <http://www.adstandards.com>.

ASC. *Ad Complaints Report.*
    <http://www.canad.com/en/Standards/
    Complaints_Report/1997ReportE.pdf.>.

ASC. *Gender Portrayal Guidelines.*
    <http://www.adstandards.com/en/
    standards/gender.asp>.

Bourque Newswatch.
    <http://www.bourque.org/>.

Boyce's Paper.
    <http://www.magma.ca/~brich>.

Canadian Broadcasting Corporation.
    <http://cbc.ca>.

Canadian Newspaper Association.
    <http://www.cna-acj.ca>.

Canadian Public Relations Society.
    <http://www.cprs.ca>.

CANOE news. <http://www.canoe.ca>.

CAUT (Canadian Association of University
    Teachers). <http://www.caut.ca>.

Common Cause.
    <http://www.commoncause.org>.

Counterpunch. <http://counterpunch.org>.

Cursor. <http://www.cursor.org>.

Democracy Watch. <http://www.dwatch.ca>.

Energy Probe. <www.energyprobe.org>.

FAIR (Fairness and Accuracy in Reporting).
    <http://www.fair.org>.

Fisk, Robert. <http://robert-fisk.com>.

Ha'aretz-English.
    <http://www.haaretzdaily.com>.

Honest Reporting.
    <http://honestreporting.com>.

Human Rights Watch. <http://www.hrw.org>.

Industry Canada. <http://strategis.ic.gc.ca>.

Al-Jazeerah. <http://www.aljazeerah.info>.

Khaleej Times. <http://khaleejtimes.com>.

Ontario Press Council.
    <http://www.ontpress.com>.

Philosophy Now.
    <http://www.philosophynow.demon.co.uk>.

Public Relations Society of America.
    <http://www.prsa.org>.

Public Relations Watch.
    <http://www.prwatch.org>.

Rabble. <http://www.rabble.ca>.

Straight Goods.
    <http://www.straightgoods.com>.

Truthout. <http://www.truthout.org>

UK. Press Complaints Commission (PCC).
    <http://www.pcc.org.uk>.

Village Voice.
    <http://www.villagevoice.com>.

Wired News. <http://www.wired.com>.

Z Magazine. <http://www.zmag.org>.

INDEX